After *The Passion* Is Gone

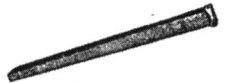

After *The Passion* Is Gone

American Religious Consequences

Edited by J. Shawn Landres and Michael Berenbaum

ALTAMIRA
PRESS

A Division of Rowman & Littlefield Publishers, Inc.
Walnut Creek • Lanham • New York • Toronto • Oxford

ALTAMIRA PRESS
A division of Rowman & Littlefield Publishers, Inc.
1630 North Main Street, #367
Walnut Creek, California 94596
www.altamirapress.com

Rowman & Littlefield Publishers, Inc.
A wholly owned subsidiary of The Rowman & Littlefield Publishing Group, Inc.
4501 Forbes Boulevard, Suite 200
Lanham, Maryland 20706

PO Box 317
Oxford
OX2 9RU, UK

Copyright © 2004 by AltaMira Press

All rights reserved. No part of this publication may be reproduced, stored in a retrieval system, or transmitted in any form or by any means, electronic, mechanical, photocopying, recording, or otherwise, without the prior permission of the publisher.

British Library Cataloguing in Publication Information Available

Library of Congress Cataloging-in-Publication Data

After *The Passion* is gone : American religious consequences / edited by J. Shawn Landres and Michael Berenbaum.
   p. cm.
Includes bibliographical references and index.
ISBN 0-7591-0814-5 (alk. paper) — ISBN 0-7591-0815-3 (pbk. : alk. paper)
1. Passion of the Christ (Motion picture) I. Landres, J. Shawn. II. Berenbaum, Michael, 1945–

PN1997.2.P39A38 2004
791.43'72—dc22
                                    2004012358

Printed in the United States of America

∞™ The paper used in this publication meets the minimum requirements of American National Standard for Information Sciences—Permanence of Paper for Printed Library Materials, ANSI/NISO Z39.48-1992.

To the memory of my teachers Walter Capps and Ninian Smart. May we honor always their legacy of humane inquiry and their commitment to integrity, dignity, and respect in the interreligious encounter.
—J. Shawn Landres

To Richard L. Rubenstein, teacher, mentor, and friend, who is now four score years of age and so strong in the years of his strength. And to Betty Rogers Rubenstein, who truly is his better half. With gratitude and love!
—Michael Berenbaum

CONTENTS

Acknowledgments xi
Introduction 1
   Michael Berenbaum and J. Shawn Landres

PART I
THE CONTEXT OF *THE PASSION* 19

   CHAPTER ONE   Almost a Culture War: The Making of *The Passion* Controversy 23
   Mark Silk

   CHAPTER TWO   Passionate Blogging: Interfaith Controversy and the Internet 35
   William J. Cork

   CHAPTER THREE   Living *in* the World, But Not *of* the World: Understanding Evangelical Support for *The Passion of the Christ* 47
   Leslie E. Smith

   CHAPTER FOUR   *The Passion* Paradox: Signposts on the Road toward Mormon Protestantization 59
   Eric R. Samuelsen

   CHAPTER FIVE   Is it Finished? *The Passion of the Christ* and the Fault Lines in American Christianity 75
   Julie Ingersoll

CONTENTS

PART II
THE PASSION IN CONTEXT 89

CHAPTER SIX The Journey of the Passion Play from
Medieval Piety to Contemporary Spirituality 93
Karen Jo Torjesen

CHAPTER SEVEN   The Gibson Code? 105
Lorenzo Albacete

CHAPTER EIGHT "But Is It Art?" A Prelude to Criticism
of Mel Gibson's *The Passion of the Christ* 115
Robert A. Faggen

CHAPTER NINE Antisemitism without Erasure: Sacred
Texts and Their Contemporary Interpretations 125
Gary Gilbert

CHAPTER TEN Theologizing the Death of Jesus, Gibson's
The Passion, and Christian Identity 137
Jeffrey S. Siker

CHAPTER ELEVEN   Manly Pain and Motherly Love:
Mel Gibson's Big Picture 149
David Morgan

CHAPTER TWELVE   *Imago Christi:* Aesthetic and Theological
Issues in Jesus Films by Pasolini, Scorsese, and Gibson 159
Lloyd Baugh, SJ

PART III
JEWS AND CHRISTIANS: REFRAMING THE DIALOGUE 173

CHAPTER THIRTEEN   Theological Bulimia: Christianity
and Its Dejudaization 177
Susannah Heschel

CHAPTER FOURTEEN   A March of Passion; or, How I
Came to Terms with a Film I Wasn't Supposed to Like 193
Stephen R. Haynes

CHAPTER FIFTEEN   The Exposed Fault Line 207
Richard L. Rubenstein

CONTENTS

CHAPTER SIXTEEN Crucifying Jesus: Antisemitism and the Passion Story 219
Stephen T. Davis

CHAPTER SEVENTEEN Five Introspective Challenges 229
David M. Elcott

CHAPTER EIGHTEEN No Crucifixion = No Holocaust: Post-Holocaust Reflections on *The Passion of the Christ* 243
John K. Roth

CHAPTER NINETEEN The Passionate Encounter: The Ethics of Affirming Your Faith in a Multireligious World 255
Elliot N. Dorff

CHAPTER TWENTY Reframing Difference: Evangelicals, Scripture, and the Jews 267
Kathryn J. S. Smith

Afterword: The Passion of War 279
   Mark Juergensmeyer
Bibliography 289
Index 331
About the Contributors 341

ACKNOWLEDGMENTS

The Sigi Ziering Institute is grateful to Mrs. Marilyn Ziering and her children Michael and Diane Ziering, Ira and Godeleine Ziering, Amy Ziering Kofman and Gil Kofman, and Rosanne Ziering; to Irma and Lou Colen; and to Maxwell and Janet Salter for their generous support of its mission and its ongoing activities. The Institute enjoys the support of President Robert Wexler of the University of Judaism (UJ). We are blessed by the legacy of Dr. Sigi Ziering of blessed memory, a German-born child survivor of the Holocaust who went on to become a brilliant scientist and active philanthropist, who wrote powerfully on the ethics of the Holocaust, and who forged a life of charity and compassion from his own ruinous history.

The symposium series "The Crucifixion of Jesus" could not have taken place without Amy Greenberg's logistical expertise and additional support before and during the UJ event from Tina Gargotta, Joshua Cohen, Sarala Chandra, and Zuzana Riemer Landres. In Claremont, thanks to Professor John K. Roth and the Claremont-McKenna College (CMC) Center for the Study of the Holocaust, Genocide, and Human Rights as well as to Bonnie Snortum, director of the Marian Miner Cook Athenaeum at CMC. At Loyola Marymount University (LMU), we thank Professor Jeffrey S. Siker of the Department of Theological Studies for coordinating the symposium, along with Professor Kristin Heyer at LMU, who organized a presymposium interreligious dialogue for UJ and LMU undergraduates. Our thanks as well to the panelists themselves—Lloyd Baugh, Stephen Davis, Robert Faggen, Gary Gilbert, John Roth,

ACKNOWLEDGMENTS

Jeffrey Siker, and Kathryn Smith—whose presentations made the idea of a "quick book" seem all too easy.

Kim Lawton of PBS's *Religion and Ethics Newsweekly*, Rob Eshman of *The Jewish Journal of Greater Los Angeles*, Tom Tugend of the *Jewish Telegraphic Agency*, and Iris Waskow of the UJ believed in the news and editorial value of our approach, and Erik Hanson of AltaMira Press paved the way for our project with enthusiasm, good humor, and speed. Evan Sagal first sketched the cover concept and Zvzana Riemer Landres helped prepare the index. Our thanks to the Reverend Ed Bacon of All Saints Church Pasadena for having the foresight to invite Karen Jo Torjesen and Susannah Heschel to give guest lectures, thereby giving us the opportunity to benefit from their insights in this book (our thanks as well to their cohosts and fellow panelists, Gregory Boyle, SJ, Rabbi Kenneth Chasen, Rabbi Joshua Levine Grater, Professor David Myers, and Kenneth Turan). Wade Clark Roof of the Department of Religious Studies at the University of California, Santa Barbara (UCSB), has his hand in the success of this volume: one of the editors (Landres) and two of the contributors (Julie Ingersoll and Leslie E. Smith) are his doctoral students. Thanks also to Randall Balmer, Caroline Walker Bynum, Stewart Hoover, Gary Laderman, Edward Linenthal, Elbert Peck, Stephen Prothero, and Jan Shipps for helpful references and good counsel.

Shawn Landres wishes to acknowledge the numerous conversation partners who helped him think through many of the difficult issues addressed here; in particular, he wishes to thank Yoav Ben-Horin, Dr. Marcy Braverman, the Reverend Dr. Thomas Breidenthal, Dr. David Elcott, Dr. Eugene Fisher, Scott Perlo, and Rabbi David Wolpe as well as his former students Leah Eve Ticker and Alyssa Uphoff. Alumni of the UCSB–Fulbright American Studies Institute on "Religion in the United States: Pluralism and Public Presence" provided important feedback on the film's reception around the world; thanks especially to Patrick Adeso (Cameroon), Chaider Bamualim (Indonesia), Oscar Celador Angón (Spain), Radovan Čikeš (Slovak Republic), Markus Glatz-Schmallegger (Austria), Lucia Grešková (Slovak Republic), Miloš Mrázek (Czech Republic), and Istvan Peter (Romania) for their reports and reactions. The members of the UJ's first-ever undergraduate course on Christianity displayed an enthusiastic spirit of experimentation: Jessica Danon, Stephanie Funk, Tina Gargotta, Amy Greenberg, Raymond Janeway, Nicole

ACKNOWLEDGMENTS

Nathanson, Mike Pavehzadeh, Zack Portman, Tamara Rettino, Rachel Saks, and Blake Shapiro. More practically, Shawn is grateful to his in-laws, Ing. Daniel and Dr. Magdalena Riemer of Košice, Slovak Republic, for allowing him to turn their bedroom into a temporary Internet-connected office every day for nearly three weeks; to Martin Bahleda and Andrea Bahledová for allowing the same in their apartment in Prague, Czech Republic; and especially to his wife, Zvzana Riemer Landres, for her love, patience, and support on two continents.

Michael Berenbaum wishes to acknowledge the distracting presence of his young children Joshua Boaz and Mira Leza and the blessing of his first grandson, Jeremy Judah Grinblat. His thanks go to Ilana and Tal and above all to Melissa. Words of praise are appropriate for his colleague Shawn Landres, who has worked tirelessly and with dedication and diligence under great pressure and an unforgiving timetable to get this book done. He has cajoled our colleagues to get their work in, edited the work that was submitted skillfully and tactfully, and done it all with style and grace. It has been both a privilege and a pleasure to watch this young scholar demonstrate his talent.

INTRODUCTION
Michael Berenbaum and J. Shawn Landres

"But how did it all begin?" asks Roberto Calasso in his magisterial recounting of the tragedies of Greek mythology in *The Marriage of Cadmus and Harmony*.[1] How, indeed?

It's Not Always about the Jews—but Sometimes It Feels That Way

"If it is history we want," Calasso answers, "then it is a history of conflict."[2] Ordinarily, Christian theological and liturgical debates are the concerns of Christians alone, and Jews have neither right nor reason to intervene. However, the matter of Christian teaching about Jews and Judaism, of course, is of great interest to those who are the subject matter of such doctrine. To be sure, many people had thought that the "problem" of Christian–Jewish relations had been settled, at least to the extent possible, in the wake of the Roman Catholic Church's Second Vatican Council and similar shifts in the mainline Protestant churches. Despite the significant advances in Jewish thinking about Christianity associated with *Dabru Emet*,[3] however, many Jews continue to associate Christianity with a series of violent persecutions of the Jews culminating in the Holocaust.

Events occur in context: in late 2002 and early 2003, when *The Passion* first made headlines, and the winter of 2004, when it premiered, American Jewish public life for many felt problematic, depressing, dispiriting, and even bleak. Antisemitic violence was on the rise both in Europe and in the Islamic world. Vandalism against Jewish institutions and violence against Jews reflected heightened tensions in the Middle East, the apparently never-ending conflict between Israelis and Palestinians. Official and popular criticisms of Israel and the Israeli government—whether legitimate or excessive—were mistaken by elements of the European populace for license to attack local Jews. This environment, dubbed "the new antisemitism," contributed to a growing sense of isolation and anguish among many American Jews. While it is highly exaggerated, dangerously misleading, and needlessly inflammatory to compare contemporary events to the 1930s, such comparisons resonate within the Jewish community and set the context in which many American Jews received the news of *The Passion*'s imminent release.[4]

Perhaps ironically, the public debate over *The Passion* began with the same emotion that the gospel accounts suggest inaugurated the Passion itself: Jewish fear. Jewish observers were the first to take cautious note that a popular politically conservative actor-director was making a film about the last twelve hours of the life of Jesus of Nazareth, the Christian Christ. That this filmmaker's father reportedly had denied the Holocaust only intensified Jewish suspicions. Thus, while the earliest media reports around the film concerned the Gibson family's traditionalist Catholicism, the "right of first reaction" went to Jewish activists, such as Rabbi Marvin Hier of the Simon Wiesenthal Center and Abraham Foxman of the Anti-Defamation League, who viewed *The Passion* through the prism of the Holocaust and the "new antisemitism,"[5] issues that are the bread and butter of their institutional life.

Hier's March 2003 statement, the first formal reaction to the film by any public figure, explicitly links the Passion narrative to "wanton slaughter of Jews" in a manner that can only refer to the Holocaust.[6] The comparison was not surprising. Many Jews associate the symbolism of the Passion with the still-recent murders of six million Jews; Elie Wiesel's image in *Night*, of God as a little boy on the gallows, remains a powerful reminder for Jews that years of suffering brought no redemption.[7] Therefore, when a traditionalist Catholic filmmaker attacked Vatican II and the transformations in the Roman Catholic Church, he was attacking that dimension of Roman Catholic history that had been most favorable to Jews, most welcoming to Jews, and most respectful to Judaism—and at a time when many Jews felt more vulnerable than they had in many years.

INTRODUCTION

The Christians and Jews who had worked so hard to achieve these gains thought—in retrospect so naively—that Gibson would honor these gains and the troubles of our time and respond accordingly. Not so!

If we judge from the responses of many within the American Jewish community, Mel Gibson's *The Passion of the Christ* seemed to be about the Jews and only about the Jews. Hier and Foxman may have tried to build up expectations that Gibson would respond to their cautions by taking steps to avoid further allegations of antisemitism or Holocaust denial. But Gibson did not respond to Hier and Foxman's demands; moreover, his defenders turned their allegation on its head: the film was not antisemitic, but the attacks on it were anti-Christian. The more Jewish spokespersons protested, the stronger the "defense" of Christianity against its "attackers."

In advancing their perspectives on Gibson's film at the same time as they drew increasing press attention to what they saw as growing worldwide antisemitism, Foxman and Hier unknowingly and unwillingly helped propel the film itself to front-page attention.[8] In its June 2003 press release on the film, the Anti-Defamation League (ADL) offered "to advise ICON Productions constructively regarding *The Passion* to ensure that the final production is devoid of anti-Semitic slander"; in February 2004, Foxman described the film as a "revision . . . of *Nostra Aetate*" and demanded that the Vatican condemn the film.[9] On the release of the film, the Simon Wiesenthal Center complained, "Had the [United States Conference of Catholic Bishops] guidelines concerning these matters been consulted, and responsible Jewish groups been involved in the process, we are certain that a new film based on the Gospels could have been made that would have been acceptable to Christians and Jews alike."[10]

Hier, Foxman, and their colleagues had misread the context in which they were operating. As a result, Gibson and his allies skillfully exploited them as a marketing tool to generate unprecedented level of prerelease publicity. The frequent ADL and Wiesenthal Center statements on *The Passion* reflected their persistent assumption that Gibson would wish to involve outside groups, let alone Jewish ones, in the realization of his personal cinematic vision; furthermore, the statements revealed at best their insensitivity and at worst their ignorance with respect to Gibson's traditionalist Catholic religious beliefs and his relationship, or lack thereof, with the Vatican. Gibson's defenders "spun" these press statements as evidence that there was a conspiracy to destroy the film and discredit Christianity. This allowed Gibson to perceive himself—and be perceived by others—as a martyr and hero. *Imitatio Dei*, Gibson could see himself as being crucified by the Jews.

When *The Passion of the Christ* finally appeared in theaters, its blockbuster success marked one of the rare times in recent American history that the Jews have sensed themselves as cultural outsiders. The film was a financial triumph, grossing more than $350 million between Ash Wednesday and Easter Sunday 2004[11] and bringing into the theaters a new audience that seldom sees R-rated movies and views Hollywood with suspicion and disdain. Viewers left movie theaters silent and humbled, moved, and often tearful. Critic after critic commented on the response of the audience. But the Jews in attendance did not seem to understand that response; they did not understand Christian friends who were moved by what they had seen. For a generation of Jews who are accustomed to see themselves as an integrated part of American culture and as shapers and movers of American culture, not mere participants and certainly not bystanders, the experience of being an outsider was quite unnerving.

Paradoxically, and therefore perhaps confusingly, the reiteration of Jewish outsider status came at the same time that American Jews were beginning to come to grips with the reality of their social and political influence. As *The Forward* opined in the wake of *The Passion*'s controversial success, claims by Foxman, Hier, and others that Jews would be the film's victims fell on incredulous ears to Americans accustomed to seeing Jews as "an influential group." Jews no longer easily can "win sympathy as vulnerable underdogs," *The Forward* observed. "More and more, it's our opponents who claim the victim's mantle. The rules have changed, and we're clueless to respond. That's what's scary."[12] Even the much vaunted "new antisemitism" plaguing Jewish communities is an expression of anger by violent but ultimately powerless actors on society's margins against a group they perceive to be the engine and beneficiary of globalization.[13]

For some Jews, as Michael Lerner suggests, *The Passion* controversy reinforced Jewish "fears generated by 1700 years of Christian oppression" and thereby gave some Jews another excuse not to come to grips with let alone "acknowledge their own power."[14] Others, conversely, had the uneasy sense, as one Jewish reviewer put it, that *The Passion*'s Jewish defenders, many of whom had built alliances with conservative Christians over shared political interests both in the United States and in Israel, had opted, "in their zeal to keep Judaism safe from the less traditional hordes, . . . to align themselves with the most fundamentalist people and ideas, even at risk to the very religion they are presumably dedicated to preserving."[15] In and of itself, *The Passion* was an uncomfortable reminder of Jewish otherness in American culture. At the same time, *criticism* of the film risked reinforcing that otherness by damaging the evangelical-Jewish alliance on Israel that provides the power base for center-right American Jewish political influence.

It's Not Only about the Jews—Expanding *The Passion* Debate

The media-driven controversy over the film—was it or wasn't it antisemitic?—overshadowed a larger challenge that the film posed to Christian theology and to Christian–Jewish relations. Left unsaid and unseen in Gibson's film is any account of Jesus's popular religious appeal; almost no account is given of the teachings of Jesus of Nazareth. Gibson's portrayal of Jesus's last hours sparked controversy among Christian scholars of religion, such as Martin E. Marty, who argued before the film's release that "Christians believe that Jesus was and is the Christ, the Anointed, and they are to find meaning in his sacrificial love and death, not to crawl in close to be sure they get the best sight of the worst physical suffering."[16] Indeed, contrast Gibson's resurrected Jesus with the one Jack Miles depicts in his landmark study *Christ: A Crisis in the Life of God*. Absent from *The Passion of the Christ* is any sense of the transcendence that Miles observes in Jesus's resurrection: "the same act that exposes all authority as provisional renders all revenge superfluous. And because the death of God does this, it functions within the myth as not just another death but a redemptive death, one that saves us from the violence that we might otherwise feel justified in inflicting on one another."[17]

One reason for the difference is Gibson's own religious commitment to penitential theology. As Karen Torjesen notes in chapter 6 of this volume, Gibson's conviction that Jesus's suffering is what saved him from certain damnation closely resembles the medieval belief that in order for Jesus's death to be redemptive, his suffering had to be proportionate to the iniquity that was cleansed. For Gibson, then, Jesus's Passion—his grievous suffering—is *the* story that matters, so that is what is projected on the big screen. In this view, Jesus's death is not quite sufficient: it is the passion, or *suffering*, of the innocent that becomes the foundation of Christian belief.

Here is where Jews and Christians might have had a more meaningful interreligious engagement about the film.[18] Even for Christians who do not subscribe to penitential theology, there seems no question that Jesus's suffering at the very least contributed to his redemption of the world and that "suffering is part of the life of a Christian."[19] The Passion narrative and the Easter holiday with which it culminates celebrate God's victory over suffering and death: Jesus's sacrificial death at the hands of the Roman imperium secures humanity's eternal life in the kingdom of heaven.[20] To recall the suffering of Jesus is to reclaim his humanity and social peripherality, especially for those who continue to feel themselves powerless on society's margins.[21] For Jews, however, suffering does not redeem but rather wounds, injures, and destroys; the *memory* of suffering is what matters, and whether that memory can be redemptive depends on how people behave in the aftermath of suffering. The persecution that the earliest Christian martyrs suffered at the hands of the Romans during the first three hundred years of Christian history is a much longer and more recent memory for Jews.[22] Images of the suffering of the innocent inevitably evoke memories of the Crusades, the Inquisition, and the Holocaust.

If for Christians the question is how to take up the cross, how to make suffering redemptive, then for Jews the question is how one lives in the face of suffering. What portrayal of suffering is most likely to engender the Christian dignity, solidarity, and decency of faith, hope, and love? How can the memory of suffering be used to perform the Jewish commandment of *tikkun olam*, repairing the world? Such questions are the stuff of interreligious dialogue at its best. But as Peter Steinfels of the *New York Times* dryly observed, "Pain, personal or empathetic, notoriously blocks thought and concentrates the mind rather than expanding it."[23] In any event, national conversation about the nature of suffering was unlikely during a period of continuing economic recession and an increasingly troublesome U.S. military occupation of Iraq.

While others have glibly spoken of the war between civilizations, it is clear that contemporary religious life is characterized by a war within religious traditions: liberal and conservative, fundamentalist and traditionalist, quietistic and activist. Both the marketing campaign for *The Passion of the Christ* and the debate over the film demonstrate that the fault line in American Christianity is not between Protestants and Catholics or indeed between evangelical and mainline Protestants. The fault line is between messianic progressives and pietistic conservatives. We use each term with care. Messianic progressives are committed to realizing the Kingdom of Heaven on earth: at one end of this spectrum are liberal world-redeeming Protestants and Catholics like Jim Wallis and Dorothy Day; at the other end are R. J. Rushdoony–style postmillennialist Christian reconstructionists. Pietistic conservatives pursue an inner-oriented separation/isolation from the "wider world" that is deeply individualistic—even atomistic—at its core. They range from meditative ascetics and quietists like Thomas Merton to premillennialist activists like Jerry Falwell. Gibson's *Passion* is a paean to pietistic conservatism, and its critics are mostly messianic progressives disappointed by its detachment from the world.

Moreover, contemporary religious affiliation is as much if not more about belonging than about endorsing doctrinal propositions; affiliation, rather than belief, better predicts and describes Judaism and Christianity in contemporary America. Therefore, when they perceived themselves "attacked," evangelical and fundamentalist Christians emerged alongside traditionalist and conservative Catholics to defend their turf. Had Jews stayed out of the headlines, there likely would have been an inner-Christian skirmish pitting literalists against nonliteralist Christian readings of the Crucifixion and engaging the serious scholarship of faithful Christian scholars to recover an understanding of the Jesus of history.[24]

Why *This* Book?

Recently, one of us saw a bumper sticker that read, "God said it. I believe it. That settles it." This simplistic sentiment—that the Bible requires no interpretation—is a popular one. Indeed, *The Passion of the Christ* has exposed the basic ignorance even of seemingly informed men and women regarding the Gospels. *It is therefore a teaching moment*, an opportunity for everyone to study the Gospels and to understand this most formative text of Western tradition. Let us be clear: Mel Gibson has the right to make and distribute almost any kind of film he likes, but the rules of civil society and scholarship require that he and his defenders respect the rights of critics, scholars, and others to analyze and evaluate the film. Whatever else it may be, *The Passion of the Christ* is not a fifth gospel, and therefore even and especially for the most literalist of inerrantists, it must remain open to interpretation and criticism. Shortly after *The Passion*'s release, the conservative film commentator Michael Medved, a self-identified Orthodox Jew, praised the film for its success, noting that "a religious movie can achieve major success even if prominent organizations find it offensive." Moreover, he wrote, it "teaches future filmmakers that they need not feel timid about affirming religious values out of fear of public conflict; in fact, they might even welcome such attacks as a means of winning attention."[25] As scholars and concerned public intellectuals, we do not share Medved's joy at the prospect of an American society further wracked by polarization and recrimination, nor do we accept the conclusion of conservative Roman Catholic political commentator Patrick Buchanan that the debate over *The Passion* is "a religious war going on in our country for the soul of America . . . a cultural war, as critical to the kind of nation we will one day be as was the Cold War itself."[26]

We have no cause to criticize those who defend the film on its own merits; while we do not agree with those who refuse to make the distinction between the film as an artistic production and the story it tells, nonetheless we acknowledge their right to do so. However, we draw the line when the film's defenders and critics—whether Catholic, Protestant, or Jewish—use threatening or demonizing language to denigrate those who do not share their views. The neoconservative Rabbi Daniel Lapin, one of *The Passion*'s few Jewish defenders, asserted that "those who publicly protest Mel Gibson's film lack moral legitimacy."[27] Some commentators characterize criticism of the film as tantamount to treason, suggesting that it "draws attention" away from threats emanating from fundamentalist Islam not only to Judaism but also to all of Western civilization.[28] Patrick Buchanan launched an attack on *The Passion*'s Jewish critics. Openly accusing Jews of having "a touch of 'guilt and perfidy,'" he wrote that one Jewish critic of *The Passion* "stands truth on its head" and gleefully noted that another is "at risk of having [his] lights punched out" for "insulting millions of Christians."[29]

Some defenders of the film charged that to criticize *The Passion* was to attack Christianity itself. Gibson himself told Peter Boyer of *The New Yorker* that "modern secular Judaism wants to blame the Holocaust on the Catholic Church."[30] Albert Mohler of the Southern Baptist Theological

Seminary argued that "the Passion has offended the usual parties—those who accuse the Gospel of anti-semitism"; he specifically named Foxman, "officials of the Simon Wiesenthal Center," and the "mainstream interfaith movement."[31] And in a nationally televised debate with the Wiesenthal Center's Hier, William Donohue of the Catholic League for Religious and Civil Rights charged that Foxman and others "have . . . a deep-seated need to find anti-Semitism and then to attack Christians," asking, "So are we all a bunch of bigots, Rabbi Hier?" Donohue charged that Hier was "poison[ing] relationships between Christians and Jews" by purposefully lying about potential "pogroms" and by "bringing up the Holocaust and everything to make Christians feel on the defensive."[32] The anonymity of the Internet gave some activists cover to attack *The Passion*'s Jewish critics as "enemies of God" and to invite their readers to "pray that the ADL and other Jewish leaders . . . repent on their knees for their sins against all of humanity in need of Christ's message for opposing this film."[33]

Defenders of *The Passion* also made implicit threats against the film's critics. Seven months before the film's release, in a comment revealing much about the agenda of so-called "Christian Zionists," Ted Haggard, president of the National Association of Evangelicals, implicitly tied Christian theological support for Israeli territorial maximalism to American Jewish acquiescence on *The Passion*:

> In the current global clash of civilizations, I'm surprised that some Jewish leaders would protest a movie portraying the final hours of Christ's life. There is a great deal of pressure on Israel right now, and Christians seem to be a major source of support for Israel. For the Jewish leaders to risk alienating 2 billion Christians over a movie seems shortsighted.[34]

Not surprisingly, the indirect threat evoked sharp criticisms, but given the opportunity to clarify his comments, Haggard merely restated his comment and assigned clear responsibility for Jesus's death not to "some" Jews or Romans but to "the Jewish people" and "the Roman people."[35] For his part, Buchanan wondered, "Is it wise to keep up this vendetta against a movie that Christians have embraced, when millions of these Christians give uncritical loyalty to Israel?"[36]

Of equal concern was the reaction to *The Passion* in some quarters of the diverse community of American Jews. Some accused the Gospels of antisemitism; others leveled the same charge at Christianity. Still others criticized the movie for failing to adhere to Roman Catholic guidelines regarding the portrayal of the Passion, even though the filmmaker is not in communion with the Church.[37] Rabbi Shmuley Boteach referred to certain gospel passages as "cheap forgeries" inserted by "falsifiers" of the New Testament.[38] The independent centrist Jewish monthly *Midstream* published a commentary charging that "what passes as history in the Gospels is, quite clearly, only Christian propaganda."[39] Rabbi Bentzion Kravitz of the antimissionary organization Jews for Judaism criticized "Christian misinterpretations" of the Hebrew Scriptures and urged that they be "read correctly."[40] The ADL's Foxman traveled to Rome to demand that the Vatican condemn the film; despite the Gibson family's disaffiliation from the Vatican, according to news reports, Foxman maintained that the Roman Catholic hierarchy had the "responsibility to set the record straight on its teachings."[41] At least one Jewish Democratic activist tried to use *The Passion* as a political weapon in party politics when he suggested that "the fallout over weapons of mass destruction, budget deficits, and even gay marriage and the controversy over 'The Passion of [the] Christ' movie have further weakened [President Bush's] position within the Jewish community."[42] Ironically, the most damning prediction—in the incendiary words of antimissionary activist Rabbi Tovia Singer, that "by the time the first nail is hammered into the cross, viewers in Germany will be passing around knife sharpeners in the theater"[43]—not only was inappropriate but also proved itself entirely wrong, as Germany was the only country in which the leaders of the Roman Catholic, Protestant, and Jewish communities cooperated to issue a joint statement criticizing *The Passion*.[44]

This book attempts what too many of *The Passion*'s defenders, as well as some of its critics, refused to do: to engage in reasoned scholarly discussion. Thus, there are contributors to this volume who find the film, in whole or in part, to be powerful and moving testimony for the Christian faith. There are contributors to this volume who find the film, in whole or in part, to be an antisemitic reflection of a retrograde theology. There are contributors who do not take a position on the film at all but rather seek to understand why certain groups supported or opposed it. In all cases, however, these contributors do so in a spirit of collaborative scholarly inquiry that acknowledges the possibility of other positions even as it respects each person's right to assert his or her own viewpoint.

INTRODUCTION

Martin Buber writes that the secret of the Hasidic Master is that "he elevates their need, before he satisfies it."[45] For Christians, conversations about *The Passion of the Christ* should invite a return to the Bible but also an encounter with traditions of interpretation and the need for interpretation. For Jews, it should invite a reading of the text most sacred to their neighbors, one that also is representative of one dimension of first-century Judaisms. We intend this book to model of how diverse, conflicting, and controversial views can be presented in a context that permits serious exchange and deep discourse.

One of us directs the Sigi Ziering Institute: Exploring the Ethical and Religious Implications of the Holocaust at the University of Judaism; the other has developed the university's first-ever undergraduate course on Christianity. While both of us were concerned about the tenor of Gibson's forthcoming film, we knew enough about Christian theological and cultural diversity to be certain that regardless of any bias, the film would not receive unanimous approval. However, we were surprised and appalled by the lack of sophistication with which those Christians and Jews who were speaking publicly at the time had resolved themselves into opposing camps.

It was obvious to us, long before the film's February 2004 release, that there had to be a better way to ask and answer important questions that were being ignored. A month before *The Passion* debuted, the Sigi Ziering Institute organized a forum on the theme of "The Crucifixion of Jesus," in which Jewish and Christian scholars spoke to audiences at three local universities; the University of Judaism, which is the home of the Conservative movement's Ziegler School of Rabbinic Studies; the Roman Catholic Jesuit Loyola-Marymount University; and Claremont-McKenna College, a secular college adjacent to a mainline Protestant seminary. The panel discussions, which took place two weeks before, the evening before, and two weeks after *The Passion*'s Ash Wednesday release, were balanced: Jews and Christians, Catholics and Protestants, fundamentalists, evangelicals, conservatives, and liberals. The intent was that the discourse, however intense, would be civil and serious and we would speak *to* one another and *with* one another, not *at* one another. Buber's principle of dialogue would be upheld. Far more quickly that we imagined, the dialogue moved from the general (Jesus's crucifixion) to the specific (Gibson's *Passion*).

Building on the success of the symposium series, we solicited additional essays from scholars across the country whose work provides critical context within which to understand both the film itself and its American religiocultural context. In part I, contributors assess the cultural milieu within which Gibson produced and released his film. Mark Silk and William J. Cork give histories of the debate, Silk by tracing the attempt to create a media-driven "culture war" and Cork by following *The Passion* as it emerged as a topic of discussion on the Internet. Leslie Smith explores the film's appeal among evangelical Protestants, whose ardent support for and attendance of the film helped generate its record box office receipts. There was conflict over the film, however, even among secular culture's harshest critics. Eric R. Samuelsen places the dilemma felt by Mormons over the film within a context of the debate over the continuing protestantization of the Church of Jesus Christ of Latter-day Saints. And Julie Ingersoll considers the fault lines in American evangelical and fundamentalist Christianity that the film exposed.

Part II considers the medium of film as heir to a lineage of literature and drama that itself has a genealogy and a history of interpretation. Karen Jo Torjesen examines *The Passion* as heir to a dramatic tradition that emerged from medieval penitential theology. Lorenzo Albacete, Robert Faggen, and Gary Gilbert consider the extent to which the "text" of the film can be read prior to the context within which it appears; through their exploration of antisemitism in Gibson's *Passion*, Faggen and Gilbert arrive at rather divergent conclusions. Jeffrey S. Siker and David Morgan consider the film as a reaction against liberalizing trends in American Christianity, Siker through an analysis of the film's theology and Morgan through his psychoanalytic interpretation of the film's imagery in the context of the history of what he calls American "visual piety."[46] Finally, Lloyd Baugh considers Gibson's film in the context of two other controversial treatments of the Passion, those by Scorsese and Pasolini.

Finally, both the film and the discussion it generated can tell us something about the limits, possibilities, and urgencies of interreligious engagement in our time. Susannah Heschel opens part III with a history of the interreligious debate in nineteenth-century Germany over the religious identity of the "historical Jesus." Stephen R. Haynes and Richard Rubenstein take different positions over the extent to which antisemitism and anti-Judaism in Gibson's *Passion* reinforce an impassable barrier between Christians and Jews; Stephen Davis argues that the question of Christian antisemitism must be assessed independently from that of the film. David Elcott and John Roth call for greater introspection within their respective faith traditions, noting that such self-reflection and even self-criticism must accompany, if not precede, critiques of other faiths for elements and attitudes that are also are present in one's own. Elliot Dorff offers a guide to meaningful interreligious engagement in a post-*Passion* era, one which Kathryn Smith independently models in her exploration of ways in which evangelicals might engage one another—and Jews—about contextual and covenantal questions regarding Christianity and Judaism.

To be sure, there are important perspectives not represented in this book, such as those of African American scholars and theologians.[47] There are no Muslim reflections and none by scholars who are not part of the great textual traditions. But Christians and Jews alike interpreted this as an intramural issue, and our book reflects that approach. Moreover, while some polemicists attempted to appeal to the need for common ground against a dangerous Islamic "other," we specifically reject such objectification. However, ours may be the first word, but it surely is not the last. In his afterword, Mark Juergensmeyer moves beyond such facile "us-versus-them" appeals to explore the resonance of the film in the post-9/11 world, a world that Gibson seems to believe is a "battlefield for the cosmic forces of good and evil" and his film "a weapon in that war."[48]

The Passion of the Christ is a disquieting phenomenon that appeared during unsettling times. Within and well beyond the Jewish community, we live at a time where fundamentalism is the driving passion of our day, whether it is Islamic fundamentalism, Jewish fundamentalism, Christian fundamentalism, Hindu fundamentalism, or what many in the world call the fundamentalism of the rhetoric and politics of "American freedom." In many cases, it is a fundamentalism with a political agenda, a fundamentalism that excludes rather than includes, that demonizes instead of welcoming the other, that curses the sinner and not just the sin and regards the sinner as irredeemable. Fundamentalists regard liberal religious thought as too compromised, too rational, and unable to answer the question of meaning for many postmodern men and women. It does not seem to be redemptive enough for those who are lost.

How do we begin? Of that we are uncertain, but begin we must. In editing this volume, we have bracketed but not set aside our own conflicted opinions about the film; the contributors to this book express better than we can the concerns that we have about both Gibson's *Passion* itself and its effect on Christian and Jewish communities in the United States. For his part, Gibson is a man of considerable talent and significant means who has brought his own personal vision to the giant screen, claiming all along that his own idiosyncratic reading is the truth, the whole truth, and nothing but the truth. Gibson's wealth and standing gave him the capacity to use the medium of film to challenge what he apparently perceives as the liberalism not only of Hollywood but also of the Roman Catholic Church.

Competing rhetorics of "victimhood" and "outsider status" made it difficult, if not impossible, for many Christians and Jews to recognize one another's concerns.[49] Combined with the fundamentalist fear of change, the rhetoric of victimhood denies the possibility for progress and transformation: according to this worldview, *The Passion*'s Jewish critics are irredeemably "anti-Christian," and the film's defenders (not to mention the entire continent of Europe) are always and forever murderous antisemites. As Mark Silk notes, Dennis Prager's observation that Christians and Jews saw two different films helped defuse the brewing culture war (indeed, Patrick Buchanan's antisemitic jeremiad may reflect his frustration and anger that they gave a war but nobody came).[50] At the same time, however, American religious culture further polarized to the extent that Jews were unable to recognize the Christian perspective on the film and Christians could not see the film through Jewish eyes. The former were blinded by the depiction of the Jews, the latter by the majesty of the Passion.

Mel Gibson's *The Passion of the Christ*[51] and the controversial public discussion that surrounded it was a major episode in American religious culture. To be sure, *After* The Passion *Is Gone: American Religious Consequences* is appearing well before the 2004–2005 awards season, perhaps well before the passion has faded and just as the DVD's effect is being felt. Inevitably, there will be a new debate over whether or how to acknowledge the cinematic efforts that resulted in the film. And it will be at least two years and perhaps as long as a half decade before we can measure with any accuracy the worldwide impact of the film and its DVD editions. However, enough has occurred in and around the film's production, release, and reception to generate both popular and scholarly interest. This volume is one outcome of that interest.

INTRODUCTION

The enormity of the public response to Gibson's film disproves Jack Miles's argument that "a premodern response to the miraculous is virtually impossible for any contemporary adult."[52] At the same time, however, the film amply demonstrates Miles's contention that what attracts potential believers to the biblical narrative are not Protestant-Catholic polemics or the doctrinal propositions that characterized premodern Christianity; rather, Miles suggests, "What attracts viewers, believing or unbelieving, to the great rose window of the Bible is neither what can be seen through it nor how the glass for it was stained and assembled, but what the window looks like in and for itself and what all those jagged fragments of light and color, working together, make happen behind the eye of the beholder."[53] It is our hope that this collection of chapters sheds light on the jagged fragments that formed the public debate around *The Passion of the Christ* and that readers indeed see through the film to the great assembly of American religious culture beyond.

Notes

1. Calasso 1993, 4 and passim.
2. Calasso 1993, 7.
3. Frymer-Kensky et al. 2000.
4. Berenbaum, "In 2003, We Are Strong: In 1933 We Were Weak," 2003.
5. See Cork (chapter 2 in this volume) and Silk (chapter 1 in this volume).
6. Simon Wiesenthal Center 2003.
7. Wiesel 1960, 75–76; see also Anisfield and Terry 2001, 115–19.
8. See Watanabe 2004; Cattan 5 March 2004; Rosenblatt 2004.
9. Anti-Defamation League 24 June 2003; Winfield 2004. Foxman further requested that "Gibson go on camera at the end of the film to tell audiences that it was wrong to blame the Jews alone for Jesus' death" (ibid.).
10. Simon Wiesenthal Center 2004.
11. MovieWeb 2004.
12. *The Forward* 12 March 2004.
13. Berenbaum, "The Top Ten Reasons Why Today Is Different," 2003.
14. Lerner 2004.
15. Newhouse 2004.
16. Marty 2004.
17. Miles 2001, 12.
18. See, for example, Gellman and Hartman 2004.

19. Anisfeld and Terry 2001, 127.
20. Pettit 2004.
21. Franklin 2004.
22. Landres 2004.
23. Steinfels 28 February 2004, A13.
24. See, for example, Cattan 30 January 2004.
25. Medved 14 March 2004.
26. Buchanan 2004.
27. Lapin 2003.
28. Medved 21 July 2003; International Fellowship of Christians and Jews 11 February 2004; Coulter 2004; Buchanan 2004. Rabbi Lapin's (2004) defense of the film even included an implicit call for mass conversion from Islam to Christianity: "Should one billion Moslems convert to Christianity, does anyone really believe that the world would be a worse place?"
29. Buchanan 2004.
30. Boyer 2003. See also Wolpe 2004.
31. Mohler 2003.
32. Zahn 2004. Michael Medved (24 December 2003) suggested that Hier's own criticism of the film was the cause of antisemitism: "The hate-filled calls and letters that the Rabbi has received . . . represent the indignant (and utterly predictable) reaction to Rabbi Hier's own ceaseless denunciation of Gibson's work."
33. Support Mel Gibson! [website].
34. National Association of Evangelicals 2003.
35. Greenberg 8 August 2003. Haggard told the Christian World News that "I think it would be wise for the Jewish community to understand that Bible-believing Christians are supporters of the Jewish people, and defenders of the Jewish people, and defenders of the state of Israel. . . . Now, I don't want to make that too strong of a statement, because certainly the Jewish people and the Roman people were involved with the crucifixion of Christ" (Little 2003).
36. Buchanan 2004.
37. "Live Chat with LA Cardinal Roger Mahony" 2004.
38. Boteach 2003.
39. Urekew 2004, 23.
40. Board of Rabbis of Southern California 2004; Kravitz 2004.
41. Winfield 2004.
42. Hallow 2004.
43. Singer 2003.
44. Spiegel, Lehmann, and Huber 2004. We are grateful to Susannah Heschel for bringing this statement to our attention.
45. Buber 1958, 61.

46. Morgan 1998.
47. See, for example, Franklin 2004.
48. Drew 2003.
49. Landres 2004.
50. Prager 2003; Buchanan 2004. In a similar vein, writing for the progressive *Pacific News Services*, Christian columnist Andres Tapia reminded his "Jewish friends" that evangelicals "find Jews quite irrelevant to their own personal experience with Jesus" (Tapia 2004).
51. Gibson 2004.
52. Miles 2001, 284.
53. Miles 2001, 289.

Part I
THE CONTEXT OF *THE PASSION*

The opening section of *After* The Passion *Is Gone: American Religious Consequences* features five chapters that place the film in its religious and political context and explore both the ways in which the controversy developed and the many public forums in which discussions were held.

Mark Silk traces the origins of the conflict regarding *The Passion of the Christ* from the first article published in the *New York Times Magazine* by Christopher Noxon, a Los Angeles–based freelance writer, whose father learned that a Hollywood film star was building a traditionalist Catholic chapel near his Malibu home. Somehow Rabbi Marvin Hier got wind of the forthcoming story and expressed concern about the portrayal of the Jews in the film that Gibson was contemplating. Instead of taking some steps toward ameliorating a potential controversy, which is standard in Hollywood, Gibson and his allies turned the tables on Hier and other Jewish critics by accusing them of being anti-Christian. Using conservative media outlets to buttress the claim and to intensify the pressure upon their critics, *The Passion*'s supporters determined that the best defense would be an aggressive offense: a culture war. Accusations that Gibson was being crucified and allegations that the United States Conference of Catholic Bishops and the Anti-Defamation League had trafficked in a stolen script quickly established a pattern. Silk argues that America was headed toward a culture war, at least until Jewish neoconservatives broke ranks with their evangelical and conservative Catholic allies, beginning with Dennis Prager, who understood that the majesty of the Crucifixion blinded Christians to the portrayal of the Jews and that the portrayal of the Jews made it impossible for Jews to encounter the majesty of the Passion. The loss of key conservative allies quickly doused the flames of battle despite the media's apparent interest in feeding the frenzy.

The last time a movie about Jesus sparked a major public controversy was in 1988, long before the Internet revolutionized public debate and made it possible for anyone with a computer and online access to take part in the discussion. This time, much of the dispute took place in cyberspace. William J. Cork provides us with an important guide to the world of cyberspace and to the way that the Internet gave a forum for the expression of views regarding *The Passion*. His observations are stark and confirm Silk's perceptions. "The most ardent defenders of the film chose to use it as a wedge to divide the true believers from the infidels, seemingly angry that some people refused to acknowledge 'The Truth.'" The difference was not the message but the medium. Weblogs, or "blogs," are Web diaries that permit layered commentaries on a topic and provide a conversational forum for like-minded communities. Cork traces the way in which blogs were used to promote the film, to attack the film, and, on too few occasions, to wrestle with the film. Exchanges of ideas that began in cyberspace were soon reflected in print, on television, and later in theater attendance. *The Passion*'s supporters used the Internet as an alternative means to publicize the film and build broad allegiance to it. Cork's experience blogging *The Passion* demonstrates that weblogs and similar technologies are increasingly important sites for public discussion and debate.

Leslie E. Smith provides us with an informed guide to the evangelical Protestant world that, perhaps surprisingly to outsiders, embraced a film with strong traditionalist Catholic overtones and nonbiblical depictions of the Passion. Smith shows that the film resonated emotionally with these evangelicals "because it privileges emotional experience, it appeals to traditional American consumerism, and it asserts supernaturalism and moral absolutism." Emotions often trump theology, and evangelicals saw in *The Passion* an opportunity for conversion experience on a massive scale. The materiality of the film appealed to evangelicals because it helped them bridge the gap between being "in the world" but not "of the world." Finally, the absolutism of the film and of the debate around it echoed the binary "good-versus-evil" and "us-versus-them" thinking of many evangelicals. Gibson's self-portrayal also resonated with a community that views Hollywood as antireligious. The perception by many evangelicals that criticism of the film constituted an amoral or antimoral secular attack on Christianity itself only reinforced their sense of alienation and victimization.

Eric R. Samuelsen explores the response to *The Passion* by members of the Church of Jesus Christ of Latter-day Saints (LDS). Mormon understanding of the significance of the last twelve hours of Jesus's life differs from that of other Christians in that they believe that the Atonement—the act whereby Jesus redeemed the world—took place at Gethesemane, not on the cross. Thus, the cross, so prominent in Gibson's film, has limited religious significance for the Mormons and often is seen simply as an instrument of Roman torture. Moreover, the violence in the film created a dilemma that juxtaposed culture against theology: most conservative Mormons avoid R-rated movies, but this one was about a sacred theme. Why, then, did the film prove so popular among conservatives, who otherwise would be the most likely to defend Mormon particularism? Samuelsen sees the reaction to the film as further evidence of the growing alliance—political and experiential—between Mormons and conservative Protestants. Despite the persistence of anti-Mormon feelings among evangelicals and fundamentalists, this "protestantization" of the LDS Church has softened some deep differences and created bonds where one would have suspected that none could exist.

Had questions of "antisemitism" and "anti-Christianity" not taken center stage in the controversy surrounding *The Passion*, Julie Ingersoll's depiction of the fault lines in American Christianity might have been the real story of *The Passion* debate. Instead, it has become an important sideshow but nonetheless one that reveals religious divisions in what outsiders mistakenly perceive to be a unified conservative right. One might have expected Catholics to embrace *The Passion* and Protestants to reject it. However, acceptance and rejection defied religious boundaries. Liberals of both faiths felt more comfortable with each other. As Ingersoll notes, sectarian Protestants and Catholics have drawn closer in recent years around their efforts to defend traditionalist gender culture. Their battles against common enemies—feminism, abortion, homosexuality, and same-sex marriage—redrew the dividing lines. *The Passion*, however, introduced new fissures into the conservative alliance. Fundamentalist Protestants offered serious theological critiques of the film, attacking its

PART I

attention to the Roman Catholic Mass, the Stations of the Cross, and other elements of Catholic tradition; its devotional focus on Mary; and its use of nonbiblical sources. For some, the very depiction of Jesus himself was idolatrous. For many years, Ingersoll notes, a common cultural agenda had bridged a theological divide. However, she concludes, the conservative response to *The Passion* suggests that theological differences may be putting stress on the political coalition.

CHAPTER ONE
ALMOST A CULTURE WAR: THE MAKING OF *THE PASSION* CONTROVERSY
Mark Silk

The controversy over *The Passion of the Christ*, which began a year before the movie opened, threatened to turn into one of the uglier culture wars that have bedeviled American society over the past couple of decades. That it didn't quite do so can be explained, in part, by the specific course of events, which tended to keep the combatants from fully engaging each other, and even more by strongly divergent views of the film that ultimately emerged within the conservative coalition that normally fights as a united front. This chapter seeks to explore the roots of this near-culture war by looking closely at the early media coverage of *The Passion*. In today's world, a culture war is, virtually by definition, a media war. Telling the story means recounting how the ink was spilled and the electrons hurled; the war narrative is a metanarrative of stories told and spun.

When the first reports that Mel Gibson was making a movie about the death of Jesus began to surface in August 2002, there was not a whiff of anticipated controversy. A *New York Daily News* article, for example, announced that Gibson was scouting hillscapes in southern Italy to shoot the film.[1] In September there were news flashes that shooting would start in November. Gibson himself was rather blithe. His favorite quote, repeated more or less verbatim again and again, had to do with his decision to film the story in Latin and Aramaic—two dead languages. "They think I'm crazy, and maybe I am," he said. "But maybe I'm a genius."[2]

By January 2003, however, the auteur was beginning to complain that there were people, muckraking journalists, who were out to get him. The most detailed of the denunciations came in an appearance that month on Fox television's *The O'Reilly Factor:*

> *Gibson:* Since I've been in Rome here, for example, I know that there are people sent from reputable publications who . . . start digging into your private life. . . . And then they start bothering your friends and your business associates and harassing your family, including my 85-year-old father. And I find it—it's a little spooky.
>
> *O'Reilly:* We have heard that there is a reporter trying to dig up dirt on you, and who has bothered your 85-year-old father, trying to get provocative statements from him, and trying to portray you as a fanatic and perhaps a bigot, that this guy is operating right now. He's trying to dig up dirt on Mel Gibson. And do you believe it's because you're making this movie about Jesus?
>
> *Gibson:* I think it is, yes. I think he's been sent. So, that's the way it is. . . . I'm a big boy and I can take care of myself. . . . But if you start picking on my family when I'm out of town, get ready.
>
> *O'Reilly:* But I'm surprised that someone would go after somebody as well-liked as you are and as powerful as you are. And you really believe it's because you're making this movie about Jesus?
>
> *Gibson:* Yes, I think so. Yes, I think there's a lot of things that don't want it to happen.[3]

Months later, in the second of what turned into four articles on the film and its maker, the *New York Times*'s Sunday culture columnist Frank Rich charged Gibson with ginning up hostility to his project when none was there.[4] However, it turned out that a writer had indeed been doing the things that Gibson charged, if not in the ominous spirit portrayed. He was Christopher Noxon, a Los Angeles freelancer who had successfully pitched a story about Gibson, his faith, and his new movie to the *New York Times Magazine* after learning the Gibson was building his own church in the hills near his Malibu home. In an e-mail he sent me in January 2004, Noxon explained the background to the story:

> Two years ago, my dad noticed surveyor stakes on a hill near his home in Agoura Hills. Along with other neighbors active in a local homeowners group, he met with a church leader, who explained that it was a tra-

ditionalist congregation and that services would be conducted entirely in Latin. The $2.8 million construction was being picked up by a single congregant, who he described as "a very spiritual figure on the world stage."

Gibson's involvement was an interesting celebrity tidbit, but it wasn't anything I felt particularly compelled to write about. Mr. Gibson's longtime marriage, seven children and conservatism are well known in Hollywood, and while it didn't sound like his congregation was practicing garden-variety Catholicism, I certainly didn't have any interest in poking around a guy's church just because he's famous.

But over the next few months, other signs that something serious was going on with Gibson convinced me the story was worth pursuing. First came news of "The Passion," which in addition to representing a huge commercial and artistic risk, is also an open effort to evangelize. Then, poking around on the Internet, I learned about his father, his books and the Alliance for Catholic Tradition. I went to parochial school myself but never knew anything about the traditionalist movement—it was fascinating stuff, and with Mr. Gibson's involvement I knew there was a story to be told. . . .

It's important to note that while I did have a family connection to the story, my father didn't oppose Mr. Gibson's church. After reviewing the plans and coming to an agreement covering such issues as parking, signage and hours of operation, his neighborhood group gave the project their stamp of approval. By all accounts, that review was a routine process and the relationship between the church and the neighbors was entirely amicable. Mr. Gibson's lawyer Martin Singer has subsequently threatened to take action against me, the *Times* and even my father and his neighbors, on the grounds that my piece was an act of retribution linked to a land dispute. This is nonsense, and easily confirmed as such.[5]

Gibson himself had declined to be interviewed for the article, so Noxon focused much of his attention on the eighty-five-year-old Hutton Gibson, a leading figure in the Catholic traditionalist movement. According to the published article, Hutton was more than happy to welcome the young journalist into his Houston home and treat him to a full dose of sedevacantism[6] and antisemitism. While Noxon made it clear that Mel Gibson did not necessarily share all his father's views, he did suggest that the younger Gibson was no fan of the Vatican, having been quoted in the Italian newspaper *Il Giorno* as attacking the Vatican as a "wolf in sheep's clothing." Overall, if it was not a flagrantly hostile piece, it could hardly be considered the kind of advance notice that a producer-director would want for his $25 million high-risk exercise in religious filmmaking.

The week before the article appeared, Rabbi Marvin Hier, founder and dean of the Simon Wiesenthal Center in Los Angeles—the *New York Times Magazine* apparently having shown him an advance copy—issued a statement expressing concern about the forthcoming movie. "Obviously, no one has seen 'The Passion' and I certainly have no problem with Mel Gibson's right to believe as he sees fit or make any movie he wants to," Hier said. "What does concern me, however, is when I read that the film's purpose is to undo the changes made by Vatican II. . . . If the new film seeks to undo that . . . it would unleash more of the scurrilous charges of deicide directed against the Jewish people, which took the Catholic Church 20 centuries to finally repudiate."[7]

Gibson and his production company, Icon, responded by drumming up support at the conservative end of the media spectrum. On 6 March, three days before publication of Noxon's *Times* article, a Q-and-A interview with Gibson appeared in Zenit, an international news service dedicated to covering the Catholic Church. Zenit is owned by the Legion of Christ, an ultraconservative order of priests founded in the mid-twentieth century by a Mexican priest.[8] Asked how he could be so sure that his film was accurate, Gibson told Zenit, "We've done the research. I'm telling the story as the Bible tells it. I think the story, as it really happened, speaks for itself. The Gospel is a complete script, and that's what we're filming."[9]

The next day, the *Wall Street Journal* ran, with a "Rome" dateline, a puff piece on the shooting of the film written by the news director of EWTN, Mother Angelica's Eternal Word Television Network, another expression of ultraconservative Catholicism, which bills itself as the world's largest religious television network. The article's final paragraph reads, "'I look at myself as a conduit here—a tool, using what God gave me,' Mr. Gibson says. For those who still doubt the power of faith and the merits of sacrifice, one has only to peek into Studio 5 to see them in bold, passionate flower."[10] Three days later, on 10 March, NewsMax.com, a conservative American online news service, picked up Gibson's Zenit interview.[11] Like Zenit, NewsMax served as an early and ongoing principal source of pro-Gibson news and commentary. On 11 March, for example, it took up cudgels against Rabbi Hier; on 26 March it ran a column titled

"Crucifying Mel Gibson."[12] Fully eleven months before the film's release, the forces engaged in regard to *The Passion* were divided, on the one side, between Noxon's *New York Times Magazine* article and Rabbi Hier and, on the other, a clutch of religiously and politically right-wing Gibson defenders on television, in print, and online.

Then onto the field marched the United States Conference of Catholic Bishops (USCCB), a soon-to-be-notorious committee of Roman Catholic and Jewish scholars, and the Anti-Defamation League (ADL). The scholars' committee was assembled by Eugene Fisher, associate director of the Secretariat for Ecumenical and Interreligious Affairs (SEIA) of the USCCB and the bishops' professional liaison for Catholic–Jewish relations. Noxon's article had prompted Fisher to suggest to Icon that it might be useful for a group of Catholic and Jewish scholars, acting under the auspices of the SEIA and the ADL, to review the screenplay.[13] Icon did not reply formally, but a copy of what turned out to be the shooting script somehow found its way to Rabbi Yehiel Poupko, the head of an education center at the Chicago Jewish Federation. Poupko took it to Father John Pawlikowski, a leading figure in national Catholic–Jewish dialogue with whom he had been engaged in interfaith discussions. Pawlikowski in turn sent the script to Fisher, who informed Icon that he had the script and would give it to the scholars for review.[14] As of 22 April, Easter Sunday 2003, the scholars had their copies. As it happened, however, the same day the *Los Angeles Times* published a story headlined "Scholars Concerned about Film's Fallout."[15] It quoted two members of the committee, Sister Mary Boys of the Union Theological Seminary in New York and Eugene Korn, then the ADL's director of interfaith affairs. Both expressed worries about how the film would portray the story of Jesus's death. Neither indicated that they had seen the script; indeed, Korn was quoted as saying he would wait "a suitable amount of time" for Gibson "to respond to the request for a panel of scholars to read the script." It seems clear that the interviews took place before Fisher, let alone the scholars, had received the script.

Not long thereafter, according to sources at the USCCB, an extended phone conversation took place between Fisher and Gibson himself. While Gibson, not surprisingly, was less than happy with the *Los Angeles Times* story, he apparently expressed interest in what the scholars would have to say about his screenplay; there were no angry demands that this "purloined" or "stolen" script, as it came to called, be returned to its rightful owner.[16] In the middle of May, Fisher sent the scholars' eighteen-page report to Icon, with the understanding that this was a private communication. The report, which was not made available to the public until after the movie was released, turned out to be highly critical of Gibson's version of the Passion story; it expressed particular concern about its representation of the Jews.[17] After a couple of weeks of silence, Icon responded by demanding that the script be returned immediately along with an apology. Failure to comply, Icon threatened, would result in lawsuits against both the USCCB and the ADL. Meanwhile, the existence of the report became known via a 30 May Zenit story that displayed considerable familiarity with its contents.[18] Representatives of Gibson and Icon later claimed that the scholars were responsible for leaking the document, but it is highly unlikely that scholars would have gone to Zenit, virtually a Gibson house organ, to bring their particular concerns to light.

At USCCB headquarters in Washington, there was a sense was that the Gibson people were spoiling for a public fight. Unlike the ADL, however, which simply ignored the threatened lawsuit, the USCCB responded by returning the copies of the script and tendering a tepid apology. Not that the USCCB considered the threatened lawsuit anything to worry about—to the contrary. Rather, it seems, there was concern that Fisher, a lay professional staff member, had acted too independently: no bishops' committee or secretariat formally had authorized the report, which had been sent to Icon with a cover letter on USCCB letterhead. The apology made all this clear and put off until the actual appearance of the movie a judgment on the merits.[19]

Like any other complex institution, the USCCB is home to people of differing views and perspectives—including, of course, the bishops themselves. Indeed, the 30 May Zenit story that broke the news about the "Scholars' Group" report begins by mentioning a defense of Gibson by Denver's Archbishop Charles Chaput, who two days earlier had attacked those he called "some critics and scholars."[20] The criticism, he wrote, "seems based on an earlier, working draft of the script that Gibson says was stolen and leaked; in other words, an inaccurate text that was acquired—to put it politely—by unauthorized means."[21] Chaput allowed as how he hadn't seen the film or read "the final script," but the following month he saw the film and turned into the film's strongest promoter among American Roman Catholic bishops.[22]

Even as the USCCB declined to take up Gibson's gauntlet, Icon did what it could to exaggerate the extent of the USCCB's apology, creating an indelible impression that the scholars had stolen the script and that they had criticized the film on behalf of a politically correct ecumenist agenda that had nothing to do with church norms. As William J. Cork observes in chapter 2 in this volume, no one did more to solidify this impression than William Donohue and his Catholic League for Religious and Civil Rights.[23] On 24 June, the ADL issued the kind of careful statement that, in the best of all worlds, would have come from the SEIA as well. It expressed support for the scholars report and laid out the reasons for concern about how the screenplay portrayed Jews and Judaism.[24] The next day, the Catholic League issued a news release, "ADL Attacks Mel Gibson," followed a week later by another, "Catholic Bishops Did Not Condemn Gibson Movie." Subsequent releases accused *The New Republic* of libeling Gibson and defended the film against criticism by the ADL's Korn and Foxman, who saw a private screening of the film in Houston on 8 August.[25] That Donohue, a self-appointed defender of the institutional church, should take up cudgels on behalf of an irregular Catholic like Gibson says something about the ideological politics of Roman Catholicism today.

Amid the controversy that broke out in June, Gibson began showing cuts of the film to friendly columnists and religious leaders, the majority of them not Catholic. With apparently the sole exception of the Houston screening for Foxman and Korn, only the most ideologically friendly Jews—people like Rabbi Daniel Lapin and movie critic Michael Medved—were included among the early invitees. Later, flocks of evangelical ministers were invited to screenings around the country; all they had to do was sign a pledge in which they agreed to keep confidential their "exposure, knowledge and opinions of the film"—while at the same time they were "free to speak out in support of the movie and your opinions resulting from today's exposure to this project and its producer."[26] This clever marketing campaign resulted in waves of enthusiasm from the like-minded pundits and pastors, while almost all those who might be critical were left waiting for the movie to appear.

With the notable exceptions of the *New York Times*'s Frank Rich and Paula Fredriksen of the scholars' committee, who wrote a lengthy article in *The New Republic*, those who might otherwise have taken up cudgels against the Gibson partisans' attacks on the scholars and the ADL for the most part held their peace.[27] After all, they had not seen the film and were in no position to judge for themselves. The most important story about the movie to appear over the summer of 2003, Peter J. Boyer's *New Yorker* article "The Jesus War," was a good deal more sympathetic to Gibson than to his critics. (Boyer himself was shown an early cut of the film, which he said he found "riveting and quite disturbing.")[28]

The apotheosis of the publicity effort was the apparently successful effort by the Gibson folks to get a copy of *The Passion* into the pope's own DVD player. After one high-ranking Vatican official reported that John Paul II had pronounced that "it is as it was," a welter of claims and counterclaims ensued, culminating in a categorical denial by Archbishop Stanislaw Dziwicz, the pope's private secretary, that John Paul had made any remark at all about the film. In the United States, the story spun into a media *Twilight Zone*. Rod Dreher, a conservative columnist for the *Dallas Morning News*, declared,

> Here's what I think. The pope was quoted accurately, but, for some reason, Vatican officials became uncomfortable with it. So they changed their official story. If doing so makes honorable filmmakers and journalists, Catholics among, come off as sleazebags or dupes—well, that's life.[29]

Regular members of the Vatican press corps, such as John Allen of the *National Catholic Reporter*, fumed. "Reporters, myself certainly included," Allen wrote, "look like naïfs who have been spun every which way, or worse yet, like willing partners in someone's dishonesty." Allen went on to say of the Vatican, "Even if officials were acting for the noblest of motives, they have stretched the meaning of words, on and off the record, to their breaking point. Aside from the obvious moralism that it's wrong to deceive, such confusion can only enhance perceptions that the aging John Paul II is incapable of controlling his own staff, that 'no one is in charge' and the church is adrift."[30] It appears to have dawned on the pope's courtiers that if a serious denial was not issued, the planet was going to be inundated with DVDs—not to mention posters and television commercials—featuring the testimonial, "It is as it was—Pope John Paul II."[31]

The Vatican takes a very dim view of using the pope's name for commercial gain. At the same time, the fracas likely did not upset Gibson himself in the least: not only was it boffo for business, but it also reflected badly on that "wolf in sheep's clothing" occupying the Vatican. Still, whatever else it did, this papal contretemps served notice on Gibson's U.S. Roman Catholic supporters that the Vatican might have some problems with Gibson's movie—and possibly with Gibson himself. By January, at any rate, they seemed to be keeping their enthusiasm for *The Passion* under control.[32] (The same could not be said for the film's evangelical enthusiasts, however.[33])

Already muddled by the confusion over the pope's purported endorsement, the nascent culture war over the film was stymied after the film's release when one wing of the right's staunchest culture warriors went AWOL. Since the beginning of America's post-Vietnam culture wars, Jewish neoconservatives have been key players. Unlike many of their coreligionists, they have been happy to link arms with conservative Christians, who, following Israel's victory in the 1967 Six-Day War and its emergence as a strong pro-Western outpost in the Middle East, have to show increasing support for Israel and Judaism. During 2003, therefore, support from Jewish neoconservatives like Lapin and Medved seemed to predict that the neocons would support Gibson and his film as part of the larger fight for "values" in Hollywood. It didn't happen. There were hints that it wouldn't as early as October, when Dennis Prager—a neocon commentator acclaimed in conservative Christian circles for his tireless promotion of "traditional family values" in the Jewish community—began advancing a "two movies" thesis about the film in secular, Christian, and Jewish media outlets. "For two hours, Christians watch their savior tortured and killed," wrote Prager, who had previewed the film at Gibson's invitation. "For the same two hours, Jews watch Jews arrange the killing and torture of the Christians' savior."[34] Although he contended that "many Jewish groups and media people now attacking 'The Passion' have a history of irresponsibly labeling conservative Christians anti-Semitic," he wrote that, nonetheless, "I cannot say that I am happy this film was made." By granting the legitimacy of both critics' and advocates' reactions—and including himself among the critics—Prager undermined the "either/or" logic of the brewing culture war.

That logic collapsed further on the film's release in February 2004, when prominent Jewish voices on the right—columnists like Charles Krauthammer, William Safire, Mona Charen, and Jeff Jacoby; historian and neocon elder stateswoman Gertrude Himmelfarb; and Rabbi Yechiel Eckstein of the philo-Christian International Fellowship of Christians and Jews—roundly attacked the film.[35] Their consternation seems to have had some impact on their Christian ideological soul mates; Gibson's mainstream supporters largely ceased their attacks on critics of the film, contenting themselves with praising the film and its obvious appeal to masses of Americans.[36] They stopped portraying Gibson as the innocent victim he made himself out to be and his critics as uniformly anti-Christian or antireligious or politically correct zealots. The one notable exception was columnist and sometime GOP presidential aspirant Patrick Buchanan, who, in the pages of his magazine, *The American Conservative*, assailed the film's neoconservative Jewish critics—his longtime archrivals in the conservative movement. By Buchanan's lights, "Those who hate *The Passion* are almost all on the other side" in the culture war that he had announced in his famous speech to the 1992 Republican National Convention. "Braveheart," he concluded, "has led and won a great victory in the crusade that is the culture war that will determine the fate of the civilization that came out of what happened on Calvary and on that first Easter morning."[37] But Buchanan notwithstanding, by the time *The Passion of the Christ* had (with a brief resurrection at Easter) yielded its top box office position to *Dawn of the Dead* and *Hellboy* and *Kill Bill II*, the clearing smoke suggested that Gibson's crusade had come up short.

Notes

1. Rush et al. 6 August 2002.

2. United Press International 2002; Herbert 2002. For a variant, see Zenit 2002: "Many think I am mad, and perhaps I am. Or maybe I am a genius."

3. O'Reilly 2003.

4. Rich 3 August 2003. Rich's subsequent columns appeared 21 September 2003, 18 January 2004, and 7 March 2004.

5. Noxon, personal communication. The article itself appeared in the *New York Times Magazine* on 9 March 2003.

6. The belief that the pope is illegitimate and therefore that the See of Peter is "vacant." Contemporary sedevacantists hold that all popes beginning with John XXIII are illegitimate; therefore, the See of Peter has been vacant since 1958, and none of the Roman Catholic's teachings since then have any authority, least of all the statements associated with Vatican II.

7. Simon Wiesenthal Center 2003. The statement received national attention on 13 March when Fox News featured an interview with Hier on *The O'Reilly Factor* (O'Reilly 2003).

8. For an account of the Legion, see Berry and Renner 2004, 1–221. Unconfirmed reports suggested that there were Legionaries on the *Passion* set during filming; in any event, the movie's credits thank the Legion of Christ.

9. Zenit 3 March 2003.

10. Arroyo 2003.

11. NewsMax.com is run by Christopher Ruddy, one of the cadre of right-wing journalists who made names for themselves by attacking the Clinton administration. Ruddy is the author of the 1997 book *The Strange Death of Vincent Foster*. Advertising itself as "America's News Page," NewsMax features an array of punditry from the Rush Limbaugh wing of the Republican Party.

12. Hirsen 2003; Brennan 2003.

13. For a detailed chronology of this episode from the perspective of one of the scholars involved, see Fredriksen 2003. For an account of the "Scholars' Group" controversy as it played out in the media, see Silk 2004, the sources for which also inform my analysis here.

14. In the subsequent controversy, Gibson's defenders took to asserting that the script reviewed by the scholars was a preliminary one—presumably much revised prior to the filming—but that turned out not to have been the case.

15. Levine 2003, E3.

16. Less than three weeks after Zenit broke the scholars' committee story, Tracy Connor of the *New York Daily News* already was referring to the script as "purloined" (Connor 2003). On 14 August 2003, William A. Donohue of the Catholic League for Religious and Civil Rights wrote to the *New York Times* that "Mr. Gibson has had his script stolen." See also Parker 2003.

17. Boys et al. 2003.

18. Zenit, 30 May 2003. William J. Cork (chapter 2 in this volume) notes that he received an e-mail copy of the report on 26 June; who put it into the electronic pipeline I cannot say.

19. Whether the USCCB would have beaten such a retreat had the procedural faux pas occurred on a different matter I cannot say. Nevertheless, if the bishops had responded to Icon's demands by supporting the scholars' concerns about of the script—instead of hanging them out to dry—much of the ugliness that followed might well have been avoided.

20. Chaput 2003.

21. Chaput 2003, quoted in Zenit 30 May 2003.

22. In his 28 January newspaper column, Chaput (2004) urged his flock to purchase tickets for a special advance screening to be shown on 28 February; at

that time the archdiocese's home Web page featured a display ad for the special screening, with a note to the effect that the proceeds would "benefit our archdiocesan seminaries and formation programs" (Archdiocese of Denver 2004).

23. William J. Cork (chapter 2 in this volume).
24. Anti-Defamation League 2003.
25. Catholic League for Religious and Civil Rights 25 June 2003, 1 July 2003, 21 July 2003, 12 August 2003.
26. Kennedy 2004.
27. Fredriksen 2003.
28. Boyer 2004.
29. Dreher 22 January 2004.
30. Allen 23 January 2004.
31. Outside the United States, that is exactly what happened. For example, in strongly Roman Catholic central Europe, the epigraph appeared in promotional material for the film.
32. Indeed, growing pressure to state clearly whether Gibson was in communion with the Church culminated in a statement by the archbishop of the diocese in which Gibson lives, Cardinal Roger Mahony of Los Angeles, on 20 February 2004. In a live online chat on Beliefnet.com, Mahony stated that Gibson "does not participate in any parish of this Archdiocese" and that "he, apparently, has chosen to live apart from the communion of the Catholic Church." Mahony concluded his statement with the rather damning words, "I pray for him" ("Live Chat" 2004). However clear the statement, nonetheless it is instructive that Mahony's comment appeared in an extremely obscure forum, so obscure that the national media took no notice of what might have been a major story on the eve of the film's release.
33. See Leslie Smith (chapter 3 in this volume).
34. Prager 2003; see also Eckstein 9 April 2004.
35. Krauthammer 2004; Safire 2004; Charen 2004; Jacoby 2004; Himmelfarb 2004; Eckstein 16 February 2004.
36. See Ingersoll (chapter 5 in this volume) for a discussion of the debate that emerged at the evangelical/fundamentalist fringe.
37. Buchanan 2004.

CHAPTER TWO
PASSIONATE BLOGGING: INTERFAITH CONTROVERSY AND THE INTERNET
William J. Cork

Mel Gibson's *The Passion of the Christ* became the subject of intense discussion more than a year before its release. News coverage of the controversy focused on speculation and criticism by scholars and religious organizations as well as statements by celebrities and public relations professionals. But discussions also were taking place around workplace water coolers, in church and synagogue parking lots, and in our contemporary *Stoa*, the Internet.

The creation of the World Wide Web and hypertext by Tim Berners-Lee in the early 1990s had transformed the Internet from a network of university computers roamed by programmers and technicians into a new public forum. By the mid-1990s, anyone with a PC could surf for information as well as interact with others through e-mail, subscription-based e-mail discussion lists, and Web-based discussion "bulletin boards" and "chat rooms." The latest in this series of labor-saving devices for the Internet is the weblog, or simply blog, an electronic diary-cum-soapbox from which an individual can stand before the world and speak his or her mind on the issues of the day, from the Iraq War to *The Passion*.

The simplest definition of a weblog is that it is a Web page of "links with commentary, with the new stuff on top."[1] Today there are upwards of 4.12 million hosted weblogs, of which more than one hundred thousand are updated weekly.[2] Blogs have caught on for various reasons.[3] From a reader's perspective, they serve as guides to the Web, providing links to information that surfers might never happen to find. Blogs provide context for the sources they link to, both through commentary (especially useful if the blogger has expertise in the area) and by bringing together multiple links on a subject. Blogs are information filters with a personal touch, with readers drawn to particular blogs because of the uniqueness of the blogger.[4] When a blog has comment boxes, it facilitates community formation.

This chapter examines how bloggers wrote about *The Passion* even before its release.[5] How did bloggers approach the controversy? What is the potential of blogging for interfaith dialogue? Using my own experience of blogging about *The Passion* as a starting point, this chapter explores themes that arose in evangelical Protestant and Jewish conversations, particularly those illustrating how approaches differed across confessional lines.

Blogging *The Passion*

In December 2002, Amy Welborn became the first Catholic blogger to take note of Gibson's then-forthcoming film.[6] I mentioned it for the first time in January 2003 and referred to a *Time* magazine report from Gibson's set.[7] I made no mention of anything controversial about the film until 9 March, when I linked to Christopher Noxon's *New York Times Magazine* piece. I called Noxon's story "bizarre" and a "hatchet job" because it seemed to be a scattered attack on everything from the movie to Gibson's traditionalist Catholic beliefs, hints of which Noxon discerned in earlier Gibson films such as *Signs* and *We Were Soldiers*.

A key element of blogging is "linking," or creating a hypertext Internet link to another website, especially that of a media outlet. The appearance of news articles, opinion pieces, and other Web material often drives blogging debates. Thus, both the controversy and my blogging about it intensified in June 2003, when Gibson threatened a lawsuit against the Anti-Defamation League (ADL) and the United States Conference of Catholic Bishops (USCCB) for their role in facilitating a "Scholars' Report" based on a copy of the shooting script.[8] On 22 June, I linked to my brother's report about having seen an early preview of *The Passion* at the Atlanta Eucharistic Congress the previous day.[9]

More information about the script review became available on 25 June, and the blogging community took note. I criticized the media for not representing the nature of the criticisms accurately. Links abounded: I linked to an "ADL Statement on Mel Gibson's 'The Passion'" (24 June;

their first on the subject), which itself was responding to a press release from the USCCB distancing the Bishops' Conference, as well as the Bishops' Committee for Ecumenical and Interreligious and Affairs (BCEIA), from the "Scholars' Report."[10] The ADL press release, though careful not to criticize the USCCB, nonetheless linked to a 17 June statement in which the four Catholic members of the "Scholars Group" (the panel that had authored the report) defended their findings.[11]

The point and counterpoint of the press releases launched a series of blogs debating the issue: was the ADL overreacting, or "hyperventilating," as Mark Shea put it?[12] Were Catholics being censored, as Phil Lawler suggested?[13] I posted a summary of the facts known to date and concluded that I did not believe it was the ADL that was "hyperventilating." I linked to a press release from William Donohue of the Catholic League for Religious and Civil Rights[14] that in my view set the tone for future defense of Gibson by conservative Catholics. It focused not on the substance of the criticisms but on the "stolen" script and sought to drive a wedge between the Scholars Group and the BCEIA and between Christians and Jews. The themes introduced by Shea and Lawler, that the criticism was motivated by "fund-raising" and perhaps anti-Catholicism, also would recur, there and elsewhere.

On 26 June, I received an e-mail copy of the "Scholars' Report." The same day, blogger and screenwriting consultant Barbara Nicolosi announced, "I saw *The Passion*." The screening Nicolosi attended was the first in a series of private screenings to which Gibson invited those he thought would respond positively. Confidentiality agreements ensured that only positive reviews would get out. Nicolosi called *The Passion* "a stunning work of art," "devout," an "act of worship." It was, she said, "no more anti-Semitic than is the Gospel. . . . Having seen the film now, I can only marvel that the attacks are pretty much demonic." She concluded with an invitation, "I'll take questions." When I sent questions based on the Report, she replied,

> Would it help if I said that some of the Romans in the movie are shown as being cruel, twisted and blood-thirsty? Does that make you feel better? I'm not going to answer these specific questions because they come from an unpublished version of a script that was then unfairly trashed and copied. I can't comment on anything that came out of that vile and disgusting process.

I noted the exchange on my blog and commented, "This is unfortunate. She could clear up a lot of rumor and misunderstanding, but is apparently choosing not to do so." My posts from that date began to reflect my growing concern that emotional defense of the film was preventing objective discussion of the questions that it raised.

"I was still pretty neutral before I saw the reactions to the trailers and to this screening," I wrote; "now I'm worried. This film is showing the capability of stirring up raw emotion, emotion which is convinced that it is right and that those who question are 'demonic.'"[15]

As I continued to follow the controversy, I began to get accusatory e-mails from a few readers of my blog, repeating arguments made by Nicolosi, Donohue, Shea, and Lawler. Some denied that antisemitism was a concern today; to show that it is, I began linking to websites showing that antisemitism remains alive on the traditionalist fringe of Catholicism.[16] I also linked[17] to a *USA Today* article that detailed how several recent movies (*The Incredible Hulk*, the *Lord of the Rings* trilogy, and the *Star Wars* series) had been the subject of Internet rumor and debate long before they were released, yet, unlike Icon, the producers and directors of those films reacted positively to the fan involvement.[18]

Gibson next began to show the movie to prominent Jews with conservative political leanings, partly in order to delegitimize the ADL's criticism. The tactic did not calm the debate in the blogosphere.[19] My blogging on the movie increased following a Houston screening on 8 August attended by a number of my friends. As more of my readers attended *Passion* screenings in subsequent months, I increasingly could comment on specific issues in the film itself (rather than in one version of the shooting script) as well as on how Jews and Catholics were experiencing the film differently.

On 16 January, I attended a screening in Denver and thereafter began commenting on the film as I had seen it. At first, I did so indirectly, but in February, as more reviews began to appear in other sources, I posted an in-depth analysis.[20] The discussions in which I participated on the blogs and in person, after August, however, followed the pattern already established. I wanted to discuss the positives and negatives of the film, but the film's most vigorous defenders seemed interested only in polarization. Though some bloggers have provided balanced coverage (notably Amy

Welborn), the attitude of Barbara Nicolosi was more typical (27 February, "Why do the heathen rage?"):

> I was marveling this morning at the horrific vitriol that some secularists are spewing towards Mel and his film—which is now really "our film" in the way that the Sistine Chapel and the Pieta are ours. I really have to take the Maureen Dowds and the Dominic Crossans, and the Christopher Kellys at their word that this bloodied, tortured Jesus in *The Passion of the Christ* is no one that they know. . . .
>
> Sorry, I just don't believe the protesters. I don't believe the journalistic outrage, the cultural pundits spewing warnings, and liberal scholars tearing their theological garments. I don't buy any of it. They are missing the one thing that would validate their claims to authority: quiet tears.

The most ardent defenders of the film chose to use it as a wedge to divide the true believers from the infidels, seemingly angry that some people refused to acknowledge "The Truth."

Conservative Protestant Reactions

Gibson's decision to target the marketing of the movie to evangelical Protestant organizations such as James Dobson's Focus on the Family proved to be a tremendous success. A number of publishers dedicated websites to *Passion*-related resources such as sermon helps, bulletin inserts, tracts, and discussion guides. The Web page of the North American Mission Board of the Southern Baptist Convention exemplifies the conservative Protestant approach. Refusing to be drawn into a debate about details of the movie, these organizations chose to concentrate instead on the opportunity before them:

> How do you use a motion picture event such as "The Passion of the Christ" to introduce people to Christ, while at the same time taking care not to endorse elements of an R-rated movie?
>
> This website is a resource for you and your church to use in order to use the impact of this movie to relate the rest of the story about the saving and redemptive power of the gospel.[21]

An indicator of the attention they paid, however, to marketing the film is that prominent evangelical clergy and educators took time to blog about *The Passion*. Albert Mohler, president of the Southern Baptist Theological Seminary, defended the film from the charge of antisemitism:

> The mainstream interfaith movement has decided that the gospels are inherently anti-Semitic and thus must be "corrected" by modern scholarship. Of course, what this means is that liberal scholars will cut and paste the New Testament to meet their modern standards of political correctness. . . .
>
> The issue of anti-Semitism is not even really relevant to the discussion. It tells us far more about the despisers of Christianity than about Christianity itself.[22]

Some conservative Protestant discussions of the film revealed a not-so-latent anti-Catholicism. Apologist James White blogged his concern about the presence of "unbiblical and extraneous Marian elements." He asked, "Could an Evangelical successfully 'filter out' the extraneous stuff? I suppose so, but it would take a conscious effort." His conclusion: "It is not nearly as accurate as we were told; it is truly a prize for Rome."[23]

Themes on Jewish Blogs

Jewish bloggers noticed the film before Catholics did; at least one, Naomichana, knew controversy would follow: "Where can I get into the betting pool on whether the absurdly-left-wing Jewish groups or the absurdly-right-wing Christian groups will condemn this project first?"[24] When controversy did erupt, many Jewish bloggers blamed the ADL for "harping on the issue."[25] They expressed concern that "restrictions on speech will always rear back and bite you on the ass. And make you look small and desperate too."[26]

There were, however, certain concerns that Jewish bloggers viewed as legitimate. One was the potential for violence.[27] Another was Gibson's stance on the Holocaust, which most likely caused the greatest concern among Jewish bloggers despite the delicacy and hesitancy with which they raised the issue.[28] Some hoped controversy would encourage honest dialogue.[29] While many were skeptical of critics of the film who had not seen it, some Jewish bloggers were even more critical of those who supported the film sight unseen.[30] Jewish bloggers paid more attention to *The Passion*'s evangelical Protestant defenders than to Catholics, perhaps because of the comments by one evangelical leader suggesting that Jewish criticism of "Passion" might weaken evangelical support of Israel.[31]

The controversy prompted many Jewish bloggers to learn about the Gospels, Passion plays, Christianity, and a German nun named Anne Catherine Emmerich.[32] Judith Weiss distinguished between Gibson's use of the gospel accounts and his use of the writings of Anne Catherine Emmerich; she linked to my blog and review and emphasized that Gibson was "adding scenes *not* in the Gospels."[33]

Reflections

Over the past year, I have often wondered whether we were in danger of losing forty years of progress in Jewish–Christian dialogue and to what degree that dialogue has influenced the grassroots. The release of *The Passion*, however, has brought about a revival of dialogue not only among academics and professionals but also in parishes and synagogues. These conversations, both online and in the "real world," are a sign of life and hope to me. They show that people are interested, even if they are at times ill informed or if they react emotionally when first presented with an opposing opinion.

As discussion forums, blogs are sites for exchange and debate; as links to other stories and perspectives, blogs are information filters, indeed gateways to a world of knowledge and opinion that can be daunting if approached without a guide. It seems to me that the major issue in ecumenism and interfaith dialogue today is not how to produce new statements but how to pass on to a younger generation what we have already learned and shared. Blogs could serve as such a tool, provided that they be used effectively for education and understanding.[34]

Pippa Norris has written about "the bridging and bonding role of online communities."[35] Some human communities are characterized by "bonding," in which individuals of similar belief or background come together for mutual purposes and to strengthen their common ties. Other community types seek to bridge differences, creating an inclusive community that can help overcome potentially dangerous divisions in society.

This distinction is true of online communities as well. People tend to be drawn toward those communities made up of people like themselves; this is true of both the Catholic and the Jewish blogging communities;

their online interaction is a bonding experience. However, the Internet can also bridge differences, bringing together people of different backgrounds or beliefs who might never meet in the brick-and-mortar world. Norris suggests that Internet communities could serve to mediate conflicts in strife-torn territorial communities, such as Belfast, Northern Ireland.

Blogging is a new technology, and to date a small percentage of Internet users are aware of the concept. Like all technologies, it has limits, but it also offers unexplored possibilities for community building and information dissemination. My own experience suggests that blogging could be useful in bridging faith divisions since it provides information and commentary as well as opportunities for building community. My role in blogging *The Passion* was to attempt to focus not only on the issues raised by scholars but also on the different perspectives of Catholics and Jews; this brought numerous new readers to my blog, both Christian and Jewish, living in places as distant from me and from one another as Jerusalem and California. Jewish readers wondered if any Christians could see the movie as they did and whether Christians could listen with respect to Jewish fears. Christians sought insight into the nature of the controversy, the history of interfaith dialogue, and the sources used by Gibson. They found, in my blog and others, a place where they could meet.

Weblogs Cited

Carter, Joe
   The Evangelical Outpost. http://www.evangelicaloutpost.com.

Cork, James R.
   JessnJim. http://unsinkablecork.com/jessnjim/weblog/.

Cork, William J.
   Ut Unum Sint. http://billcork.blogspot.com.

Horowitz, David
   "David's Blog." *FrontPage Magazine.* http://www.frontpagemag.com/blog/.

Lawler, Phil
   "Off the Record." *Catholic World News.* http://www.cwnews.com/offtherecord/offtherecord.cfm.

Lynn B.
   In Context. http://incontext.blogmosis.com/.

Mohler, Albert
    [Personal blog.] CrossWalk.com. http://www.crosswalk.com/news/weblogs/mohler/.

Naomichana
    Baraita. http://www.baraita.net/blog/.

Nicolosi, Barbara
    Church of the Masses. http://www.churchofthemasses.blogspot.com.

Pax, Salam
    Where Is Raed? http://dear_raed.blogspot.com.

Shea, Mark
    Catholic and Enjoying It. http://markshea.blogspot.com.

Smash, LT.
    LT Smash. http://lt-smash.us.

Solomonia
    Solomonia. http://www.solomonia.com/blog/.

Susanna
    Cut on the Bias. http://bias.blogfodder.net.

Volokh, Sasha, and David Bernstein
    The Volokh Conspiracy. Edited by Eugene Volokh et al. http://volokh.com.

Weiss, Judith
    Kesher Talk. http://www.hfienberg.com/kesher/.

Weiss, Steven I.
    Protocols. http://www.protocols.blogspot.com.

Welborn, Amy
    In Between Naps. http://amywelborn.blogspot.com.

White, James
    Apologetic Blog. Alpha and Omega Ministries. http://www.aomin.org.

Winer, Dave
    Scripting News. http://www.scripting.com.

Notes

1. Blood 2002, 3. The early history of blogging is covered by Blood 2000; see Barrett 1999 for an essay that helped define the genre.

2. See Henning 2003. The remaining four million blogs rarely are touched or were simply abandoned once the novelty had worn off. People under the age of thirty write more than nine out of ten blogs; more than half of all bloggers are female.

3. Blood 2000; Blood 2002, 10–17.

4. During the Iraq War, popular bloggers "LT Smash" (a Naval Reserve officer at a base in Kuwait) and "Salam Pax" (a twenty-nine-year-old Iraqi architect) brought the headlines to life as we read war news through their eyes. Pax's journals have been republished in book form (Pax 2003).

5. Writing about blogging presents unique challenges, as one must take into consideration the articles to which the blogger has chosen to link, the comments made by the blogger (and his readers, if he has comment boxes), how other bloggers react, and how these conversations flow over time.

6. Welborn 21 December 2002. See Weblogs Cited list on pages 42–43. All weblogs have archive pages accessible from the main page and organized by date. While some bloggers write under their own name, some use pseudonymous "screen names" that usually are nicknames, anonymous pseudonyms, or variations on their own names.

7. Bill Cork 20 January 2003; see also Corliss and Israely 2003. I had begun blogging in June 2002, when the community of Catholic bloggers known as "St. Blog's Parish" was experiencing rapid growth. Like other Catholics who began blogging at that time, my initial posts reflected a preoccupation with the sexual abuse crisis; blogging was a way to follow and share stories and to vent frustration. Soon, however, I began to concentrate on ecumenical and interfaith issues, and I christened my blog *Ut Unum Sint* (John 17:21, "that they might be one"). See Serafin, "Some Catholic Blogs," for a list; Drake 2002 and Linner 2004 discuss Catholic blogging.

8. See Silk (chapter 1 in this volume). On 22 June, I linked to a *National Catholic Register* article announcing that the bishops had apologized to Gibson for making use of a preliminary script. This was the first source to report that Dr. Eugene Fisher of the USCCB's Secretariat for Ecumenical and Interreligious Affairs and the ADL's Rabbi Eugene Korn had assembled a team of Jewish and Catholic scholars to review Gibson's script. See Walther 2003; Boys et al., "Report," 2003.

9. James Cork 2003.

10. USCCB 2003.

11. Boys, "Dramatizing the Death of Jesus," 2003.

12. Shea 25 June 2003.

13. Lawler 25 June 2003.

14. Catholic League 2003. Donohue was the first to accuse the Scholars Group of using a "stolen screenplay." He rejected accusations that the film was either antisemitic or too violent.

15. Bill Cork 27 June 2003.

16. Ciaccio 2003; "The Jews and the Passion"; "Against the Heresies"; "The Secret of the Masons" 1954; Cain 21 January 2004; Cain 10 February 2004; St. Joseph's Men Society 2004; White 2004.

17. Bill Cork 1 July 2003.

18. Bowles 2003.

19. See Shea's claim (31 July 2003) that the criticisms constituted "blind prejudice," an ad hominem "attack" on Mel Gibson, and the advancement of a "liberal agenda." I had not acknowledged publicly that I had a copy of the "Scholars' Report," but it was guiding my selection of material to post as well as the questions I was raising on the blog. In my response to Shea (1 August 2003), I defended the questions as an effort "to seek truth—and that's what Mel says he is about." See also my posts on 3 August 2003 and 6 August 2003.

20. The analysis (13 February 2004, with subsequent revisions) also reflected a consolidation of my earlier blog posts on *The Passion*.

21. North American Mission Board 2004.

22. Mohler 2003. Some evangelicals questioned the Jewish criticism of the film, especially in view of a newly emergent Evangelical–Jewish alliance over Israel. Ted Haggard, president of the National Association of Evangelicals, issued a not-so-veiled threat: "There is a great deal of pressure on Israel right now, and Christians seem to be a major source of support for Israel. . . . For the Jewish leaders to risk alienating 2 billion Christians over a movie seems shortsighted" (Greenberg 2003).

23. James White 2004. See Ingersoll (chapter 5 in this volume) for an extended discussion of this issue.

24. Naomichana 24 September 2002.

25. Solomania 30 January 2004.

26. Weiss 27 August 2003.

27. See, for example, Weiss 25 July 2003.

28. See, for example, the interchange between David Bernstein and Sasha Volokh on "The Volokh Conspiracy," 30 January 2004.

29. See, for example, Naomichana (16 October 2003). Judith Weiss first described *The Passion* somewhat tongue-in-cheek as a new form of interfaith dialogue (14 March 2003) but later (16 August) speculated that interfaith dialogue might have motivated Gibson to make changes to the film and she hoped that the film would create "a great opportunity for education." Susanna (9 March 2003), however, warned that dialogue should not become an "'I'm OK, You're OK! umbrella' that suggests all religions are the same." She feared that *The Passion* would "inspire more overheated rhetoric and sadly unscholarly accusations."

30. Steven I. Weiss (31 July 2003) felt that "even more unjustified is the support of it by those who haven't viewed it," particularly evangelical Protestants.

31. Judith Weiss (21 August 2003) said, "If conservative Christians are such fair-weather friends of Israel that they are willing to retract their support of Israel over Jewish discomfort with Mel Gibson's Passion play, why on earth should Jews kiss their butts to make them stay? Friends like that we don't need." See also Weiss 27 August 2003.

32. See, for example, Weiss 25 July 2003.

33. Weiss 24 February 2004.

34. Glenn 2003.

35. Pippa Norris 2004.

CHAPTER THREE
LIVING *IN* THE WORLD, BUT NOT *OF* THE WORLD: UNDERSTANDING EVANGELICAL SUPPORT FOR *THE PASSION OF THE CHRIST*
Leslie E. Smith

I'm not a preacher, and I'm not a pastor. But I really feel my career was leading me to make this [movie]. The Holy Ghost was working through me on this film, and I was just directing traffic. I hope the film has the power to evangelize.... Every one [*sic*] who worked on this movie was changed. There were agnostics and Muslims on set converting to Christianity.

—Mel Gibson[1]

At an early screening of *The Passion of the Christ* for evangelical Protestant pastors and church leaders, Mel Gibson encouraged his listeners to use the movie as a form of spiritual outreach. One conservative Christian commentator present at the screening remarked of it that "Mr. Gibson has wisely taken the message straight to the people who can evangelize for Christ—believers like you and me."[2] Asked for whom he created the film, "the church or the unchurched," Gibson replied, "Oh, that's easy, the unchurched."[3] What seems most clear about the film, despite the many questions that surround it, is that its creator sees it as a masterpiece with a mission.

American evangelicals went to great lengths to juxtapose their message of personal salvation and transformation with Gibson's cinematic work. They set up pro-*Passion* websites, circulated e-mail petitions supporting the film, and hired out entire theaters for free public screenings. In their eyes, Mel Gibson took a bold stand for Christian values with an equally bold film that serves as a stunningly powerful conversion tool.

That evangelicals should take advantage of what one observer called "the best evangelism opportunity in 2,000 years"[4] hardly is surprising—except that the traditionalist Catholic theology of Gibson's *Passion* contradicts the very ideological commitments that define evangelical Protestants as a group. Because evangelicals adhere strictly to the biblical text and believe that Christians are saved exclusively through the individual's personal faith in Jesus, they do not adhere to "tradition" in the Roman Catholic understanding of the term, nor do they grant theological authority to extrabiblical sources. To be sure, contemporary evangelicals are less likely to shun Catholicism per se than in earlier years, preferring instead to inquire whether the individual, Catholic or Protestant, has a "personal relationship" with Jesus Christ, meaning the sense of an ongoing connection between the individual and Jesus that enriches the believer's spiritual growth. Nevertheless, Catholic doctrines, traditions, and ritual practices—of the kind that appear throughout Gibson's *Passion*—do not sit easily with them.

Why did evangelical Protestants so eagerly embrace a film with such strong traditionalist Catholic overtones and clearly nonbiblical scenes?[5] And why a film produced and directed by a Hollywood actor known for cinematic portrayals of violence, especially considering how often evangelicals have targeted the mainstream entertainment industry for contributing to America's moral decline? How, indeed, did evangelical beliefs create a culture of enthusiasm for *The Passion of the Christ*?

I propose that Gibson's movie was met with great support in evangelical circles because it exemplifies many of the qualities of modern American evangelical culture: it privileges emotional experience, it appeals to traditional American consumerism, and it asserts supernaturalism and moral absolutism in a rationalistic, postmodern society. *The Passion*'s synthesis of these three ideas preaches to and reaches an eager choir of evangelicals who believe that the film is yet another example of how they "live *in* the world" but are "not *of* the world."[6]

Who Are Evangelicals?

Like almost all conservative Christian theology, evangelical theology begins with the conviction that Jesus is the begotten son of God and that his life and death are part of a divine design to save humanity from its sinful nature. The Bible, which evangelicals believe to be the inerrant word of God, is the revelation that informs Christians of the details of this divine plan, whose centerpiece is Jesus's death and resurrection.[7] Evangelicals take the Bible both seriously and literally. They contrast themselves with those who consider it an example of mythology or who believe that its "spiritual truths" are purely metaphorical.[8]

While contemporary evangelicalism is defined by its desire to engage the world, such involvement has not always characterized the movement. For the majority of the twentieth century, conservative Christians were remarkable more for their separatism than for their cultural participation. Beginning in the 1970s, however, a segment of this group began to reach out to other Christians and nonbelievers; fueling this effort was, in large part, the sense that American values were moving in a direction contrary to Jesus's teachings. The mobilization of religiopolitical organizations, such as the Moral Majority and the Christian Coalition, and the artful use of televangelism generated a new wave of conservative Christians who were ardently committed to rescuing society from its sinful demise. Satan's tactics are cunning, indeed, this group argued, and no more so than in sexualized media images, moral relativism, liberalized education, and the constant scourge of abortion and homosexual rights groups that manipulated otherwise wholesome values like equality and justice in order to bolster their positions.[9] Known as evangelicals, the group's connection with culture at large distinguished it from its fundamentalist counterparts who "sought ways to withdraw, to fight back, and to exist in spite of" the modern world rather than to recognize and build on its rationalistic and pluralistic tones.[10]

Over the past quarter century, American evangelicals have come to define themselves in large part through their outreach to non- and nominal Christians; one of their defining characteristics is their desire to "seek out and save the lost."[11] They cite Jesus's "Great Commission" as their inspiration to evangelize the world: "Go therefore and make disciples of all nations, baptizing them in the name of the Father and of the Son and of the Holy Spirit, teaching them to obey everything that I have commanded you."[12] Saving the lost means guiding nonbelievers to a "personal relationship" with Jesus. This is a minimum criterion for evangelicals, for if one does not believe in Jesus, one believes very little.

Evangelicals remain true to their chosen mission to seek the lost—and to fight for them—by becoming part of the very culture they wish to transform. Their narratives often portray the culture of the "wider," nonevangelical world as a secular postmodern enemy. One part of their weaponry is surprising savvy with various media, from books and periodicals to music, television, and film, all of which have turned Sunday mornings or, indeed, entire weekends into impressive multimedia affairs. Evangelical megachurches (congregations whose attendance rivals that of major sporting events) offer members an encounter with religion like no other. The first and still perhaps the most noteworthy of these is Willow Creek Community Church, located in South Barrington, Illinois, a prosperous suburb north of Chicago. "Through drama, multi-media presentations, contemporary music and practical messages," Willow Creek "present[s] the ageless truths of the Bible in a format that's easy to understand, even if you've never been to church."[13] Willow Creek's offerings include a service for "Generation Xers" that exists alongside the more "traditional" (read: adult contemporary) worship atmosphere, a reception for new members that meets in the church's food court (which features a cappuccino bar and bookstore), and appearances by celebrities including figures such as country singer Randy Travis and quarterback Kurt Warner of the St. Louis Rams.[14] Truly, religious expression for twenty-first-century evangelicals is taking forms unimaginable to their counterparts from the past. Mastering the media and, in turn, the public has been a task that evangelicals have taken very seriously as they mobilize to fight cultural and spiritual corruption. With this in mind, it is easy to see how *The Passion of the Christ* had a ready-made fan club even before its release.

The Right Kind of Accuracy

A few weeks after *The Passion of the Christ* hit theaters, I attended a study group of evangelical Christians who were discussing the film's significance with the aid of a workbook titled *Experiencing the Passion of Jesus*, coauthored by Lee Strobel, former teaching pastor of Willow Creek Community Church.[15] Strobel, a former reporter, is known on the popular circuit for his series of books written as journalistic investigations into the "claims" of Christianity; his *Case for Easter* was released as a mass-market paperback to coincide with the release of Gibson's film.[16] The workbook is dotted with quotes from figures as varied as Aleister Crowley ("If one were to take the Bible seriously, one would go mad. But to take the Bible seriously, one must be already mad."); Pope John Paul II, who, after viewing the film, allegedly said, "It is as it was"; and Gibson himself ("My sins were the first to nail him to the cross.") in a format designed to lead the reader through various questions about Jesus's death to a clearly soteriological interpretation.[17]

One might expect that Gibson's historical and artistic license in creating *The Passion* would turn away evangelicals, whose commitment to biblical accuracy and literalism is well established. However, the members of my discussion group insisted that *The Passion* was a wholly reliable reflection of the Bible. Although they were able to find some degree of mismatch between Gibson's film and the biblical narratives of Jesus's death, the people with whom I spoke gauged *The Passion*'s accuracy not by measures of specific historicity but rather by the emotions the film evoked in the viewer and the extent to which it could lead to a conversion experience. To put it simply, this group of evangelicals assessed the realism of the film by its emotional impact. There is historical precedent for this response. Evangelicalism's lineage, in great part, is the story of long revivals, persuasive messages, and fiery preachers whose ability to evoke emotional responses generated thousands of conversions.[18] Strobel echoes this sentiment in his published reaction to the film:

> For the first time in my life I felt as if I were really *experiencing* what Jesus had endured. Book research, library studies, and interviews with scholars had given me cognitive knowledge, but now my heart engaged with history as never before. Tears flowed freely. The emotional impact of the film forever changed the way I would think about the crucifixion. . . . It wasn't until I endured the visual intensity of Gibson's film that I was able to absorb the emotional impact of the passion of Jesus.[19]

Similarly, Del Tackett, executive vice president of the conservative Christian group Focus on the Family, included in his official endorsement of *The Passion* a description of his emotional reaction to the film:

> I can't stop thinking about it nor can I stop talking about it. I have never seen a film that has so affected my life. It is powerful, moving, and disturbing. In re-telling one scene to my wife, I broke down. The film is true to the Bible and other historical evidence, yet it is alive with emotion and

the harshness of reality. I do not want to see it again, but I will be compelled from within to do so—not only again, but again and again.[20]

Strobel's and Tackett's testimonies demonstrate the natural partnership between the evangelical style and cultural forums, such as films, that incite an emotional response while focusing on a biblical theme. Since there is little to validate a conversion other than a new Christian's own conviction, he or she has only subjective emotional experience on which to rely in settling questions of religious accuracy. For this reason, it is easy for evangelical groups that emphasize emotion to elevate movies like *The Passion* to epic status.

Converting the Consumer

The primacy of emotionalism and individual subjectivity within evangelical religion arguably—and ironically—makes evangelicalism a quintessentially postmodern movement. Indeed, many modern evangelical groups attract converts by customizing services, sermons, and doctrines to align with widespread cultural trends or preferences. Through a contemporary worship atmosphere, various small-group formats, a certain informality on the part of both the leadership and the congregation, as well as engagement with themes and trends in popular culture, many evangelical "seeker services" attempt to prove that the individual's way can also be God's way.[21] This also means that evangelicals use consumer language to talk about the "individual."

Like the Chicago area's Willow Creek Community Church, Saddleback Church of Lake Forest, in southern Orange County, California, has reached megachurch status through its focus on creating personalized worship experiences. Saddleback is one of the nation's largest congregations, boasting an attendance of almost 24,000; its 2004 Easter services were the largest in record, with more than 39,000 attending.[22] The bulletin for the weekend after *The Passion*'s American release advertised twenty-five support groups, a café serving gourmet coffee and treats, and five different services that allowed the churchgoer to choose the style of music, service format, and even, in some circumstances, the demographic of the persons with whom one wished to worship. Featured prominently in church publications was the opportunity to engage in various studies of Gibson's *Passion*.[23]

Saddleback's senior pastor, Rick Warren, perhaps is best known for his books: *The Purpose-Driven Church* and *The Purpose-Driven Life*.[24] Warren, who founded Pastors.com, a website designed to support evangelical ministry leaders, has led the evangelical force in preaching, marketing, and supporting Gibson's endeavor.[25] Coupled with Warren's sermons on the film, which use catchy alliteration, multiple references to popular culture, and simple, clear-cut language, the Saddleback approach to *The Passion* transforms the torture and crucifixion of Jesus into an easily digestible theological tidbit.[26] When a columnist for *Christianity Today* expressed concern over the film's hype, wondering why the excitement over the movie was any different than "adult contemporary praise music, electing Republicans, or a new booklet or tract,"[27] Warren responded with a defense of his approach to evangelical "seeker" Christianity:

> In a culture where visual imagery is the main language for many, it [*The Passion*] is the perfect post-modern evangelistic tool. It doesn't preach; it just tells the story in an unsanitized and authentic way, and all of America is discussing it right now. The church should be leading that discussion.[28]

Warren's approach is based on the belief that if evangelicals ever hope to be heard by the wider culture, they must communicate through the venues of the same culture they are trying to reach. His efforts demonstrate how seriously and successfully evangelicals vie for the public's loyalties while also creating a product that can be the object of public demand.

However, some inevitable "sanitation" occurs through the marketing of the film despite what Warren describes as Gibson's efforts to the contrary. Various websites using *The Passion* name provide evangelicals opportunities to lighten their wallets, all in the name of witnessing to the lost. One website features a large selection of *Passion* T-shirts, coffee mugs, tote bags, and ball caps; at the same time, it reaches out to a younger, hipper crowd with wall clocks, coasters, infant bibs, and the "Passion Fashion pink camisole," all donning the slogan, "Christ Is My Passion, & I'm His Passion Too."[29] Included among the movie's officially licensed products is a necklace pendant in the shape of a nail used to affix Jesus to his cross. It is available in either pewter or silver. Bob Siemon Designs, creator of the pendant, markets it and other Passion memorabilia as "a unique and powerful way to express and share your faith."[30]

The materialistic quality of the response to *The Passion of the Christ* demonstrates that evangelicals are willing to spend, both economically and culturally, in ways that blend American consumerism with traditional revivalist fire. In a sense, they *have to* spend, for evangelicalism today is less about adopting theological tenets than about buying into a cultural identity.[31] Movies, clothing, and other cultural fanfare represent a mode of communication that creates a specific sense of community among believers while simultaneously fulfilling the ever-important responsibility to evangelize. Those who wear the T-shirts and leave coffee rings on *The Passion* coasters are sending not-so-discreet messages about who they are (or *whose* they are, evangelicals would counter), using a medium that society will understand. Employing the stuff of capitalism to communicate these messages is essential to evangelicalism's survival, for it long ago figured out that the "living in the world, but not of it" maxim has its limits. Reaching the lost in the American context means speaking the language of the lost as well.

Friends or Foes?

Although evangelicalism readily adapts itself to and is fueled by postmodern consumerist popular culture, paradoxically it simultaneously sees itself as the victim of that very culture. As such, another key reason for the success of Gibson's *Passion* is that it provides a rallying point for evangelicals who feel that American culture long has waged war on their values and deprived Christians of their share of positive cultural attention. Secular culture, they argue, ridicules conservative religious belief and the moral absolutes on which these beliefs are founded.

To the extent that evangelicals identify with *The Passion*, they understand criticisms of the film to be criticisms of evangelical Christianity or even as attacks on Jesus himself. Thus, many condemnations of the movie are read by evangelicals as symbolic recapitulations of the very events the film purports to chronicle. Some (including Gibson) have even likened critics' negative comments as evidence of the hand of Satan.[32]

This is why charges that the film displays unnecessarily graphic violence and antisemitism found little sympathy among evangelicals; most evangelical critics likely would charge that ulterior motives were at play in these accusations. For instance, one conservative commentator noted that "while pop-culture priests defend movies filled with sex, perversion and blasphemy in the name of free speech and tolerance, the same inquisitors plot crucifixion for a Jesus film that threatens to be faithful to the Gospels."[33] Focus on the Family founder and popular radio commentator James Dobson echoed the same sentiment when he remarked,

> In my estimation, the liberal backlash against *The Passion of the Christ* is incredibly significant. Shaky charges of "anti-Semitism" are really just a smokescreen. I believe that the real problem the liberal establishment has with this movie is that it has the audacity to portray Christ as He really was—not only as an historical figure, but as the Savior of mankind. That is an offense to the postmodern sensibilities of our morally relativistic culture. The fact that Mel Gibson actually hopes to use his movie as a vehicle for *evangelism* only adds fuel to the fire.[34]

One of the most prominent themes of *The Passion* is the experience of victimization.[35] The representation of the innocent victim kindles battle imagery very familiar to most evangelicals, who often see themselves as engaged in a struggle with a postmodern culture that not only counterattacks but, moreover, denies their very legitimacy. Thus, evangelicals see in the suffering Jesus a mirror of what they believe is their own persecution.[36] Because *The Passion* portrays a Jesus with whom, by all accounts, audiences of all backgrounds deeply sympathize, evangelicals have reason to cry victory: the audience response not only is a sign of legitimacy but also is one more battle won in the greater war to save all souls for Christ. Hence the significance of a comment left for Gibson on a pro-*Passion* website: "Thanks for finally recognizing the Christians!"[37]

Linda Kintz, a scholar of women and the religious right, notes that the products of contemporary culture's postmodernity—among other things, social fragmentation, lack of an "anchoring effect," and a general sense of unease—actually create the conditions that make conservatism both possible and popular.[38] Without the perception of social instability, there is little need for the absolutist moral and theological positions that evangelicalism provides. As such, if there is a "victory" for evangelicals in the promotion of *The Passion*, it is to be found in the middle ground, where familiar popular cultural forms make possible an appreciation of the rhetoric of absolutes.[39] Indeed, the evangelical preference to reform rather than eradicate "evil" institutions indicates their continuing necessity.

James Dobson's Focus on the Family website recognizes this when it addresses the concern that support for *The Passion* merely lines the pockets of media producers:

> If "Hollywood" producers want to make movies about Jesus, even if they stay true (as Gibson has) to the biblical "script," we should do everything we can to encourage them. What difference does it make if their past lives are morally imperfect or their doctrinal perspectives don't completely match our own? The Word of God retains its power in spite of human motives and agendas.[40]

Evangelicals, it seems, view a Hollywood transformed as better than no Hollywood at all if in its transformation it affords evangelicalism even a small degree of social legitimacy.

Conclusion

Understanding American evangelical support for *The Passion of the Christ* requires us to acknowledge the dynamics that created both phenomena; these dynamics are rooted in the way conservative Christians create and maintain their social groups. In this case, emotionalism, consumerism, and tension with the larger culture were the common elements that linked evangelicals to *The Passion* and, indeed, created a symbiotic relationship for them. The attention paid to *The Passion* was alluring to evangelicals because of the legitimacy that it granted both their group and their message.

To be sure, we should not overlook the fact that *The Passion* is, simply, an "easy sell" for evangelicals. In a world where their conservative values are being dislodged from places of privilege by pluralism's alternatives, evangelicals can invite the unchurched to experience the crux of the gospel story merely by watching a movie and can avoid those difficult conversations about morality and lifestyle.[41] This, perhaps, is the most interesting part of the equation, for if evangelicals hope to reach those they consider "lost," they must speak the language of the lost; if they seek to separate themselves from the world, they first must become a part of it. Gibson's film provides a reference point for evangelicals to see that when the hearts and minds of a pluralistic public are at stake, living in the world often means living *of* the world.

Notes

1. Gibson's statement is featured in Dobson 2004.
2. Landsbaum 2004.
3. Reid 2004, 5.
4. See McLaren 2004.
5. It is often just as troubling to many evangelicals to see biblical depictions that are out of context as it is to encounter nonbiblical materials that are presented as biblical. Examples of the former from the film include scenes that depict Jesus crushing a snake with his foot (a reference to Genesis 3:15) and his comments to Mary, his mother, while carrying the cross: "See, Mother, I make all things new" (a reference to Revelation 21:5). These images do not appear in the gospel accounts of Jesus's death. For more commentary on the variance between the film, the gospel accounts, and Christian theology, see Ingersoll (chapter 5 in this volume).
6. Claiming to live "*in* the world" but not to be "*of* the world" is a popular evangelical Christian saying that finds its roots in biblical passages such as 1 John 2:15–16: "Do not love the world or the things in the world. The love of the Father is not in those who love the world; for all that is in the world—the desire of the flesh, the desire of the eyes, the pride in riches—comes not from the Father but from the world."
7. Kellstedt et al. 1998, 175. See also Ingersoll (chapter 5 in this volume), who provides some historical background on the classic divisions within American Christianity that have played a role in the debate over *The Passion*.
8. Harding 2000, xv.
9. Ruether 2000 provides an excellent synopsis of the relationship between the Christian Right and its family-oriented agenda, the result of the political mobilization referenced here. See also Frankl 1998.
10. Ammerman 1987, 7.
11. Luke 19:10.
12. Matthew 28:19–20.
13. Willow Creek Community Church 2004.
14. Willow Creek Community Church 2004.
15. Strobel and Poole 2004.
16. Strobel 2004.
17. Strobel and Poole 2004, 34, 35, 20.
18. See, for example, Hatch 1989; Butler 1990.
19. Strobel and Poole, 2004, 5–6.
20. Tackett 2004.
21. Corbett 2000, 174.

22. Saddleback Church 2004; Saddleback Church Bulletin 28–29 February 2004. On a smaller scale, one need look no further than the corner church to find that congregations without the glamour and glitz are still tuning into the cultural wave, as sermons and small-group meetings on *The Passion* abound.

23. See Saddleback Church Bulletin 28–29 February 2004.

24. Warren 1995, 2002.

25. See Saddleback Church Bulletin 28–29 February 2004.

26. Warren, "Understanding the Passion," 2004.

27. McLaren 2004.

28. Warren, "Catching the Passion Wave," 2004.

29. "Passion Movie Inspired Gear" 2004. Evangelical material consumer culture has a long history, beginning with products associated with nineteenth-century temperance campaigns. In the 1990s, evangelicals launched a chastity campaign called *True Love Waits,* replete with "chastity rings," "TLW" clothing, and even a musical. See Landres 1996.

30. "Passion Jewelry" 2004.

31. I am indebted to both Brett Miller and Shawn Landres for helping me think through the implications of this point.

32. Neven 2003.

33. Vieth 2004.

34. Dobson 2004.

35. See Elcott (chapter 17 in this volume).

36. As an example of this, John 15:19–20 reads, "If you belonged to the world, the world would love you as its own. Because you do not belong to the world, but I have chosen you out of the world—therefore the world hates you."

37. Blankenship 2004.

38. Kintz 1997, 60–61.

39. This rhetoric of absolutes plays out in other cultural venues; one need look no further than the popular *Lord of the Rings* trilogy (Jackson 2001–2003) to see another battle between good and evil.

40. Focus on the Family 2004.

41. I thank Shawn Landres for noting this important point.

CHAPTER FOUR
THE PASSION PARADOX: SIGNPOSTS ON THE ROAD TOWARD MORMON PROTESTANTIZATION
Eric R. Samuelsen

Perhaps the central paradox of contemporary Mormonism has to do with the issue of assimilation, the ways in which Mormonism has moved from a radically transgressive nineteenth-century Christian heresy—millenarian, polygynous, eschatological, and communitarian—to one of the most respectable and mainstream of contemporary American Christian cultures. This shift, from what sociologist Armand Mauss has called "the predicament of disrepute" to the "predicament of respectability,"[1] might help explain such phenomena as the growing corporatization of the Mormon hierarchy, greater emphasis on issues of authority and obedience from the pulpit, and growing intolerance for theological speculation, cultural dissent, and doctrinal heterodoxy. On the other hand, most Mormons generally would discount this analysis and would agree with Jan Shipps that the perception that "Mormonism is merely one more slightly idiosyncratic form of Christianity" is wrong.[2] Mormonism, in Shipps's view, actually has not changed doctrinally very much at all, and the perception that it has changed radically represents nothing more than the triumph of an effective public relations strategy by the Church.

In fact, however, both Mauss and Shipps are right. The perceived protestantization of Mormonism (to use Mauss's phrase for it) has greater cultural than theological significance, and the doctrinal differences between Mormons and Protestants remain genuine and profound. Mormonism not only has aligned itself culturally with mainstream conservative middle-class society but has also actively sought alliances with evangelical Protestants on a variety of political and cultural fronts.

ERIC R. SAMUELSEN

The Church hierarchy also has made a point of distancing itself from the word "Mormon" and publicly embracing and highlighting the official title, The Church of Jesus Christ of Latter-day Saints (LDS). At the same time, Mormon doctrines remain exotic and peculiar as compared with most contemporary Christian theologies and are actively obnoxious to evangelical Christians. The debate over Mel Gibson's *The Passion of the Christ* within Mormon culture, therefore, is quite revealing insofar as it both defines and delimits the boundaries of Mormon protestantization.

Although Gibson's film was as controversial within Mormon culture as it was in other Christian cultures, the controversy did not always involve the same issues. Within Mormon culture, the debate over *The Passion* tended to function within larger debates over a wide range of other issues to which the movie is related only tangentially, such as the following:

- Hierarchy and authority within the LDS Church
- The ways in which Mormons tend to approach political questions
- The relationship between Mormon culture and American popular culture
- The still-evolving relationship between Mormonism and certain strains of evangelical Protestant culture
- The ways in which Mormon culture has become embroiled in larger American cultural wars
- The ways in which some Mormons have sought to align themselves culturally and politically with the Christian Right

The LDS Church did not release any official response to *The Passion of the Christ* in connection with its release or in connection with the 2004 Easter holiday. This is not surprising. Church leadership generally has been very unwilling to speak out on specific cultural events, preferring instead to offer general counsel on broad cultural and moral issues and allowing general Church membership to make up their own minds about specific works. The only two exceptions to this policy have involved films about Jesus. In 1971, the Church officially condemned the musical *Jesus Christ Superstar*, and in 1988, the Church urged members to avoid Martin Scorsese's *Last Temptation of Christ*. On the latter occasion, the Church statement emphasized the official name of the Church and encouraged "all people to truly seek the Savior and the eternal truths he taught, and to shun those things that detract from the dignity and spirit of his divine mission."[3] I do not know of any instance where the Church officially has endorsed any film or dramatic work.

Much of the debate within Mormon culture about Gibson's *Passion* involved speculation about what the unofficial position of the Church might be. One of the most hotly contested issues relating to the film within the culture was whether Mormons were justified in going to see the film at all since the Motion Picture Association of America (MPAA) had given it an "R" ("restricted") rating. Although the Church has no official policy regarding the rating system, the Church's then-president, Ezra Taft Benson, in 1986 urged LDS young men not to "see R-rated movies or vulgar videos or participate in any entertainment that is immoral, suggestive, or pornographic."[4] Since that talk, other general authorities of the Church have given talks applying that counsel to choices made by young women and adults. Since active Latter-day Saints regard the president of the Church as a prophet of God, many Mormons regarded Benson's statements as canonical. In some Mormon cultural circles, the "R-rated movie" has been seen as synonymous with "immoral, suggestive and pornographic," however strangely those words might apply to *The Passion*.[5]

In practice, however, Mormons *do* attend R-rated films, with a variety of justifications. Nonetheless, active Mormons generally are reluctant to disregard the counsel of President Benson as irrelevant to their decisions. Therefore, many Mormons who choose to see R-rated films look for other statements that might suggest a softening in what might represent the Church's unofficial position on an issue about which no official position has been taken. For example, Mormons might point to a 1997 address in which LDS Apostle L. Tom Perry, one of the fifteen highest-ranking leaders of the Church, wondered if Latter-day Saints "can trust others to make rating decisions for us."[6] This suggested to some that perhaps the Church leadership now considered the MPAA system suspect. Moreover, moderate to liberal Mormons might be inclined to see the comments of both Benson and Perry as offering counsel only, that is, as advice that reasonable people can embrace or reject as they choose.

At any rate, Mormons tend to see the MPAA rating system as providing a plausible guide to the movie choices of adults as well as children, and some in the culture see avoiding R-rated films as an act of faith and obedience to the LDS Church. For many people, the ever-evolving doctrine of "continuing revelation," in which the words of living Church authorities are presumed to be the revealed word of God today, has led to an oppressively rigid emphasis on individual obedience to Church authority; for others, continuing revelation provides an anchor of moral stability in a frighteningly relativistic world. Inevitably, much of the public comment about the film focused on the issue of the film's MPAA rating and whether Mormons were permitted to see it. In other words, in some quarters, debate over the film centered on a larger debate to which the film is essentially peripheral and of which the ratings debate itself is only a small part.

To orient the film within this larger debate and to make that debate intelligible beyond the Mormon community, it may be helpful to outline a kind of hierarchy of Mormon canonicity. First of all, Mormons believe in four books of canonical scripture, beginning with the Book of Mormon, the Doctrine and Covenants, and the *Pearl of Great Price*, with the Bible regarded as slightly less authoritative than the other three. Mormons believe that all four of these books are genuine communications from God. However, issues of translation and transmission affect the Bible in a way that they do not affect the other books, which God revealed directly to Joseph Smith.[7] Official statements by the three-member First Presidency of the Church are regarded as authoritative statements of Church policy. As indicated previously, many consider as canonical statements made by the president of the Church, whom Mormons believe to be a prophet. Statements by and writings of members of the Quorum of the Twelve Apostles are good indicators of the direction Church policy is taking, as are statements of other general authorities of the Church, which include the Quorum of the Seventy and the presiding bishopric. Statements from local ecclesiastical leaders rank still lower in this hierarchy of Mormon canonicity, just above books and articles by scholars in the Church.

To the rather limited extent that terms such as "liberal" or "conservative" meaningfully describe points on the Mormon cultural continuum, they generally refer to these issues of authority and canonicity within the theological context of continuing revelation. Liberal Mormons generally would not consider statements by contemporary general authorities to be canonical automatically, let alone frequently. More conservative Mormons, on the other hand, might regard any talk given from the pulpit by any general authority to be as scripturally authoritative as Paul's Epistle to the Romans. For that reason, the statement, "The prophet said we were to avoid R-rated movies," is one with tremendous authority, even if—especially if—no official statement of the Church has been issued regarding the issue. As such, for conservative Mormons, two positions toward *The Passion* emerged. On the one hand, for some, this was simply another R-rated movie to be avoided. For others, it was the one R-rated film they were likely ever to see. When I saw the film for the first time, as I was walking out of the theater, an elderly couple walking ahead of me discussed the film, and I overheard the woman say, "So, that's what R-rated films are like!"

Hence the following irony: since "liberal" Mormons are less likely than "conservative" Mormons to consider President Benson's comments about R-rated films authoritative guides to their own entertainment choices and "conservative" Mormons generally would avoid seeing R-rated films as a matter of faith and testimony, one might presume that conservative Mormons would have avoided and disliked Gibson's *Passion* and that liberal Mormons would have embraced it. In general, in fact, that is the way Scorsese's *The Last Temptation of Christ* was received. However, the strongest positive Mormon reactions to *The Passion* came from people generally regarded as conservatives, such as Robert Millet, the former chair of Brigham Young University's Department of Religion; the science fiction novelist Orson Scott Card; and the Academy Award–winning filmmaker Keith Merrill. Meanwhile, the journal *Sunstone*, the unofficial organ of Mormon liberalism, solicited two review articles critical of the film.[8]

While many conservative Mormons chose not to see the film because of its R rating, the most positive responses to the film came from "conservative" Mormons themselves. This suggests, in part, that Mormon culture has become embroiled in larger American cultural wars and that some Mormons have begun to align themselves culturally and doctrinally with the Christian Right. Thus, the debate over *The Passion* is a valuable signpost on the road to what Mauss has called the protestantization of the Mormon Church.

At least some of the Mormon rhetoric surrounding the film certainly had evangelical echoes. Orson Scott Card's popular fantasy novels in the Alvin Maker series echo Mormon history so exactly that they have become, to some circles, akin to a Mormon *Left Behind* series. His response to the charge that the film might have antisemitic overtones provides a good example of "evangelicized" Mormon rhetoric:

> What I find truly disturbing, as an American, is how the American Left, which supposedly glorifies free speech and cultural inclusion, should so brutally reveal their true colors. The fact that Gibson could not find distribution for this film, and had to turn his production company, Icon, into a distributor (a very expensive and difficult process), speaks volumes—there was no such problem over *The Last Temptation of Christ*, which apparently was acceptable because it would offend Christians and denied the accuracy of the scriptural account. Hollywood touts itself as courageous—just like the rest of the PC Left—whenever they stomp on Christians. It's part of the elitist war on Christianity that's clearly going on. Other people's ethnic heritage or "folk beliefs" can be celebrated in school—but Christian customs and beliefs can hardly be mentioned.[9]

Card's talk of an "elitist war on Christianity" invites comparison, for example, with David Limbaugh's take on the film,[10] which Merrill's review cites approvingly: "How ironic that when a movie producer takes artistic license with historical events, he is lionized as artistic, creative, and brilliant, but when another takes special care to be true to the real-life story, he is vilified."[11] The rhetoric in both citations suggests a specific sort of political polarization: the devout Christian pitted against infernal forces of political correctness and hypocritical liberalism. In this model, the writer rhetorically constructs "Hollywood" as "elitist" and as at war with Christian customs and beliefs. Conversely, "Christian," in this context, is a specific cultural term that refers to people who like *The Passion* and who see it as a historically accurate depiction of mainstream Christian belief. Neither of these reviews acknowledges the possibility that other Christians may be equally sincere in their beliefs, such as Christians who doubt the historicity of the Gospel of Matthew, embrace "higher criticism" of biblical texts, or reject biblical inerrancy. This is particularly ironic since many evangelicals—whose language Card and Merrill embrace—refuse to acknowledge Mormons as legitimate Christians. Is it not as legitimately "Christian" to embrace higher criticism, to detect a political agenda in Matthew's text, to question whether Matthew wrote it, or to question whether Jewish high priests incited a full-scale riot in order to get Jesus crucified as it is to embrace biblical inerrancy? Indeed, to say "As a Christian, I didn't care for this film" is as legitimate as to say "As a Christian, I was profoundly moved by it." However, in Mormon circles, evangelical Protestants seem to enjoy a presumption of sincerity and authenticity that mainline Protestants and liberal Catholics do not, at least with respect to doctrines and claims of inerrancy. It is here, at these rhetorical parallels between Card, Merrill, and Limbaugh, that the response to *The Passion* provides evidence for the "protestantization" of Mormon culture.

To be sure, this alliance has limitations, and here another irony presents itself. Despite efforts by Mormon conservatives to align themselves culturally and politically with the Christian Right, the most ferocious and unremitting attacks on Mormons from other Christians have come almost entirely from the Christian Right, from the very forces of evangelicalism that some Mormons seem so anxious to join. Evangelicals have persisted in calling Mormonism a cult and in insisting that Mormons are not Christians.[12] Evangelicals have sent missionaries to Utah, and evangelical street preachers protest every Mormon General Conference. Evangelical bookstores often have more anti-Mormon tracts on their shelves than most Christian publishers have in their catalogs.

I certainly do not mean to imply that all evangelical congregations are uniformly anti-Mormon or that there have not been genuine efforts from both sides to bridge differences.[13] Nonetheless, the concerted efforts of the LDS Church in recent years to foreground its Christian identity largely have been a response to evangelical attacks on Mormon Christian authenticity. Moreover, the more insistently Mormons press claims of Christian legitimacy, the more strident those evangelical attacks have become. From a theological perspective, those attacks are not without foundation: Mormon views on such foundational Christian doctrines as the nature of God, the nature and importance of the Incarnation, priesthood authority, and salvation genuinely are at odds with the views of most Christian faiths.

Given the uneasy relationship between *The Passion*'s Christian theology and mainstream Mormon Christian theology, then, positive responses to Gibson's film by some Mormon conservatives, which echo the positive responses of many evangelicals to the film, seem even more peculiar. While much intra-Christian debate centered on Gibson's penchant for violence, his choice and interpretation of gospel texts, and his extracanonical additions,

LDS Church theology presents a somewhat different theological framework within which to consider the film. That framework itself derives from the heavy reliance Mormons place on extrabiblical canonical works, the very existence of which are, of course, anathema to most evangelical Christians. For the most part, Mormons base their theological understanding of Christ's atonement and their interpretation of such events as the scourging and crucifixion not on the Bible or on the Book of Mormon but rather on the Doctrine and Covenants, especially as clarified by subsequent writings of general authorities of the Church.

Mormons do not believe that Christ's atoning sacrifice for the sins of humanity took place on the cross. Rather, Mormons believe that the atonement took place in the Garden of Gethsemane before Jesus's arrest. There are two books about Christ and the atonement that most Mormons find particularly authoritative in this regard, in large measure because apostles wrote both of them. James E. Talmage wrote *Jesus the Christ* under the direction of the First Presidency of the Church, who also approved its contents before publication. Bruce R. McConkie's later, multivolume work, *The Mortal Messiah*, is more comprehensive, but it agrees with Talmage on every major point of doctrine and indeed quotes Talmage extensively. Talmage points out that the hierophany takes place not at Golgotha but at Gethsemane:

> Christ's agony in the garden is unfathomable by the finite mind, both as to intensity and to cause. . . . In some manner, actual and terribly real though to man incomprehensible, the Savior took upon himself the burden of the sins of mankind from Adam to the end of the world.[14]

For his part, McConkie, quoting from the Doctrine and Covenants, posits that Jesus's victory over suffering in the Garden of Gethsemane is the real spiritual climax before the "denouement" of the "shame and humiliation and pain of the cross." He writes, "It was on the cross that he suffered death in the flesh" even as many have suffered agonizing deaths, but it was in Gethsemane that "he suffered the pain of all men, that all men might repent and come unto him."[15]

Talmage's and McConkie's books present a unified theological core of atonement beliefs. The atonement was a cosmic event that involved intense spiritual suffering beyond human comprehension. It took place in

Gethsemane and was of a magnitude that dwarfed the subsequent suffering that Jesus endured on the cross. Speaking again of Gethsemane, the Doctrine and Covenants presents Christ's own description of "suffering which caused myself, even God, to tremble because of pain, and to bleed at every pore."[16] As a result of the atonement, all people have the opportunity to repent from their sins and be received into God's presence after the resurrection. When Card echoes Talmage and McConkie in his review of Gibson's film, he is expressing nothing more than a straightforward Mormon understanding of the Passion:

> I believe that Christ's real suffering was the anguish he felt as he bore the horror of complete spiritual separation from God—taking upon himself to an infinite degree the torment that is the natural spiritual consequence of sin. The remorse and despair we feel (or will feel) to varying degrees because of our disobedience to or rejection of God, he felt so utterly that we cannot imagine it. In this context, what was done to his body was almost a distraction. Many people have borne as much.[17]

Since the atonement took place at Gethsemane and not on the cross, Mormon homes and churches usually do not display crucifixes of any kind. For Mormons, a cross is not any sort of instrument for human salvation; it is simply a Roman torture device. Therefore, Gibson's depiction of Christ's suffering in the scourging and crucifixion is irrelevant to the question of his atonement, and the epigraph with which Gibson begins his film, "by his stripes we are healed," has a very different significance for Mormons than it does for the traditionalist Catholic filmmaker.[18]

Gethsemane's prominence at the beginning of *The Passion*, however, itself dictated by Gibson's focus on the liturgical Stations of the Cross, makes it possible for some Mormons to project their own theology onto the film. Card resolves the dilemma of the film's subsequent violence by interpreting it as an external representation of Jesus's inner torment at Gethsemane:

> The problem is, the inner, spiritual suffering could not be filmed. So even for someone who believes as I do, the torment of Jesus's body stands as an outward representation of the inner torment. Viewed in this way, the violence is not excessive at all; it is all the glimpse that we can bear of the inner torment he suffered for us.[19]

In other words, although Gibson's depiction of physical suffering may not be wholly theologically consistent with the Mormon understanding of the Christ's atonement, conservative Mormons seem to have chosen to see *The Passion* as a powerful and evocative complement to that understanding. Keith Merrill, who directed the film *Testaments* under official Church auspices, a film that focuses on the Book of Mormon's presentation of Christ, sums up his own reaction to the film as "an emotional supplement in my quest to know the Christ."[20]

It is possible that this effort to project one understanding of an event onto a very different cinematic depiction of it might echo the Maussian "protestantization" of Mormon culture and might represent genuine cultural change within Mormonism. Alternatively, it might be nothing more than a Mormon movement toward some version of ecumenicism.[21] Such a trend toward inclusion and openness was reflected in much of the Mormon criticism of Gibson's *Passion*. In general, Mormon liberals who reviewed the film—Richard Bugg, chair of Southern Utah State University's Department of Theater; *Sunstone*'s Robert A. Rees; and LDS publisher Scott Parkin of the Association for Mormon Letters—did not differ greatly from conservative Mormons in their responses to the theological content of the film, but liberals and conservatives alike reflected in their criticism this larger search for common ground among Christians.[22] In the past, Mormon liberals have tended to distance themselves from the Christian Right politically and culturally, but that interest did not appear to find much expression in reviews of Gibson's *Passion*. Instead, there appears to have been a genuine effort, through the film, to seek common cause with fellow Christians. Parkin, for example, acknowledges the basic legitimacy of Gibson's approach even as he quibbled with its details:

> It became clear to me that the filmmaker wanted me to understand that Jesus was the Christ, the literal son of God.... This new dramatization created a new way of thinking about my assumptions and beliefs and conceptions of those events, and in so doing gave me another chance to appreciate the power of the passion of the Christ and to consider its meaning and impact on my life. Which is what this film was about—an expression of testimony about the Christ, the condescension of God himself to descend below all things and redeem the world of its sin while in the midst of that sin. I found that testimony to be powerful and worthwhile. I found myself spiritually uplifted in a far

more subdued, less ecstatic sort of way than I was used to. Perhaps not the method I would have chosen to come to that testimony, but a valid and powerful acceptance nonetheless—regardless of the relative orthodoxy of the presentation.[23]

To be sure, there were less positive conservative and liberal responses to the film. W. Jeffrey Marsh, who teaches ancient scripture at Brigham Young University, faulted the film for not focusing more intensely on Gethsemane; and Steve Farrell, the former managing editor of *Right Magazine*, a Christian Right Internet magazine based out of Wheaton College, published a negative review of *The Passion* that denounces the notion of a punitive, vindictive God as incompatible with his faith:

> Irritatingly, superstitious elements, from apocryphal writings and elsewhere, were added, which serve to taint the Christian message as fantastic and inconsistent. . . . Jesus forgave his slayers—that was magnificent—but God then sends down a crow to pluck out the eye of the poor soul suffering on the cross next to him, just because he struggled with his faith on the cross? Thus, we have the inaccurate portrayal of a God who moves from being merciful to vengeful, from a God who permits men to carry out their agency, even unto death, to a street bully who exercises arbitrary justice upon those who commit lesser crimes. . . . Why add such ridiculous nonsense as "attention getters"? Similarly, there was the inventive use of children taunting and torturing Judas because he was "cursed." By contrast, the Biblical Jesus spoke of the innocence of little children, that of such were the kingdom of Heaven. So why this demeaning-to-children baloney?[24]

For some Mormons, the film was too Catholic, too violent, and too foreign to the Mormon religious experience to have much positive resonance. *Sunstone*, the most reliable venue for Mormon liberal scholarship, solicited two negative reviews of the film.[25] The Brigham Young University student newspaper, *The Daily Universe*, published two editions devoted to the film, and the vast majority of responses were negative, mostly because of the film's MPAA rating.[26]

In contrast to other Christians and many Jews, most Mormons appeared to be unified in their disagreement with the charge that *The Passion of the Christ* is antisemitic. The reasons for this have to do primarily with issues of inerrancy. The Mormon position is somewhat less rigidly inerrant than the position taken by some evangelicals. Mormons believe, for example, that the Bible is the word of God "as far as it is translated correctly."[27] However, they generally reject biblical higher criticism. As such, Mormons generally regard as authoritative Matthew's account, with "chief priests and elders" leading a crowd to shout "His blood be on us and on our children!"[28] The Book of Mormon further complicates this issue. It includes a prophecy by Jacob—a contemporary of Jeremiah and the son of Lehi, a wealthy Jerusalem merchant—that the Messiah "should come among the Jews, among those who are the more wicked part of the world; and they shall crucify him—for thus it behooveth our God, and there is none other nation on earth that would crucify their God." Writing in the seventh century B.C.E., as Mormons believe (and not the American frontier of the 1830s), Jacob continues his jeremiad against the wicked Jerusalem leadership of his day:

> For should the mighty miracles be wrought upon other nations they would repent, and know that he be their God. But because of priestcrafts and iniquities, they at Jerusalem will stiffen their necks against him, that he be crucified. Wherefore, because of their iniquities, destructions, famine, pestilences and bloodshed shall come upon them; and they who shall not be destroyed shall be scattered among all nations.[29]

Just as Jeremiah is not considered antisemitic, neither is Jacob. And Mormons have never regarded this passage in 2 Nephi as excusing antisemitic attitudes, let alone acts of antisemitic violence. On the contrary, Mormons see Jacob's denunciation of a nation sufficiently wicked that "none other nation on earth that would crucify their God" as referring only to a specific generation of specific misled people who lived in a particular time and place.

To be sure, while Jacob's comments in the Book of Mormon were clearly intended to have a very specific and limited application, some Mormons have applied them more broadly. Nonetheless, the Mormon historical experience, in which our ancestors were driven from state to state, persecuted, robbed, and murdered, generally has led to strongly pro-Jewish cultural leanings. Like many evangelicals, Mormons have also tended to support Zionism politically.[30] At the same time, lingering vestiges of antisemitism, or at least insensitivity to Jewish concerns, can be found in at least a few Mormon cultural contexts.[31]

Since Mormons generally do stress commonalities between the Mormon historical experience and the Jewish one, charges of antisemitism are particularly galling. Nevertheless, the charge of antisemitism against Gibson's film led to an unfortunately defensive public response by many Mormons. Rather than carefully and thoughtfully examining the charges on their merits—as, for example, the LDS Church attempted to do in 1995 in discussions with the Simon Wiesenthal Center—and rather than using the film to open a dialogue with fellow Christians and with our Jewish brothers and sisters, Mormons tended to respond as Card did in his review with wild charges of political correctness and angry denunciations of "liberal elites." It is here that we see most clearly and publicly the increasing and strangely paradoxical cultural alliance between Mormons and evangelicals. Although the *Left Behind* novels, with their radically apocalyptic eschatology centering around Israel and Armageddon, do not have the same cachet in Mormon culture as they do in evangelical circles, they have been given increasingly prominent display in Mormon religious bookstores.[32] While the Rapture is not the centerpiece of Mormon apocalyptic sermonizing that it is from evangelical pulpits, many Mormons do believe in it. And while Mormons did not flock to see *The Passion* in anywhere near the numbers that evangelicals did, Mormons who saw the film were equally certain that the film is not antisemitic and that Gibson's difficulties finding funding for the film provides irrefutable evidence of Hollywood's anti-Christian bias.

In the wake of *The Passion*'s release, there were no official pronouncement by the Church about Gibson's *Passion*, nor did any current general authorities speak about it. During the 3–4 April 2004 General Conference of the Church of Jesus Christ of Latter-day Saints, there were three talks by general authorities discussing issues surrounding Christ and the Passion, but none specifically referenced the film. This is not unusual. Given the publicity surrounding *The Passion*, it is hardly surprising that Church leadership would find the occasion of the film's controversy an appropriate time to remind Church membership of what the Church actually teaches about Christ's atonement. At the same time, it is equally unsurprising that the Church should avoid embroiling itself in the controversy over the film: for the institutional Church, a film like *The Passion* is best approached with caution.

Mormons have come to value a certain skill akin to Kremlinology: the ability to read between cryptic statements and through broad generalizations in order to decipher where the Church might stand on certain issues. This is an important skill since most active Latter-day Saints are unwilling to take issue publicly with positions taken by general authorities; Mormons do tend to align themselves with the Church. Therefore, Mormons approached *The Passion* cautiously. Should one see the film? How applicable are President Benson's comments on R-rated films? What do the three conference talks on the subject suggest? The Church publishes an annual pamphlet, *For the Strength of Youth*, offering counsel and guidance for LDS teenagers. At one time, that pamphlet urged youth to avoid R-rated movies. The more recent versions of that pamphlet no longer mention movie ratings. Is this significant? Should something be read into that?

It is at this point that folklore begins to fill the gap. I received e-mails from four different friends regarding comments supposedly made by various general authorities, either in private conversations or in talks about *The Passion* given at local congregations. Two of these mythical accounts declared the film to be a faith-promoting masterpiece, with only minor doctrinal discrepancies from orthodox LDS views; the two others apparently said the film was to be avoided by all practicing Latter-day Saints. Whether in reviews of the film or invented conversations by mythical Church leaders, then, Mormons generally divided between those who embraced it despite the film's doctrinal differences from Mormon theology and those who found the theological implications of the film more troubling.

Mormon differences with Protestants remain real and profound. However, culturally, on at least some issues, at least some Mormon conservatives have grown closer to evangelicals than their doctrinal differences would ever seem to allow for. The protestantization of Mormon culture remains incomplete and fraught with tensions, contradictions, and paradoxes. It is a real phenomenon nonetheless.

Notes

1. Mauss 1994, 5.
2. Shipps 1985, 148.
3. Lindsay 1988.
4. Benson 1986.
5. Indeed, Robert Millet, a Brigham Young University professor of ancient scripture, told the *Salt Lake Tribune* that the R rating of Gibson's *Passion* "is another experience where the rating system has betrayed us" (Stack 2004).

6. Perry 1997.

7. The Book of Mormon is regarded as a genuinely ancient text, engraved on plates of gold by prophets living in the American continents, given to Joseph Smith by an angel, and translated by the power of God. The Doctrine and Covenants is a compilation of revelations received by Joseph Smith and others. The *Pearl of Great Price* is a slight volume, including Joseph Smith's inspired rewriting of the first three books of Genesis called *The Book of Moses*, an inspired translation of papyri called *The Book of Abraham*, and Smith's own history.

8. Stack 2004; Rees 2004; Samuelsen 2004.

9. Card 2004.

10. Limbaugh 2003.

11. Merrill's response was first published on the conservative online Mormon magazine *Meridian*. The *Meridian* website included four reviews, not all of them positive. See Card 2004; Farrell 2004; Marsh 2004; Merrill 2004.

12. There are hundreds of evangelical websites that declare Mormonism to be a cult: see, for example, Connor 1998; Hein and Hein 2001; Miesel [n.d.]; "The Mormon Cult" [n.d.].

13. See, for example, Robinson and Blomberg 1997.

14. Talmage 1915, 613.

15. Doctrine and Covenants 18:11; McConkie 1981, 128.

16. Doctrine and Covenants 19:18.

17. Card 2004.

18. Isaiah 53:5. Mormons believe that the scourging and crucifixion were necessary, a humiliating public death leading to Christ's resurrection. Our "healing" simply means resurrection.

19. Card 2004.

20. Merrill 2004.

21. Mormons believe that the primitive Church collapsed in complete apostasy in the second and third centuries C.E., leaving only vestigial ecclesiastical and theological remains, until God effected a restoration through Joseph Smith in 1830. This leaves very little room for genuine ecumenicism. Still, Mormons do try to get along with their Christian neighbors, and efforts have been made in recent years to clear the Mormon mind-set from exclusionary excesses. See, for example, Ballard 2001.

22. For example, despite their observations that Gibson's portrayal of Mary, the mother of Jesus, reflects his own Mariolatry, nonetheless Merrill, Card, Bugg, Parkin, and Millet all found Gibson's depiction of Mary profoundly moving in a human, if not specifically theological, sense (Bugg 2004; Card 2004; Merrill 2004; Parkin 2004; Stack 2004).

23. Parkin 2004.

24. Marsh 2004; Farrell 2004. Ironically, there are fringes of Mormon culture that echo the vision that Farrell criticizes. See, for example, Lundwall 1952 and the response to it in Oaks and Hill 1975.

25. Rees 2004; Samuelsen 2004.

26. See Williams 2004; Nelson-Stowell 2004; *The Daily Universe* 7 March 2004; *The Daily Universe* 18 March 2004.

27. The Eighth Article of Faith. It is generally included as part of the *Pearl of Great Price*, one of the four standard works that Mormons regard as canonical.

28. Matthew 27:25.

29. 2 Nephi 10:3–6.

30. Mormons believe that the spiritual beginning of the modern Zionist movement occurred when Elder Orson Hyde, then a Mormon apostle, visited the Mount of Olives in October 1840 and offered a prayer in which he dedicated Israel for the return of the Jewish people.

31. The LDS Church's international reputation for genealogical research is based on the Mormon belief that people who did not have a chance to hear the gospel in this life should be given a chance to accept it in the next, through proxy baptisms and marriage sealings, for those who have died. Genealogical efforts initiated in order to generate names for these ordinances have led to clashes with some Jewish organizations for which this practice is a repugnant reminder of forced conversions and baptisms; the use of lists of Holocaust victims has generated sharp criticisms. Despite the Church's agreement in 1995 to remove hundreds of thousands of Jewish names from its database, the controversy has been revisited periodically (see Thiessen 2004).

32. LaHaye and Jenkins (1995–2004).

CHAPTER FIVE
IS IT FINISHED? *THE PASSION OF THE CHRIST* AND THE FAULT LINES IN AMERICAN CHRISTIANITY
Julie Ingersoll

In 2003 and 2004, Christians across America raised their voices in support of a major Hollywood movie. They became an important component in one of the most innovative prerelease film promotions in history. Long before the release of *The Passion of the Christ*, Christian churches trained to use it as an evangelistic tool, and religious publications such as *Christianity Today* devoted extensive space to discussing the film. Icon, Gibson's production company, arranged special prescreenings for selected churches. "Christians" seemed more or less united in their enthusiasm for Mel Gibson's latest work.

Critics, religious leaders, and filmgoers have debated charges that the film would exacerbate historic divisions between Christians and Jews and perhaps even fuel antisemitism, but little has been said about the ways in which this film made visible long-standing cleavages within American Christianity itself—cleavages that result in divisions and alliances that are complex and often paradoxical.

I have in mind several specific strains of Christianity present in early twenty-first-century America. For the purposes of this chapter, I am calling them mainstream Catholicism, traditionalist Catholicism, mainstream Protestantism, evangelical Protestantism, and fundamentalist Protestantism. It is helpful to think of these strains of Christianity on a "church–sect continuum," as described by Finke and Stark,[1] with the defining characteristic of traditionalist Catholicism and fundamentalist Protestantism being their tension with the surrounding culture. For my purposes here, I want to circumscribe very narrowly the group I describe as "fundamentalist"; leaders who might be considered fundamentalists in other discussions may not be so here.

The Rise of Mainstream Christianity

Through the nineteenth century, the dominant form of Christianity in the United States was a broadly evangelical, revivalist Protestantism. There was widespread suspicion of Catholicism on the part of those Protestants: Catholics owed their loyalty to a "foreign power," their development of a parochial school system was "un-American," and their fundamental religious sensibilities were thought to be "undemocratic."

In a now familiar story, the turn of the twentieth century brought the development of two distinctive strains of Protestantism: one embracing the values and criticism of modernism and the other seeking to shore up evangelicalism. It also brought similar divisions within Catholicism that culminated in election of the nation's first non-Protestant president and, abroad and at home, the midcentury reforms of Vatican II. Though they express their faith in a variety of denominational forms, mainstream Christians (Catholic and Protestant alike) now are more likely to embrace mainstream versions of other denominations than they are to adopt sect-like versions of their own.[2]

The Rise of Sectarianism

Finke and Stark have argued convincingly that as religious institutions become more "churchly"—that is, more worldly and in less tension with the surrounding culture—alternative institutions develop to meet the demand for high-tension religion. While the rise of fundamentalism at the turn of the twentieth century has been explained variously,[3] I believe that it is much less useful to try to see this movement in cohesive theological terms than as the coalescence of a variety of subcultures in opposition to modernism, which is a much more compelling view.[4] This underlying model is especially helpful in looking at the relationship between sectarian Protestantism and Catholicism.

To American Protestants, the face of American Catholicism initially looked—literally—foreign: ethnic tensions fed opposition to parochial schooling, the Know-Nothing Party, and even the temperance movement.

By the middle of the century, opposition to Catholicism was widespread and at the center (along with antisemitism) of the theological and political worldview of the "old Christian Right."[5]

Ethnic tensions were also expressed in theological language as a key factor in the development of the antimodernist, evangelical strain of Protestantism was the growing acceptance of premillennial dispensationalism, which labeled the pope the "Antichrist" and saw the Roman Catholic Church as apostate.[6] The growing importance of this eschatology in popular conservative Protestantism was both a result of and a source of anti-Catholic nativism.

From the middle of the twentieth century, an analogous strain of sectarian Catholicism began to develop and burst into broader public consciousness in the wake of Vatican II.[7] This sectarian Catholicism rejected the reforms of Vatican II. "Traditionalist" Catholics placed renewed emphasis on many of the theological issues that divided Catholics and Protestants to begin with: the centrality of the Mass—in Latin, the role of the Virgin Mary, and the authority of the pope.

A funny thing happened on the way to the twenty-first century. Despite a widening theological gap between the sectarian versions of Protestantism and the sectarian version of Catholicism, these two groups made peace with one another. What they agreed on was the defense of a traditionalist gender culture[8] that rejected abortion (and contraception for Catholics but also often for Protestants as well), rejected homosexuality and gay and lesbian rights, endorsed hierarchical models of heterosexual marriage, and placed limitations on women's roles as religious leaders. During right-to-life sit-ins at abortion clinics during the late 1980s, Protestants singing "Just as I Am" sat next to Catholics praying the rosary. "Saving babies" took center stage, while disagreements over the meaning of communion or Mary, Mother of God, were pushed to the background. The New Christian Right had dropped the anti-Catholic nativism of its forebear.

So, what does this have to do with *The Passion*? Well, everything. First, the place of these groups in the larger context of American Christianity shaped the response of these various groups to the film. Second, there is some evidence that, around the margins of this unusual Pax Americana, there may be some disintegration of the coalition.

One might have expected Catholics to approve of the film and Protestants to oppose it. Listening to media coverage of the responses to the film, one might think that Christians of every stripe are flocking to the film and that they all perceive their viewing of it as a profound religious experience. In fact, however, there are both positive and negative responses to the film, and they cross the Catholic–Protestant divide.

The Passion of the Christ clearly represents Mel Gibson's ante- and anti-Vatican II sensibilities: the graphic and violent portrayal of the crucifixion as substitutionary atonement as the central aspect of the gospel, the use of Latin and Aramaic, and the central role played by Mary, to name a few key examples.[9] Conservative lay Catholics and some clergy praised the film—the more traditionalist the Catholic, the more exuberant the praise. A review from the traditionalist Catholic paper *The Remnant* commends Gibson for the bloodiness of the film, a bloodiness made necessary by the evil of the fallen world:

> This is His Precious Blood, made Precious because it is the Blood sacrificed to the Father in atonement, as the reparation for the sins of the world. His precious Blood had to be shed, among thousands of other causes, because parents in our time would love their own children so little as to allow them to be killed in the womb.
>
> In a post–Vatican II Church that has turned its eyes away from the Passion of Our Lord, Mel Gibson has shoved this hard Truth before the eyes of the world. In their pristine, sentimental new order temples of felt banners and eagles wings and liturgical dancers and altar girls and resurrecifixes [*sic*] and kisses of peace and lay ministers and Father Bobs and Father Mikes and social justice, where has the Precious Blood been located?[10]

Evangelical Protestants were as enthusiastic as Catholics. They saw the film as providing a unique opportunity to deepen their own appreciation for the significance of Christ's sacrifice as well as an opportunity to share the Protestant gospel with non-Christians and even Catholics.[11] I include within this category conservative Protestants who made common cause with the Catholics as part of the Christian Right—not only leaders who often are considered fundamentalists, such as Jerry Falwell and Pat Robertson, but also more recognizably evangelical figures, such as Billy Graham, James Dobson, Bill Hybels of Willow Creek Community Church, and Rick Warren of Saddleback Church. These are the folks that *The Passion* marketing team targeted to promote the opening and taught to use the film for evangelizing—those for whom conservative Catholics produced lapel pins and "witnessing cards." *Christianity Today* put it this way: "In the history of Evangelical enthusiasms, Mel Gibson's *The Passion of the Christ* seems to be joining "What Would Jesus Do?" (WWJD) bracelets and Promise Keepers' conferences as cultural markers."[12]

In widely quoted comments following a preview of the film, leading evangelist Billy Graham said,

> I have often wondered what it must have been like to be a bystander during those last hours before Jesus' death. After watching *The Passion of the Christ*, I feel as if I have actually been there. I was moved to tears. I doubt if there has ever been a more graphic and moving presentation of Jesus' death and resurrection—which Christians believe are the most important events in human history. The film is faithful to the Bible's teaching that we are all responsible for Jesus' death, because we have all sinned. It is our sins that caused His death, not any particular group. No one who views this film's compelling imagery will ever be the same.[13]

These two groups (moderate to traditionalist Catholics and evangelical Protestants) see themselves as allies and interpreted the film in similar ways. Such an alliance makes sense in view of Wuthnow's thesis about the restructuring of American religion. Both groups play up the theological issue of substitutionary atonement (the idea that a physical human sacrifice was required to make up for human sin and that Jesus "substituted" himself for us). Both groups share the conviction that there is a real Satan and that there are demons active in this world.[14] The two groups also share cultural religious sensibilities that might be labeled populist: an emphasis on what they believe to be literal readings of Scripture and an emphasis on individual religious devotion and piety. They also share the broader cultural values discussed previously, many of which they also express politically. To follow James Davison Hunter, they are the "orthodox" side in what they perceive to be an ongoing culture war.[15] Finally, both groups see the film as an opportunity to share the gospel.[16]

Among mainstream Christians who criticize the film, Catholics and Protestants also have aligned. In keeping with Wuthnow's point that liberals are likely to have more affinity for other liberals in other denominations than for conservatives in their own denominations (and vice versa), we find commonalities in the responses from mainstream Catholics and

Protestants. Mainstream Catholics charged that the film violates Church teaching on the presentations of the Passion of Christ. The review by the United States Conference of Catholic Bishops concludes,

> Although the film's brutality poignantly conveys the depth of Christ's love by showing him freely enduring such extreme agony for the redemption of all sinners, the graphic nature of the raw visuals is played to diminishing returns.

It points out that although Vatican II rejected the historical connection between Christianity and antisemitism, the film seems to fall short on that point:

> While it is the film's assertion that responsibility for Christ's torture and death rest squarely with the Roman authorities, and away from the collective Jewish populace, the movie presents a historically skewed depiction of the Temple elite's sway with their imperial overlords.[17]

Catholic scholar Philip A. Cunningham finds the film's Catholic Christology utterly inadequate:

> The film's graphic, persistent, and intimate violence raises theological questions from a Catholic perspective. It closely resonates with an understanding of salvation that holds that God had to be satisfied or appeased for the countless sins of humanity by subjecting his son to unspeakable torments. This sadistic picture of God is hardly compatible with the God proclaimed by Jesus as the one who seeks for the lost sheep, who welcomes back the prodigal son before he can even express remorse, or who causes the rain to fall on the just and unjust alike.
>
> This understanding of salvation is constricted because it fails to incorporate the Incarnation. The Word of God enters into human history not to pay back in pain some debt that the Father will not otherwise remit. No, among other things the Word became flesh to take on human mortality and overcome it.
>
> By focusing on Jesus' torments, the film minimizes the central and defining reality of the resurrection for Christian faith. Christ has conquered death. Therefore, all creation is being renewed.[18]

Mainstream Protestants make similar criticisms, having moved from the emphasis on Jesus's death as the center of the gospel to an emphasis on his teaching, particularly his teachings on justice. Martin E. Marty makes this point in what he takes pains to point out is not a review of the film:

> The humanistic and theological point: pain is pain, suffering is suffering, torture is torture, and horrible pain-suffering-torture is horrible, and I don't think there are grades and degrees of these. Today, all over the world, people are suffering physically as much as the crucified Jesus. The point now is not to accept grace because we saw gore. The issue is not, were his the worst wounds and pains ever, but, as the gospels show, the issue was—and is—who was suffering and to what end. Christians believe that Jesus was and is the Christ, the Anointed, and they are to find meaning in his sacrificial love and death, not to crawl in close to be sure they get the best sight of the worst physical suffering.[19]

While for mainstream Protestants and Catholics the torture and death seem to be missing the larger point about the life of Christ, for sectarian Christians the suffering and sacrificial death is exactly the point. As Wuthnow's work leads us to expect, American Christians have divided—not as Catholics and Protestants as in the past but as liberal and conservative, mainstream and sectarian.

The Fundamentalist Critique

The picture, however, is more complicated than just a liberal–conservative split. I hinted previously that there were changes afoot in what I called the Pax Americana, that is, the détente that developed between the conservative Catholics and the evangelicals partially as a result of their shared political agenda. However, if the ecumenical détente between evangelicals and Catholics signals a growing worldliness in religious organizations and a lessening of tension with the surrounding culture, then we should also find what Finke and Starke describe as the "self-limiting" character of secularization wherein new high-tension movements appear. In this chapter, I reserve the label "fundamentalist" for such groups.

Given my argument about the way in which concern over abortion during the 1980s brought together Catholics and some of the most fundamentalist Protestants, it is perhaps ironic that much of the conservative Protestant critique of *The Passion of the Christ* comes from the most radical corners of the right-to-life movement. These critics explicitly place themselves in the "reformed tradition" and focus entirely on the degree to which this film is "Catholic."

One extensive critique, titled "The Animated Crucifix," claims that this film is a "two hour commercial for Catholicism." Surveying nearly twenty-five websites and articles criticizing the film from this perspective,[20] I found some common themes in the criticism:

1. The violent replaying of the crucifixion is interpreted as a Catholic Mass in and of itself. Of course, one of the dividing lines between Protestants and Catholics always has been transubstantiation and the question of whether the mass (or communion) is a literal re-creation of the sacrifice of Christ or merely an act done in remembrance. Alan Yusko, editor of the *Rapture Report*, took up this point in his review:

   > Next let's take a quick look at the Mass, which is a re-sacrifice of the Lord Jesus in a bloodless way for the sins of the people. This is done because Catholics do not believe what was done on the cross was enough. They do not believe that the sacrifice on the cross was complete. All sins are not covered by what the Lord Jesus did on the cross. Only some sins were covered by the Lord Jesus on the cross. This is heresy![21]

2. The film is thought to replicate other Catholic rituals, such as the devotion at the Stations of the Cross:

   > Catholics used a little Bible and much imagination to invent them (the stations of the cross), and Mr. Gibson based his movie's scenes on them. They include Veronica wiping Jesus' face with a cloth, which supposedly left an image for a relic. They include Mary encouraging Jesus to Calvary. Three of them are Jesus falling, though He does not fall in the Bible. They include Mary holding the dead Jesus, which is the Pieta for Mariolaters [*sic*].[22]

3. For fundamentalist Christians, adding to the material contained in the Bible is as forbidden as deleting material. Gibson's additions are called satanic:

What I did find personally disgusting was the "falling off a bridge" and falling 5 times on the way to the crucifixion. These were inventions in addition to the gospels, and I couldn't help but wonder what kind of devil would actually find it necessary to ADD to the sufferings of Christ?[23]

4. The depiction of Christ is considered idolatrous. In a lengthy review for the Presbyterian Church in America's Web page, a pastor writes,

> We do, already, possess "the image of God in the Church today, not in pictures or carvings or photographic reproductions, but in the Bible account of historical witnesses, in the preaching that repeats and sets forth their witness, and in the Sacraments."
>
> New Testament Christians are still prohibited from making any image of the deity—even in a movie or in art. The reason is that it is impossible for any artist to depict the godhead or spiritual matters, but more importantly, no matter how necessary or essential we might believe a movie to be, God has said "No." That ought to be more than sufficient for us.[24]

5. Finally, perhaps the most strident opposition to the film focuses on the central role Gibson gives to Mary, as the mother of God.[25] Pastor Matt Trewhella, founder of the right-to-life group Missionaries to the Preborn (which actively advocates illegal activity—and defends the use of violence—in the fight against abortion), circulated his review for the film, in which he wrote,

> The film is wrought with an unbiblical fixation on Mary, the mother of Jesus. What's more disturbing and disgusting is the reason for the fixation. Mel Gibson clearly presents Mary as the co-redemptress with Christ in his film, a belief and teaching found in Roman Catholicism, and which is contrary to Scripture. Because of this, Mary, who is mentioned only once in the Bible during the timeframe Gibson's film covers, is the focus of Gibson's cameras nearly as much as Jesus.

Trewhella then gives several illustrations of the ways in which Mary is presented as "co-redemptress," of which the following passage is a representative example:

> In another scene, Jesus is hanging on the cross. Mary walks right up to Jesus and kisses His feet. Blood is now smeared on her face. The imagery screams co-redemptress. She then says to Jesus "Flesh of my flesh, heart of my heart" (and here I cannot remember the further exact wording, but she says something to the effect of) "Can I not die with you?" Gibson was hellbent on getting his belief of co-redemptress across to the viewers.[26]

Nearly half of Trewhella's review focuses on this particular concern. Trewhella is "disgusted" and "disturbed"; the film is "abhorrent" because of the centrality of Mary. The tone of his comments is as important as the words themselves. It is instructive that the role of Mary is what produces such a visceral response in Trewhella. Trewhella's choice of the term "redemptress" as opposed to the more Catholic term "redemptrix" seems to underscore the gender-based aspect of his opposition. It is reminiscent of the term "priestess" as used by opponents of women's ordination. The term also calls attention to Mary's gender in a way that will be recognizable to Trewhella's audience.[27]

Conclusion

The divisions, boundaries, and alliances in American religion are constantly shifting. As helpful as they are, models like Hunter's culture wars and even Wuthnow's restructured liberals and conservatives are seriously limited in that they can show us the cleavages in only two dimensions. The focused response to *The Passion of the Christ* provided a rare opportunity to see those divisions, boundaries, and alliances in American Christianity as complex and multidimensional. Specifically, there are conservative Protestants who might have been expected to endorse the film but who rejected it for reasons different from the mainstream Protestants. Ironically, the agreement on a gender culture that seems to have brought the Catholics together with the evangelicals is the very point at which the fundamentalists are criticizing the film as "too Catholic." This is the area where, for some, the edges of the right-to-life alliance seem to be deteriorating.

I have argued elsewhere that gender is a key component of evangelical identity, an essential dividing line between conservatives and liberals, and a focal point for conflict within the evangelical subculture.[28] The various responses to the film reflect this rift. The Catholic view of Mary can be seen as both empowering to women and limiting: her traditionally determined role as mother clearly circumscribes whatever "redemptive power" she has. Protestants, however, have a much more complicated relationship with Mary. For mainstream Protestants who have embraced feminism, Mary—even as co-redemptor—poses no serious challenge. Evangelical Protestants, on the other hand, have incorporated an evangelical version of feminism into their theology and into their culture. They expect women to play specific significant roles, and they feel especially at ease when those roles flow from women's maternal functions. Drawn to *The Passion* with its straightforward, albeit graphic, depiction of the role of the crucifixion in atonement, the presentation of Mary as a devoted mother did not trouble these evangelicals.

The Protestants I have called fundamentalists, though, saw the film's portrayal of the crucifixion as decidedly Catholic, and they found the centrality attributed to Mary unacceptable because the blurry distinction between Mary and the Trinity threatened their symbolic reality and the strict order it represents. Dismissing Gibson's *Passion*, a Hollywood blockbuster despite its theme, was a way for them to draw a line between themselves and the rest of culture. Understanding gender and gender-related issues is increasingly important as conservative Christianity continues to exercise influence on American culture and politics. Within the conservative Protestant subculture, norms and expectations regarding gender are part of a larger process of cultural production. The debate over *The Passion* is only the most recent chapter in a continuing history.

Notes

1. See Finke and Stark 1992.
2. See Wuthnow 1998.
3. See Marsden 1980; DeBerg 1990; Harding 2000.

4. See Marsden 1991, "Preachers of Paradox."
5. See Ribuffo 1983.
6. Nineteenth-century evangelicals largely were postmillennialist. They believed that it was the task of Christians to build the Kingdom of God on earth—hence to social reform efforts—and that Jesus would return after they had done so. John Nelson Darby developed an alternative eschatology—premillennial dispensationalism, popularized by the study notes in the Scofield Reference Bible—that held that humanity is approaching the end of the "dispensation," called the church age, and that there is about to be a Great Tribulation, the rapture of the Christian Saints, and a final battle between good and evil at Armageddon that would usher in the Second Coming of Jesus and the Kingdom of God. For an excellent treatment of this tradition, see Weber 1997.
7. See Weaver and Appleby 1995.
8. See Ingersoll 2003, 106–8, 143–47.
9. For development of this idea, see Morgan (chapter 11 in this volume).
10. White 2004.
11. See Smith (chapter 3 in this volume).
12. Neff 2004.
13. WorldNetDaily 2004.
14. Compare the presence of demons in *The Passion* with those in the *Left Behind* novels (1995–2004) or the earlier Frank Peretti novels (1986, 1989).
15. Hunter 1991. See, for example, *The Remnant*'s Mark Alessio (2004) description of *The Passion*'s prerelease critics, which follows the logic of a culture war between traditionalist Catholics and "enlightened" ecumenical "elitists":

> Here was a cabal whose elitists were telling Joe Q. Public that his religion was hateful, that his cherished sacred texts were defective, that he had to be sensitized and reeducated into a brand new mindset whose truths and values would be determined by those who were more "enlightened" than he was. If he refused to acquiesce to this new deconstruction and defilement of his ancient beliefs, well, then he would be labeled either a hate-monger or a simpleton, and be dismissed as unworthy to contribute to the prevailing "spiritual" climate.

Alessio concludes, "There *is* a 'threat' looming, but it is leveled against those Catholics already distanced from the Traditional Catholic Faith and who are easy prey for the insatiable wolves of ecumenism."

16. At the same time, they understand the gospel differently; they still have profound theological disagreements—not to mention the fact that the Bible may be the literal inherent Word of God for the evangelicals, but the Catholics use a different Bible. For these two groups, however, these points are relegated to the position of "nonessentials."

17. United States Conference of Catholic Bishops 2004.
18. Cunningham 2004.
19. Marty 2004.
20. The fact that there were twenty-five articles is not, in itself, significant. The number demonstrates clearly that more than a few critics make the arguments discussed here. For other research, I am on a number of e-mail lists for right-to-life groups that defend the use of violence to stop abortion; the people on those lists directed me to these websites. A list of some of the sites is at the end of "The Animated Crucifix" (Let God Be True 2004).
21. Yusko 2004.
22. Let God Be True 2004. See also Fortner 2004: "James Caviezel said, referring to his role (as the Son of God!), 'I think it's very important that we have mass every day. . . . I need that to play this guy. . . . If I was going to play him I needed the sacrament (mass) in me.' Still unconcerned?"
23. Malone 2004. Ironically, *The Remnant*'s Alessio, in an "open letter to Mel Gibson," warns, "One word . . . one phrase . . . altered or removed from the Gospel accounts is a small victory, not for Truth, but for those who despise 'the Way, the Truth, and the Life'" (14 October 2003). Alessio did not comment on *The Passion* after its release.
24. Gleason 2004.
25. Additional analysis of this aspect of the film can be found in Morgan (chapter 11 in this volume).
26. Trewhella 2004 "*The Passion of the Christ* or The Emperor's New Clothes."
27. I am indebted to editor Shawn Landres for this observation. Oppenheimer (2003, 166) notes the term's "superstitious connotations" when used by opponents of the ordination of women in the Episcopal Church. The term "redemptrix," though arguably more accurate, is at the same time less familiar in common usage that the "-ess" to denote the feminine.
28. Ingersoll 2003.

Part II
THE PASSION IN CONTEXT

The seven chapters that follow place *The Passion* in context as a cinematic offering, an argument about history, a spiritual form, a theological statement, a work of art, and an expression of the psychology of our generation.

Karen Jo Torjesen sees the root of Gibson's *The Passion of the Christ* in medieval Passion plays that brought the sacred world of the churches into the town square and the marketplace, precisely where contemporary movie theaters are situated. The artistic vision, she writes, touches deeply embedded images in our collective religious imagination. While early Christian authors attended to the life, teaching, and resurrection of Jesus, medieval thinkers—like Gibson—focused on Jesus's suffering and death. *The Passion* reflects the influence of Irish monastic penitential theology and of atonement theology. Why does this medieval imagery resonate so deeply in contemporary American life, especially to evangelical Protestants, whose churches are adorned with empty crosses and not the crucified Christ? Like so many entertainment offerings and especially the nightly news, this film offers "vicarious participation in violence." Torjesen believes that we share with medieval culture the idea that only the material and the physical are real. "The divine must be physically present." The "raw physicality" of the film makes the story of the crucifixion more real.

When Msgr. Lorenzo Albacete first was invited to view *The Passion of the Christ*, two questions were of central concern. Was the film antisemitic? Was it faithful to the Gospels and to history? These questions, however, did not concern Albacete as much as Gibson's paradoxical devotion to text and rejection of history. Albacete revisits the central divide between Protestants and Catholics over ecclesiastical authority and the interpretive history of Scripture. The story of Jesus's life and death as well as his resurrection, he argues, cannot be separated from the larger context of Christian faith and the life of the church. Despite Gibson's traditionalist Catholicism, Albacete suggests, Gibson seems to want to embrace the Protestant tradition of *Sola Scriptura* ("Scripture alone"). However, *The Passion* is unrestrained in its religious emotionalism and is not "just the facts." In many ways, he concludes, *The Passion* betrays an ahistorical and anti-Judaic Gnostic sensibility, one that cannot be resisted except through involvement in the life of the church and attention to church teachings.

For Robert A. Faggen, films should be judged neither as histories nor as political documents but as works of art. Thus, a film cannot be antisemitic, but its viewers can. They choose how to behave in response to the artistic work, whether to perpetrate hate or to engage in acts of love and kindness. Faggen proposes to shift the question from "Who killed Jesus?" to "Why did Jesus die?" In focusing on the former, Faggen suggests, *The Passion* obscures Jesus's Jewishness and his ongoing dialogue with the Hebrew Scriptures. Moreover, it ignores the notion that the prime mover in the Passion narrative is God, who has chosen suicide in order to change the terms of the covenant. Faggen concludes that artistic judgments about *The Passion* must rest on the extent to which it is accessible to an empathetic viewer; religious judgments must rest on the extent to which the film encourages devotional faith. The rest is up to the viewer.

Given Gibson's apparently premodern absolutist value system, Gary Gilbert finds that *The Passion* employs a surprisingly postmodern form of artistic creation, deconstructionism, most especially the technique of erasure, whereby the film is not antisemitic but rather ~~antisemitic~~ (the technique reminds us that "erasing" an idea never deletes it completely). That most audiences are focused not on the Jews but on the crucifixion does not mean that the film is not antisemitic, only that the its antisemitism is very subtle. Moreover, the loud debate over the inclusion of the "blood curse" (Matthew 27:25) and Gibson's subsequent deletion of the line from the subtitles only hid the remaining signs. The "good Jews" are those who have accepted Jesus. The film makes clear that those whose heads are covered, especially by prayer shawls, are the enemy. After the crucifixion, *The Passion* provides a powerful visual dramatization of supersessionism, the doctrine that Christianity has taken the place of Judaism, when God's tear sends an earthquake that shatters the Temple but leaves the Roman palace untouched. Fully one-third of the film has no biblical basis; even then, Gibson chooses selectively among the gospel accounts. Gilbert concludes that debates over individual anti-Jewish expressions, over claims to history, and over doctrinal differences "cannot erase antisemitism wherever it occurs, including in film."

Jeffrey S. Siker discusses the post-Holocaust, post–World War II developments of Christian thinking regarding the life, death, and resurrection of Jesus, changes that Gibson seems to vehemently oppose. The film virtually ignores the life of Jesus, his teaching, and his identity as a Jewish teacher in the prophetic mode. According to Siker, Gibson relates "to a community that is both historically and theologically more conservative" than the theological shifts of biblical scholars and Christian theologians. The greater Jesus's suffering, the greater his redemption of sinners; in *The Passion*, Christ's sacrificial death overshadows Jesus's life and resurrection. *The Passion* has touched a "a raw nerve" with Christians who believe that scholars and church leaders are selling out some of the deepest doctrinal commitments of faith. It is "reactionary counterpunch," Siker concludes, and fully intended as such.

David Morgan points to another distinct aspect of *The Passion*, namely, the role of Mary and her competition with Satan for Jesus's loyalty. Moreover, Joseph is absent, and the film suggests, through images of the occluding moon and sun, that God is withdrawing as well. Predominant is the mother–son relationship, which is playful and gentle and which underscores Mary's devotion to Jesus and her helplessness to prevent the impending slaughter. Mary's competitor is Satan, whose offer to end Jesus's suffering is one that Mary cannot match. Morgan suggests that the film should be read in the context of shifts over the course of American religious history in depictions of Jesus's masculinity or femininity. The frustration that his pleas to his heavenly father go unanswered is compounded by the tug-of-war between Mary and Satan for his maternal allegiance. Morgan traces the conflict between intimacy and rage as reflected in the film and probes for their larger meaning.

Lloyd Baugh, SJ, reminds the reader that *The Passion of the Christ* is neither the first nor the last controversial film on the theme of the life

PART II

and death of Jesus. In fact, the intensity of the initial controversy may have obscured the nature of Gibson's work and the issues that he raised. Contrasting *The Passion* with Pasolini's *The Gospel according to Saint Matthew* and Martin Scorsese's *The Last Temptation of Christ*, Baugh reminds us that a contemporary understanding of the film may not endure for long and that once the dust settles and the passion fades, the value of the film may be rather different. Baugh rejects the argument that the filmmaker's biography is predictive of a film's orthodoxy or heterodoxy; despite Gibson's reported traditionalist Catholic beliefs, the film approaches docetism in its implicit suggestion that Jesus only appeared to be human, that no normal human being could have survived the punishment and risen again. Moreover, Baugh finds that Gibson's narrowly individualistic and joyless portrayal of Jesus's resurrection is "fatally flawed" because it gives no sense of its hopefulness or of its broader historical implications for the newly born Christian community. These flaws, in addition to the film's obsession with penitential atonement theology, Baugh argues, likely will emerge when later critics have the opportunity to revisit the film.

CHAPTER SIX
THE JOURNEY OF THE PASSION PLAY FROM MEDIEVAL PIETY TO CONTEMPORARY SPIRITUALITY

Karen Jo Torjesen

A Medieval Passion Play

To what genre does *The Passion of the Christ* belong? Is it a historical account of the trial and crucifixion? A retelling of the gospel narratives? A staging of a theological drama? A catechetical retelling of the gospel stories? An artistic work of religious imagination?

The use in the film of Aramaic and Latin appears to be a gesture toward historical accuracy to the extent that the use of these ancient languages creates a deeper sense of historical authenticity for theatrical audiences. However, Greek rather than Latin was the lingua franca of the day; the use of Latin in the film suggests that the film derives its power from the sensibilities of a different era. Moreover, Gibson originally intended to show the film without any subtitles; he wanted the powerful message of the film to be carried by the action alone. Neither is the movie a simple retelling of the gospel narrative. The devil in the garden and her appearances throughout are not part of the Gospels, nor are the scenes of pools of blood, the multiple falls under the weight of the cross, the scourging with the cat-o'-nine-tails, the encounter with Veronica (the woman with the scarf), or the crowd of children that become demonic tormentors.[1] According to the film's credits, Gibson's only consultant—on matters theological or historical—was the Jesuit priest who translated the script into Aramaic, Hebrew, and Latin; Gibson apparently did not consult any of the considerable work done on first-century Roman Palestine, Second Temple Judaism, or early Christianity.

While Gibson's *Passion* is a work of the imagination like any other creative work and while it does bear distinctive marks from his earlier movies—such as in *Lethal Weapon* the prisoner pushed off the bridge and caught by his own chains—nonetheless it represents an artistic vision that goes beyond one man's imagination. Christian audiences who sobbed through the brutal scenes of the movie were responding to images deeply embedded in a collective religious imagination. Indeed, the artistic development of the movie, its pace, its focus, its structure, and most of all its impact on the audience are best understood by understanding the movie as a contemporary version of a medieval Passion play.

The rhythm of medieval life in Christian Europe divided the calendar year into cycles of sacred time. Liturgical festivals marked these cycles through the celebration of saints' feast days and events in the life of Christ. Medieval church dramas served to educate a nonliterate society. Holy Week was the most solemn of all the festivals.[2] The Passion play itself was the enactment of a Latin text that could be neither read nor understood by the laity, who spoke in the vernaculars of their day—Italian, French, Spanish, German, and English. However, the deeper purpose of the Passion play was to cultivate a distinctive medieval spirituality, an affective piety in which the emotions were the true register of theological understanding. The drama of the Passion play was intended to produce in its audience a range of emotional responses from horror to grief, from grief to sympathy, from sympathy to remorse. Moreover, the liturgical drama of the Passion play spilled out from the sacred space of the church or cathedral into the town itself, transforming the profane marketplace into a sacred place.

Gibson's *Passion* seeks to effect the same outcome on its contemporary audiences that the Passion plays did on their medieval audiences. However, with his cinematic depiction of the Christ's suffering body, its tormented and torn flesh, and its prodigious loss of blood, Gibson's representations of the Passion go well beyond what medieval actors were able to dramatize. The camera remains riveted for what feels like hours of theater time on scenes of scourging and beating that he renders in fervent and adoring detail. For these scenes, Gibson admits that he has done both historical and medical research on the body's capacity for suffering.[3] The body of the Christ is the focus of his drama, not the actions; the body, more than the person, has primacy. The drawn-out scenes of suffering emphasize the passivity of the victim so that suffering itself becomes the primary message. Relentless blood is the visual motif that unifies the movie.

This constellation of the body, suffering, and the power of blood calls for further exploration. What contemporary theatrical audiences have seen in record numbers and what some Christians continue to find profoundly moving is a spirituality that in fact emerged historically nearly a millennium after the death of Jesus and the birth of Christianity. For the contemporary student of religion, the fascinating question posed by this popular response to Mel Gibson's film is this: Why does this distinctively medieval spirituality find such a resonance in contemporary culture?

The Missing Crucifix

Early Christians did not preoccupy themselves with the broken body, the suffering victim, or the spilled blood. When Matthew and Luke revised and expanded the Gospel of Mark, it was not the details of Jesus's suffering that they elaborated.[4] John's retelling of the Jesus story elaborates miracles and proclaims Jesus's divinity with philosophical fervor. Rather than with a birth narrative, the Gospel of John opens with a theological affirmation of a preexistent cosmic Christ who becomes incarnate in Jesus's body. Even Paul's letters, the earliest records of the Christian church, give little attention to the crucifixion and virtually none to the suffering victim and the spilled blood. Paul's life-changing encounter on the road to Tarsus was not with the suffering Jesus but with the resurrected Christ.

In the earliest extant baptismal formulas, Christians confessed to the historicity of a Jesus who "was crucified under Pontius Pilate, and was dead and buried, and rose again the third day."[5] Beyond this simple statement, little was made of the fact that the trial and crucifixion involved suffering and bloodletting. One reason was that these were not particularly distinctive aspects of Jesus's biography; scourging and crucifixion were routine Roman penal procedures. More important, however, early Christians were struggling to assert the divinity of a Jesus who lived and died as a mortal. Gods were immortal, not subject to change, not involved in the material world, and not limited by a body. To Gentile ears, the Christian claim that the divine subjected itself to bodily existence within the world of time and change bordered on the blasphemous.

Romans, Greeks, and Mithraists readily could accept a human Jesus who was as an emissary of God or a divine intermediary but not someone who was the full embodiment of the divine. Christian apologists asserted Jesus's divinity on the basis of his fulfillment of scriptural prophecies, his miracles, and his ethical teachings.[6] The "ordinary" physical suffering of a common prisoner and the execution of that prisoner under the Roman judicial system detracted from the early Christian proclamation of Jesus's divinity. Given the extent to which precisely this image has pervaded Western culture, it is difficult to show how absurd this claim would have sounded to first-century ears: a rough contemporary analogy would the claim for the divine status of a John Walker Lindh after his trial, conviction, and execution by lethal injection. The vulnerability to shame and ridicule provoked by an image of a crucified Savior is captured in a Roman graffito that depicts a hastily scrawled cross with a donkey's head and torso on it under which is scrawled, "Alexander is worshiping his god."[7] Contemporary language still describes an awful person as a "horse's ass"; imagine being accused of worshipping one.

Because the cross was an uncomfortable reminder of Jesus's apparently ordinary mortality, it is not surprising that early Christian art features almost no representations of the cross or the crucifixion.[8] From the catacombs to the basilicas, early Christian art portrays Jesus as a wonderworker, a teacher, a healer, and a ruler—but never as a crucified convict. Not until the tenth and eleventh centuries do we find the first representations of Christ on the cross.[9]

Heroic Suffering

Narratives about early Christian martyrs prominently feature their suffering bodies and their blood. These stories also are set against the backdrop of the Roman justice system and include, like the Passion, narrative stories of the arrest, trial, and investigation under torture, which included not only flogging but also other forms of torture. Martyrs' stories culminated in a criminal's execution; citizens were beheaded, but others died by fire or at the claws and teeth of wild animals in the Roman arena.

Martyrdom counted as a second baptism, a baptism in blood. To die a martyr was an active choice, and the suffering, endurance, heroism under torture, and fearlessness in the face of death was clear evidence of the triumph of the divine presence within. In spite of the fact that they were caught in the net of the Roman judicial system and suffered imprisonment, torture, and death, the early church made it clear that martyrs were not helpless victims: a favorite metaphor for the suffering martyr was the victorious gladiator. Their bodily death in the Roman arena marked their spiritual victory in the kingdom of heaven. Martyrs bought their freedom at the price of their lives; in their death and through their death, they conquered death and triumphed over Satan.

Penitential Spirituality

Since themes of body, suffering, and blood dominate the stories of the martyrs' suffering, we might have expected Mel Gibson to draw on martyrologies in depicting a triumphant Jesus victorious through his suffering. However, this is not the case. Indeed, Gibson's Jesus is passive, almost a helpless victim. He pulls on our emotions, forcing even the stoniest heart to feel a compassion that borders on pity. The source for such imagery originates not with the early Christian martyrs but in the Irish monastic roots of medieval penitential piety.

Planted on native Irish soil just outside the reach of what remained of the Roman Empire, Irish Christians created a practice of penance so daunting, expressive, and formidable that it transformed and reformed Roman Christianity on the European continent. The suffering naked body on the cross, the suffering flesh, and the open bleeding wounds became powerful religious symbols and took deep root in the religious imagination as a popular penitential piety. By the eleventh century, this piety had helped form a cultural context within which the doctrine of the atonement placed a passive, suffering Christ at the center of Christian theology.

While secular priests and bishops were preoccupied with the major sins that ordinary people commit,[10] the monastic life appealed to those who withdrew from the world in a spiritual quest for perfection. Monks concerned themselves even with the smallest of sins and were determined to root out sin from the most hidden core of the human self. It was a sin to speak crossly to a brother, to answer back to a superior, and even to forget to say "Amen" at the end of grace before meals. Just as beatings were the primary form of domestic household discipline for errant slaves, children, servants, and wives, so too were beatings imposed for sins against

God and the community: two blows for raising one's voice and six blows for shouting, six blows for talking while eating and ten blows for cutting the table with a knife.[11] Sinfulness expressed itself through bodily suffering; penance for sin involved bodily punishment.

The warrior cultures of the Celts in Ireland and of the continental European Goths, Saxons, Angles, and Vikings were early sources for the religious meaning of the pain and suffering borne in the body.[12] When Germanic customs supplanted Roman law in northern Europe, early medieval Christianity assimilated ideas about blood revenge (that blood can be expiated only through the shedding of blood) and compensation (that restitution or satisfaction must be made for an offense).

As the monastic disciplines themselves, such as fasting, vigils, and chanting, came to be understood as practices that had the power to expiate sins, so too did physical punishments, such as beating, withholding of food and water, and extreme vigils, come to be understood as acts of satisfaction or restitution for sins. Shorter and more extreme forms of penance could substitute for longer, milder practices. Again, the notion of substitution and satisfaction or compensation lies at the heart of this spirituality.[13] The body was the site of both passion and penitence.

In the eleventh century, the northern European theologian Anselm of Canterbury used Aristotelian logic to apply the system of penitential piety to Jesus's crucifixion itself. According to Anselm, Jesus's physical suffering and death functioned as a satisfaction to God's offended honor for all human sinfulness. Because Jesus was without sin and infinitely good, he was able to use that sinlessness and goodness as compensation for humanity's sin and evil. His undeserved suffering and self-sacrifice created an infinite store of merit that could paid on behalf of all those who needed to make satisfaction for their sins.

We can see the influence of Anselm's theology on Gibson's *Passion*: "Turn your eyes away from his divinity for a little while and consider him purely as a man. You will see a fine youth cruelly beaten and covered with blood and wounds. Look at him diligently now, and be moved to pity and compassion."[14] Anselm's atonement theory placed a strong emphasis on Christ's suffering and cultivated a piety based on a desire to suffer with Christ, in a sense to help Christ pay humanity's debt to God. Anticipating Gibson by a millennium, Anselm urged his monks to focus their devotions explicitly on Christ's sufferings, for "since Christ was scourged and his blessed flesh and delicate limbs were grievously torn with knotted thongs, and his beautiful body was covered with wounds and bruises and died in blood, a valiant soldier in Christ ought to chastise his body by mortification and penance that it may not stubbornly resist the Spirit."[15] Indeed, the biblical Passion narrative provided a model for these meditations in the figure of Mary, the Mother of God. Mary's spiritual suffering on gazing on the broken body of her son—greater than all the physical suffering of the martyrs combined—became the basis for vivid meditations on the scourging, the beating, the flayed flesh, the open wounds, and the agony of the crucifixion. In Gibson's *Passion*, Mary plays this role and serves as the mediator for the audience's participation in Jesus's suffering.

The penitential practices of mortification and penance also counted as physical participation in the suffering of Christ. This participation in Christ's suffering gains for the penitent access to the merits of Christ's satisfaction. As Anselm insists, "Surely they would imitate him in vain if they did not share in his merit."[16] The grammar of "*compassio*," as Jennifer Lane calls it, links the merits of Christ's Passion with the reception of those merits through participation in Christ's suffering. Christ suffered for us in order to pay our debt; by suffering with him, we are able to receive that payment.[17]

Throughout the twelfth and thirteenth centuries, monks (and later the lay public) sought ways to participate in Jesus's suffering. Franciscan monks in particular wove these powerful emotive practices into lay spirituality. After they received custodianship of the holy places of Jerusalem from the Mamluks in 1342, they transformed the Jerusalem pilgrimage itself into a meditation on the Passion of Christ. Those who could not make the trip to Jerusalem could follow the Way of the Cross through passionate meditation and receive the same benefits from the treasury of merit as those who are able to make the trip. Hundreds of devotional books promised the same experience of participation in the sufferings of Christ through the heartfelt and heartrending *compassio* in response to those sufferings. The fourteenth-century *Meditations on the Life of Christ* urged readers to "look at him well then as he goes along bowed down by the cross and gasping aloud. Feel as much compassion for him as you can placed in such anguish and renewed derision."[18]

In the fifteenth century, this piety of *compassio* or participation in the sufferings of Christ through an emotive identification gave rise to meditations on images of Stations of the Cross, specific times and places in the last twelve hours of Jesus's mortal life. By the end of the seventeenth century, the number of images that made up the Stations of the Cross was standardized at fourteen.[19] These fourteen images were so influential that the Jerusalem pilgrimage itself was reorganized to conform to the European meditational practice of the Via Dolorosa (literally, the way of suffering), as the Stations of the Cross came to be known.[20] This radical transformation of the gospel accounts of Jesus's progression from the Garden of Gethsemane to Golgotha made room for a distinctive piety framed within an atonement theology. Following the Via Dolorosa moved pious pilgrims from compassion to remorse as they participated spiritually in Jesus's sufferings at each station. And it is this narrative path that structures Mel Gibson's *Passion*.

The Medieval in the Modern

The enormous success of Gibson's film returns us to the original compelling cultural question: Why does this medieval piety find such a powerful resonance in contemporary culture? Even more interesting is the question, Why did evangelicals flock to see this movie? Evangelicals are inheritors of Protestant Christianity. Their churches have empty crosses. Their images of Christ are either a robust redheaded Jesus or the more reflective and spiritual long-haired Jesus of Warner Sallman. In no case do they devote themselves to the suffering, bleeding, scourged, and dying Jesus. Furthermore, Protestant Christianity repudiated the medieval penitential system as having no salvific value: faith—that Christ died for humanity's sins and was born again—is the only effective route to salvation. Spiritual participation in Jesus's suffering no longer gave access to the merits of his Passion. Indeed, even the post–Vatican II Roman Catholic Church has revised radically the remnants of the penitential system and has reclassified confession and penance as a "rite of reconciliation."

Nonetheless, there are interesting resonances between the context of contemporary spirituality and medieval penitential spirituality. Although Protestants rejected the penitential piety of medieval Christianity and with it the idea that participatory suffering (as acts of penance) accrues merits, Anselm's atonement theology remains central to Reformation theology. And post-Reformation blood piety appears not in art (the Calvinist reform eschewed images) but in the hymnology of Protestant worship.

William Cowper's nineteenth-century hymn, "There is a fountain filled with Blood, drawn from Immanuel's veins, and sinners plunged beneath that flood lose all their guilty stains," is but one example.[21]

Atonement theology sees Jesus's death as a substitutionary death in which Christ bears the punishment for all humankind. His death propitiates human sin. But this presupposes an angry God, to whom propitiation must be made—and for this reason theologians have struggled with it since the Middle Ages. Did sin offend God's honor? Did it insult God's justice? What had to be propitiated? Why couldn't God forgive sin without the sacrifice of a son? Atonement theology seems to make of God an abusive father who wreaks terrible suffering on his son to satisfy his own sense of honor.[22] Christ's passive suffering is essential to a theology of atonement. Christ is the helpless and willing victim whose suffering is redemptive; all that is required is consent to suffering.[23] Gibson's *Passion*, as steeped in pre–Vatican II Catholic piety as it is, has found a profound resonance among evangelical Christians because it reinstates atonement theology as a historical fact. Atonement theology is what gives the brutality of the violence its powerful religious meaning.[24]

Contemporary society also shares with medieval culture the conviction that the real is located in the material and physical. For the divine to be real, it has to be physically present and accessible in a material way. For medievals, the reality of the presence of Christ in the Eucharist could be affirmed only if that presence were physical and material; thus, the doctrine of the transubstantiation of the material elements of bread and wine into the body and blood of Christ became dogma. Relics of the saints—bits of their clothing, bones, and objects associated them—were meaningful because their physicality and materiality constituted the protective presence of the saints. The scientific worldview that characterizes contemporary culture shares a similar sensibility that what is real is what is physical, tangible, and material.[25] The raw physicality of the Passion of Gibson's Christ makes the story of the crucifixion more real. Devout Christians leave the movie with a deeper sense of the reality of the events because the film so graphically renders the physical dimensions of their spiritual experience.

Gibson's *Passion* re-creates in the modern genre of cinema the medieval vision of the Passion of Christ. The meditations on the life of Christ that late medieval devotionals used to evoke spiritual suffering in the reader— the images of the body and its brokenness, the suffering of the flayed flesh, and the blood pouring from wounds—belong to a spirituality that has roots in the tribal cultures of northern Europe during the Middle Ages. To be sure, it would not be unreasonable to argue—historically—that the penitential piety of Gibson's *Passion* has deep roots in the medieval culture of Gibson's *Braveheart*. The spirituality of the late medieval church was rooted in the values of a warrior culture that valorized the power of physical suffering and in a legal code that required retribution and satisfaction and a monastic penitential piety that understood self-imposed physical suffering as profound acts of penance and forms of restitution for the impossible burden of the sinful self.

Attention to physical suffering indeed is something contemporary culture also shares with medieval culture: a fascination and obsession with violence in its most immediate forms—the battered, broken, and bleeding body and the blood it sheds. The warrior culture of slashing swords and piercing arrows, of brutal cudgels and pools of blood, were medieval culture's stock in trade—as they are the currency of contemporary popular cinema. Medieval artists and storytellers rendered in gory details the suffering of the saints; torture and executions were public spectacles. In much the same way, Gibson the storyteller builds on a rich tradition of Hollywood violence, of which he himself is a major producer; *The Passion* both benefits from and contributes to the popularity of cinematic violence. Historians of medieval Christianity have accounted for that period's brutal religious imagery by referring to the tenor of violence in late medieval society: terrible plagues, devastating wars, famines, and religious persecutions.[26] We also have this in common. Like medieval society, contemporary society seems to have an insatiable appetite for representations of violence, for vicarious participation in violence through entertainment. Our fascination with violence also reflects the struggle to come to terms with violence in our homes, in our communities, and in our world.

Notes

1. Many of the additional elements come from the collected meditations of an eighteenth- to nineteenth-century nun, Anna Katharina Emmerich (1911).

2. The following traditional meditations determine the structure of Gibson's *Passion*: the Five Sorrowful Mysteries, the Agony of Jesus in the Garden, the

Scourging of Jesus at the Pillar, the Crowning with Thorns, the Carrying of the Cross, and the Crucifixion and Death of Jesus.

3. See, for example, Sawyer 2004.

4. See Mitchell 2004.

5. The earliest known creedal statement comes from Hippolytus's account of 215 C.E. See "Hippolytus's Account of the Baptismal Service."

6. See, for example, Origen 1953.

7. As of 1982, this graffito still was visible in the palace of Maxentius on the Roman Forum.

8. The one exception, striking in its singularity, appears on the great carved doors of the fifth-century Roman Church Santa Sabina. One of the wooden panels depicting the life of Christ represents the three crosses on Golgotha.

9. There are tenth-century depictions of Jesus on the cross, but it is not the dying Christ but rather a Christ with arms extended and eyes wide open and fully clothed in an act of teaching—far removed from the image of a suffering or dying Christ.

10. Throughout the first five centuries, only three sins disbarred erring Christians from participation at the communion table: murder, adultery, and apostasy. Such offenders could be restored to fellowship with the church after an extended period of public penitence. The public character of this penitence imposed a certain humility on the penitent and was itself a sign of genuine conversion.

11. *Common Rule of the Brethren* from the sixth-century *Rule of St. Columban* (McNeil and Gamer 1938, 258–59).

12. Bynum 2002.

13. The old Irish Table of Commutations proposed substituting extreme forms of penance, such as the cross vigil, in which the arms extended to form an image of the cross for the entire night while the monk sang repeatedly Psalm 119 (the longest psalm). A more extreme form was a ritual of genuflection in which the palms were thumped on the stone floor that left the hands bloodied by the end of the night. An even more extreme penance was to sleep with a corpse in the grave—for, as Columba explained, "Who is not implicated in some way in the killing death of another?"

14. Bonaventure and Green 1961, 330–31.

15. Anselm, quoted in Ludolph the Saxon 1887, 193.

16. Anselm of Canterbury 1976, 134.

17. Lane 2003, 108.

18. Bonaventure and Green 1961, 33.

19. Thurston 1906, 159–62.

20. Lane 2003, 269.

21. Armstrong 2004, 42.

22. See Morgan (chapter 11 in this volume) and Rubenstein (chapter 15 in this volume).

23. Feminist theologians have challenged atonement theology because it valorizes passive suffering and makes the victim a role model. Women, far more often than men, are called on to emulate the self-sacrificing Christ because the traditional virtues of womanhood, submission, self-sacrifice, patience, and longsuffering are reinforced by the theology of a self-sacrificing Christ. See, however, Ingersoll (chapter 5 in this volume) for an analysis of the role of gender in evangelical and fundamentalist Protestant disagreement over Gibson's *Passion*. Ingersoll's suggestion that "pro-*Passion*" evangelicals are comfortable with women playing an active but limited role in redemption would not be inconsistent with my focus on atonement theology if that role were understood as an "active" commitment to passive submission and self-sacrifice.

24. Jensen (2004, 45–47) makes precisely this point.

25. Even conservative Christians who support creationism over Darwinian evolution refer to their positions as "creation science" or the "theory of intelligent design."

26. See, for example, Bieler 1975; Russell 1994; Swanson 1995.

CHAPTER SEVEN
THE GIBSON CODE?
Lorenzo Albacete

In the autumn of 2003, I received an invitation to view the then-current version of Mel Gibson's *The Passion of the Christ*.[1] At that time, the two major controversies surrounding the film were questions regarding its fidelity to the Gospels and its potential antisemitism. I had grown up in Puerto Rico in a culture where plays and movies about the Passion and death of Jesus were standard Holy Week fare. Antisemitism was not an issue then (most of us had not met a single Jew) and fidelity to the sources even less important. In some of the productions, the entire cast assembled at Calvary for Jesus's death, including the magi and the shepherds associated with the story of his birth. The productions also placed people at Calvary who are not present in the biblical narrative but for whom Jesus had performed a miracle, like the widow of Naim and her resurrected son, the man born blind, Lazarus, the woman with a hemorrhage, and others.[2] No one cared about precise historical accuracy. Instead, what mattered was the ultimate truth of the story: God had subjected himself to human cruelty because of our sins and in solidarity with the poor and the victims of injustice. I did not think Gibson had much to worry about regarding his film in this cultural context.

People attended these productions with great devotion. Many prayed during the show. You could hear the whispers of parents and grandparents explaining to the children what was happening on stage. Once, as in Mario Vargas Llosa's semi-autobiographical novel *Aunt Julia and the Scriptwriter*, I was present at a production in which Jesus fell from the cross to the religious horror and dismay of the audience and even of the other performers.³ Beyond doubt, these presentations were not simply show-business events but ways of handing down a cultural tradition. People left the theater feeling that they had been participants, not mere spectators.

As a child and young adult, I always understood the Passion and death of Jesus as part of a larger narrative that had thoroughly penetrated our culture. The purpose of the Passion plays was not to portray the events for neutral viewers but rather to renew our sense of belonging to a particular history, a history that still had relevance in our contemporary lives. Moreover, these productions did not take place in a social vacuum: the Church always was there to guide the strong emotions aroused by the spectacle. I remember talking with my pastor after a particular production had moved me especially, and he said, "Well what are you going to do about it now? Go to confession!"

Neither two thousand years ago nor today can the Passion narrative be understood without references to the traditions that gave birth to the biblical accounts and to the cultural context within which contemporary audiences understand those accounts. What has made possible the antisemitic and other misinterpretations of the gospel narratives themselves has been their detachment from those traditions and contexts. And the cultural contexts that once guided our strong emotional responses to the Passion narrative—such as my priest at home—no longer exist everywhere or even in places where they once did. There has been much debate about whether Mel Gibson's *The Passion of the Christ* gets the facts of Jesus's crucifixion right. However, this discussion has largely missed the point. The greatest problem with Gibson's *Passion* is that it fetishizes the facts of Jesus's crucifixion above all else and separates the story of Jesus's death and resurrection from the larger context of Christian faith and the life of the Church. Separating the Passion story from its origin in the traditions of the early Christian communities has led not only to antisemitic interpretations but also to distortions of the Christian view of God as a bloodthirsty judge demanding reparation for human offenses. Jewish sacrificial language has been understood in pagan terms. Elsewhere, the death of Jesus has been interpreted politically, and his cross has been used to bless military adventures. Critics of Christianity have called it a religion of slaves that encourages submission to unjust authorities and promises heaven to those who suffer passively.

In my view, therefore, even if Gibson's *Passion* itself may not be antisemitic, nonetheless, its shocking emotional provocations, separated from the original traditions behind the gospel narratives, could foster antisemitic responses.[4] The real danger of antisemitism lies in the way antisemites caricature it and indeed the Passion narrative itself to support their agenda. Even though I found *The Passion of the Christ* to be, at some level, powerful, nonetheless Gibson's reduction of the Passion to an emotionally wrenching story is problematic. To separate the facts of the Passion from their proper context is to open the door to unchecked religious emotionalism. The link between past and present is crucial because without it, the Passion can be used to manipulate emotions contrary to its purpose. This is what worries me about Gibson's film. What is one supposed to do about this story? Cry? Be inspired to make sure things like that do not happen again? Why not seek revenge (as antisemites throughout the ages have done)? None of these is the intended purpose of this narrative.

To be sure, Christians are divided on the question of how the Passion should be linked to the present. Catholics believe that the Church makes present—and relevant—the events of Jesus's life; without it, the Passion is just a story that can provoke sadness, anger, or any range of emotions. True faith is something more than having your heartstrings pulled by a moving story. Acknowledging the link between Jesus's death and the present requires acknowledging the developing nature of Christianity. Moreover, doing so means accepting Vatican II, which absolved Jews of responsibility for Jesus's death.

As a Catholic priest who frequently is asked questions about Gibson's film in particular and the Passion narrative in general, I consider it my obligation to familiarize myself with both the Vatican II documents and the general progress that Jewish and Christian scholars have made in overcoming and preventing antisemitic interpretations of the gospel accounts of the conflict between Jesus and his opponents. Contemporary scholars have a much better understanding of the historical context of the various communities involved in the composition of the Passion narratives. This progress in understanding is very well documented and easily available to anyone.[5] It demonstrates clearly that extremely complex historical questions must be answered in order to reconstruct the part played by various individuals and groups in the execution of Jesus. It also reveals the rich and complex religious and political panorama that characterized first-century

Judaism, when the gospel narratives were being compiled. There is no excuse now for antisemitic caricatures based on simplistic views of the teachings of the Pharisees, Temple worship, Jesus's attitude to the Torah and its interpretations within Judaism, and the characteristics and strength of the messianic expectations of that period in Israel's history.

All this, of course, is inconvenient for Gibson because he is a traditionalist Catholic who does not accept Vatican II. That is why his film is out of touch with current Catholic doctrine in its portrayal of Jews. But it also explains why *The Passion* is out of touch with the spirit of Catholicism in its "just the facts" approach to the Passion story. The priests who attended the Puerto Rican Passion plays of my youth took care to emphasize that the life of the Church was the place to deal with the emotions that the story of Jesus's death unleashed. Of course, the Catholic Church cannot send an official to all screenings of *The Passion*. Nevertheless, precisely because Gibson was so determined to present a context-free version of the Passion, it is crucial that Church officials try to mediate Catholics' understanding of the movie as best we can. Indeed, the effort to prevent the antisemitic interpretations of the gospel accounts should be an overriding preoccupation not for purposes of political correctness or diplomacy toward the Jews but as a matter of safeguarding the nature of the Christian faith itself.

Christian faith depends entirely on historical facts, on historical events, on things that happened. The gospel narratives are the product of the interpretation of the experiences of the first Christian communities in light of the events of the life of Jesus. As *Nostra Aetate* declares, the Gospels themselves are compilations of narratives that select "some things from the many that had been handed on by word of mouth or in writing, reducing some of them to a synthesis, explicating some things in view of the situation of the Churches, preserving the form of proclamation, but always in such a fashion that they tell us the honest truth about Jesus."[6] To separate the Passion accounts from this context, therefore, is to ignore their intended purpose.

A forced harmony between the different gospel accounts for purposes of telling a single story ignores the method on which Christianity depends to justify its claim about the identity and mission of Jesus. The Christian claim is based not on stories about past events in order to inspire, guide, or teach us, but rather on current events, through which Jesus verifiably remains in the world after having defeated death. Current and verifiable means that if what happened then does not happen now, Christianity is at best a beautiful illusion, if not a cruel hoax.

To sustain the Christian claim, it will not do to present the Passion and death of Jesus as an emotionally wrenching story of the past that will move us to be good today. How is one to respond to what happened two thousand or so years ago? The reduction of Christianity to an abstract ethical or philosophical system has been its greatest historical deformation. This possibility is particularly strong today, when the split between faith and reason no longer is "only" a factor in the divisions between Christians but indeed has become a very powerful cultural preconception.

Gibson's *Passion* powerfully appeals to the viewer's emotions. It is not simply a presentation of "just the facts." Indeed, it is surprising to see how concise and devoid of detail the Passion accounts in the Gospels are. One could read all four of them during the time it takes to watch the flagellation scene in Gibson's film. The film is a work of Gibson's artistic imagination and talent designed to make us share his view of the events in question. In addition, there are scenes that are not in any of the gospel accounts.[7] For example, Gibson's depiction of Mary, the mother of Jesus, is entirely the result of his Catholicism. Of course, there is nothing wrong with that—Michelangelo's *Pietà* is no less an expression of the sculptor's faith. What response does Gibson expect from us? When I left the theater after seeing his film, my priest was not waiting for me to counsel me and to send me to confession. How, then, can the response to Gibson's work be guided?

The intended purpose of the gospel narratives is to invite people to join the community where these events are experienced as occurring in the present. The possibility of being a "contemporary" of these events is in fact what the resurrection of Jesus is all about, and Christianity stands or falls with it. To separate events from their proper context is to open the door to a religious emotionalism gone wild, and we are presently suffering enough from that. Christian leaders who enthusiastically welcome Gibson's movie now have the overriding responsibility to lead an educational effort that will prevent unleashed emotions from spawning intolerance, discrimination, and violence.

The Christian proposal about Jesus and his mission depends entirely on how we understand the link between present experience and past events associated with the life of Jesus of Nazareth. Christianity holds that Jesus's mission was in fact to educate and guide the human religious quest, and that this takes place within a tradition that faithfully links his followers today to his original community of disciples. In fact, the only reason we have those gospel accounts and not others is that their ultimate truth was verified through the experience of the presence of the risen Christ in the first Christian communities. Outside this tradition, all is up for grabs, and then there is really reason to fear the powerful emotions unleashed by spectacles such this powerful film.

The truth of the Christian claim cannot be separated from the method of its transmission.[8] This concern about method is crucial. In fact, we might view much of the current debate about the effects of Gibson's film precisely as a clash between different views of the appropriate method with which to verify the claims of the Christian proposal.

The first possibility is the attempt to discover the "historical Jesus" through the current methods of historical investigation. Jesus is a fact of the past and should be studied as such. This includes understanding the cultural and social context of his time; gathering, classifying, and evaluating all available information; and including in the analytical process the role of the preconceptions of the present investigator.[9] This is how the so-called search for the historical Jesus has been carried out.[10] Those who believe that this is the only rational approach to connect us to Jesus of Nazareth will of course reject the film as naively dependent on the Passion narratives.

The problem with this method is that it necessarily excludes the truly new, the unexpected, and the unforeseen. Although a historical studies approach can help us understand better the significance of the events that faith recognizes as the numinous—that is, the appearance within history of the Mystery that haunts the religious quest—such an approach cannot account for the novelty of these appearances. This method a priori excludes the possibility of verifying the reasonableness of belief in Christianity's claims and moreover consigns it to a realm of "pure faith" that has no basis in experience.

Another method, often a reaction against the historical approach, is to consider the link to Jesus as an "inner experience" brought about by the Holy Spirit through contact with biblical texts or preaching. The problem is that this makes Christian faith depend on powerful feelings. Moreover, these feelings, which can be manipulated, are subjective and therefore lead to a plurality of often-contradictory views of the consequences of the Christian message. Moreover, this method seems to ignore Christianity's specific claims about the incarnation—namely, that the invisible, the transcendent, and the divine manifested itself as a fully human reality in all its dimensions, not just in terms of subjective feelings.

The controversy within Christianity concerning this question of method can be understood as a clash between the Protestant tradition of *Sola Scriptura*, namely, that the Bible is the only source of divine revelation, and the Catholic insistence that Scripture can be validly interpreted only in fidelity to the "tradition" of the Church. Vatican II sought to go beyond this "one or two sources" way of expressing the problem by proposing that both Scripture and tradition are the fruits of the events of revelation. This seems to me to be much more faithful to the way we human beings think for ourselves. We link our present with our past by interpreting our present experiences within the cultural contexts generated by the powerful experiences of past events. In fact, there is no such thing as *Sola Scriptura*. There always is a cultural context within which the text is understood, and we are deluding ourselves if we fail to acknowledge that and take responsibility for it.

In terms of method, the first Christians' experience of the truth of the resurrection of Jesus—that is, of his living Presence in human form today—was inseparable from that of belonging to a community created and sustained by its power. This "unity of believers" itself was seen as the contemporary form of Jesus's presence in history that believers can encounter today. This method conceives of the Christian claim as the invitation to a present and wholly human experience—an objective encounter with that objective human reality called the Church.

It was in the light of this experience that the Passion and death of Jesus was interpreted and expressed in the religious language of the first Christian community of apostles and disciples, the language of Israel's experience of election, liberation, atonement, and mission.

As such, historical criticism of the movie's facts is not enough. Excluding context, leaving out the community's own experience of the narrative leads to claims about textual fidelity that simply are false. Jesus's life story is important not simply because it happened but because it is part of a larger historical narrative—and because, like the Passion plays I attended growing up, it can speak to us today. To separate the Christian proposal from its origin and its traditional method of transmission is to do violence to the method through which Jesus is revealed and experienced as a living Presence today, as a fact that truly matters. It leads to an "abstract," indeed Gnostic, Christ, a figure detached from the limitations of human flesh who can be interpreted according to contemporary ideological prejudices.

This "disincarnation" of Christ still haunts Christianity. Its attraction can be seen in the current love affair with Gnosticism evident in the popularity of the novel *The Da Vinci Code*.[11] The early Church fought relentlessly against the Christian Gnostics, who saw the Christian message as an interior experience of illumination through self-knowledge completely separate from the emerging structures and traditions of the Christian community. Such a detachment from history made possible Gnostic antisemitism alongside its radical separation of the Hebrew Scriptures and the New Testament. Indeed, it was the Gnostics who coined the phrases "Old Testament" and "New Testament" in order to highlight their belief that the creator God of the Old Testament demanded obedience, while the redeemer God preached by Jesus in the New Testament was loving and merciful. Gnostics saw the *ekklesia* as an obstacle to the understanding of the true meaning of Scripture, which was entirely spiritual and subjective. This is precisely the view of the Church in the *The Da Vinci Code*, where the Church is portrayed as the main obstacle to the search for the truth about Jesus.

Gibson's film moves people emotionally, but unless they have access to the context that gives the events of the Passion their intended meaning through an adequate catechesis, this movie could become a cinematographic *Gibson Code*.

Notes

1. Apparently, Gibson was interested in gauging the reaction of "Hispanic Catholics" to the film. I declined the invitation because although I was born in Puerto Rico, I could not honestly present myself as a "focus group sample" of the varied and complex Hispanic world.
2. Luke 7:10–12; John 9:1–41; Matthew 9:20–22; John 11:1–41; Luke 8:43–48.
3. Vargas Llosa 1982.
4. To be sure, *The Passion*'s view of the bloodthirsty Temple authorities, the agitated mobs demanding the death of Jesus, and the vacillations of the Roman

procurator Pilate looking for ways to release him, for example, all have been used in the past for antisemitic purposes.

5. See, for example, Bishops' Committee for Ecumenical and Interreligious Affairs 2003. The BCEIA republished this collection in 2004 in response to Gibson's *Passion*.

6. See Pope Paul VI (*Nostra Aetate*) 1965, § 4.

7. See Cunningham (2004) for a complete list.

8. See Giussani 2001. Much of the following discussion is based on his analysis of methods with which to assess Christianity's claims.

9. There are contemporary philosophical positions that deny the possibility of ever attaining such an understanding, but taking such a position of course precludes the possibility of any reasonable discussion between different evaluations of historical claims.

10. See, however, Heschel (chapter 13 in this volume) for a discussion of the consequences of this approach.

11. Brown 2003.

CHAPTER EIGHT
"BUT IS IT ART?" A PRELUDE TO CRITICISM OF MEL GIBSON'S *THE PASSION OF THE CHRIST*
Robert A. Faggen

Mel Gibson has embarrassed the twenty-first century. He has made a film—a highly sophisticated representational technology of the present moment—about a two-millennium-old religious mystery with an emphasis on a form of faith that intellectuals had relegated to the Middle Ages and to the early modern era and a way of belief that many still hold but feel somewhere between uncomfortable and ashamed to discuss in public. Instead of focusing on the question of whether Mel Gibson's film *The Passion of the Christ* succeeds as a devotional work of religious art and about the future of Christian art or religious art of any kind, much of the debate has hovered around the politics of antisemitism and Jewish and Christian relations.

Admittedly, the problems of art and politics are not readily separable. However, I have not heard such a debate surrounding any recent performance of Bach's "St. Matthew Passion" or his "St. John Passion." Instead, Gibson's film—obviously because it is a film and because it is a Mel Gibson film—has been regarded as crude and irresponsible populist effort, analogous to the most crude and inflammatory Passion plays, such as the Oberammergau Passion play. I would prefer to hear questions about the film such as "Is this good art?" or "What is 'good' religious art?" and "What is the relationship of art to religion in our time?" If the focus is to be on content and ideology, I would prefer more direct and, I believe, honest questions, such as "Is Christianity bad?" or "Is religion bad?"

Instead, the primary question among critics has been political: "Is the film antisemitic?" or "Is this film potentially antisemitic?" The sanitized version of the question in most of the popular media has been "Who killed Jesus?"[1] or "Who *really* killed Jesus?"[2] Those questions rarely are transformed into a more sophisticated and important question, "Why did Jesus die?" The media have tended to treat the film as something it most definitely is not: a conspiracy docudrama in the tradition of Oliver Stone's *J.F.K.*

The approach taken to the film by such media entities as *Newsweek* and *Dateline NBC* to investigate historically who bears responsibility for the killing of Jesus will do nothing to resolve or ameliorate any potential tensions between Christians and Jews. Moreover, such an investigation misses the point about judging the film as a work of art. Sending Stone Philips to Jerusalem[3] will not give us any better understanding of the Passion story than having Stone Philips sit in a room with several copies of the Bible before him.

History Is Not the Answer

History, perhaps, could provide some insight, but there is very little historical evidence about Jesus, though there is somewhat more information about Pontius Pilate. I am not sure that historical evidence is ever likely to persuade people about the meaning of the life and death of Jesus more than Scripture itself. We have volumes of evidence and documentation about the death of John Kennedy, much of it supporting very strongly the theory that there was a lone gunman. However, that has not stopped about half the population from believing that there was a conspiracy.

The story of Jesus is one of faith—the substance of things hoped for and the evidence of things unseen—and of mystery. I am quite content to address the question of "who killed Jesus" in terms of Holy Scripture. As a teacher of literature and of stories, I am well acquainted with the power and mystery of storytelling. I am, therefore, quite willing to take the Bible the way many Jews and Christians take it—as an inspired text. Gibson's claims to the truth are based largely on Scripture, and I think it is reasonable to preface what he has done with some serious regard for that source. It may provide a better answer to questions about the mystery of culpability than a search for historical fact. We can regard the Bible as an inspired work that itself can be interpreted best by other inspired works. If Gibson's own form of puritanical Catholicism has occasioned a renewed look at the relationship of Jesus to Judaism, what I am engaged in here is a somewhat puritanical or fundamental examination of the relationship of the New Testament to the Hebrew Bible and of Jesus and Christianity to Judaism. Understanding the mystery of that relationship is essential to understanding what is at stake in the telling of the story of the Passion or evaluating a representation of that story.

When I hear the assertion, as I do from time to time in conversation with students and in their papers, that "the Jews killed Christ," I am less inclined to say, "That's not true" or "How do you know?" than to begin with some clarifications. It might seem obvious, if not condescending, to say, "Jesus, who some thought was the anointed or 'the Christ,' was not only a Jew but a rabbi." But when I hear Diane Sawyer, an experienced television journalist with great research engines available to her, asking Maia Morgenstern, the Romanian Jewish actress who plays Mary in the film, "What was it like to be Jewish and play the mother of Jesus?,"[4] I realize it may be worthwhile to remaining truly "unassuming" about what people generally know or do not know.

Jesus and Scripture

It is important, as many have tried to point out, that Jesus first was regarded as a Jew and indeed a rabbi. His teaching and his story are fundamentally Hebraic. When Jesus says, "You search the scriptures because you think in them you have eternal life; and it is they that testify on my behalf,"[5] he both echoes and alters one of the holiest parts of Torah, God's commandment to "Keep these words that I am commanding you today in your heart. Recite them to your children and talk about them when you are at home and when you are away, when you lie down and when you rise."[6] Jesus emphasizes keeping the heart and the spirit of the commandments.

The beginning of the Gospel of John underscores the relationship between God and the Word: "In the beginning was the Word, and the Word was with God, and the Word was God."[7] This calls attention to the connection between the God of the Hebrew Bible (Genesis in particular) and the God of the New Testament. Jesus's penultimate words on the cross, "Eloi, eloi, lama sabachtani?" are based on the second verse of Psalm 22, and it makes a great deal of difference whether one recognizes that or hears only a cry of despair.

Jesus is in continual dialogue with the Hebrew Scriptures, and he himself highlights that dialogue in the Sermon on the Mount: "Do not think that I have come to abolish the law or the prophets; I have come not to abolish but to fulfill. For truly I tell you, until heaven and earth pass away, not one letter, not one stroke of a letter, will pass from the law until all is accomplished."[8] One radical aspect of Jesus's teachings is his desire to make universal a religion heretofore connected exclusively to a particular people and nation. That desire is also present in the Hebrew Prophets, who are dissatisfied with national corruption. We can understand the drama of Jesus's life and death only in relation to the Hebrew God and the Hebrew teachings, of which, Christianity claims, Jesus became the incarnation.

Jesus's major teachings all can be found in the Torah, the Prophets, and the Writings of the Hebrew Scriptures (the *Tanakh*), and he knows this quite well. When a lawyer among the Pharisees asks Jesus which is the greatest of the Torah's commandments, Jesus replies, "You shall love the Lord your God with all your heart, and with all your soul, and with all your mind." This is the greatest and first commandment. And a second is like it: "You shall love your neighbor as yourself." On these two commandments hang all the law and the prophets.[9]

In his answer, Jesus consciously shifts from the language of the Decalogue to the language of the Holiness Code:

> You shall not take vengeance or bear a grudge against any of your people, but you shall love your neighbor as yourself. . . . When an alien resides with you in your land, you shall not oppress the alien. The alien who resides with you shall be to you as the citizen among you; you shall love the alien as yourself, for you were aliens in the land of Egypt.[10]

His answer also echoes the recapitulation of Deuteronomy: "You shall love the LORD your God with all your heart, and with all your soul, and with all your might."[11] Jesus no doubt knows that those commandments in Leviticus and Deuteronomy were revisions or developments of the law as originally presented in Exodus. Jesus's answer recapitulates both the Torah and the Prophets, and it anticipates Paul. The Deuteronomist reminds Israel that "the Lord your God will circumcise your heart and the heart of your descendants, so that you will love the Lord your God with all your heart and with all your soul, in order that you may live";[12] and Jeremiah exhorts Israel to return to God's law and "circumcise yourselves to the

LORD, remove the foreskin of your hearts."[13] Jesus's interpretation of the Scriptures thus anticipates Paul's own shift of the definition of a Jew from one who has undergone the physical rite of circumcision to one whose heart is circumcised spiritually.[14]

The connection between the Hebrew Bible and the New Covenant or New Testament, both in content and in pattern, is inextricable. How could one possibly follow those teachings or commandments and still practice hatred of Jews, Christians, Muslims, Buddhists, or anyone else for that matter? How could one fail to recognize that Jesus's reforms were fundamentally Hebraic in character?

From "Who Killed Jesus?" to "Why Did Jesus Die?"

Much to Gibson's credit, Satan is a definite presence in the film. Satan really is a gift of late Temple Judaism and early Christianity, the strong figure against which God and his Messiah make war.[15] We may ask, as many theologians and poets have done, Where in God's name did the Devil come from? This gets us into very difficult, perhaps impossible theological trouble, and I do not think it is quite necessary at the moment to dive into such Augustinian depths. It may be that theology cannot answer such questions and that they remain mysteries. However, where the logic of history, philosophy, and theology cannot go, the complex symbolism of art can go. Gibson's film incorporates an important and dramatic but elusive change in the biblical story: God's war no longer is with Pharaoh or the Canaanites or the Romans or even corrupt Israelites. God's new war or, better, struggle is with the Devil and with death.

What Jesus says to Pilate makes it clear that the ultimate source of the drama also is the ultimate source of power: God. God killed Jesus. And readers of the Hebrew Bible are familiar with this kind of story, in which God uses figures of history—in apparently impossibly cruel ways—to accomplish what God wants accomplished. God commands Moses to ask Pharaoh to free his people. But God also hardens Pharaoh's heart against Moses's cause. As a result, Pharaoh brings (God's) plagues on Egypt and on himself. Thus, God wills that his people be free but also that Pharaoh fail to free them. The outcome is that God and no one else, neither Moses nor Pharaoh, frees the Israelites from bondage. Similarly, it is God who wills that both Caiaphas and Pilate be involved in Jesus's condemnation and execution. Unless God had willed it, there would be no Christianity. How could anyone commit "deicide" if God is indeed God? However contemptible the various players may have been, it was a dirty job, as the saying goes, but somebody had to do it.

In order to comprehend what is stake in any representation of the Passion story, it also may be worth considering that instead of punishing sinners as he had in the Hebrew Bible, God now decides to punish himself. God becomes incarnate in man and kills himself in an attempt to put an end to all of humankind's failed sacrifices and brutalities. This vision has an ancient tradition. Jack Miles has argued, following Aquinas (among others), that "Christ is a suicide by metaphysical definition":

> If Jesus is God Incarnate, then no one can have taken his life away from him against his wishes. His suicide is, in this regard, as deeply built into the Christian story as the doctrine of the Incarnation. Thus, for Thomas Aquinas, Jesus was the cause of his own death.... Thomas strongly implies, moreover, that those who actually killed Jesus, or conspired to kill him, were less than fully responsible agents, that they were tools in the hand of God, a species of human rainstorm drenching God because God wished to be drenched. There is support for the latter view in the New Testament. From the cross, Jesus says of his executioners, "Father, forgive them, for they know not what they do" (Luke 23:34). Peter, preaching in the Temple after Jesus' death, says, "Now I know, brothers, that neither you nor your leaders had any idea what you were really doing; but this was the way God carried out what he had foretold when he said through all his prophets that his Christ would suffer" (Acts 3:17–18).[16]

The prophets to whom Peter refers include Isaiah, whose account of a "suffering servant"[17] accompanies a shift within the *Tanakh* itself, a change in which God becomes more mysterious and in many respects other than or opposite to the ways of the world.

In committing suicide, Christians believe, God changes the terms of his covenant with humanity, but that change can be seen clearly only in the light of how God is in the Hebrew Bible. Miles also underscores that "what matters about the Crucifixion is not what is suffered—the Romans crucified Jews by the thousands—but who suffers it."[18] A historical or political investigation simply cannot get to the heart of this mystery, the dilemma that God—the warrior God of the Hebrew Scriptures—has chosen to change his covenant and become incarnate, suffer, and die.

Some debates about *The Passion of the Christ* have narrowed the question of culpability to a choice between, on one side, the Jews in the Temple and their high priest, Caiaphas, and, on the other side, Pontius Pilate, the Roman governor. But trying to decide whether Caiaphas or Pilate bears the greater blame is useless. It is a powerful, human aspect of the story that Jesus, a puritanical reformer within the Temple, is rejected, betrayed, or denied by the some member of his own congregation, including—especially—his own disciples. One certainly can understand that some Jews would have been outraged by Jesus's apparently blasphemous claim of divinity. This blasphemy is unmistakable when Jesus responds to his followers' question of who he is claiming to be: "Very truly, I tell you, before Abraham was, I am."[19] Both the film and the Gospels depict Caiaphas as more instrumental and political than inhuman. Caiaphas may well have feared for both his own authority and the wrath of the Roman governor because of Jesus's growing power. In the Gospels but not in the film, Caiaphas says, "You do not understand that it is better for you to have one man die for the people than to have the whole nation destroyed."[20] John adds the following commentary: "He did not say this on his own, but being high priest that year he prophesied that Jesus was about to die for the nation, and not for the nation only, but to gather into one the dispersed children of God."[21] If Caiaphas thinks he is acting instrumentally, John suggests that Caiaphas himself is God's instrument: he is part of a plan that will make the religion of the Jews not only national but universal and "gather into one the dispersed children of God."

Pilate no doubt was a bully who crucified thousands of Jews. The threat of Roman genocide haunts the Gospels. The fact that Pilate at moments seems reluctant to crucify Jesus does not make him compassionate or thoughtful. Pilate's reluctance is political and therefore even more horrifying because he appears to have the power of choice. The fact that both Pilate and Caiaphas decide that Jesus should die for political reasons tends to make each side dramatically more, not less, contemptible. Anyone who knows politics or literature will recognize the deal in which two bullies, Caiaphas and Pilate, sacrifice something good and innocent in the interest of maintaining power. The tragic power of the Passion story does not come primarily from the cruelty of political expediency. Rather, it comes from the irony that these political players do not grasp that they are but minor players in God's dramatic sacrifice of himself.

How is it that God is active in history and determines its outcome but at the same time allows his creatures freedom of will and holds them morally accountable for their actions? How can it be that Jesus can be fully divine and yet a vulnerable human being who suffers when he is tortured? These are among the mysteries that haunt the story of Jesus and some representations of the Passion. Whether we judge Gibson's *The Passion of the Christ* to be a good work of art will depend on how much we believe that it conveys the power of those mysteries in a way that enables us to see them and experience them empathetically. Whether we judge *The Passion of the Christ* to be a good work of *religious* art will depend on how much we believe that the film cuts our minds and our hearts in a way that brings us closer to devotional faith and to the experience of Christian love.

There can be little question but that for many Jews the evocation of the Passion story brings about horrific memories of abuse and atrocity perpetrated in Christianity's name. Many remember feeling uncomfortable or even frightened to walk out of their houses on Good Friday and Easter (and not only then) for fear of being taunted as "Christ killers." Sadly, no amount reading, thinking, or reasoning will deter a bigot from his hate. Even if Gibson's film somehow were clearly antisemitic (and I do not believe that it is), I would contest the view that one should censor the film or demand of its maker that it be amended for fear that it somehow would incite or inflame antisemitic feeling. Here, I agree with what Milton wrote in the *Areopagitica*: "They are not skilful considerers of human things, who imagine to remove sin by removing the matter of sin."[22] Milton himself is on the edge of a mystery: How can one uphold God's power and foreknowledge but not hold him culpable for humanity's transgressions and degradation? How do we uphold justice against brutality and evil and at the same time enact the kind of mercy that the Passion story might want us to embrace? The fault of antisemitism does not lie in a film or in a story but in the will and actions of people who decide to perpetrate hate. One can condemn a film as expressing hate-filled views. One even can suggest that the pleasure or good feelings one has from viewing the film are actually evidence that something is very wrong with the viewer. Still, the viewers themselves, not the work of art, are responsible for their actions.

Notes

1. Meacham 2004.
2. *Religion and Ethics Newsweekly* 2004.
3. See Phillips 2004.
4. Sawyer 2004.
5. John 5:39.
6. Deuteronomy 6:6.
7. John 1:1.
8. Matthew 5:17–18. What Jesus meant by "until all is accomplished" is open to much interpretation.
9. Matthew 22:37–40.
10. Leviticus 19:18, 33–34.
11. Deuteronomy 6:5. Jesus apparently substitutes "mind" for "might"; this is further evidence that he prefers the (universal) will of the heart to the force of the (particularistic) law.
12. Deuteronomy 30:6. Earlier, Moses cautions the people, Israel, "Circumcise, then, the foreskin of your heart, and do not be stubborn any longer" (Deuteronomy 10:16).
13. Jeremiah 4:4.
14. Romans 2:29: "Rather, a person is a Jew who is one inwardly, and real circumcision is a matter of the heart—it is spiritual and not literal. Such a person receives praise not from others but from God."
15. A "satan," or accuser as a type of angelic skeptic, makes cameo appearances in such canonical works as Job (see Job 6–12).
16. Miles 2001, 169–70.
17. Isaiah 53. Christians understand the "suffering servant" to be the awaited Messiah; Jews understand the "suffering servant" to be Israel itself.
18. Miles 2001, 175.
19. John 8:58.
20. John 11:50.
21. John 11:51–52. See also John's reminder (18:14) that "Caiaphas was the one who had advised the Jews that it was better to have one person die for the people."
22. Milton 1959, 527.

CHAPTER NINE
ANTISEMITISM WITHOUT ERASURE: SACRED TEXTS AND THEIR CONTEMPORARY INTERPRETATIONS
Gary Gilbert

Will he or won't he? That was the question buzzing in the media for several weeks before the opening of *The Passion of the Christ*. Would Mel Gibson include the infamous words from the Gospel of Matthew in which all the people cry out, "His blood be on us and on our children"?[1] For centuries, the misuse of these words has encouraged Christians to denounce Jews as Christ killers. Early accounts reported that Gibson had indeed shot the scene with the line but was unsure whether it would make the final cut. In September 2003, in an interview with *The New Yorker*, he said, "I wanted it in.... My brother said I was wimping out if I didn't include it. It happened; it was said, but man, if I included that in there, they'd be coming after me at my house, they'd come kill me."[2] Although Gibson hinted that he would leave the line out, the final disposition did not become clear until the U.S. release of the film. The line was in, sort of: viewers heard the words spoken in Aramaic but did not see the translated line in the film's subtitles. Gibson had engineered a resolution that allowed him to remain true to his vision of the story and at the same time gave him cover against charges of antisemitism. The words are there but also not there. The simultaneous presence and absence of a controversial biblical verse that long has been used to foster antisemitism not only reflects an uneasy tension in how the film depicts Jews but also helps explain how the same film can be inspirational to some and offensive to others and offers a perspective on the continuing problem of antisemitism in the twenty-first century.

GARY GILBERT

From Corinth to Oberammergau to Matera: The Use and Abuse of the Passion Narrative

The Passion tells a story, but it is more than a story.[3] Over the past two thousand years, the telling of the Passion has produced its own history. Whereas the story of Jesus's death and its theological message of atonement have brought inspiration and comfort to countless Christians, the history of the Passion narrative often has been one of hate.[4] This darker side of the Passion goes back to the very origins of the story. Paul's Epistle to the Thessalonians describes Jews as those who killed Christ, and the Gospels intensify the Jewish responsibility for Jesus's through their grossly complimentary and ahistorical portrayal of Pilate.[5] Of particular relevance to the controversy over Gibson's film is the Gospel of Matthew, which, whether because of intracommunal antipathy or for some other reason, develops the theme of Jewish culpability in a way unique among the Gospels. Building on Mark's depiction of Pilate and a Jewish crowd, the Gospel of Matthew has Pilate literally wash his hands of the matter and declare, "I am innocent of this man's blood." The traditional interpretation of the next line understands the Jewish mob to accept guilt for the killing of Jesus not only for itself but also for all Jews in generations to come: "His blood be on us and on our children."[6] In subsequent generations, Christian writers echoed the charge of deicide and came to understand the crucifixion as an act that led God to revoke the old covenant and destroy the Temple.[7]

The long historical association between Passion plays and antisemitism[8] led many early critics of the film to voice justifiable concern whether Gibson's *The Passion of the Christ* would be any different.[9] Gibson and his supporters denied the charge of antisemitism and defended the film on three grounds: the film, they claim, avoids invidious portrayals of Jews found in previous Passion dramatizations; it includes several positive Jewish figures; and, finally, it records the events as they happened and telling the truth cannot be considered antisemitic. Although these arguments have a kernel of validity, in general they ignore the many ways in which the film perpetuates negative images and ideas that have long been associated with Passion plays and with antisemitic rhetoric more generally. Not only does Gibson's *Passion* fail to erase antisemitism, but indeed through the development of certain characters and the subtle inclusion of nonbiblical materials, the film offers an interpretation of the Passion story that is itself antisemitic and reflects the continuing challenge of antisemitism.

While many viewers, including journalists, scholars, and religious leaders, have recognized the film's troubling portrayal of Jews, many people who have seen the movie deny any presence of antisemitism. Nor has the film caused them, for the most part, to express any animosity toward Jews. It is almost as if viewers see radically different versions of the film. Accounting for the difference is not easy. Several factors may explain why many American viewers have found little if any antisemitism in the film. To be sure, the limited reaction is due in part to the brief and somewhat obscure way the most objectionable scenes are presented; they go largely unnoticed or unremembered by most viewers. Second, many of the most problematic scenes are intelligible as such only to the most careful viewers and perhaps only to those familiar with how the Passion has been visualized and dramatized over the centuries. Third, many viewers were interested only in the film's theological message and not in its choice of narrative details.

Those who have seen the film speak often about being moved and touched by what Jesus went through for them. The film confirms and deepens their appreciation for the great love that Jesus had and for the reconciliation that his suffering and death brought to the world. These comments suggest that most viewers are interested and engaged primarily with what happened to Jesus and "its iconography of God's supreme love for humanity" and less, if at all, with how it happened.[10] In this way, *The Passion* is not tremendously different from other Jesus movies. The "ultimate goal of nearly all Jesus films is to address the question, what did the life (and resurrection) of Jesus mean? In particular, what does it mean to us today?"[11] In short, the theological message of *The Passion* overwhelmed and obscured the finer details of the film's story, many of which present invidious depictions of Jews.

Compared to earlier Passion plays, *The Passion of the Christ* dispenses with many of the most egregious stereotypes and degrading images of Jews, such as horns, hooked noses, and references to "perfidious Jews." While largely cleaned up for public consumption, the film nonetheless retains several conspicuous images that mark at least some Jews as worthy of contempt. Moreover, the costuming reinforces negative ideas about

Jewish authorities, if not about Jews in general. The film creates a striking contrast between the conspicuously resplendent priests with their golden embroidered robes and the simple attire of the "good" people, such as the disciples or Simon of Cyrene. The richness of the priests' clothing reminds one of Jesus's denunciations of the scribes who walk around in long robes[12] and of the scribes and Pharisees who outwardly appear beautiful but within are full of dead man's bones and uncleanness.[13] These words of condemnation need not be spoken; the costumes speak for themselves.

Many of the film's supporters refute charges of antisemitism by pointing to several Jewish characters who are honest and sympathetic to Jesus. As important as these characters are in the story, they are numerically fewer than the overwhelming assembly of Jews who denounce Jesus before the Sanhedrin, cry out for his crucifixion in the courtyard of Pilate's palace, and cast verbal abuse and stones as he travels toward Golgotha. Moreover, the film draws distinctions among Jews. Male Jews who oppose Jesus are often seen wearing shawls over their heads. By contrast, the good Jews, the disciples, and Simon of Cyrene go bareheaded. According to the film's own visual code, a good Jew is one who not only accepts Jesus but also has shed, both literally and figuratively, his Jewish identity.[14] The film leaves largely unsettled whether a Jew who has not acknowledged Jesus or remains connected to their religious heritage can ever be considered good.

Finally, Gibson and his supporters assert that the film cannot be antisemitic because it reports the events as they actually happened.[15] Telling the truth, the argument goes, is not antisemitic. This is a particularly pernicious argument and exists as a corollary to the modernist position later embraced by fundamentalism that truth is ascertained from that which is empirically verifiable. The argument assumes, of course, that the Gospels are historically reliable, a claim disputed not only by biblical scholars but by many churches as well.[16] The main problem with *The Passion* and its treatment of Jews is not that the film restricts itself to the Gospels but in its selective use of the gospel traditions and insertion of nongospel materials.[17]

The Passion does not so much faithfully record the Gospels as it selectively appropriates materials from different Gospels. As in previous Passion plays, *The Passion* presents a synthesis of differing and sometimes inconsistent accounts of the last twelve hours of Jesus's life. In depicting the brutal scourging of Jesus, for instance, Gibson had a choice to follow either the synoptic Gospels and place the event after Pilate's final judgment for crucifixion or the Gospel of John and portray the scourging as Pilate's attempt to punish Jesus without actually killing him. Either version would be faithful to Scripture. For whatever reason, Gibson chose to film the event as reported in John. As a result, the film deepens the Jewish crowd's blood lust by not only having them cry out for Jesus's execution but doing so only after the Roman guards have inflicted the most horrendous beating imaginable and in the presence of the bloodied Jesus.

Moreover, this argument refuses to acknowledge that the Gospels themselves contain language that is decidedly hostile toward Jews.[18] Regardless of whether such rhetoric better is understood as antisemitic or anti-Jewish or internal Jewish polemic, nevertheless these claims and counterclaims laid the foundation for the relationship between the followers of Jesus and other Jews in the first century. In light of a theology in which Christianity supersedes and indeed replaces Judaism, the texts themselves, and not just the centuries of venomous interpretation, come to construct an anti-Judaic myth. The myth, as Rosemary Ruether termed the problem, is not superficial or secondary to Christianity thought but finds its very roots in the New Testament.[19] Many Christian communities have recognized the animosities inherent in these texts and worked to mitigate their effect.[20]

The claim that the film is not antisemitic because it is based on the Gospels fails because so much of the film, as much as one-third, has no biblical basis.[21] To be sure, some recent films, such as *Jesus of Montreal* and *The Last Temptation of Christ*, intentionally have downplayed the Jewish role in Jesus's death. As Adele Reinhartz has noted, "These films negotiate the tension between fidelity to scripture and the desire not to appear to be antisemitic by omitting some features of the Gospel narrative and introducing elements not found in the canonical accounts."[22] *The Passion of the Christ* takes a noticeably different approach: its extracanonical sources form the basis for the film's antisemitism. Many of the scenes are taken from later sources, such as the nineteenth-century nun Anne Catherine Emmerich, and present some of the most antisemitic elements of the film. The first example comes early in *The Passion* when we see priests scurrying through the streets of Jerusalem, knocking on doors and thrusting bags of money on the Jewish residents. No dialogue accompanies the action, but it is clear that the Jewish leaders are seeking to bribe Jews to come and bear false witness against Jesus. The basis of this scene is not the Gospels but the visions of Anne Emmerich; through the mixing of sources, the image of Jews as financially evil takes on a quasi-scriptural basis.[23] The scene is brief, but its presence perpetuates long-held stereotypes that Jews use money to gain influence in society and that Jews will do anything for money. These accusations go back centuries and became a mainstay of antisemitism throughout European societies.[24]

Condemnations of Jews based on economic factors are confined neither to the past nor to neo-Nazi and other hate groups in the present. In October 2003, Gregg Easterbrook, editor at *The New Republic*, accused Jews in the entertainment industry of being more interested in money than morality and asked if it is "right for Jewish executives to worship money above all else, by promoting for profit the adulation of violence?"[25] Although he apologized almost immediately thereafter for his comments,[26] the ease with which Easterbrook wrote these charges, however, attests that the stereotype of Jews as preoccupied with money and power remain deeply ingrained in the psyche of Western culture. Easterbrook's message, as well as Emmerich's as portrayed in *The Passion*, is clear: Jews value money over their religious and moral commitments and use their wealth to achieve harmful results.

A second example of implicit antisemitism concerns the figure of Barabbas. The Gospels offer a typically laconic description of the man. We learn almost nothing beyond the various references to him as a notorious prisoner, rebel, leader of an insurrection, murderer, or robber. In the film, however, he appears as dirty and disheveled; he speaks no recognizable words and only grunts. This portrayal of a grinning, laughing lunatic, completely absent from the Gospels, serves not only to flesh out a minor character but also to comment on the choice made by the Jewish crowd. The film transforms the crowd's decision from misguided to ludicrous. The buffoonish, almost subhuman depiction of Barabbas renders the crowd's selection of Barabbas all the more inexplicable and unjust.

Even following Jesus's death on the cross, the film incorporates anti-Jewish elements into its visual representation of the consequences of Jesus's death. *The Passion*, like the Gospels, records an earthquake at the moment of Jesus's death on the cross. In the film, however, as the tremor spreads, we see that Pilate's palace shakes vigorously but sustains no damage: Pilate may lack a sense of virtue, but his failure is not of his doing.[27]

In a pointed contrast, the earthquake devastates the Jewish Temple, the symbol of Jewish religious life of the time. The walls shatter, and the floor splits apart. As the priests move through the damaged hall, Caiaphas weeps. The Gospels of Matthew and Mark speak of the rending of the Temple veil—a symbolic gesture that mirrors the Jewish mourners' practice of rending one's clothes—but neither mentions any additional damage.[28] The film draws a direct causal connection between the death of Jesus and the ruin of the Temple, a completely ahistorical version of events not found in the Gospels but taken largely from Emmerich.[29] This addition to the Passion story echoes the long-held Christian belief that through the destruction of the Temple, God punished the Jews for killing Jesus and moreover annulled the Sinaitic covenant with Israel.[30] Since no one asserts that Emmerich or any other similar visionary nonbiblical source is an accurate historical account, the claim that the film simply "tells the truth" cannot serve as a defense against antisemitism.[31] The problem, therefore, lies not only in the film's inclusion of nonbiblical scenes that express antisemitic and anti-Jewish views; by weaving this nonbiblical material together with the biblical accounts, the film extends the authority over the nonbiblical elements.

Antisemitism and *The Passion of the Christ*

Was the concern justified that *The Passion* might inspire antisemitic and anti-Jewish attitudes and actions?[32] On the day of the film's U.S. release, a Pentecostal minister in Denver, Colorado, set up a sign in front of his church that read "Jews Killed the Lord Jesus . . . Settled!" The minister defended his actions by saying that he was only quoting Scripture,[33] the same argument Gibson used to defend the film against antisemitism. A few weeks later, several Jewish students in Overland Park, Kansas, faced taunts and vandalism. They were called "Christ killers," and one had a swastika drawn on his jacket.[34] The film may not have made these people hate Jews, but they felt they had permission to do so. This perhaps is the real danger of Gibson's *Passion*: at best it validates antisemitism, and at worst it encourages people like those in Colorado and Kansas to express their hatred against Jews. It makes antisemitism seem acceptable.

Despite the story he presents on screen, Mel Gibson often has said that he is not into the "blame game."[35] According to Gibson, all human beings, through their sins, are to blame for Jesus's death. This venerable and widely held Christian belief, however, stands in marked contrast to the story presented in the film. Unless the viewer brings this theological understanding into the theater, nothing in the film will suggest it. The film itself presents only two groups active in the crucifixion of Jesus, Romans and Jews, and focuses blame on the latter. Gibson and the supporters of the film act as if speaking about universal guilt obviates and erases the antisemitic images found in the film. However, while the theology ascribes guilt to all humanity, Gibson's *Passion* casts Jews as the primary culprits and apparently has convinced many in the United States that Jews bear the responsibility for Jesus's death.[36]

The attempt to erase the portrayal of Jews as the main perpetrators of Jesus's death by overlaying a theology of universal guilt is similar to the deconstructionist strategy of putting words under erasure, *sous rature*. Erasure acknowledges a certain ambivalence toward language. On the one hand, the words we use to communicate our ideas are inadequate, but we cannot communicate without them. Martin Heidegger would often write the word "Being" but print it with lines through it (~~Being~~), thus "warning the reader not to accept them at philosophic face value."[37] This graphic technique is meant to dislodge meaning. Jacques Derrida uses erasure "to claim that he can use the language of Western philosophy without that use committing him to a belief in its concepts or any of its principles."[38] Without pushing the analogy too far, I think we reasonably can consider Gibson, albeit unintentionally, to have used a similar technique. The film is a text (albeit one with both words and images) in which Jews appear as evil and function as persons responsible for the death of Jesus. In interviews, however, Gibson uses the theological doctrine of universal guilt to cross out or erase the antisemitic meaning presented in the text. The film's language, while necessary to tell the story, does not in Gibson's mind carry the meaning often ascribed to it. *The Passion of the Christ*, therefore, is not antisemitic; rather, it is ~~antisemitic~~.

The postmodernist technique of erasure has taught us about the instability of language and revolutionized the way we think about the relation between text and meaning; it also has received significant criticism. A critique of Derrida, for instance, is that "he relies on language to put his arguments across, while simultaneously claiming that language is unstable and meaning indeterminate."[39] Similarly, Gibson has played his own "confidence trick" by relying on several antisemitic motifs to tell the story but simultaneously denying that these elements have any antisemitic meaning. The same weakness in the postmodernist technique renders Gibson's denial of antisemitism rather tenuous. The theological claim of universal guilt attempts to reinterpret the story so as to erase any antisemitic meaning, but the erasure is at best incomplete, and the negative images themselves remain clearly visible to any viewer who takes the time to see them.

Supporters of *The Passion of the Christ* have hailed it as an unparalleled evangelistic opportunity; both its supporters and its critics agree that the film and the debate over the film is a unique teachable moment. The film already has proven itself a potent instrument for shaping the way millions of Christians think about the death of Jesus. Films do not necessarily cause behaviors, but they do have the ability to facilitate and legitimate both attitudes and actions. At its best, the film has prompted Christians and Jews to engage in substantive discussions about matters central to their histories and beliefs and allow each community to develop a better understanding of the other.

At its worst, *The Passion of the Christ* has reopened the wounds of antisemitism, given comfort to antisemites, and encouraged anti-Judaism, including evangelism targeted at Jews.[40] In discussing the recent rise in global antisemitism, Cardinal Roger Etchegaray, former president of the Pontifical Council for Justice and Peace, observed of antisemitism that "not acknowledging [it], not calling it by its proper name, is an unconscious way of accepting it."[41] However inspiring *The Passion* may be to millions of people, its antisemitic elements must be named. Pruning away crude anti-Jewish expressions, making claims to history, and citing well-intentioned theological doctrines cannot erase antisemitism wherever it occurs, including in film.

Notes

1. Matthew 27:25.
2. Boyer 2003.
3. The death of Jesus, the film's climactic event, forms the basis of most Christian theology. The Gospels ascribe considerable narrative and theological importance to the Passion (see Sloyan 1995). See Torjesen (chapter 6 in this volume) and Sloyan (1995) for accounts of the way early and medieval Christian theologians

built on the understanding of Jesus's death as the universal expiation of human sin and construct complex doctrines of atonement, reconciliation, and satisfaction.

4. For a different view on how the Gospels ascribe blame for the death of Jesus, see Stephen Davis (chapter 16 in this volume). Robert Faggen (chapter 8 in this volume) has a different view on the question of antisemitism in Gibson's film.

5. In what may be the earliest extant Christian writing, the Epistle to the Thessalonians speaks of the Jews who killed the Lord Jesus (1 Thessalonians 2:14–15). The Gospels assign responsibility for Jesus's death to the Jews in a variety of ways, but no more so than through their portrayal of Pontius Pilate as a weak and easily manipulated administrator who reluctantly succumbs to the cries of the Jewish crowd and the machinations of their leaders. Outside the New Testament, Pilate is better known among his contemporaries (see, for example, Philo 1971, 294–309) for his brutality and uncompromising rule in Judaea.

6. Matthew 27:24–25.

7. Origen 1953, 4.32; Ambrose Letter LX. By the second century, the charge that the Jews as a category are responsible for Jesus's death had emerged as a normative aspect of Christian thought. See Richard Norris 1980; Sloyan 1995.

8. See Mork 2004.

9. Passion plays regularly depicted Jews as filthy, corrupt, cruel, and treacherous people who bore exclusive responsibility for Jesus's death. Passion plays also were notorious for inciting hatred and violence against Jews. See Shapiro 2000. For a discussion of *The Passion*'s relationship to traditional Passion plays, see Fredriksen 2003.

10. United States Conference of Catholic Bishops 2004. For a sample of reactions, see "See the Passion."

11. Flesher and Torry 2004.

12. Mark 12:38; Luke 20:46.

13. Matthew 23:27.

14. See Kathryn Smith (chapter 20 in this volume) for a discussion of the erasure of Jewish material culture from representations of Jesus and his contemporaries.

15. Gibson thought it "absolutely necessary to adhere as faithfully as possible to those four Gospels" (Stammer 2004).

16. The Roman Catholic Church (1988, § C.1.b), for instance, understands that "the Gospel authors did not intend to write 'history' in our modern sense."

17. This argument is also rejected by the National Conference of Catholic Bishops (1988), who explicitly state that "it is not sufficient for the producers of passion dramatizations to respond to responsible criticism simply by appealing to the notion that 'it's in the Bible.' One must account for one's selection."

18. See, for example, Matthew 27:25; Matthew 23; John 8:44.

19. Ruether 1974. See also the recent essays by biblical scholars and theologians on the need and process for rereading and reinterpreting the New Testament in light of the legacy of antisemitism (Linafelt 2002).

20. The most constructive work has been accomplished within the Roman Catholic Church, which has developed specific guidelines on how to teach the Gospels and dramatize the Passion. The Church (1988, n. 13) urges "the greatest caution . . . in all cases where it is a question of passages that seem to show the Jewish people as such in an unfavorable light." See also Vatican Commission for Religious Relations with Jews 1985.

21. Cunningham 2004.

22. Reinhartz 2004.

23. Emmerich (n.d.), § 138; Flesher and Torry 2004.

24. Penslar 2001.

25. Easterbrook 13 October 2003.

26. Easterbrook 16 October 2003.

27. *The Passion* presents Pilate as somehow caught between Caesar and Caiaphas, as if Pilate's power in Judaea were not absolute. The Gospel of John more convincingly places the political conundrum at Caiaphas's feet. Indeed, the high priest cautions the Sanhedrin that "it is better for you to have one man die for the people than to have the whole nation destroyed" (John 11:50). However, both the verse and the complex political realities of first-century Judaea are both absent from the film.

28. Even early Christian writers, who describe not only the tearing of the veil but also the fracturing of the Temple's lintel and the breaking of its hinges, do not imagine the extensive destruction depicted in the film (Brown 1994, 2.1116–18).

29. In fact, the Romans destroyed the Temple in 70 C.E., some thirty-five to forty years after Jesus's crucifixion.

30. Matthew and Mark seem to present the rending of the Temple veil as violating the sanctuary's holiness or purity and therefore signaling its future, physical destruction (Brown 1994, 2.1104). The Gospels, however, do not present this action as punishment for anything done by Jews or their leaders.

31. The introduction to Emmerich's visions states clearly that "they have no pretensions whatever to be regarded as history" (Emmerich [n.d.], § xi).

32. Mork (2004) claims that almost any depiction of the Passion has the ability to inflame animosity toward Jews: "the dramatization of the suffering of Jesus the Christ *can* provide the opportunity to teach people to hate the Jews" (emphasis in the original).

33. 1 Thessalonians 2:14–15; D'Ambrosio 2004; Kohler 2004.

34. Lipman 2004.

35. See, for example, Sawyer 2004.

36. Just over one quarter of Americans believe that the Jews were responsible for Jesus's death; this belief is more prominent among those who have seen *The Passion* than among those who have not (Pew Research Center for the People and the Press 2004).

37. Christopher Norris 1982, 69.

38. Sim 2001, 240.

39. Sim 2001, 240–41.

40. See Rutten 2004 for a description of one evangelical leader, Mike Evans, who expressed concern that the film might spark antisemitic reactions outside the United States; see, however, Kathryn Smith (chapter 20 in this volume) for an assessment of the larger implications of Evans's kind of philosemitism. For a discussion of the evangelical support for the film, see Leslie Smith (chapter 3 in this volume).

41. Agence France-Presse 2003.

CHAPTER TEN
THEOLOGIZING THE DEATH OF JESUS, GIBSON'S *THE PASSION*, AND CHRISTIAN IDENTITY

Jeffrey S. Siker

The intersection of historical reconstruction, deep faith convictions, theological critique, and popular culture occasioned by Mel Gibson's movie *The Passion of the Christ* offers a rich opportunity for engaged and even charged conversation across religious traditions, academic disciplines, and popular forums that takes place all too rarely. While the Christmas and Easter issues of *Time* and *Newsweek* routinely feature surface discussion about modern interpretations of Jesus and the endless historical questions that arise, the release of Gibson's *The Passion* seems intended to spark deeper conversations and debate about the meaning of Jesus's death for Christians past and present as well as timely discussion about Jewish–Christian relations.

I confess as I approached the release of Mel Gibson's *The Passion* and its possible consequences for relations between Christians and Jews that I had no small personal interests at stake. I grew up in a household with a Jewish father and a Roman Catholic mother. I had an uncle who was a conservative rabbi and a great aunt who was a mother superior. Somehow, this mixture turned me into a Presbyterian minister who works primarily as a professor teaching and writing about early Jewish–Christian relations at a Roman Catholic University. Ironies abound. Along the way, I have also become very interested not only in Jewish and Christian origins but in the history of biblical interpretation as well and especially with how Christians today make use of their Scriptures in relationship to Jews and Judaism. Since my own personal and professional identity has been tied so closely to Jewish–Christian relations, the release of the Gibson movie has provided a significant place for both personal and critical reflection as a Christian theologian who teaches not only about Christian origins but also about the appropriation of these roots in contemporary film.

The most important thing to note about the death of Jesus is that Christians have been trying to make sense of it since the day it happened, since Good Friday itself, and since before there were even Christians and before the horrible death of Jesus came to be envisioned in any sense as good. In this chapter, I want, first, to explore several early Christian interpretations of the Passion of Jesus in light of important recent changes in scholarship on early Jewish–Christian relations and then to turn to more contemporary Christian interpretations of Jesus's death, especially in light of Mel Gibson's *The Passion*. As I hope to show, reflection on the death of Jesus can serve as a helpful barometer both for external relationships between Jews and Christians and for internal relationships among Christians.

When we turn to the earliest Christian sources, the Gospel of Luke gives us the only narrative we have from early Christianity where we are told anything about what the followers of the earthly Jesus were thinking after his death and before they became convinced of his miraculous resurrection from the dead. In Luke 24, we read about two disciples of Jesus on the road to Emmaus (about seven miles from Jerusalem). A stranger comes and joins them on their way. Christians know the story well. The stranger is none other than the risen Jesus, and the two disciples "were kept from recognizing him"; they do not know who he is.[1] And so along the way this stranger asks them what they've been discussing, and they ask incredulously if he is the only person who hasn't heard what has just happened, about Jesus of Nazareth, a prophet mighty in word and deed, "and how our chief priests and leaders handed him over to be condemned to death and crucified him."[2] Then comes the very first response to the death of Jesus on record: "But we had hoped that he was the one to redeem Israel."[3] Clearly, according to Luke, the followers of Jesus had had messianic hopes about Jesus. But his death has ended these hopes that Jesus was a redeemer figure. The first interpretation of the death of Jesus, at least according to Luke, tells us that far from being redemptive in any way, the death of Jesus was purely tragic. So goes the only preresurrection interpretation we have.

However, of course, that is not the end of the story for Luke or for any Christian. The earliest followers of Jesus came to the stunned belief that

THEOLOGIZING THE DEATH OF JESUS

Jesus in fact had been raised from the dead. Why had he died? The hidden yet risen Jesus himself provides the first answer: "Was it not necessary that the messiah should suffer these things and then enter into his glory?"[4] Necessary? Why necessary? This Luke does not answer. It apparently has something to do with fulfilling the Scriptures. The risen Jesus even offers a citation: "Thus it is written, that the Messiah is to suffer and to rise from the dead on the third day."[5] The only problem is that there is no clear proof text from the Jewish Scriptures to accompany this assertion. Why did Jesus die? It was necessary. It fulfilled the Scriptures. Such became another early Christian response to the death of Jesus: to make sense of his death in light of Scripture.

The death of Jesus and its significance is located at the heart of Christian faith. Apart from belief in the resurrection, this death lies meaningless and powerless.[6] In light of the resurrection, however, Jesus's Passion is full of meaning and full of power. Exactly what it means and how it is powerful has been the point of considerable debate and dispute in Christian tradition from the beginning until today. Indeed, interpretation of the death of Jesus truly is a theological barometer, as the meaning and significance one derives from the death of Jesus says a great deal about one's identity as a Christian in relation to others claiming the same identity. It also says a great deal about one's identity as a Christian in relationship to non-Christian Jews and to Judaism as a whole. Mel Gibson's *The Passion* is but another "take," as it were, in the long history of Christian theologizing about the death of Jesus, its significance for Christian faith, and how it positions Christians in relationship to Jews and Judaism. In short, Christian reflection and theologizing on the meaning of the death of Jesus has always been an important barometer of both internal Christian identity and Christian relations to external groups, especially Jews and Judaism.

As the earliest Christians continued to theologize about the death of Jesus, they developed various images and metaphors that acknowledged the troubling death of Jesus but saw in it various redemptive features. Jesus was the following:

- The "suffering servant" who bore our iniquities (quoted at the beginning of Gibson's film)[7]
- The "suffering Son of Man" who would come again in triumph[8]

- The unblemished Passover lamb that atones for sin[9]
- The sinless sacrifice who "bore our sins on the cross"[10]
- The conquering Lamb who would return in apocalyptic splendor[11]
- The great high priest who offered himself as the ultimate sacrifice for sins once and for all[12]
- The sacrifice of atonement in whom forgiveness of sins were found[13]
- The new Adam who was obedient to God, even unto death[14]

The early Christians were convinced that great meaning was to be found in the death of Jesus precisely because they experienced him as raised by God from the dead, his life and death vindicated by God. If he had been raised from the dead, then surely he must have died for a divinely appointed reason—to bring about human salvation.[15] By identifying themselves with this life and death, Christians could in faith align themselves with his eternal life and eternal kingdom that would come in the fullness of God's time. Such were some of the earliest Christian responses to the death of Jesus and its significance in light of resurrection faith.

In general, early Christians began rereading their Jewish Scriptures with these faith convictions in view. Rather than read the Jewish Scriptures in order to learn who the messiah would be, early Christians, having been convinced that Jesus was the messiah, decided that they now knew how to read the Scriptures.[16] If they had not originally expected the messiah to suffer, die, and rise from the dead, now they knew to search the Scriptures with such images and convictions in view. They therefore landed on such passages as Isaiah 53 and Psalm 110. And so they began to reinterpret their Jewish faith and Jewish Scriptures in light of their faith in Jesus, increasingly convinced that the prophets of old had been fulfilled, convinced that soon the promised kingdom proclaimed by Jesus would arrive, all in the course of God's great providence.

There also was a troubling side to these newfound Christian faith convictions, a certain anti-Judaism that started as an intramural Jewish fight between Christian Jews and non-Christian Jews but that eventually broke out into an interreligious battle between Jews and Gentile Christians. This was an extramural fight in which Christians used the Jewish Scriptures now recast as the "Old Testament" to portray Jews as Christ killers and Judaism as the religion that rejected its own messiah. If the death of Jesus expressed the depth of God's sacrificial love, this death also was interpreted as expressing the fulfillment of and break with the Jewish covenant tradition embodied in the Mosaic law.[17] Thus began the long road of Christian anti-Judaism, again with the focus on the death of Jesus and whether one believed in the salvific meaning of this death and resurrection. As Rosemary Ruether noted a generation ago, anti-Judaism has been the backhand of Christology.[18]

Nevertheless, some twenty centuries later, things are by no means the same. Indeed, over the past century, scholarship on early Jewish and Christian origins has made important steps toward a new understanding of these origins. A generation ago, scholars of early Judaism and Christianity held to a model of Judaism as a "parent" that gave birth to Christianity as its "offspring." However, many scholars now argue that both early Christianity and early rabbinic Judaism grew up as sibling rivals out of the same dynamic first-century Jewish setting. In this view, the earliest adherents of rabbinic Judaism and Christianity engaged in serious intramural fights over issues related to the Jewish law, the interpretation of Scripture, the messianic identity of Jesus, and the status of Gentiles, among other things. In short, they were the two versions of Judaism left standing after the Jewish War of 66–70 C.E., with rabbinic Judaism embracing Torah observance and the Jewish Christians embracing a highly messianic interpretation of Jewish tradition that subordinated Torah observance to adoration of Jesus and opened the door to Gentile converts at the same time. The Jewish scholar Alan Segal has used the image of "Rebecca's Children" to describe the relationship of such sibling rivalry, replete with the kind of intense animosity that can form only between siblings.[19] Both groups claimed to represent the true interpretation of the promises made to Abraham, to Moses, and to David. Both groups vilified each other. Still, both groups survived and indeed thrived, though only with significant tensions between them that ebbed and flowed over the years, indeed to this very day.

A development related to this new understanding of Jewish and Christian origins has been the realization of Christian scholars over the past generation, especially since World War II and the Holocaust, that a certain anti-Judaism had become part of the way that Christian scholars had told the story of Christian origins. A generic version of this story goes something like this: Once upon a time, there was a vibrant Jewish religion, especially as it was animated by the prophetic literature. Then, after the destruction of the Second Temple, there was a slow and steady decline of so-called late Judaism, a dry and dusty legalistic religion, that finally gave birth to the brilliant light of early Christianity, which rejected law observance, welcomed Gentile believers, and essentially replaced Judaism as the true religion. Fortunately, both Christian scholars, such as E. P. Sanders,[20] and Jewish scholars, such as Susannah Heschel,[21] have shown how Christian theological convictions provided the context for this kind of misrepresentation of Judaism at the time of Christian origins. This new understanding has helped move most Christian scholars and many seminarians beyond the explicit and latent anti-Judaism of previous generations, has resulted in a renewed appreciation for the Jewishness of Jesus,[22] and has led to the possibility of true constructive dialogue and engagement between Jews and Christians as friends. Most mainstream Catholic and Protestant church traditions now reject calls to evangelize Jews and call instead on the need for Christians to recognize and respect the vitality of the Jewish covenant traditions.

A second development relates to the first, and it has to do with the ways in which many Christians have rethought the significance of the death of Jesus. As a result, many in the Roman Catholic Church and in the mainline Protestant denominations have moved toward a somewhat different understanding of the death of Jesus than was the case even just two generations ago. While the death of Jesus has remained central to Christian self-understanding, in the mainstream Catholic and Protestant traditions the death of Jesus has been interpreted more in terms of the political realities of first-century Palestine, especially in light of Roman rule, and less in terms of a kind of theological blame game against the Jews. While such difficult passages as the so-called blood curse, the cry of the Jewish leaders that Jesus's "blood be upon us and upon our children,"[23] continue, understandably, to be very difficult for Jewish audiences to hear in the Christian Scriptures, these same passages have been largely defanged in many Christian traditions. While such passages remain in Christian Scriptures (and are important witnesses to the tensions that existed between emerging Christianity and emerging rabbinic Judaism), they have been increasingly deauthorized in Christian tradition and theology. Indeed, the Roman Catholic Church has in many ways gone the farthest to issue official instructions on how the death of Jesus should not be presented; that is, it should not be read as though everything took place at the insistence of the Jewish mobs pleading for Jesus's death against a hapless Pilate.

This change in mainstream Protestant and Catholic thought also represents a very real change in Christian atonement theology over the past two generations, an intense internal debate that continues within the Christian tradition.[24] Two generations ago, it was common to hear a strong emphasis on the atoning death of Jesus in which his death pays the price for the sins of the world (much in the sense that Anselm had argued). Today, however, there has been a shift away from concentrating on this kind of an atonement theology and its emphasis on the bloody sacrifice of Jesus and movement instead toward a greater emphasis on the ministry of Jesus, a ministry that saw many conflicts, a ministry that eventually led to his death. While much of evangelical Protestantism and various forms of fundamentalist Christianity continue to stress the atoning sacrificial death of Jesus and the significance of his blood poured out for the sins of humanity, significant theological developments continue to be made among Christians who are increasingly uncomfortable with the notion that God offered Jesus up in sacred violence as a blood sacrifice to atone for human sin, even though such language can be found in the New Testament Scriptures.[25] The shift, basically, is away from salvation coming as a result of the sacrificial and atoning death of Jesus and toward a view that salvation comes from the faithful obedience to God that Jesus embodied, obedience even unto death, a death that God redeems in resurrection. Christians are called to follow as disciples of this Jesus and to trust in God's redemption of human suffering and death.

So where do these changes in scholarship and Christian theology leave us in relation to the phenomenon of Mel Gibson's *The Passion*? Fundamentally, there are two observations I would offer in this regard. First, Gibson's film gives voice to an important and significant part of the Christian community that is both historically and theologically more conservative than the scholarship and theological shifts I have outlined here. Scholars, as is their want, have introduced serious new ways of thinking about developments in early Christianity. They have highlighted the authorial role of the gospel writers as theologians in their own right and not as mere scribes writing down history (contrary to Gibson's view of things). They have also made problematic the traditional understanding of Christianity arising as the superseding fulfillment of Jewish tradition (again, contrary to Gibson's apparent understanding). And church leaders, for their part, have sought to pay serious attention to these developments, seeking to foster a more educated and reflective community of faith, especially in relationship to Jews and Judaism. Gibson has touched a nerve with Christians who believe that scholars and church leaders alike are selling out some of the deepest doctrinal commitments of their faith.

Second, Gibson's film can be seen as a kind of embodiment of these more conservative voices, a reactionary counterpunch to current developments in historical research and in constructive Christian theology. This was certainly my sense when I first saw *The Passion* before the film's release at a small private screening, with Gibson and actor Jim Caviezel (who played Jesus) in attendance for conversation afterward. While I was watching for elements that might prove anti-Jewish, what struck me initially was how the film really speaks to the intramural fight within the Christian tradition over the degree to which the death of Jesus functions as a sacrificial atonement for sin (ironically borrowing the very Temple imagery that the death of Jesus is supposed to supplant). Gibson has been vocal in his criticism of developments in the post–Vatican II Roman Catholic Church, even going so far as to build his own private chapel for worship. The emphasis in the film is Gibson's highly personal testimony to how much Jesus suffered for the sins of the world and how important that suffering is for Gibson's personal faith, an approach to Jesus's suffering and death shared by millions of other Christians. As many critics have noted, the actual life of Jesus seems to matter little in the film—the whole focus is on his sacrificial death. The bottom line seems to be the more suffering, the more redemption. The more pain Jesus endures, the more sins are forgiven.

One scene in particular stands out to me. Gibson takes the scene of the Romans beating Jesus before he is brought out and condemned to death. The beating scene is developed at length and gets divided into two parts. In the first part, a couple of Roman soldiers take turns beating Jesus nearly senseless with thick leather whips. When they are done, a slumped Jesus slowly drags himself to his feet, and the look in his eyes suggests that he has not yet suffered enough for the sins of humanity, so he needs to be beaten some more. The Romans gladly oblige by now taking whips with pieces of metal in them, and they brutalize Jesus for another fierce lashing that rips flesh from bones and leaves Jesus completely bloodied, with only enough strength left to carry his cross, and so show even more how much he suffered. The movie is so over the top on the suffering endured by Jesus that Gibson's point and his theology is clear: Jesus suffered and died to atone for human sinfulness. The movie communicates that Jesus lived in order to die, and to die as an atoning sacrifice, His was the ultimate bloody sacrifice. Jesus himself seems intent on being the "suffering Son of Man." Who killed Jesus? Gibson's answer seems to be that the sins of the world nailed him to the cross. His film reminds me of a T-shirt a student once wore to class. It had a bloody Jesus with a crown of thorns on the front of the shirt, and on the back it had what I'm sure the student saw as a profound statement, one with which Gibson would seem to concur (in my own view a rather trite theological commentary); the T-shirt read "His pain, your gain." This vision of the death of Jesus is highly individualistic as a "death for you," on behalf of your sins. And while it finds resonance in much of the New Testament,[26] many Christians today are moving away from the kind of sacred violence implicit in this interpretation of the Passion narrative. Instead, they are calling attention to the life that Jesus lived, the life that got him in trouble with the governing authorities, the life that led to his death, rather than emphasizing his death apart from an equal emphasis on the context of his life. Ironically, though the film provides gory detail of the suffering of Jesus in the flesh, the Jesus presented comes across at the same time as highly docetic—so divine that his life truly matters only insofar as he dies and dies suffering more than any "human being" in history. Indeed, no human could have endured what Gibson puts him through; only God could.

The reactionary character of the movie can also be seen in Gibson's treatment of the Jews (and, arguably, Judaism). It is safe to say that Gibson maximizes the responsibility of the Jews for the death of Jesus (with no real clear motive) and minimizes the responsibility of the Romans. The earthquake at the death of Jesus (borrowed from the Gospel of Matthew) provides a parallel greater indictment of the Jews than the Romans. Pilate's palace shakes, but nothing is destroyed; by contrast, not only does the Jewish Temple suffer the familiar torn curtain, but the foundation of the Temple itself suffers a devastating fissure—apparently Gibson's commentary on the status of Judaism after the death of Jesus. Is

Gibson commenting on the need for Jews today to see the salvation God offers in the sacrificial death of Jesus? Gibson's complete disregard of official church guidelines on the depiction of Jews in relation to the death of Jesus should be seen for what it is: a simple shrug and dismissal of the direction of church teaching on the subject, a throwback to a defiantly naive reading of the Gospels.

One final comment. After the film, I had a chance to have a conversation with Gibson. I asked him about the movement in the Roman Catholic Church since Vatican II away from talking about the "sacrifice of the Mass" in referring to the Eucharist and toward talking about the Eucharist as the joyful feast of the people of God. Where was there room in his vision for the community of the people of God, the church? His response was that he thought the church was moving in the wrong direction, that the sacrificial death of Jesus was everything, as it helped to remind him of his own sin and his need for constant redemption. In my view, his focus on his own identity as a thankful sinner before his crucified and risen Lord overshadows any view of the larger community of faith and other powerful symbols of Christian faith that can help transform suffering and death to healing and new life. Still, the debate continues within the Christian community, and this film, as others before it, continues to spark debate about the significance of the Passion of Jesus for Christian identity and Jewish–Christian relations alike.

Notes

1. Luke 24:16.
2. Luke 24:20.
3. Luke 24:21.
4. Luke 24:26.
5. Luke 24:44–46.
6. See 1 Corinthians 15:17–19: "If Christ has not been raised, your faith is futile."
7. Isaiah 53; on the use of that passage in early Christianity, see especially Bellinger and Farmer 1998.
8. The Gospel of Mark apparently coined the notion of a suffering Son of Man. The character of a "son of man" was known in both prophetic (for example, Ezekiel) and apocalyptic literature (for example, Daniel, 1 Enoch) within Jewish tradition. On the "suffering Son of Man," see Brown 1994; Burkett 1999; Hare 1990.

9. John 1:29; John the Baptist's declaration draws on the imagery of sacrifice in the Jerusalem Temple.

10. 1 Peter 2:22–24.

11. Revelation 5.

12. Hebrews 4–5.

13. Romans 3:21–26.

14. Romans 5; Philippians 2.

15. Perhaps the classic formulation of the reason for Jesus's death remains the medieval theologian Anselm's *Cur Deus Homo* (Why God Became Man). In this view, Jesus died as a substitutionary atoning sacrifice on behalf of humankind to satisfy the debt incurred to God by human sin. Anselm's theory of atonement has come under significant critique in modern theologizing on the death of Jesus. See, for example, the discussion in Weaver 2001.

16. See, for example, Juel's fine study (1988).

17. This is a common interpretation of Paul's language in Romans 10:4.

18. Ruether 1974.

19. Segal 1986.

20. See, for example, Sanders 1977.

21. Heschel 1998; see also chapter 13 by Heschel in this volume.

22. See, for example, Vermes 2003; Meier 1991.

23. Matthew 27:51.

24. See Weaver 2001; see also Bartlett 2001; Ray 1998; Winter 1995.

25. See especially the work of René Girard (1977, 1986); see also Williams 1995.

26. See, for example, John 3:16.

CHAPTER ELEVEN
MANLY PAIN AND MOTHERLY LOVE: MEL GIBSON'S BIG PICTURE
David Morgan

In the wake of America's bloodiest war, the war that did more to define the nation than any before or since, many nineteenth-century American Protestant and Catholic men inaugurated a decisive turn in the nation's portrayal of Jesus. In the antebellum period, Christian mothers had become enthroned in the home as the principal purveyors of religious formation. Middle-class mothers molded their children in all things spiritual as fathers made their way into the worldly marketplace of office, bank, and factory. Popular iconography from the mid-nineteenth century commonly shows young children gathered about a stately mother, the modern Madonna, but also the modern Jesus blessing the children. She reads Scripture and primer and prays with her children, nurturing in her sons and daughters alike the sentiments of faith that were to guide them throughout adulthood.[1]

The baptism of the Civil War transformed the experience and the ideology of manhood. Men learned to define themselves more in terms of their relations with other men. Advocates of an increasingly "muscular" Christianity stressed the importance of male formation on the sports field and the frontier, employing metaphors of the military drill and field of honor as tropes for the new masculinity. Membership in male fraternities mushroomed, and a new sensibility among many Christian men recognized in male bonding, physical exertion, and hardiness the appropriate measure of masculinity. Special contempt was reserved for sacred art that had, as the denunciation commonly went, too long portrayed Our Lord as a wimp, as effeminate, as a woman with a beard (Morgan 1999, 298–301,

328–30). Jesus had thrown the merchants from the Temple and spent long days at heavy labor. Surely, his artistic depiction ought to match the virility of his life. Indeed, Bruce Barton proclaimed in the early twentieth century that it was Jesus's portrayal in Sunday school imagery as a tender child, as "meek and lowly" and the "lamb of God," that kept boys and men from attending church. "Mary's little lamb," he complained. "Something for girls—sissified" (Barton 1925, ii). In an earlier work, Barton regretted the inability of young men to identify with Jesus as he was pictured in Sunday school art in contrast to the attractive role models visualized in images of other male biblical figures: "We do not feel close to Him—not as we [feel] close to Samson and David, nor to Moses with his wand and brass snake" (Barton 1914, xii).

Mother and Son in Mel Gibson's *Passion*

Bruce Barton's contempt for images of the coddled Jesus and his cloying mother pervade late nineteenth- and twentieth-century American commentary on Christian art. In his own way, Mel Gibson struggles to come to terms with Mary's claim over her son. But the dynamics are notably different. The prominence of the Holy Mother is one of the most striking features of *The Passion of the Christ*, in part because that relationship typically has received less emphasis in Jesus films in the United States. Gibson responds to the Victorian mother and the feminization of American Christianity, but he does so within the register of a peculiar form of Roman Catholicism. He emphasizes Mary not in order to minimize the masculinity of Jesus but rather, in a strange way, to underscore it. Like virtually every Christian image maker in the twentieth century, Gibson has commented that his portrayal of Jesus avoids the effeminacy of other cinematic treatments of Jesus. His focus on the Mother–Son connection contrasts with most films of the life of Christ, which have focused on different relationships between Jesus and those whom he knew. Judas, Peter, John, John the Baptist, and Mary Magdalene have all enjoyed special emphasis. But not Mary, and not without reason: the New Testament Gospels suggest that Jesus distanced himself from her as his public career unfolded.[2] Therefore, in light of the American history of Jesus and the question of his masculinity, it is noteworthy that Gibson gives special attention to the moving relationship between mother and son in *The Pas-*

sion of the Christ, even surcharging their bond with the dark antithesis of Satan's anti-Marian parody.

The operative relationship in Mel Gibson's film and the crux of its treatment of evil is the affection between Mother and Son. Gibson describes the depth of the affection not only in Mary's heartrending sorrow as she witnesses her son's torture and death but also in the serene flashbacks to his childhood. The film is about the violation of this relationship, its sudden loss. Thus, surely it is significant that Joseph is never present, never even mentioned in the film. In one flashback, an adult Jesus crafts a table—something like a northern European altar or mensa, the instrument for the celebration of the Mass, perhaps—and jests about it with his mother. Their playful, affectionate relationship does not miss a father. Jesus even seems to replace him. Another flashback, occasioned by one of the several times that Jesus falls beneath the heavy load of the cross on the way to Golgotha, recalls for Mary an instance in which a very young Jesus fell and cried out for her comfort. The tender moment tugs mercilessly at the viewer's heart. Now Mary can do nothing but watch her son be led away to slaughter.

Curiously, her helplessness is set in relief by his submission to abuse. Consequently, if viewers feel compassion for Mary, indignation grips many of them as they watch malicious Roman soldiers mistreat Jesus. Anger eclipses the sorrow that many might have been expected to feel for the victim of such sadistic abuse. In crafting this cleft between compassion and indignation, however, the film pairs empathy and rage as either side of the relationship of its two leading characters. Several of my students told me that they resented what they considered the film's attempt to make them feel guilty about Christ's excessive suffering—as if their sorrow for him was being twisted into blame and personal responsibility. I wonder, though, if the film's deeper emotional aim with respect to Jesus was anger. The film clearly directs the viewer's compassion to Mary for the pain she must endure. Her complete helplessness is unmistakable. Jesus, however, willingly submits himself to torment and death. And his resignation contrasts sharply with the giddy enthusiasm of the Roman soldiers, who gleefully flay him in a shower of blood and torn flesh and then follow him all the way to Golgotha with an unrelenting hail of abuse, pausing only to catch their breath. Is one meant to feel sorry for Jesus—or to hate his heartless torturers?

With the exception of Mary, all parties to the event are culpable and despicable. The film's treatment of Jesus's assailants is unswervingly negative. It portrays even his disciples as weak and cowardly. Pilate is impotent and indecisive. The Jewish leadership is hostile and hateful. And Gibson spares no contempt for the agent of the Christ's arrest, Judas Iscariot, whose depiction is utterly unsympathetic. Though he tries to repent of his betrayal, according to Matthew, Judas's will in the matter is unimportant. The reason for his treachery was demonic or Satanic possession, as the Gospels of Luke and John report.[3] We watch him tortured at first by his own regret and then by demonic children and a rising mania that drives him to suicide as the just punishment for his deed. He receives what he was due, even though a dark force had compelled him, one over which he had no control. We are not to sympathize with Judas: he is at best a warning, a taunting cautionary tale, and at worst the vehicle of Satan's attempt to foil Jesus's ministry of sacrificial atonement.

Why does the film glorify Mary, particularly in view of the tensions between mother and son recorded in the Gospels?[4] What does Gibson seek to accomplish by pairing pity and indignation in mother and son? The answer surely lies in the piety that Gibson seeks to champion in telling his version of the Passion. His film foregrounds Mary's and the viewers' emotional response to her travail, which reaches its apogee in the tableau vivant at the foot of the cross, when Mary holds the dead Jesus and poses in the traditional manner of the Pietà, along with John and (Mary) Magdalene. Mary fixes her bereaved gaze on the viewer's eyes and holds forth an imploring hand, inviting our pity—for herself as violated and victimized Mother as much as for her deceased son.

The mother's (nonbiblical) words to her crucified son underscore the film's Marian emphasis: "Heart of my heart . . . my son, let me die with you." The identification of Mary with her son's suffering was part of a late medieval piety that was conveyed visually in Rogier van der Weyden's well-known *Escorial Deposition* (c. 1435), an altar painting in which the gesture of Mary's body parallels the form of Christ's corpse as it is lowered from the cross. The participation of Mary in Christ's suffering took on theological substance in the Middle Ages as she acquired a salvific role, even being elevated to the fourth member of the triune configuration of Father, Son, and Holy Spirit. Mary became co-redemptrix by virtue of her sharing in the Passion. Of course, authorities much closer to Gibson's time than the fifteenth century underscore the justification for this foregrounding of Mary. In her much cited recounting of mystical visions of the Passion, Sister Anne Catherine Emmerich (1774–1824) stated that, "filled with intense feelings of motherly love, [the Virgin] entreated her Son to permit her to die with him."[5]

From the Son to the Mother?

Gibson's film redirects the emotional attention of the devout filmgoer from the figure of Jesus to the Mother. It is to Mary who mortals must turn for access to the Son, whose suffering strikes one not as a demonstration of his humility and self-effacement but rather as the measure of his obedience to the Father. In other words, in this film, Jesus does not suffer in this film to invite viewers' identification with and compassion for him. He suffers as egregiously as he does because that is what God the Father demands of him. The drum roll and grim determination evident in his expression and stride in the final seconds of the film's resurrection scene further suggest that this is not a tender savior. It is now Christ's turn for indignation. This leaves Mary as the focus for human petition. She has earned the right to receive the prayers of sinners and has even accrued merit of her own. Since her angry son has been reconciled to his absent and angry father, the devout will welcome this maternal advocate.

Still, the satisfaction of God's righteous demand for holiness is not the only reason that Jesus suffers in this film. Why, one must ask, does Jesus suffer the way he does—so long, so graphically, so violently, at the hands of such orgiastic and sadistic Roman soldiers? The history of art that portrays the Passion is full of the instruments of Jesus's torture and the ugliness and contempt of the soldiers and Jewish officials who conducted his abuse and execution.[6] Gibson did not invent those features. But his sustained and mounting display of violation both intensifies the visual tradition and stresses the passivity of Jesus, who patiently submits himself to one humiliation after another. One wonders why, watching his unbearable trek from Pilate to Calvary. It is tempting to consider a psychoanalytic interpretation of the point. Some will conclude that a son whose father's rage pulverizes him is punishing himself for having desired forbidden relations with his mother. The complete absence of Joseph from the film might be read as accenting this dynamic. Jesus submits himself to the punitive task of appeasing his heavenly Father. This is no easy undertaking. Even at the point of death, hanging on the cross, Jesus fears that the One whom he seeks to please has abandoned him. Mary would join Jesus in death, but Jesus will not allow any union with this mother and so replaces himself with another son, John, "the Beloved Disciple" (the same John, it should be remembered, to whom tradition assigns authorship of the fourth Gospel, which is the primary source of Gibson's *Passion*).

Satan as Counter-Mother

From a psychoanalytic perspective, it is tempting to regard the excessive violence to which Jesus submits himself in the attempt to please his father as a self-imposed masochism motivated by guilt for the desire of his mother.[7] Psychoanalytical interpretation can easily stretch credibility. But it can also illuminate irrational aspects of plot and subject matter. Consider the role of Satan in Gibson's film. A female actor portrays the androgynous figure, who dresses in a manner recalling Mary. Among the characters she or he appears with and among, only Jesus and Mary see or interact with Satan (Judas sees a demon and demonic children but apparently not the figure of Satan). Satan parodies the Madonna and Child in an especially repellant scene during the scourging of Jesus. Floating across the screen in a kind of silent, slow-motion specter, Satan coddles (suckles?) a deformed, white, bald creature that turns its head to smile grotesquely at the scene of Jesus's flaying. As the anti-Mary, Satan may be taunting Jesus with the very thing he desires, his mother, who looks on from the entrance of the courtyard in which her son is being lashed.

Satan plays an important role in the film, far more than in any other cinematic portrayal of the life of Christ. As the film begins, viewers hear and see Jesus struggling at prayer in the Garden of Gethsemane. Many Christians will be familiar with common pictures of a prayerful Jesus, images that show him quietly kneeling, clothed in billowing robes, hands clasped and brow furrowed. Nothing could be further from Gibson's vision. His Jesus stutters, gasps, faints, and stumbles, dizzy with despair in an eerie gloom. He shares the darkness with a black-robed figure whose pasty, hairless face appears female but who speaks in a masculine voice. This is an unusually disturbing rendition of Satan, who has come to tempt Jesus, to convince him that he is alone, a failure, cut off from his beloved

Father, whom Jesus repeatedly and pathetically beseeches. Christ's suffering and Satan's malicious taunting of him go hand in hand. The film puts evil and pain together in order to proclaim that the meaning of Jesus's Passion was victory over evil. But evil does not mean social inequality or cruel people or a corrupt state. These are all manifestations of the dark mother who wants the Son for herself. The battle rages between libidinous mother and demanding Father. Though Jesus suffers horribly in the struggle and his body is the very site of the battle's violence, ultimately his Father accepts him. By overcoming evil, whose defeat is heralded at the end of the film by a flashing scene of Satan writhing in a hellish vision of Calvary, Jesus overcomes his Oedipal desire and is reconciled to the absent Father who demanded his son's self-sacrifice.

Gender and Religion in American History

This conjectural but perhaps suggestive reading is bolstered by the immediate historical setting of representations of the Passion and popular conceptions of Christology in nineteenth- and twentieth-century America. *The Passion of the Christ* should be situated in the history of gender and religion in the modern United States, which I quickly sketched at the outset of this chapter. The task, though, is not to explain what Mel Gibson thought, as if exposing his intention will exhaust interpretation. If that were all we required, securing his production notes (and a psychiatric evaluation, if that were available) would be the sole task of analysis. It seems more important to show the historical context in which the film operates as a cultural representation. This context informs the film and invests it with meaning by bringing to light the film's debt to practices, values, symbols, and ideas that are larger than Mel Gibson and that his film, wittingly or not, transmits, modifies, or rejects. To be sure, this is not the only meaning of the film. A study of the director's intentions will reveal further significance, as will careful examination of the film's reception. However, I wish to apply a psychoanalytic reading to the relationship between the film and its historical setting in the modern United States in order to discern correlations of the logic of the psyche and the circumstances of historical specificity.

In the context of nineteenth- and twentieth-century American Christianity, Gibson's Jesus faces a choice between maternal and paternal religion.

Will he found a feminized church or a manly one? In fact, the film wants it both ways: Jesus does the manly deed of heroic self-denial, satisfying the demands of Father, while bestowing on Mother the cult of intercession. He refuses Evil its place—the control of maternal desire over the son—but mitigates the Father's anger by elevating devotion to Mother. In this manner, Gibson may be seeking to reestablish the spiritual economy of intercession that the Council of Trent had endorsed in opposition to the Reformation.[8] By stipulating that Christ's paschal sacrifice was the singular mechanism of salvation, the Reformation eliminated the role of Mary in the dynamics of redemption. As a result, one of the iconographical preferences of the German Reformation was Christ blessing the children.[9] Jesus himself acquired the feminine role of tenderly blessing the children, which his male companions, the disciples, sought to censor. The theme remained a favorite among Protestants and became one among Catholics, particularly in nineteenth- and twentieth-century America, when the mother became the primary figure in the spiritual formation of children, both in practice and in a middle-class ideology of domestic Christianity.[10]

Gibson and the Return to Catholic Tradition

Gibson's film separates the two functions, masculine and feminine, and reaffirms the role of Mary—not simply because he may wish to rebuke Protestantism but perhaps because he objects to the "Protestantization" of American Catholicism since Vatican II, which many observers of the Church have noted.[11] When Mary and the Magdalene swab up the blood of Jesus on the stone floor where he was whipped, I recalled the angels in fifteenth-century woodcuts and paintings who hover about the cross, holding chalices to collect the blood dripping from Christ's wounds. This is the blood of the Eucharist,[12] which we see gush out of Christ's side, spraying the centurion, John, and Mary at the foot of the cross, and which is glimpsed trickling down the cross beneath Christ's punctured feet. Add to this the Veil of Veronica and the careful choreography of the Fourteen Stations of the Cross, and *The Passion of the Christ* clearly is a film endorsing a premodern version of Catholicism. Gibson's big picture is a worldview abandoned by the Reformation in particular and by modernity in general, including, Gibson might assert, Vatican II. The sacramental sensibility of Christ's suffering, the mystical significance of his blood, the theological work of his execution as a sacrificial atonement, and the apparatus of merit dispensed by an economy of intercession keyed to such devices as images like the Veil of Veronica: all these constitute a premodern Roman Catholicism that the film seeks to recover and merge seamlessly with the historical event of the last day of the life of Jesus.

Powering this theological and ritual reclamation is the engine of compassion and indignation. Does Gibson seek to champion the return of a religious system that, at its core, is structured by a troubled relationship with male authority and by a profound emotional affinity with (and desire for?) the mother? This is not simply an expression of his psyche but part of a reaction to modernity. His big picture therefore may appeal to anyone who needs to balance if not resolve feelings of intimacy and rage. The present (modernity, maternity) must be transcended by returning to the absent (father, past), namely, the right version of the Catholic Church. The violence of Christ's suffering and death as portrayed in Gibson's film seems meant to quicken the sense of this need and to hasten the recovery of paternal honor.

Notes

1. For examinations of this iconography, see Morgan 1998, 97–123; Morgan 2005, chap. 6.
2. See Matthew 12:46–50; Mark 3:32–35; John 2:4.
3. Luke 22:3; John 6:71, 13:2.
4. See Ingersoll (chapter 5 in this volume) for a discussion of the conservative Protestant reaction to this attention to Mary.
5. Emmerich 1983, 283.
6. Excellent considerations of this imagery are found in Clifton 1997 and Finaldi 2000, 140–67.
7. Carroll (1986, 99–112) has considered the mythological and psychoanalytical symbolism of the "Mary cult."
8. Schroeder 1941, 215–17.
9. Christensen 1979, 134–36.
10. McDannell 1986.
11. Fox 2004, 373.
12. See also Bynum 1982.

CHAPTER TWELVE
IMAGO CHRISTI: AESTHETIC AND THEOLOGICAL ISSUES IN JESUS FILMS BY PASOLINI, SCORSESE, AND GIBSON
Lloyd Baugh, SJ

Mel Gibson's *The Passion of the Christ* is the latest of more than one hundred and thirty films focusing on the life of Jesus Christ. In this rich and varied tradition and given the background, the faith position, and the aesthetic choices of the director, each one of the Jesus films provides the viewer, the believer, and the critic with sometimes-thorny issues and problems. Three of the Jesus films stand out for the often violent controversy they have stirred up both before and after their release: *The Gospel according to Saint Matthew* (1964), *The Last Temptation of Christ* (1988), and now Gibson's *The Passion of the Christ* (2004). In this chapter, I propose to investigate how the controversies sparked by these three particular films, sometimes around important issues, sometimes around nonissues, have obscured other important, even critical, questions, effectively denying them the voice and the analysis they deserve.

The Scandal of a Sexual Jesus in Scorsese's *Last Temptation*

Controversy over its treatment of Jesus's sexuality dogged Martin Scorsese's *The Last Temptation of Christ* even from before its release. First the Greek Orthodox Church and then the Roman Catholic Church had condemned Nikos Kazantzakis's novel *The Last Temptation of Christ* (1955) for its all-too-human portrait of Jesus and for its representation of his temptation to sexual activity. When Scorsese announced in the early

1980s that he would be making a film based on Kazantzakis's novel, Protestant and then Catholic fundamentalist groups began a campaign of protest against what they considered its disrespectful, even blasphemous, approach. Although a commission of "eminent theologians"[1] convened by Paramount Pictures recommended that the film be made despite some risks, Paramount nonetheless terminated the project in 1983. Jack Lang, the French minister of culture and an admirer of Scorsese, offered to help, but the Catholic archbishop of Paris, Cardinal Lustiger, protested directly to the president of France, saying that public funds should not be used "for a project founded on subverting scripture."[2] French support quickly faded away. Only in 1987 did Universal Pictures agree to produce the film but slashed its budget from $15 million to $6 million.

Unprecedented controversy greeted the film's release in 1988. In America, the protests came from both Protestant televangelists and Catholic archbishops.[3] In Italy, Franco Zeffirelli, the Catholic director of the classic *Jesus of Nazareth* (1977), condemned the film—without having seen it—as "truly horrible and totally deranged" and subsequently blasted "that Jewish cultural scum in Los Angeles, which is always spoiling for an attack on the Christian world."[4] The critiques of the film went from the reasonable sublime—that the film was "equally defective on the theological level and on the esthetic level"[5]—to the passionate ridiculous, with prayers to God to rain down nuclear bombs on the cinema in Manhattan showing the film. In the end, the United States Conference of Catholic Bishops called for its first-ever "nationwide boycott" of Scorsese's movie.[6]

The target of most of the protests was a long sequence in the film in which Jesus, hanging dying on the cross, is visited by Satan one final time. Satan tempts him to renounce his salvific act, come down from the cross, marry Mary Magdalene, and live a life of quiet domesticity. In this temptation/fantasy sequence, Scorsese represents Jesus in connubial union with Magdalene and, when she dies, with Martha and Mary; from these unions issues a large family. Using the language of cinema, Scorsese makes it abundantly clear that he is representing a temptation, not a real event. The conclusion of the film shows Jesus resisting the temptation, returning to the cross, and dying victorious.

Most of the protesters misread the temptation sequence as "real" and allowed themselves to be scandalized and angered by it. However, the issue of Jesus's sexuality clearly is part of normal theological reflection on Christology and essential to the mystery of the Incarnation: if Jesus was a human being, he certainly had a sexuality. By focusing so narrowly on this theme, the protesters missed a wide variety of much more serious and troubling issues in the film, such as its deeply flawed low Christology and the problematical anthropology it projects on Jesus, both of which clearly contradict critical cornerstones of Christian belief.[7] Christians believe that Jesus, the incarnate Logos, the Son of God, was in full and deep communication and communion with God. He lived in an integrated way the dynamic of his human and divine natures, came to understand that his prophetic words and ministry would lead to his death, and chose, out of love for God and for humanity, to be faithful to his mission and go to his death. God crowned his act of love with his Resurrection, a victory for Jesus, a victory for all humanity. These—and not sexuality—are the most important issues of Scorsese's film, but they were effectively obscured in 1988 by protests based on a superficial misreading of the film.

Since 1988, the controversy around *The Last Temptation of Christ* has died down. I show the film every year in my theology classes at the Pontifical Gregorian University in Rome. My students, who come from many parts of the world and many varied cultures, reflect calmly on the film, justly noting that in many dimensions of style and content, Scorsese's *Last Temptation* already is quite dated. At times the students even laugh at the scenes that in 1988 threatened the faith of many people and caused the dramatic expense of much ecclesiastical and scholarly energy. With a healthy *sang-froid* and certainly with no threat to their faith and morals, they easily locate, appreciate, and analyze the theological weaknesses and errors of this film.

The Problematic Ideologies of Pasolini and His *Gospel*

The storm of controversy that swirled around Pier Paolo Pasolini's *The Gospel according to Saint Matthew* is of an entirely different order. First of all, the source of the film is the Gospel of Matthew—it would be difficult to find a more orthodox reference—and indeed all the dialogue of the film, except for a few verses from Isaiah, is taken directly from that gospel.[8] There is nothing obviously shocking or scandalous in the narrative content of the film, which follows very closely the narrative of the gospel. The controversy stemmed rather from the person and activity of the director himself.

The thoroughly Catholic Italy of 1964 had been ruled by the Christian Democratic Party since the end of World War II. Pasolini, on the other hand, was an enfant terrible of the political Left, a former member of the Italian Communist Party, an avowed atheist, a militant homosexual, and a veteran of several run-ins with the law over these issues. The church–state establishment judged it unacceptable for Pasolini to make a film on the life of Christ. And when his understanding of Matthew as "a revolutionary" and so his intentions for the content and style of his film became clear—"The Christ [of Matthew] who moves through Palestine is really a revolutionary whirlwind: anyone who comes up to two people and says, 'Throw away your nets, follow me, and I will make you fishers of men,' is totally revolutionary"—it became equally clear that both he and the film would face opposition.[9]

Pasolini's film-in-progress became a hot issue of public debate and clearly affected the way in which people and critics in particular reacted to the film. On the evening of the film's premiere at the Venice Festival, anticipating a violent negative reaction from the far Right, the police chief of Venice tripled the usual number of police and *Carabinieri* around the *Palazzo del Cinema* at the Lido. Though the noisy Fascist demonstrators outside did not prevent the overall warm reception of the film and, more important, did not prevent its being awarded the Special Prize of the Jury, *The Gospel* alienated politically powerful and vociferous conservative Catholics. Using illogical and blatantly ad hominem argumentation, they blamed Pasolini's communism for his angry Jesus, whose character they deemed nothing but "an anti-bourgeois guerrilla"; evidently, they had forgotten that Jesus, especially Matthew's Jesus, was "troublesome, a sign of contradiction."[10] At the other end of the Italian political spectrum, members of the Left were "highly critical of the idea of a serious film on Christ . . . [and attacked] the film on the basis that it did not deny Christ's divine nature."[11] The Vatican's reaction to Pasolini's *Gospel* was at best guarded; the review in the official *Osservatore Romano* was very negative,[12] at least in part because of the moral and political implications (in 1964) of seeming to approve of a film made by an atheist communist. In 1996, however, reflecting the intrinsic validity and value of Pasolini's film, the Vatican rehabilitated it spectacularly by including it on its published list of the fifteen greatest religious films of all time; moreover, it was the only Jesus film to be so honored.[13]

As with Scorsese's film, time revealed what the 1964 political-ideological controversy obscured: for a variety of reasons, Pasolini's film is a masterpiece that stands far above all the other Jesus films. Its great respect for the spirit and the words of the gospel, both in its narrative structure and in the strong preaching style it gives to Jesus, is unique in the Jesus film tradition. The film's disciplined, uncompromising, challenging style matches the uncompromisingly challenging style and content of the Gospel of Matthew: sharp, stark black-and-white images, like the word of God, "living and active [and] sharper than any double-edged sword."[14] Vigorous editing imitates the gospel's elliptical style; a handheld camera gives the viewer the sensation of following Jesus. Often surprising contrapuntal excerpts of classical music modulate and give a theological thrust to the images.

Pasolini's *Gospel* is exceptional for its strong portrait of a prophetic Jesus, a conscious and radical contrast to the altogether soft and sentimental quality that characterizes most other film icons of Jesus. Pasolini's cinematic Jesus, like Matthew's, is a vigorous, energetic man who is sure of himself, accepts and lives his mission with courage and integrity, and dramatically breaks with his religious tradition to proclaim the "good news" and to challenge all people to accept the liberating love of God. He also is a profoundly human figure who loves life and embodies God's gentle love and mercy in his healing miracles. At the same time, Pasolini's portrayal of Jesus's mysterious relationship to God reveals his divine nature.

Pasolini's film is not without its limits. The angry tone and world-renouncing stance of Jesus at times grates on the viewer. One critic refers to him as "a fiery young first-century revolutionary, [a] sort of a young Fidel Castro."[15] Pasolini also edits some of the discourses of Jesus, omitting references to the Kingdom of God, and he cuts several episodes from Matthew, such as the Transfiguration,[16] that underline Jesus's divine nature. Moreover, the director inserts a number of autobiographical and gay-ideological allusions,[17] but these are distracting only to someone who knows Pasolini's personal struggles well. Still, the Jesus of the Gospel of Matthew is an angry, forceful, prophetic preacher. However, this is a sharp contrast for the viewer who judges Pasolini's Jesus according to the norms of other, less challenging filmic portrayals of Jesus: "the point is, of course, not so much that we are in front of a Marxist Christ, as that He is not the gentle, all-loving Jesus of conventional Catholic iconography."[18]

Despite these limitations, in taking the risk of challenging and exploding the traditional film iconography of Jesus, Pasolini comes closer than any other director to representing the Jesus of history, the Jesus of Scripture, the Jesus of the Christian faith. Unfortunately, the early and largely unjustified political controversy stigmatized both the film and its author and obscured for many years the exceptional moral and theological impact of the clearest, most eloquent, and most accurate cinematic representation of Jesus as the Christ.[19]

Mel Gibson's *Passion* in Context

Gibson's *The Passion of the Christ* generated great deal of comment and controversy both before and after its release, and a highly charged and often polemical atmosphere developed around it. Partisans enlisted theologians, pastors, and senior Church authorities to bolster their positions. They unjustly and unfortunately pulled the ailing Pope John Paul II into the fray, on the one hand claiming that he saw and liked the film and on the other maintaining that the pope does not comment on films and prefers to leave that to experts.[20] Of course, even if the pope did see and like the film, his purported comment that "it is as it was" hardly has the theological and binding authority of an ex cathedra proclamation. It will take some time to predict the ultimate significance of the film and its controversy.

There were accusations and counteraccusations regarding the film's alleged antisemitism and the extent to which it could unleash new pogroms against Jews.[21] In response, some people dismissed far too quickly the valid concerns and fears of the Jewish community and defended the integrity, doctrinal orthodoxy, and esthetic excellence of the film by insisting illogically that "Mel is a good Catholic, and so. . . ." On the other hand, those who have seen the film and seem to want at all costs to defend it made a number of highly emotional points, one of which is that the overwhelming performance of the film at the box office is evidence that the film "must be" a most valid representation of the person and Passion of Jesus.

The positive experience of filmgoers also is an element with which to be reckoned. A catechist in the parish I occasionally serve in on Sunday, whose ministry is to prepare adults for the sacrament of baptism, after I had voiced some discrete reservations about Gibson's film, confronted me with fervent conviction. "Father!" she exclaimed. "You're a priest! How can you be against such a holy film about Jesus?!" I suspect that no answer I could have given her would have made any difference.

Much as in the cases of Scorsese's and Pasolini's films, these two extreme poles of the Gibson/*Passion* controversy created so much noise that they drowned out any attempt to highlight crucial film-aesthetic and theological issues that remained dangerously unaddressed and unresolved. For example, the grossly exaggerated and extended violence of the film's representation of the physical torture of Jesus reflects Gibson's dangerously skewed traditional theology of atonement more than it does any historical or biblical reality. Gibson proclaimed repeatedly and proudly that he wanted to push the filmgoer "over the edge."[22] Artificially amplified by the giant screen, extreme close-up shots, digital special effects, violent editing, and a dense soundtrack in THX, the violent images pound us down under an extreme-reality crucifixion that no one, not even Jesus, ever could have experienced. The hermeneutical clues, which Gibson intended should give theological and spiritual significance to the Passion—a couple of brief flashbacks to Jesus's blessing of the bread and wine at the Last Supper—effectively are lost to all but the most theologically astute in the borderline pornographic orgy of physical violence.

Another critical issue has to do with the nature of the reality presented by the film. Icon Productions and other elements of the media have touted *The Passion* as the truest and most accurate film version of the Passion and death of Jesus ever made.[23] This assertion and the "more-real-than-real" quality of any powerful film experience convinced many spectators that it really is in the cinema as it really was that day on Calvary; the not entirely historically accurate use of Latin and Aramaic serves to highlight this tone of historical reality.[24] However, far too many specific elements of the film, patently unhistorical and unbiblical, give ample evidence that the film's historical authenticity is dubious: a cross being built in the palace of Caiaphas, a weak and indecisive Pontius Pilate, Jesus falling under the cross seven times on the way up to Calvary, and a cosmic tear from the eye of a mourning God that falls to earth and sets off an earthquake that destroys the Temple but barely shakes the palace of Pilate.[25] Furthermore, this Jesus is completely separated and isolated from his Jewish cultural and religious heritage; the Last Supper, for example, gives not the least evidence of being a Seder. Gibson's cinematic text, while claiming historical accuracy, clearly shifts back and forth among elements of the Gospels, traditional Catholic devotional practices, material from the visions of Anne Catherine Emmerich,[26] and Gibson's own faith experience.

Perhaps the most critical problem with Gibson's film is the dangerously docetist Christology of Gibson's representation of Jesus. Its name derived from the Greek *dokesis*, or "appearance," docetism is a very early Christian heresy. Docetists maintained that Jesus only appeared to be human; he only seemed to live and suffer and die. He was God merely pretending to be human, going through the charade of living and suffering and dying but never actually doing it. Some docetists go so far as to deny Jesus's human nature altogether. The superhuman strength and physical resistance of Gibson's Jesus point directly to the docetist error: no normal human being would have survived until the crucifixion. Another indicator is the tranquil self-assurance with which, having fallen yet again under the cross, Jesus says to Mary, "See mother, I make all things new."[27] This is something that Jesus did not say, and to have him say it is to deny a critical truth about the Incarnation in general and the Passion in particular: Jesus experienced intense mental anguish and desperation at having been abandoned by his disciples, by the people he had served, and even by God.

The Issue of Personal Belief and the Resurrection Scene as a Useful Paradigm

In the many and varied controversies raised by the three films we have considered, polemicists paid a great deal of attention to the belief or nonbelief of the films' directors but little or no attention to the way the films represent the Resurrection of Jesus as the Christ. A much overworked truism of the Jesus film tradition is that the orthodox Christian belief of the director necessarily makes for a valid, orthodox portrait of Jesus in the film and, conversely, that the nonbelief of a director disqualifies his image of Jesus. The Catholic critic John May puts the question succinctly: "The assumption is that intention or belief—or lack of it—inevitably governs artistic achievement."[28]

Following the cue of Paul Ricoeur in this theory of phenomenological hermeneutics, I prefer to focus on the film text. In particular, I propose that the most revealing test of the validity or orthodoxy of a portrait of Jesus lies in the film's representation of the Resurrection. The Christian faith is built on the experience of the Resurrection: God's guarantee of the final validity and effectiveness of Jesus's salvific life and death. Without the Resurrection as the victory of Jesus for all humanity, the life, prophetic and healing ministry, Passion, and death of Jesus are meaningless. Moreover, unless a film image of Jesus clearly represents the social and ecclesial dynamic of his Resurrection, that film is flawed, perhaps fatally, because such an absence renders the depiction of his life, struggle, and sufferings of his Passion devoid of real meaning.

Martin Scorsese is clear about his own religious identity—"I am a Catholic"[29]—and belief: "I believe that Jesus is divine." Regarding the Resurrection, his position is quite orthodox, if not too sophisticated: "I do believe in the Resurrection. I can't exactly say what it means, beyond a kind of transcendence."[30] Well aware of the difficulties of imaging the metahistorical event of the Resurrection and of the largely unsuccessful solutions of most of the films in the Jesus tradition, Scorsese offers an abstract-symbolic interpretation of the event: a rapid montage of flashing colors, with yellow and white dominating. Lasting eighteen seconds, with vigorous drums and jubilantly ringing church bells on the sound track, the sequence comes close to suggesting the power of the Resurrection, but three elements subvert it. In the visuals of the montage, two material shots of torn sprocketed film clash with the abstract poetry and confuse the viewer; on the sound track, Scorsese includes the sounds of wailing female voices. Heard at the death of Lazarus and during the crucifixion scene, these voices are at best ambiguous and troubling signs. However, the most troubling dimensions of Scorsese's abstract Resurrection are first the theological problem of its total discontinuity with the concrete person, life, and ministry of Jesus of Nazareth and second the cinematic suggestion through color and sound that the event is a victory neither for Jesus nor for the people of God.

Mel Gibson's faith commitment in the Roman Catholic tradition is well known, especially from recent interviews, and it is evident in some dimensions of his *Passion*.[31] But Gibson's traditional beliefs do not seem to inform the conclusion of his film. His Resurrection scene is fatally flawed, for it shows none of its implications for the people who have lived the Passion with Jesus, the nascent Christian community. Gibson places his camera inside Jesus's tomb, which at first is in the dark and then, as the stone is rolled back, gradually suffused by light from outside. The camera lingers on the shroud of Jesus as it mysteriously collapses, a transparent reference to the Shroud of Turin. Then Jesus kneels into the frame: we see him in profile in a tight head-and-shoulders shot, all the marks of his Passion gone from his face. On the sound track, we hear the beating of drums striking a military rhythm—a curious choice since the Resurrection of Jesus the Christ certainly is not a military victory. As the beats grow stronger, Jesus slowly steps out of the frame. Fade to black.

Gibson represents the Resurrection event not as the pivotal event of human history and a cosmic victory for Jesus and all women and men of all times but rather as a private experience that touches neither Jesus's disciples nor the viewers of the film. There is no joy or hope in the scene; Mary, Mary Magdalene, John, and the converted Roman soldier remain suffering and passive in the Pietà tableau of the previous scene, separated from the Resurrection first by a screen that is held black for six seconds and then by a self-centered and isolated Lord once again alive. From the beginning of the film, Gibson shows us a Mary who has such a strong psychospiritual mother–son communion with Jesus that even at a distance she feels his pain and he feels her presence and love. This is a mother–son communion whose renewal is promised when Gibson has Jesus whisper to her with authority, promise, and even joy the words from Revelation, "See, mother . . . I make all things new." Surely this communion, so brutally broken off by Jesus's death, would, could, and should have been renewed manifestly in the Resurrection. However, Gibson, caught up in the extreme preoccupation with the sins of humanity that informs his atonement theology and much of the action of his film, forgoes his chance to give hope to all of us sinners.

About his faith and in contrast to both Scorsese and Gibson, Pasolini enigmatically commented, "I don't believe that Christ is the son of God, because I am not a believer, at least not consciously. But I believe that Christ is divine: I believe that in him humanity is so lofty, strict and ideal as to exceed the common terms of humanity."[32] However, this atheist, in a film recognized for its gritty, material, almost documentary texture, offers an uncompromising, clear, and most effective Resurrection. In a scene resounding with the mystery of Resurrection victory, Pasolini is most convincing about his Jesus when he represents "the disciples running joyously towards the risen

Christ in a burst of visual energy that sweeps the emotions of even the most skeptical spectator along with it."[33] Pasolini develops a fifteen-second-long shot of Jesus, avoiding close-ups that would be too sentimental and too material. As his followers run excitedly toward him, the resurrected Jesus strongly and urgently proclaims from a hilltop the concluding words of the Gospel of Matthew: "Go therefore and make disciples of all nations . . . I am with you always."[34] On the sound track, an explosion of sacred music—the Gloria of the Congolese Missa Luba, with its pounding drums and joyful voices—underlines the significance of this Resurrection as a cosmic victory not only for Jesus but for the entire people of God, a victory with a clear communitarian and missionary thrust, a victory for us.

Conclusion

It will take some time for serious researchers to analyze and understand all the dynamics of the phenomenal reaction to Gibson's *Passion*. My hope is that when the dust clears, as in the case of Scorsese's and Pasolini's films, we will make the kind of dispassionate critical appraisal of *The Passion of the Christ*, in all its positive points, limits, and weaknesses, that proved so elusive in the wake of its release.

Notes

1. Ehrenstein 1992, 112; see also Kelly 1991, 176.
2. Scorsese, Thompson, and Christie 1990, 122.
3. These included Protestant televangelists Pat Robertson, Jerry Falwell, Jimmy Swaggart, and Jim Bakker; Catholic Archbishops Roger Cardinal Mahony (Los Angeles) and John Cardinal O'Connor (New York); the Catholic Mother Angelica of the Eternal Word Television Network; and Christian pop singer Pat Boone (Ehrenstein 1992, 112–13). Others included the conservative Catholic political commentator Patrick Buchanan and the fundamentalist Protestant Don Wildmon of the American Family Association, "which added 60,000 new members during the campaign" against the film (Keyser 1992, 184–86). Wildmon and his people, armed with antisemitic slogans, picketed the Los Angeles home of Lew Wasserman, the Jewish chairman of MCA, the parent corporation of Universal Pictures.
4. Ehrenstein 1992, 113. Zeffirelli later denied having made the remarks.
5. Serre 1988, 55.

6. Keyser 1992, 186.

7. For a detailed analysis of Scorsese's badly skewed anthropology, see Baugh 1997, 48–71.

8. All the dialogue of the film is from Matthew, but not all of Matthew's dialogue is in the film.

9. Pasolini and Halliday 1992, 89.

10. Douin 1988, 38.

11. Viano 1993, 134.

12. Ciaccio 1964, 6. The review reflects a pre–Vatican II sensibility that understands the Gospels as historical-documentary accounts of the life of Jesus; Ciaccio also missed the many references in the film to Jesus's divinity.

13. Manin (1996) notes that the list included fifteen films of lasting cultural and moral value and fifteen popular entertainment films. Sadly and ironically, Franco Zeffirelli, director of the worldwide hit film *Jesus of Nazareth*, protested his film's absence from the Vatican's list and launched a thinly veiled attack on his archrival Pasolini, insisting that the director's atheism and homosexuality should have disqualified both him and his film from receiving any Vatican recognition.

14. Hebrews 4:12.

15. Wall 1970, 53.

16. Few if any directors include the Transfiguration, perhaps the most mysterious episode of the New Testament, in their Jesus films.

17. Baugh 1997, 101–2.

18. Viano 1993, 142.

19. For a more extensive treatment of Pasolini's portrait of Jesus, see Baugh 1997, 94–106.

20. See Allen 2004. The Catholic News Service reported that the pope's private secretary, Archbishop Stanislaw Dziwisz, denied the pope's positive comment; Gibson's production company, Icon, maintained that the Vatican press secretary, Joaquín Navarro-Valls, confirmed the pope's laudatory judgment.

21. I discuss at some length the antisemitism question in Baugh 2004.

22. See, for example, Sawyer 2004.

23. See, for example, Associated Press 27 June 2003.

24. Certainly Jesus and the disciples would have spoken Aramaic among themselves. The Romans in Palestine, however, used Latin for military matters and Greek for all matters of general civil administration. Therefore, it is more likely that in encounters with Pilate, both Jesus and the Jewish authorities would have used Greek rather than Latin.

25. Matthew 27:51 and Mark 16:37, in theological-symbolic and not historical references, state only that the veil of the Temple was torn in two.

26. See Emmerich 1928. The visions of Emmerich, an eighteenth-century German seer, include a number of points to which Gibson's film alludes: the construction of Jesus's cross in the Temple precincts, the excessive and nonbiblical physical violence against Jesus during the hearing before Caiaphas, and Pilate's angry criticism of Caiaphas for the abuse of Jesus. Emmerich's "diaries" are notoriously and embarrassingly antisemitic.

27. People I have spoken to insist this is something Jesus actually said. In fact, the line is from Revelation 21:5; it is a theological-soteriological statement understood by the later Christian community in the light of the Resurrection. It clearly is out of place in this film.

28. May 1982, 27.
29. Henry 1988, 8.
30. Kelly 1991, 243.
31. See, for example, Boyer 2003; Sawyer 2004.
32. Pasolini, in a letter to Lucio Caruso, quoted in Siciliano 1982, 270.
33. Bondanella 1990, 184.
34. Matthew 28:19, 20.

Part III
JEWS AND CHRISTIANS: REFRAMING THE DIALOGUE

The Passion of the Christ has now played in movie theaters at in the United States and elsewhere. Initial press interest has waned, and it is now the task of a few to inquire as to the state of Jewish–Christian relations in the post-*Passion* environment. Where are we? What have we learned from the controversy, and what does the future portend? In the chapters that follow, eight scholars raise these questions and offer preliminary answers.

Susannah Heschel suggests that the dejudaized Jesus of Gibson's *Passion* is heir to a genealogy whose roots lie in the counterhistories of German Reform Judaism and the theology of the Christian "historical Jesus" movement. The tension at that time within Christian theology—between affirming Jesus's continuity with his Jewish origins and asserting the uniqueness of his voice—led to the emergence of a thoroughly racialized Aryan Jesus, partly in reactionary response to the reclamation of Jesus's Jewish identity and the self-identification of Reform Jews as the religion of the historical Jesus. Dejudaization of Jesus, Heschel argues, requires a spiritualization and dehistoricization of the Christian message in order to remove from it any taint of Judaism. The result culminated in an attempt by Third Reich theologians to purge the Gospels and the Christian liturgy of anything Jewish, an attempt of which *The Passion*'s predilections are eerily reminiscent. Moreover, the film's metaphors of cosmic conflict both mirror and divert attention from the global conflicts in which Americans found themselves in 2004.

PART III

Stephen R. Haynes struggles to come to terms with his conflicting visions of *The Passion*: reverence, anger at perceived antisemitism, and frustration with stereotypical responses by both Christians and Jews to one another's concerns. Was the film a profitable example of Nazi-like antisemitism, or was it the most promising evangelistic tool in two thousand years? Was the violence "obscene" and "pornographic," or was it a powerful reflection of the depths of Jesus's suffering for the sins of the humanity? Was the film a cynical Hollywood product, or was Mel Gibson God's messenger to a needy world? Haynes presents the reader with a vivid portrait of the many audiences with whom he saw and discussed the film. In his chapter, he traverses "the world of academy and the world in which real people lived"; understanding the gap separating the scholar's desk and the pew, he remains on speaking terms with both by existing in between.

There is no in-between, however, for Richard L. Rubenstein, who argues that *The Passion of the Christ* reveals the irreducible fault line between Christianity and Judaism that had been blurred by the unprecedented civility of interreligious discourse in the United States. Borrowing on his earlier work, Rubenstein reiterates that what is repressed or sublimated in Judaism is made manifest in Christianity and therefore that Jewish unbelief is far more problematic for Christianity than the unbelief of others. Gibson understood this, Rubenstein suggests, and used the raw emotional power of the Passion narrative to restate the case for Christian belief. *The Passion*, Rubenstein concludes, demonstrates the limits of dialogue between scholars and their own faith communities and of dialogue between Jewish and Christian thinkers. Historical scholarship and interfaith dialogues, he argues, are "slender reeds" on which to raise hopes for interreligious understanding, even if we know all too well the dangers that lurk at the fault line when its divisiveness is not moderated.

Stephen T. Davis argues that although Christianity has a history of antisemitism, the New Testament is not antisemitic but rather reflects the strong disagreements its authors have with Jewish law and tradition. He refuses to hold the New Testament writers accountable for later antisemitism or even genocide not only because they did not intend such results but also because they could not have known how their words and ideas might later be twisted. In a parallel move, Davis rejects "theological revisionism" that downplays the Passion, death, and resurrection of Jesus in favor of an emphasis on his teachings since Christians believe that it was Jesus's death and resurrection that gave meaning to his life and teachings, not the other way around. As such, he concludes that neither Gibson himself nor *The Passion* are antisemitic but that the film may cause pain to Jews and may reinforce existing antisemitism among those who already hate Jews. However, he maintains, antisemitism is incompatible with Christian teachings, and "anyone who practices antisemitism is not practicing Christianity."

David M. Elcott challenges American Jews to reflect on the following: What do Jews know about Christianity and Christian theology? Can they trust their Christian neighbors? What unique voice do we have to contribute? Do Jews nourish sacred narratives that could foster hatred and incite violence? And are Jews prepared to stand together with non-Jews against polarization? Elcott finds that contemporary American Jews do not know enough about Christianity to be able to respond effectively to allegations of antisemitism in *The Passion* and elsewhere. The lack of knowledge is mirrored by a lack of trust by Jews in their Christian neighbors despite the statistical reality that antisemitism in the United States is largely in decline. Moreover, the lack of trust precludes Jews from recognizing the progress that Christians have made in accounting for their histories of antisemitism; "there must be room for *Teshuvah*" (atonement), he writes, "for our Christian neighbors." Elcott worries that the battle against antisemitism has left many Jews bereft of any sense of what they are *for*, not simply what they are *against*. Moreover, while Jews are quick to criticize destructive ideas and narratives in the traditions of others, they are slow to admit to the presence of the same issues in Judaism, such as the commandment to annihilate Amalek and his descendants, whoever they may be. In the wake of *The Passion*, Elcott concludes, American Jews must join forces with others not only to fight against polarization but also to assert the values of pluralism and mutual respect.

John K. Roth finds himself acknowledging the dilemma of his indebtedness to the crucifixion and Christianity for creating Western civilization and his belief that the crucifixion was a necessary, albeit insufficient, condition for the Holocaust, which has been a central concern of his for more than three decades. Gibson's film, Roth finds, shares more with pre-Holocaust Christian animosity toward Jews than it does with the reconciliation between Christianity and Judaism that occurred after the Holocaust. Gibson's *Passion*, he finds, clearly ignores the moral imperatives of post-Shoah Christianity—to be sensitive to the potential dangers of religious antisemitism and to restate Christian teaching in such a way that it does not renew such hatreds. Roth demands of his fellow Christians that they measure their Christian beliefs against both their contributions to the Holocaust and their responsiveness to it. Christian identity, he concludes, cannot be understood apart from Jewish history or in isolation from contemporary Jewish life. In the wake of the Holocaust, he calls on Christians to bear witness to three things: their shared responsibility for the acts committed by Christians of generations past, their acknowledgment that Christians are followers of the Jew named Jesus, and their responsibility to choose life.

Elliot N. Dorff proposes a Jewish ethic of interreligious responsibility and describes the religious resources that exist within each tradition to realize this ethics in action. The ethics begin with an acknowledgment of God as creator, creator of all—including the other. That we are created in the divine image means that the other is also created in the divine image. To understand the truth status of other religions, he looks to history, philosophy, and theology. History reveals the dynamics of religion, its openness to change, and its ability to absorb the changes that are required to adjust to the world that is changing. Philosophy offers an epistemology of humility: we live by the truth as far as we can tell. We do not know and cannot tell all. Theology requires us to avoid triumphalism, to avoid harm to others, and to choose interpretations that respect others.

Kathryn J. S. Smith's chapter is a fitting conclusion to this section in that it answers calls by Roth and Dorff to bear witness and to do so with respect for the other. Smith explores the broad diversity within the evangelical Protestant community regarding perceptions of Jews and Israel and implications of those perceptions for the very meaning of the Christian tradition. She notes that even conservative evangelicals are beginning to pay greater attention to Jesus's Jewishness and, perhaps more important, to the idea that "social-historical Israel is a central theological category" for Christians. *The Passion*'s attention to "*Christus Victor*, not the Christ of history," she finds, hinders important needed advances in evangelical theology regarding the church and the Jews. Smith concludes where this book began and where indeed it should end: "there is much work to be done."

CHAPTER THIRTEEN
THEOLOGICAL BULIMIA: CHRISTIANITY AND ITS DEJUDAIZATION
Susannah Heschel

Every era gets the Jesus it wants. Gibson's Jesus is not simply the product of his own religious imagination; it is an effort to shape the American cultural moment. Why the Passion and not the birth, miracles, preachings, and Last Supper that constituted earlier films about Jesus's life? The torment of Jesus in Gibson's film—a detailed account of torture found nowhere in the Scriptures, an account that Gibson allegedly holds as sacred as Scripture—is the typical gruesome, prolonged, gory horror of Hollywood films. This American Jesus sanctifies a nationalistic memory of the horrific events of September 11: a Passion of America during which innocent, defenseless Americans were attacked over and over in a most brutal fashion in an unthinkable, unprecedented, unwarranted brutal assault that killed thousands of innocent people and left thousands of families bereft.

As much as Gibson's film reflects the American cultural moment, it also mirrors a central aporia of Christianity: the clash between Jesus's Jewishness and his originality. Since the rise of the quest for the historical Jesus, it has been clear that Jesus was a Jew whose faith was Judaism. Yet by placing Jesus and his teachings in their historical context, Christian theologians discovered that he had not taught anything new or unique but simply repeated the common religious ideas of the rabbis of his day. Jewish theologians often have stressed that point, suggesting that Jesus was a pious Jew and that Christians seeking the faith of Jesus rather than the religion about him ought to turn to Judaism.

The claim that Jesus was a Jew who did not teach a new religion aroused anger among some Christians in the nineteenth century who insisted instead that Jesus was not a Jew at all but an Aryan. That idea became especially popular in Germany in the early decades of the twentieth century and was embraced by those German Protestants who sought a Christian basis for their support of National Socialism.

Gibson's Jesus is not new. He reiterates the fascist myth of the "Aryan Jesus," which emerged in Germany, long before Hitler came to power, as a German Christian counterhistory to nineteenth-century Jewish historiography about Second Temple Judaism, early Christianity, and the personality of Jesus. The myth of the "Aryan Jesus" is marked by three motifs, each of which, however unintentionally, appear in Gibson's *Passion*: Jesus was no lamb of God but a macho man, he was racially Aryan and not Jewish, and he liberated himself from the constraints of Jewish doctrine. In *The Passion of the Christ*, Jesus appears as visually and linguistically different from those whose Jewishness is clearly marked, namely, the ugly priests with their hooked noses and dark, stringy hair (a stereotype that goes back to antiquity). This Jesus, like the Aryan Jesus, is a manly Christ who withstands a barrage of physical abuse. The film challenges the viewer: are you macho enough to watch this film, man enough to be a Christian? Finally, while Gibson claims to be theologically conservative, his film repeatedly violates the text of the Gospels by inventing a narrative of torture and murder that comes not from the New Testament but from medieval Passion narratives.

As Richard L. Rubenstein notes in chapter 15 of this volume, the conundrum of Christianity is its link to Judaism; the God of Christianity is a Jewish God, and the Scriptures of Christianity include the Hebrew Bible.[1] Christianity is rooted in a theological counterhistory of Judaism. It reads the Scriptures of Judaism—the Hebrew Bible—as foretelling the advent of Jesus and doctrines of Christianity. For example, Christians read the plural "we" in Genesis's creation story as a reference to the Trinity; the Prophets' descriptions of a forthcoming messiah are understood as anticipating and being fulfilled by Jesus's own life. Christian counterhistory of biblical Judaism developed in the early generations of the church.

If Jesus is a Jew whose message was that of Judaism, then he was neither an original religious teacher nor the founder of a new religion. At the same time, if the link to Judaism is severed, Christianity loses the bases of its theological claim that Jesus fulfills the role of God's promised messiah. If the link is maintained, Christianity's originality and difference from Judaism become murky, and antisemites might have a hard time being Christian. For Christians who see Jesus as the incarnate son of God who performed miracles and was resurrected from the dead, supernatural elements can suffice as a religious grounding. For liberal Protestants, however, who reject the dogma and the miraculous, all that is left is the historical figure of Jesus and his teachings.

The intimate theological relationship between Judaism and Christianity gave rise to counterhistories, efforts revise one another's religious and historical claims. Debates over Jesus's identity began in eighteenth-century Germany, a time and place when Jews and Christians increasingly wrote in a shared vernacular, read each other's theological writings, and used the figure of Jesus as the signifier through which they gave voice to their views of each other's religion. Earlier Jewish discussion of Christianity had taken place internally, with few Christians reading Jewish texts. Formal disputations inevitably ended unhappily for the Jews. While there was no notion of religious dialogue during the Middle Ages, religious influences abounded in both directions, and each religion helped shape the other in matters of ritual as well as belief.[2] There were public disputations and polemics as well as internal discussions of the other religion that were generally not flattering.

The great medieval Jewish philosophers Maimonides and Judah Halevi, however, had viewed Christianity as an important transmitter of monotheism to the pagan world, preparing the way for the Jewish messianic era.[3] These views began to resurface in writings such as those by Jacob Emden and Moses Mendelssohn. Emden, one of the most powerful Orthodox rabbis of eighteenth-century Germany, asserted that Jesus never intended to abolish Jewish law, nor had he made any claims to divinity; rather, it was the goal of both Jesus and Paul to undertake a mission to convince Gentiles to abide by the Noahide commandments.[4] Mendelssohn, Emden's contemporary, described his respect for Jesus as a moral personality, provided that nothing supernatural was ascribed to him.[5] Indeed, according to Mendelssohn, viewing Jesus as a moral teacher was in accord with Jesus's own self-understanding because he never sought to overturn Jewish law, let alone found a new religion or claim divinity for himself.[6]

The attention to Jesus was a new phenomenon for Jews, who previously had focused their attention primarily on Christian dogma.[7] Before the fourteenth century, Judaism legally classified Christianity as idolatry for its trinitarianism. Even as Christianity was becoming a world power, Jews adopted a counterhistory of Christianity as their strategy for interpreting Christian theological claims: Christianity is not original but plagiarized from Judaism, and Jesus was not a messiah but a pious Jew about whom the early Christians invented stories and deceived the world.[8] Thus, the politics of discussing Jesus were complex and often dangerous.[9] Jews had to exercise caution in what they said in public about Jesus, whether they claimed that Jesus was a fraud or a loyal Jew. Nonetheless, by the middle of the nineteenth century, Jesus had become a frequent presence in Jewish historical writings, and in Germany those writings came to form the crux of a debate between the two theological communities that would have major ramifications for both parties during the Nazi period.

Nineteenth-century European Protestant Christianity had entered the modern world with a new conviction: a desire to hold the faith of Jesus rather than the religion about Jesus. The core of Christianity was neither dogma, nor miracles, nor the supernatural but rather the actual historical figure of Jesus and the faith he held. Protestant theologians reconstructed that faith through the historical investigation of Christian origins, a task that would preoccupy them for decades, particularly in Germany. Among Protestants, however, there was no dialogue with contemporary Jews and only a vague awareness that the historical Jesus himself was Jewish. Jesus's Jewishness first became an issue when Protestants sought the religion of Jesus rather than the religion about Jesus.[10] The problem was all the sharper because Jewish theologians themselves were engaging in their own quest for the historically Jewish Jesus. Throughout this period, the historical investigations by both Christian and Jewish theologians were affected deeply by the traditional polemics that had defined their relationship for centuries. They proclaimed—but did not attain—objective scholarly inquiry.

The quest for the historical Jesus, as the effort came to be called, demanded a contextualization of Jesus's words and actions. The context was first-century Judaea. However, most nineteenth-century Christian theologians knew little about Judaism and even less about its Hebrew-language rabbinic texts of antiquity. Instead, they relied mostly on a set of stereotypes about Judaism's legalism and narrow nationalism that made it easy for them to present Jesus's faith as a sharp contrast to Judaism.

At the same time that this formal, historical study of Christian attitudes toward Judaism began, Jews started writing Jewish history. Jewish–Christian relations were central to the Jewish historical narrative. The leaders of the nineteenth-century *Wissenschaft des Judentums*—Heinrich Graetz, Abraham Geiger, Isaac Jost, Joseph Derenbourg, and Leopold Zunz—all wrote about Christianity and its attitudes and treatment of Judaism. Wide Jewish and Christian audiences, both scholarly and lay, read their books, and their arguments participated in the ongoing scholarship on both religions.

Liberal Pharisaism and the Aryan Jesus

Let me now turn to Abraham Geiger (1810–1874), whose life was devoted to examining Jesus and early Christianity within the framework of early Judaism and whose arguments constitute an intellectual revolt against the Christian colonization of Judaism that continued to prevail in modern historical scholarship and that had led to a vision of Judaism as the other whose negation confirms and even constitutes Christianity.[11] Geiger's effort to disrupt such patterns of Christian denigration of Judaism formed the basis of his scholarly endeavors.[12] He characterized Judaism from the Second Temple to the Mishnaic period as an ongoing conflict between Pharisees and Sadducees, which he found described in apocryphal, rabbinic, and New Testament texts and implied in subtle textual emendations and mistranslations of the Hebrew Scriptures. Geiger controversially defined the two tendencies, Pharisaic and Sadducean, as a liberal and a conservative proclivity, respectively. The Pharisees, far from being the figures of hypocrisy depicted in the New Testament, attempted to liberalize and democratize *halakhah*, Jewish religious law, to make its practice easier. The Sadducees, by contrast, represented the narrow interests of the priestly aristocratic elite seeking to preserve its privileges by a conservative reading of Jewish law. Each group set forth its own *halakhah*, but the Pharisaic reading became the governing law of rabbinic Judaism, and the Sadducean interpretation, crippled by the destruction of the Second Temple, was repressed by the victorious Pharisees.

Most controversial was Geiger's claim that the Pharisees were the liberalizers of Jewish law.[13] For Geiger, proof of the freedom of the Jewish spirit was precisely the literal-minded attentiveness of the ancients that motivated their emendations of the text and alterations of its meaning through translations. This showed not that the canon was hard and fixed but rather that in every generation it underwent adjustments in response to changes in religious and political circumstances.

In a series of lectures subsequently published under the title *Judaism and Its History*, as well as in a series of scholarly articles, Geiger presented Jesus as a Pharisee, an identification that infuriated Christian scholars.[14] He argued further that Jesus had taught nothing unique or original but simply had repeated the common wisdom of the rabbis of his day; this was why his message made no great impact on his Jewish listeners. Rather, Geiger concluded, Christianity's success came when Paul brought the pure monotheism of Judaism to the pagans and polluted it with polytheistic teachings, in doing so creating a religion—Christianity—that would be more palatable to the heathens.

Geiger's scholarly agenda ultimately became central to all subsequent New Testament scholarship. Studies of the Gospels within the context of rabbinic thought and legal argumentation have become the norm, and today no one has a problem with identifying Jesus as a liberal Pharisee. In his day, however, Geiger's analysis of Christianity's derivation from Judaism greatly troubled liberal Protestants. Having rejected the supernatural and miraculous elements of the New Testament, liberal Protestants were uncomfortable with the discovery that the historical Jesus was a Jew whose faith was Judaism. The scandal over this discovery was spurred not only by Jesus's association with a despised religion but also by the theological dilemma over defining the originality and uniqueness of his faith and what relation it bore, if any, to the religion called Christianity. Perhaps most troubling for Christians, Geiger identified the Reform Judaism he was helping create as an effort to recapture the liberalism that he claimed was the hallmark of Pharisaic Judaism. Christians seeking the faith of Jesus, Pharisaic Judaism, Geiger implied, should become Reform Jews.

Not surprisingly, Geiger's work evoked hostile responses from Christian scholars. The vituperative reaction to Geiger suggests that he touched a raw Christian nerve. His arguments were met with little serious criticism or refutation; at the time, no Protestant scholars were capable of debating his readings of rabbinic literature. Instead, Geiger was attacked primarily ad hominem.¹⁵ Among the younger generation of critical biblical scholars, the attacks by Heinrich Julius Holtzmann and Julius Wellhausen were the most devastating. Holtzmann attacked Geiger's presentation of Christianity as "the old resentment against the victorious daughter religion that lies deep in the hearts" of Jews.[16] Ultimately, Holtzmann charged, Geiger was attempting to "chisel away" the name of the founder of Christianity out of the tablets of history.[17]

The turn of the century saw the publication of two best-selling books that exerted enormous influence on German cultural life and on the subsequent course of German Protestant theology. Adolf von Harnack published the manifesto of liberal Protestantism, *The Essence of Christianity*, and Houston Stewart Chamberlain published the major treatise of racial theory and German cultural superiority, *Foundations of the Nineteenth Century*. Together, both books enabled a rebellion against the Jewish Jesus promoted by Geiger and others. Their revolt laid the groundwork for the myth of an Aryan Jesus, a myth that became institutionalized as a dejudaization of Christianity, during the Nazi years.[18]

Harnack saw Jesus as a rabbi who said nothing new or unique, but he argued that the essential message shared by Jesus and the rabbis had been smothered in Judaism with trivialities and absurdities so that it was, simply, lost in the dirt and rubble piled on by the rabbis. Harnack's attempt to salvage Jesus's originality comes by constructing a negative context within Judaism for the teachings shared by Jesus and the rabbis. Judaism is excessive, dark, and dirty; Christianity is vigorous, pure, and pristine.[19]

With Houston Stewart Chamberlain, we enter the world of German theological racism, a world that was already well developed by the mid-nineteenth century, and we find the first lengthy exposition of the evidence that Jesus not only wasn't Jewish but indeed in all likelihood was an Aryan. Through Chamberlain's *Foundations*, the theory of the Aryan Jesus gained its widest publicity.[20] The book was well received in Protestant circles; the *Christliche Welt* praised the book, including its racism.[21] It inspired influential figures from Kaiser Wilhelm II to Alfred Rosenberg.

Chamberlain, like all subsequent racial analysts of Jesus, was interested far less in the genealogy of Jesus's Aryan ancestry than in the allegedly Aryan spirit of his teachings. To establish Jesus's Aryan ancestry, Chamberlain relied on scholarly arguments concerning the Galilean population of the early first century, and he relied in particular on the work of the prominent Jewish historian Heinrich Graetz. To establish the Aryan spirit of Jesus, Chamberlain simply repeated classic Christian arguments, such as the claims of Jesus's intimacy with God, Jesus's war on Judaism, and essential religious difference.

Chamberlain's fundamental break, however, is his introduction of the Aryan element.[22] Chamberlain's argument is tortured and contradictory. He claims that Jesus was racially Aryan but influenced by the Jewish religion, while elsewhere he insists that Christianity is the religious antithesis to Judaism. Such confusion was deliberate and quite effective. As a best-seller that was in fact widely read, Chamberlain's *Foundations* spread the plausibility of an Aryan Christ, creating receptivity to the radical changes in liturgy, doctrine, and even the Bible that were engineered thirty years later.

Strikingly, many German Christian scholars of Judaism became actively involved in antisemitic propaganda on behalf of the Nazi regime, including Gerhard Kittel, Georg Beer, and Karl Georg Kuhn. Walter Grundmann, a former student of Kittel's and professor of New Testament at the University of Jena, became director of the Institute for the Study and Eradication of Jewish Influence on German Church Life, which produced a dejudaized New Testament and hymnal as well as theological literature declaring Jesus an enemy of the Jews and legitimating Nazi measures against the Jews.

Ironically, it was precisely their training and expertise in Judaism that gave Christian scholars of Judaism the authority in Nazi eyes to participate in antisemitic efforts. Dejudaization required an increasing spiritualization of the Christian message to remove it from any taint of the concrete Jewish. Not the specific teachings of Jesus but their spirit became the marker of his personality. Affirmations of Judaism, such as John's assertion that "salvation comes from the Jews,"[23] therefore must have been later interpolations, falsifications of the New Testament text by Jews who had infiltrated the early Jesus movement. What was authentic was not Jesus's appearance in the synagogue but his smashing the tables of the money changers in the Temple.

The Aryan Jesus was more than racially "not Jewish"; he was the Jews' sworn enemy. Indeed, "their" crucifixion of him was "proof" of their evil nature. He was also a manly Christ, a powerful, heroic warrior who fell victim to his implacable enemy, the Jews, and whose cause the Nazis now would take up in their fight against the Jews. Finally, by rejecting selected doctrines about Jesus, theologians easily could manipulate the gospel texts and revise them to construct a Jesus in their own image. During the Nazi period, Grundmann's institute published a dejudaized version of the New Testament, one that purged the Gospels of all positive Jewish references. Some Aryan proponents even suggested that Hitler was a reincarnation of Christ.[24] Knowledge of another religion was here put to diabolical use.

At a conference in 1942 sponsored by the Institute for the Study and Eradication of Jewish Influence on German Church Life, its director, Walter Grundmann, professor of New Testament at the University of Jena and a member of the Nazi Party, proclaimed, "Our Volk, which stands above all else in a struggle against the satanic powers of world Jewry for the order and life of this world, dismisses Jesus, because it cannot struggle against the Jews and open its heart to the king of the Jews."[25] His was a theology for the Holocaust, and it expressed the conflict: how could a Nazi worship a Jewish God? His answer was not to stop persecuting Jews in the name of Christianity but to remove everything Jewish from Christianity and make it a religion that would be comfortable to Nazi antisemites.

Alfred Rosenberg, among other Nazis, recognized the difficulty of eradicating the Jewish from the Christian and mocked the efforts of Christian theologians to carry it out. Remove the Jewish from Christianity, and there will be nothing left, he insisted. Even the institute's members were not able to answer the central question: what was the Jewish that required eradication? The Old Testament from the Bible, the Jewishness from Jesus, Paul from the New Testament, Hebrew from the hymnal—the task was enormous. With each effort, a new task appeared: in 1933, Krause's call for rejecting the Old Testament was shocking; in 1939, declaring Jesus an Aryan was less troubling; in 1944, removing the Pauline epistles was going too far—it suggested that the German people had been duped for two thousand years by a stinking Jew, Bishop Walther Schultz wrote.[26]

The Consequences of Dejudaization

Was Jesus the first Christian, or was he a Jew? This was the question at the core of the dialogue between Jews and Christians in modern Germany.

The question centered on three major questions: messianism, Jesus's observance of Jewish law, and Jesus's own teachings. For Jewish theologians beginning with Geiger, Jesus did not claim to be a messiah, nor did he fulfill the biblical expectations of a messiah; his followers attributed messianic claims to him incorrectly. He did not violate Jewish law but took a liberal position toward it, as did the Pharisees. His teachings were entirely Jewish and introduced no new ideas; Paul and other theologians—not Jesus—developed classic Christian doctrines, such as virgin birth and incarnation.

The twentieth-century German theologians discussed here easily refuted these conclusions—at least according to their own terms. Jesus does not call himself a Jewish messiah but the son of God, a Gentile appellation common to Galilean eschatology. Jesus teaches neither like the rabbis nor what they taught. His teachings emanated from himself, while the rabbis cited proof texts. He did not sit in schools, like the rabbis, but rather taught while wandering. The crux of his teaching was the rejection of the Law,[27] in contrast to the rabbis' slavish legalism. In short, Jesus's teachings have nothing to do with Judaism—any similarities are interpolations, Jewish–Christian falsifications of the New Testament; it is not the Jewish Sermon on the Mount that is original but Luke's Sermon on the Plain. The rabbis follow the law; Jesus follows his heart.

The irony is tragic: during the first years of the Jesus movement, Paul and his colleagues debated whether Gentile believers could join the movement without first having to become Jews like them. In the early and mid-twentieth century, German Christians sought to purge everything Jewish from Christianity. For Paul, the question was whether one had first to be Jewish before becoming Christian. In National Socialist Germany, the answer was clear: a good Christian *could not* be Jewish in any way. And there was no possibility of dialogue or any possibility of a Jewish response. As these views were being articulated, Jews were being isolated, impoverished, deported, and murdered.[28]

The conclusions of a study of theological animosity and scholarly dishonesty are difficult to draw. As a historian, I believe that it is important to stress Jewish scholarly efforts to build bridges to Christian scholars. Geiger sought to defend Judaism by writing a counterhistory of Christian counterhistory. That is, he did not offer a monophyletic rendition of the history of Jews and Judaism; rather, he presented Jewish history in the context of his own, original counterhistory of Christianity, with the focus on Jesus and Christian origins. Geiger's efforts had a variety of motives, to be sure, including providing a historical justification for the reform of Judaism, but prime among them was ending Christian anti-Judaism with the challenge of a counterhistory of a Jewish Jesus. Geiger's arguments presented his Christian colleagues with a new challenge to their counterhistory: awareness of their ignorance of a vast quantity of primary source materials—rabbinic literature—and hence recognition of the limitations of their historical reconstructions. After Geiger and after the Shoah, Christian theologians no longer could present as counterhistory the argument that that Judaism was a sterile, petrified religion and that Jesus rejected Judaism; now they simply were false history. Persistent Christian anti-Judaism no longer reflected involuntary ignorance but rather involved a deliberate effort to pass off a false record as true.

That Gibson is popularizing a return to the most egregiously false depictions of Jews in his film indicates the failure of scholarly findings to translate to the pews. Just as troubling is the ease with which Gibson, under the veil of piety, can ignore the moral imperatives of a post-Shoah Christianity and reproduce the worst antisemitic stereotypes: Judas grubbing for his silver and fat Jewish bodies in contrast to lean Christian ones and graceful, athletic Roman ones.[29] The film dwells on the Roman leaders less to exalt Rome than provide a contrast to the Jews of Jerusalem.

Jesus's identity in the film is not entirely clear. Is he a Jew or a Christian? Despite the gospel attestations, Gibson's *Passion* makes no positive connection between Jesus and the Jews of the film or to Jewish institutions, such as Temple and synagogue. The uncertainty of identity is precisely what makes him so vulnerable to interpretation and also to gender politics: he is wounded, pierced, bleeding, victimized, and vulnerable, all classic attributes of the feminine—is he indeed a man? A similar question can be asked of his Jewishness: after the Jewish authorities and mob assault him, repudiate him, arrange his torture, and demand his death in place of a convicted murderer, is Gibson's Jesus a Jew at all?

Such antimimetic efforts occur—most significantly—when the histories of the two adversaries are connected intimately, as in the case of Christian and Jewish origins, "because the forger of a counteridentity of the other renders his own identity to depend on it."[30] Christianity depends on Judaism for its identity and always has. What is the meaning of the God of Israel or the new Israel if there is no people Israel? To wipe out the people of Israel may be a Christian fantasy of release from theological obligation, but it would bring such moral opprobrium that it ultimately would be an act of Christian self-destruction.

Why, then, is dejudaization pursued by Gibson and others? Modern theologians often refer to Judaism as the mother religion and to Christianity as the daughter religion. The choice of gender may be more useful than theologians realize. The Oedipal struggle that governs father–son relations carries with it a pattern of the son's conquest and the father's defeat.[31] However, the greater complexity of mother–daughter relations may offer an even more useful metaphor. As Marianne Hirsch explains, mothers become targets of disidentification while at the same time objects of desire.[32] The body determines the figure of the mother more intensely than it does that of the father, and the multiplicity of female positions is obvious in the figure of the mother, who always is both mother and daughter, both physical mother and abstract maternal ideal, both the source of the daughter's life and the perceived threat to the daughter's individuation. The daughter knows herself in her mother; as Jacqueline Rose writes, "The point of origin is the maternal body, an undifferentiated space, and yet one in which the girl child recognises herself. The girl then has to suppress or devalue that fullness of recognition in order to line up with the order of the phallic term."[33]

Christianity recognizes itself, its Jesus, within Judaism but has to suppress that recognition in order to differentiate itself from Judaism. That suppression ultimately is impossible because Judaism always remains within Christianity. The mother is within the daughter; Judaism's witness, its knowledge of Jesus that renders him neither original nor Christian, cannot be purged.[34] For all its efforts at a theological exclusiveness from Judaism, Christianity ends up making Judaism key to understanding its history and central tenets. Thus, for Christianity, Jewishness defines the rubrics of its destiny through the effort to deny its presence.

Judaism's presence gives rise to a longing for its absence, a desire for its eradication, for a Christianity that can be defined on its own terms, as the source of its own origins. However, that absence is not attained easily. Indeed, through the very recognition of the problem, the problem was created. Recognizing the presence of the Jewish brought with it a desire for its eradication as well as the fear that such eradication might leave nothing to Christianity. The enemy was within, and expurgating it seemed the best solution. Dejudaizing Christianity was a kind of theological bulimia, enacting a myth with long roots in Western culture.[35] Enacted on the symbolic level of theological discourse, the dejudaization of Christianity is an example of the daughter religion, Christianity, engaging in a constant, repeated process of taking in the symbolic mother, Judaism, and then regurgitating her. This is an attempt by Christians to purge themselves of a Jewish mother whose presence can never be fully eradicated from Christian theology, even as the Jewish figures who created Christianity—Jesus, Paul, the apostles—as well as the Jewish ideas that define Christianity—messiah, salvation, election, Israel—constantly are reiterated in order to shape Christian identity.

If theology is as much about politics as it is about religion, what, then, is the Gibson film trying to instill in us? Gibson surrounds his Jesus with sexual deviants: the androgynous Satan, the vulgar transvestite Herod, the repugnant homosocial clan of Jewish priests. Indeed, the only heterosexual couple in the film are Pilate and Claudia, representing the Roman Empire. Perhaps Gibson is inviting American viewers—citizens of a new empire—to identity with Mr. and Mrs. Pilate ("*Roman* Gothic"?) and, like them, to overcome skepticism and embrace Jesus. Their nonbiblical anguished ambivalence and discussions of "truth" render Claudia and Pontius the quintessential baby-boomer "seekers" of their day.[36] The historical falsity of Gibson's rendition is not far from the general disdain for history that seems to have pervaded contemporary American culture.

Whose Passion are we witnessing, we citizens of a country at war in Afghanistan and Iraq and inflicting horrific civilian suffering there? Might American viewers of Gibson's film regard Jesus's suffering as representative of the suffering of those who are casualties of American bombs? Will they identify with Pilate, who ordered Jesus crucified (despite the ambiguities of the film, which contradict the text of the New Testament)? Alternatively, will we watch the film as an expression of our own suffering, as innocent American victims of our allegedly implacable Muslim enemies? Johannes Hempel, professor of Old Testament at the University of Berlin and a member of Grundmann's institute, declared in 1942, "The opposition between the Third Reich and the Jews is a struggle for life and death."[37] Similarly, George Bush declares ours a war of "civilization against terrorism." Is September 11 to be sanctified, made into a sacred Passion that will justify our "war on terror"?

SUSANNAH HESCHEL

Notes

1. See Rubenstein (chapter 15 in this volume).

2. Although Jews endured eras of persecution, expulsion, forced conversion, and ghettoization, there also were long periods during which Jews and Christians coexisted in neighborly and peaceful relations. Indeed, relations often were intimate; Jewish women served as midwives and Christian women as wet nurses, often sharing baking ovens, if not entire households.

3. Maimonides, *Guide of the Perplexed* 3:54; *Eight Chapters*, chap. 5; *Mishneh Torah* Hilkhot Melakhim 11:4 in uncensored version, cited in Berger 1990, 149–68. See also Maimonides, *Epistle to Yemen*.

4. Cited in Novak 1989, 178 n.7; Falk 1982, 108–9; Greenberg 1978, 351–63.

5. Moses Mendelssohn, Letter to Lavater 15 January 1771, in G. B. Mendelssohn 1843–1845, 3:102–6; see also Altmann 1973, 204–5.

6. Mendelssohn further claimed that Jesus did nothing that would evoke hostility within the Jewish community and that the Jews cannot be held responsible for his trial and execution. See Catchpole 1971.

7. Ancient and medieval Jewish views of Christianity ranged from mockery to the highest respect, that of mimicry. They suggest that Jesus had learned magical secrets from the Egyptians or had stolen the ineffable name of God from the Jerusalem Temple. See Krauss 1902; Ginzberg 1928, nos. 34 and 35; Schlichting 1982.

8. Maimonides (*Epistle to Yemen*), however, argued that since Christians bring monotheism to the pagan world, they have a role in the advent of the Jewish messiah.

9. For example, Moses Mendelssohn asked, "And Jesus a Jew?—And what if, as I believe, he never wanted to give up Judaism? One can only imagine where this remark would lead me" (1770, in Bamberger 1971–, 7:59; cited in Hess 2002, 91).

10. The problem of Jesus's relationship to the Judaism of his day was intrinsic to the quest for the historical Jesus, though many historians of that quest, such as Albert Schweitzer (1906, 1910), fail to mention it.

11. See my two articles on Christianity as a theological colonization of Judaism: Heschel 1999 and Heschel 2004. Indeed, colonialist patterns prevail in the debates over Jewish emancipation in the writings of theologians from Michaelis and Paulus onward; see also Hess 1998. Christian theological studies that denigrate Judaism are, like Said's "orientalism," efforts "to control, manipulate, even to incorporate, what is a manifestly different (or alternative and novel) world" (Said 1978, 12).

12. Geiger 1857, 1860 (1928). His first book (1833) had argued that some of Islam's central teachings derive from rabbinic literature.

13. This assertion contradicted existing Christian stereotypes about the Pharisees, who, according to Christian polemicists, had falsified Talmudic texts and Targumim in order to avoid what otherwise would be proofs for the truth of Christianity. Writers from the church fathers onward made the contradictory charge that the literal-minded Jews were so absorbed in the letter of the biblical text that they could not grasp its deeper meaning, let alone appreciate its spirit or see the fulfillment of its promises in the figure of Jesus. This charge came to flourish within Lutheran theology.

14. Geiger 1864, 1865, 1910.

15. The review by Germany's grand old man of biblical studies, Heinrich Ewald (1858, 94–275), reflected commonly held scholarly prejudices of the day: it praised the absence of animosity toward Christianity but criticized Geiger's historiography. Ewald later charged that Geiger and his colleagues were "nothing but Pharisees and do not intend to be anything else" (Ewald 1864, 5:477 n.1). Franz Delitzsch, long active in evangelizing to Jews, attacked Geiger for preferring the Sage Rabbi Hillel to Jesus (Delitzsch 1866).

16. Holtzmann 1865, 225–37, 228.

17. Holtzmann 1865, 231.

18. Chamberlain argued that Jesus was not a Jew by race but an Aryan. Harnack argued that Jesus was Jewish, but his message was essentially Christian; moreover, he criticized Chamberlain's views of Jews and did not share his antisemitism. Nonetheless, Jewish theologians harshly criticized Harnack's work both for his negative views of rabbinic Judaism and for his effort to detach Jesus from Judaism.

19. Harnack's book prompted an outcry from German Jewish scholars, but their protests served only to annoy Harnack's Protestant admirers, who turned his book into an international best-seller. Geoffrey Field (1981, 239) has argued that "Chamberlain's combination of racism and theology illustrated for Jews the hostile uses to which Protestant research could be put, but it also appealed emotionally to some Christians angered by Jewish criticism of Harnack and other scholars." A number of the contributions to this volume address these dichotomies as they appear in Gibson's *Passion*; see, for example, Rubenstein (chapter 15) and Kathryn Smith (chapter 20). Both Silk's account in chapter 1 of the attempt to launch a culture war and William J. Cork's accounts in chapter 2 of the attacks on Gibson's Jewish critics echo the attacks on Harnack's Jewish critics.

20. Field 1981, 183.

21. Field 1981, 183.

22. Never clearly defined, the Aryan is shorthand for the German and is identified with spiritual qualities. Entering the northern kingdom of biblical Israel after its destruction by Assyria, Aryans brought a cultural framework antithetical to

Judaism, and Jesus was born and raised in the heart of Aryan Galilee. Like most racial theorists, Chamberlain gives us little positive information about the Aryan culture and spends most of his energy defining its antithesis, Judaism, as a religion of formalism, abstract materialism, and absence of spiritual imagination—indeed, so degenerate that it provides the perfect soil for a new conception of God to take root (1911, 1:224). For Jews, messianism is purely political and serves the Jewish "will to world domination" (Field 1981, 189).

23. John 4:22.
24. Leffler 1935, 29.
25. Grundmann 1941.
26. Schultz 2 August 1944.
27. See, for example, Matthew 23.
28. After the war, very few of the theologians active in dejudaizing Christianity and spreading vile lies about Judaism lost their positions. It was not difficult to find Judaism characterized as a violent and immoral religion. See, for example, Pastor Gruber's claim that Germany was merely the instrument of God's wrath toward the Jews (Rubenstein 1966, 53–56; 1992, 9–13).
29. See Roth (chapter 18 in this volume).
30. Funkenstein 1993, 48.
31. See Rubenstein (chapter 15 in this volume).
32. Hirsch 1989.
33. Rose 1986, 78.
34. This is a fantasy of Christian theology: there is no Judaism outside Christianity, no religion other than the Christian. However, to paraphrase Rose (1986, 131), that fantasy ultimately fails because even as Judaism becomes a "symptom" of Christianity, it persists as the place where Christians read their destiny.
35. For example, Kronos, the father of Zeus, swallowed all his children except Zeus, and when Zeus grew up, he overthrew his father, forcing him to vomit up all the sons (gods) he had swallowed. Far more commonly, however, it is not the father who vomits his children but the daughter who engages in a constant, repeated process of taking in the symbolic mother and then regurgitating her.
36. See Leslie Smith (chapter 3 in this volume).
37. Hempel 1942–1943, 212. See also Weber's 2000 biography of Hempel.

CHAPTER FOURTEEN
A MARCH OF PASSION; OR, HOW I CAME TO TERMS WITH A FILM I WASN'T SUPPOSED TO LIKE
Stephen R. Haynes

Friday Night at the Stadium

At the end of February, I received two phone calls from friends who are also editors. Both asked if I wanted to write something about Mel Gibson's *The Passion of the Christ*, one for this book, the other for a website aimed at religious seekers. To that point, I had followed the controversy closely but had avoided actually seeing the film. On that Friday afternoon, however, it became clear that if I was going to develop anything like an informed opinion of the *Passion* phenomenon, I was going to have to go to the theater to see it. Whether or not I would ultimately write something for publication, I needed to be able to answer those who asked if I thought the movie was worth seeing. And I had to decide whether I would take my own children.

That Friday afternoon in late February, I decided to see *The Passion of the Christ*. Cleverly, I thought, I would avoid the suburban theaters and head to a local art house whose patrons were less religious and less likely to respond to hype in the mainstream media. Since Friday evening is a prime moviegoing time, I drove by the theater around 5:30 P.M., where a sign on the door informed me that the 7:00 P.M. showing of *The Passion* was sold out. Determined to see the film before I lost my nerve, I purchased a ticket to the 7:15 showing at the Cineplex downtown—this time on a near-IMAX-proportioned screen. Since "big screen" tickets were the same price as "regular screen" tickets, the big screen it was.

I arrived at the theater around 6:45 and found a seat in the "stadium." Although the theater had over 500 seats, it was already nearly full. I found a seat close enough to see the screen through middle-aged eyes and far enough back to observe most of my fellow moviegoers. My first observation was the diverse makeup of the crowd—which I estimated to be about half black and half white. This racial balance surprised me; I had the impression from media reports and interviews that the film's main audience was suburban whites. Another thing that surprised me was the number of children in the theater. In the row behind me, a mother had brought four youngsters, none of them older than twelve. I found it difficult to believe that this family or any of the others present were in the habit of seeing R-rated movies together. Tonight was obviously a special occasion.

Ten minutes before the movie was scheduled to begin, two theater employees walked onto the stage in front of the screen and began to address the crowd. After welcoming us, they announced that they would be giving away movie passes to those who were the first to correctly answer Bible trivia questions. No one seemed at all surprised by this, and the contest began. The first question was, "Who can name the Ten Commandments in order?" Dozens of hands went up. A white teenager was recognized, but she stumbled over the stuff about graven images. The staff called on a little black girl who could not have been more than eight years old. She rattled off the commandments in order without hesitation or even punctuation. The crowd cheered, and she came forward to claim her movie passes. The next question was, "Which Psalm is the longest?" A man in front of me shouted, "119," but he was disqualified for failing to raise his hand. Again a little girl benefited from the miscue. The third question was something about the feet of the Son of Man. Before I could ask for clarification, someone answered the question and claimed the passes.

The projector began to roll, and, except for having my chair periodically kicked by the child sitting behind me, the next two hours were uneventful. Afterward, the crowd filed out in reverent silence. I did not notice anyone crying, but the silent faces revealed a certain degree of shock. As for me, I thought the whipping scene was excessively brutal and was annoyed by the slow-motion stumble-and-fall scenes on the road to Golgotha, but otherwise I was pleasantly surprised by how the movie kept my attention. More than anything, though, I was curious about the Bible trivia quiz. Whose idea was it? Was it offered before every showing? I lingered outside the theater until I found the young black woman who had administered the quiz. In response to my questions, she acknowledged that the quiz was her idea but that as an assistant manager it was her job to come up with ways of getting the crowd involved when "big movies" were running. She found the questions on the Internet, she said.

A Weekend at the Beach

In the days after viewing the movie, I became increasingly ambivalent about it. The movie had much to commend it. It was well acted and photographed. Moreover, the extrabiblical material it contained made it less predictable than other Jesus films. Of course, the anti-Jewish themes that were so prominent in Gibson's version of the Passion bothered me. But was the movie antisemitic? And what does "antisemitic" mean in reference to a film about the Passion of Christ?

While these questions were bouncing around in my mind, I took my family to St. Petersburg Beach, Florida, where I was to attend a "think tank" on antisemitism.[1] I knew it would be an intimate interfaith gathering that would take seriously the religious dimensions of a problem that has been at the center of my research.[2] My parents happen to live in the St. Petersburg area. The night before the think tank began, they met us for dinner at a restaurant not far from the conference hotel. Though she was sitting at the other end of the table, my mother could not resist asking me whether I had seen "the movie." My parents see very few movies, primarily because of Hollywood's penchant for violence and profanity, but they chose to see *The Passion* because of its potential to inspire. Despite their initial reservations regarding the movie's violent content, the film pleasantly surprised them.

"I don't think I ever really understood how Jesus had suffered *for me*," my mother said. This from a woman who has read and heard the Passion story for nearly seventy years.

And what did I think of *The Passion*? I said that my opinions were still in formation but that I, too, had found things to like.

Picking up my conference folder the following morning, I noticed that someone had copied and stuffed half a dozen critical reviews of *The Passion* into one of the pockets. A perusal of the titles indicated that none was positive. At the think tank's opening session, Franklin Littell reminded us that the Shoah was the "definitive event of our age" and that some churches were "still mired in the mud of venerable errors." As he surveyed recent expressions of antisemitism in the Christian world, he noted, in a reference to Gibson's *Passion*, "Nazi-type attacks on the Jews are still a profitable enterprise." Even allowing for Littell's characteristic hyperbole, I found this remark outrageous. How could linking *The Passion* with the "Final Solution" help scholars "think" about antisemitism and the Holocaust? But the comment went unchallenged by the thirty or so scholars in attendance.

Elie Wiesel's remarks about the film were more sensible and contextual. He claimed that Jewish–Christian relations had never been so good, and he worried that they would be sabotaged by *The Passion*. "Why would Mel Gibson do this?" he asked plaintively.

At lunch, I found myself sitting between two Jewish participants. When the conversation inevitably turned toward Gibson's movie, I listened attentively.

Was it antisemitic? Absolutely.

Would it worsen the situation of Jews? Without question.

Then my colleagues began to criticize technical aspects of the film: the acting was terrible, the special effects were laughable, the casting was racist, and so on. There was no point in challenging these claims, which were obviously more emotional than rational, but I did find the courage to pose a question for those sitting around me.

"Do you think the film is more anti-Jewish than the Gospels?" I asked. Noting a temporary silence, I answered the question myself. On the one hand, the film includes some extrabiblical material that may enhance the anti-Jewishness already inherent in the Passion story. On the other hand, two of the most virulently anti-Jewish texts in the canonical Gospels are conspicuously absent from the English-subtitled version of the film. These are from the Gospel of Matthew—"Then the people as a whole answered, 'His blood be on us and on our children!'"—and the Gospel of John—"You are from your father the devil, and you choose to do your father's desires."[3] Furthermore, one aspect of the gospel accounts of Jesus's life that has contributed to Christian antisemitism is the anachronistic sense one gets of "Jews" and "Christians" in conflict. In my view, however, the movie does a fairly good job of communicating that the characters in the story are either Romans or Jews, some of the latter followers of Jesus the Nazarene.

My lunch mates disagreed with this analysis but offered little evidence for doing so. The discussion regained its emotional pitch when someone talked of feeling personally assaulted by Gibson's Jew hatred. Adjectives like "obscene" and "pornographic" flew over coffee and strawberry cheesecake. I returned to the conference genuinely puzzled by these reactions. The movie was what it was. It wasn't great, but neither was it a "Nazi-like attack on the Jews" that showcased terrible acting.

However, in the afternoon session, what I had thought was anti-Gibson paranoia began to make sense to me. The agenda included a series of reports from around the globe regarding trends in attitudes toward Jews. We heard first from a spokesperson from the United Kingdom, Jane Clements of the UK Council of Christians and Jews, who lamented that things are worse for Jews in Britain than they have been in fifty years. While the Jewish population is actually decreasing, Clements said, popular estimates continue to run twelve to fifteen times higher than the actual figure. She reported a 13 percent increase in antisemitic incidents during the past eighteen months, and she spoke of British Jews who "had their bags packed." The prevalence of "salon antisemitism," Clements concluded, was something that could not be imagined five years ago.

A report by Ilya Altman, director of the Russian Research and Educational Holocaust Center, described a small and fearful Jewish population watching uncomfortably as Jew-baiting politicians sought to outdo each other. Anna Rosmus, Germany's "nasty girl,"[4] described Arab fundamentalists and neo-Nazis marching together by the thousands, united only by their common hatred for Jews. Shimon Samuels, director of the Simon Wiesenthal Center in Paris, offered more of the same in his report from France.

"Three years ago," Samuels said wistfully, "everything seemed possible." But following 9/11, the second intifada, the UN-sponsored Durban conference on racism, and academic and cultural embargoes against Israel, the world climate had become very dangerous for Jews. Samuels made an observation that put all the misgivings about Gibson's *Passion* into perspective. His concern about the film was focused not on the United States, he said, but on Latin America, eastern Europe, and the Middle East. When the film hits these places, he warned, it could ignite a volatile mixture of ideologies that are hostile to Jews and to Israel.⁵ In his closing comments, Elie Wiesel reflected the pall these reports had left over the conference. He observed that antisemitism had once again become a serious threat. It is possible, he warned, that ancient ghosts were waking up, ancient threats becoming real.

Monday Evening at the Dinner Table

After the conference, we spent the weekend with my parents. My mood was somber, my feelings about *The Passion* more conflicted than ever. Aware of my commitment to Jewish–Christian relations and familiar with the controversy surrounding the movie, my mother asked the question I had been anticipating.

"Do you think the movie was antisemitic?" Like many questions asked over the family dinner table, this one had a complicated subtext. My parents know that scholars and liberals (they regard me as both) are critical of the presumed anti-Jewish tendencies in traditional versions of Christian faith. However, they resent such criticisms since they are traditional theologically but progressive socially. For them, Christian faith simply has no place for prejudice. In fact, my parents' influence probably is the reason I have dedicated much of my scholarly career to studying interracial and interfaith relations. My first encounter with living Judaism came when my parents took my siblings and me to the home of some Jewish friends for a Passover Seder meal. Although I was no more than ten years old at the time, the experience deeply informed my understanding of Jews and Judaism, as did the messages of tolerance and respect I heard from my parents throughout my childhood.

Given their exposure to explicit racial and religious prejudice during their own upbringing, the inclusive legacy my parents passed along to my brother, my sisters, and me is a remarkable gift. Thus, sitting at the family dinner table, I wanted to communicate my concerns about the film without accusing my parents of antisemitism simply because they found the movie inspiring.

"Didn't the portrayal of Jews in the film bother you?" I asked. My mother said she blamed "sinful humanity," including but not limited to Jews, for the death of Jesus. I tried to explain that the logic of the Gospels—and the film—was to concentrate blame on the Jews and to make them the emblem and agent of "sinful humanity." My mother responded that for her at least, casting blame was not a central theme in the story. When the conversation turned toward their grandchildren, I was relieved.

The next morning, my father returned from a meeting at my parents' church with a copy of a book the minister had ordered in bulk in connection with Gibson's movie. John Piper's *The Passion of Jesus Christ* is a compilation of "fifty reasons why Christ suffered and died."[6] I accepted the book as my father's gift and read through it on the plane ride home. Piper claims to let "the Bible speak" as he catalogs the reasons for Jesus's death in a series of two-page chapters. Most of Piper's reasons why Jesus "came to die" are consistent with classical Christian theology: "to absorb the wrath of God," "to make us holy, blameless, and perfect," "to reconcile us to God," "to free us from the slavery of sin," "to rescue us from final judgment," and so on. In this sense, the book is unremarkable.

The reason my father wanted me to read the book did not become clear until I turned to the introduction, titled "The Christ, the Crucifixion, and the Concentration Camps." Piper begins by arguing that "the ultimate answer to the question, Who crucified Jesus? is: God did."[7] He stresses that "since God meant [the crucifixion] for good," its meaning lies in divine purpose rather than human cause. "God himself was the chief Actor in the death of his son, so that the main question is not, which humans brought about the death of Jesus? But, what did the death of Jesus bring about for humans."[8]

In his effort to sever the nerve of Christian anti-Judaism, Piper goes further. In a section called "The Passion of Christ and the Passion of Auschwitz," Piper writes,

> It is a tragedy that the story of Christ's passion has produced anti-Semitism against Jews and crusading violence against Muslims. We Christians are ashamed of many of our ancestors who did not act in the spirit of Christ. No doubt there are traces of this plague in our own souls. But true Christianity—which is radically different from Western culture, and may not be found in many Christian churches—renounces the advance of religion by means of violence.... The way of the cross is the way of suffering. Christians are called to die, not kill, in order to show the world how they are loved by Christ.... It is not Christian to humiliate or scorn or despise or persecute with prideful putdowns, or pogroms, or crusades, or concentration camps. These were and are, very simply and horribly, disobedience to Jesus Christ.[9]

What Christian could disagree with such sentiments? Piper goes on to highlight the Jewish–Christian connection by linking Jesus's passion and the Holocaust: "The denial that Christ was crucified is like the denial of the Holocaust . . . Jesus Christ suffered unspeakably and died. So did Jews."[10] Piper cites Wiesel's *Night*,[11] where he finds encouragement for "link[ing] Calvary and the concentration camps." Once that link has been established, Piper cannot help but wonder if there is a way

> that Jewish suffering may find, not its cause, but its final meaning in the suffering of Jesus Christ? Is it possible to think, not of Christ's passion leading to Auschwitz, but of Auschwitz leading to an understanding of Christ's passion? . . . Perhaps a generation of Jewish people, whose grandparents endured their own noxious crucifixion, will be able, as no others, to grasp what happened to the Son of God at Calvary.[12]

The anti-Judaism in Piper's book is complex and, like many Christian attempts to understand Jewish destiny, riddled with ambivalence.[13] On the one hand, Piper acknowledges the church's historic role in persecuting Jews, eschews Jew hatred, and denies (or at least overlooks) Jewish responsibility for the death of Jesus. On the other hand, he affirms supersessionism in his recital of reasons for Jesus's death ("to cancel the legal demands of the law against us," "to abolish circumcision and all rituals as the basis of salvation," "to bring the Old Testament priesthood to an end and become the eternal high priest"), and he reasserts the classic hope that the Jews' perennial suffering will bring them to Christ. It is easy to understand why this book instantly became popular among evangelical Christians engulfed in the controversy over Gibson's *Passion*. Because it simultaneously denies the deicide charge and asserts the spiritual bankruptcy of Judaism, the book deflects the charge that Christians regard Jews as "Christ killers" while confirming traditional, "biblical" notions of Jewish destiny.

When we returned home, I browsed through the stack of newspapers that our neighbor had saved for us. The front page of the Business section of the *Memphis Commercial Appeal* featured an article by Wendi C. Thomas, a young African American political columnist whose opinions I had come to respect. Her column, titled "Jews Didn't Kill Jesus; He Gave His Life for Us," offered her perspective on the purportedly antisemitic nature of Gibson's *Passion*:

> I was raised in Christian churches. And when I say raised, I mean that until I was 18, I was in church virtually every time someone took the pulpit or an offering.
> And never have I heard and never was I taught that Jews killed Jesus.
> Not at Raleigh Assembly of God, where I grew up. Not in the Apostolic church I attended in college. Not in the Baptist church where I was baptized. Not in any of the nondenominational churches I've attended since.
> Maybe some pastors preach that Jews are Jesus-killers, but where those churches are, I don't know.[14]

Thomas's conclusion was that when we focus on who killed Jesus, we miss the point that "Jesus was born to die, as a perfect sacrifice for a sinful world." *The Passion* is valuable, she wrote, inasmuch as it reaffirms that "Jesus wasn't *killed*. Jesus *gave up* his life—for Jews and Gentiles and the sins of the world."[15] While I found Thomas's dismissal of the movie's anti-Jewish potential naive, it was reassuring to hear someone who has spent a lifetime in traditional Christian churches report that she never had been exposed to the canard that Jews are Christ killers.

A few days later, my mother copied me on an e-mail message dealing with *The Passion's* R rating:

> The "R" of course is because of the violence, the gore. In movie terms "R" stands for RESTRICTED, but in this movie "R" stands for RELEVANT, for REALISTIC, for it REALLY happened for a REASON because we were REBELLIOUS we needed a REDEEMER, we needed to be RECONCILED, we needed to be RECOVERED, we needed to be REGENERATED. Jesus needed to be REJECTED so that we could have a RELATIONSHIP not just a RELIGION. The "R" is to REMIND us to REMEMBER what Jesus did to REMOVE our sin to RENDER Satan powerless, to RESCUE us from eternity in hell. The "R" rating is to show that Jesus was RESPONSIBLE for giving you REST. As a RESULT of his death Jesus RETIRED your debt. The "R" rating means that some will be REPULSED, some will REFUSE to believe, some will be RELUCTANT, some will think you are RIDICULOUS in believing that a death was REQUIRED. The "R" rating means that the RESULT of sin has been REVERSED and now through faith in Christ your REWARD is eternity and you are now RIGHTEOUS before God because you have RECEIVED him as the RULER

of your soul. What a REVOLUTIONARY and RADICAL solution to REDEEM mankind.¹⁶

A spirited defense of the film, I thought, and one that carefully avoided referring to the Jews' or anyone else's RESPONSIBILITY for Jesus's death.

Tuesday Afternoon at the Office

Before leaving for Florida, I had agreed to serve on a Rhodes College discussion panel devoted to *The Passion of the Christ*. It was a good idea, I thought, to help our students process the conflicting things they were hearing about the film. While my own thoughts about *The Passion* and the reasons it was so loved and hated were still evolving, I felt obligated to say something intelligible to the undergraduates I knew would turn out in droves.

Gail Streete, a colleague in New Testament whose rage—at the movie, Mel Gibson, his father, and the movie's marketing campaign—was poorly concealed, led off the session. She called Gibson's use of the New Testament "blasphemous" and a "bastardization of the Gospels." She offered to share with any student who was interested a document called "31 Ways Gibson's Film Is Not Faithful to the New Testament." The next panelist was Rabbi Harry Danziger, who teaches part time in our department. He described the movie as "sheer sadistic violence and cruelty" and referred to its "vicious portrayal of Jews." He worried that the film presented Jews with the same dangers as those traditionally associated with Passion plays, and he noted that a Jew watching this movie could not help but ask why God would demand such suffering. The third panelist was Patrick Gray, a junior New Testament scholar who displayed considerable courage in dissenting from the scholarly consensus about *The Passion*. He reminded us that Jesus's suffering is quite important to most Christians, whose emphasis tends to be on the necessity of Jesus's death rather than on assigning responsibility for it. Citing Josephus and other first-century sources, Gray argued that New Testament accounts of Jesus's last hours are not as implausible as some scholars have argued.

Finally, it was my turn to speak. When I said there were positive things about the film, the eyes of some students lit up. It was better than most films in the genre. Besides, it had given religion scholars a level of attention and credibility of which they usually only dream. The film was no more anti-Jewish than the canonical Gospels, I said, but the Gospels *are* quite anti-Jewish. Most Christian fans of the film simply had not come to terms with this problem. At this point, I noticed that the light in students' eyes had begun to dim.

Referring to Rabbi Danziger's comments, I noted that while much of the film's violence is gratuitous, it is precisely the violent aspect of the story that speaks to many Christians. Recapping what I had heard in Florida about the growth of antisemitism throughout the world, I suggested that the fears expressed about the film in the contemporary United States may become reality as it makes its way into other markets.

Saturday in the Park

I felt good about my contributions to the panel, but I still had no idea what I would write about *The Passion*. How could I resolve the feelings about the film that kept me suspended between criticism and defense? How would I acknowledge the dangerous effects of Christian anti-Judaism and yet maintain empathy for those who embraced a movie that reiterated the very images on which this tradition is based? And how to respond to my parents—and many others—who loved the movie but reported being unmoved by its portrayal of Jews as the prime agents in a plot to eliminate Jesus?

The time had come to examine my own psyche for the roots of my dilemma. I did so in the place where I often receive clarity—in the park near our house. While running through the forest trails last Saturday, the roots of my ambivalence began to reveal themselves. Gradually it became evident that it was not simply empathy for religious folk or respect for my parents that led me to a semidefense of *The Passion*. It was my own deep-seated affinity for images of a God who suffers. This affinity reveals itself in my cinematographic preferences as much as in my research interests.

There is a scene in *The Mission*[17] where Robert DeNiro's character (a Jesuit novice) defies his superior (played by Jeremy Irons). DeNiro's penance is to climb a rock cliff with a bag of military implements tied around his waist. It is a painful and difficult climb; as DeNiro strains to advance up the mountainside, the symbols of war bang against the rock and become caught in the brush. When the Jesuit novice reaches the top, his blood and sweat mingle with tears of contrition. I have always found this scene terribly moving; in fact, each time I see it, I cry without quite knowing why.

Then there is my obsession with the martyr Dietrich Bonhoeffer.[18] At my insistence, my wife and I spent part of our honeymoon in 2002 visiting three German concentration camps associated with Bonhoeffer and the church resistance. At Flossenbürg, I lingered in the spots where Bonhoeffer was hanged and where his Nazi executioners dumped his ashes. I simply could not imagine traveling to Germany without making a pilgrimage to the place where a pagan regime had "crucified" Bonhoeffer.

Remembering these things forced me to acknowledge that something in my understanding of Christian faith makes me want to view suffering redemptively. Ironically, my study of the Holocaust has only nurtured this desire to seek a God who suffers in and with humanity. As a Christian scholar, renditions of the Christian story that may endanger Jews concern me. As a Christian believer, however, I must affirm that suffering and death are as inseparable from incarnation as crucifixion is inseparable from resurrection. I do not claim that one *must* feel this way in order to be a Christian, but it is the way in which the faith has become meaningful for me. Thus, I continue to exist uncomfortably between the following:

- Those who see the movie as a profitable example of Nazi-like antisemitism and those who see it as the most promising evangelistic tool in two thousand years
- Those who are offended by "obscene" and "pornographic" images of religiously sanctioned violence and those whose faith is inseparable from images of a Jesus who endured the depths of human suffering "for them"
- Those who resent popular movies and the clever marketing of controversy and those who view Mel Gibson as God's messenger to a needy world

It certainly is not the first time, nor will be the last, that I have felt caught between the world of the academy and the world where real people apply real faith to real experience.

Notes

1. For about a decade, I have been an active participant in the Scholars' Conference on the Holocaust and the Churches. The 34th Annual "Think Tank" titled "Remembering the Past—Facing the Present and the Future" took place in St. Petersburg Beach, Florida, on March 7, 2004.
2. See, for example, Haynes 1995.
3. Matthew 27:25; John 8:44. In the English-language version of *The Passion*, the crowd cries out the text from Matthew 27:25 in Aramaic, but the words are not subtitled on the screen.
4. See Verhoeven 1989.
5. As of late April 2004, no such violence had occurred other than petty vandalism in the United States.
6. Piper 2004.
7. Piper 2004, 11.
8. Piper 2004, 16. My father also had given me a two-page publication that was circulating in his church, Donald Whitney's "Ten Questions to Ask about *The Passion of the Christ*." Under "Do You Know Who Killed Jesus," Whitney writes that "no one can point a finger at any other person or group for the death of Jesus. Our sins were the reason Jesus had to be crucified."
9. Piper 2004, 14.
10. Piper 2004, 15.
11. Wiesel 1960.
12. Piper 2004, 16.
13. For additional discussions of Protestant Christianity and antisemitism, see Stephen Davis (chapter 16 in this volume) and Kathryn Smith (chapter 20 in this volume).
14. Thomas 2004.
15. Thomas 2004.
16. E-mail from Jean Haynes, March 19, 2004.
17. Joffé 1986.
18. See Haynes 2004.

CHAPTER FIFTEEN
THE EXPOSED FAULT LINE
Richard L. Rubenstein

There is a fault line separating Judaism and Christianity. The Second Vatican Council (1962–1965) made a major contribution toward moderating the harshness of that separation. Mel Gibson's *The Passion of Christ* goes a long way toward restoring some of the fault line's harshest features. Nevertheless, in spite of the film's unrelieved depiction of *nonbelieving* Jews as vile and sadistic, I do not regard the film as motivated primarily by antisemitic malice. The film very well may intensify antisemitic feelings, but that was not Gibson's fundamental objective.[1]

I did not look forward to viewing the film, and I waited to do so until the media-hyped crowds had satisfied their curiosity. I knew too much about how the recital of Jesus's Passion had incited some Christians over the centuries to homicidal rages against defenseless Jews. I saw Jesus's sufferings, presented graphically on the screen, as foreshadowing all the agonies my people had endured because of the deicide accusation and the Jews' "inability" to share in the "good news" of Christ's promise of salvation. In pre–Vatican II Europe, Holy Week always was a dangerous time for Jews.

Most Christians throughout history have believed that the killing of Christ was no ordinary homicide. It was and is the *murder of God*, the fountainhead of all goodness, order, and structure. The accusation of deicide made against Jews places *unbelieving* Jews squarely in the camp of Satan, as does Gibson's film. To make his point, Gibson inserts into the narrative a perhaps hermaphroditic Satan and seven demonic young Jewish boys. The Gospels offer no warrant for either insertion.

RICHARD L. RUBENSTEIN

To me, the film's unrelieved sadistic brutality—culminating in the most graphic depiction of the crucifixion ever presented on the cinema screen—seemed to border on the obscene. I would not have subjected myself to such a spectacle had it not been for the central role Christ's suffering and death play in the religious consciousness of Western civilization. Indeed, it may very well be that Jesus of Nazareth, rather than Socrates, Plato, or Aristotle, is *the* decisive personality in the formation of Western civilization as we know it.

Gibson's film is precisely about Jesus's sufferings. Gibson gives his rationale for the lurid brutality at the very outset. The film opens with the verse from Isaiah, "He was wounded for our transgressions; he was crushed because of our iniquities. *By his stripes were we healed* (italics added)."[2] Christians traditionally have interpreted the verse as referring prophetically to the Passion of Jesus and its redemptive consequences. In choosing the verse, Gibson's theological instincts are on target. The verse gives context and legitimacy to the film's continuous depiction of the suffering and pain inflicted on Jesus. According to New Testament scholar Paula Fredriksen, Gibson's Christ is a theological figure who saves "not through dying so much as through endless, unspeakable, unbearable suffering." She rightly points out, "That's the core of Gibson's film. The rest is window-dressing."[3] Writing in *The New Yorker*, Peter J. Boyer relates that Gibson had been told by friendly audiences that *The Passion* was too violent and that seeing Jesus subjected to such an unending series of brutal assaults would "have a numbing effect on the audience, detaching them from Christ's pain."[4] Gibson acknowledged the possibility but nonetheless kept the violence and brutality in the film. Given his traditionalist Roman Catholic commitments, Gibson's instincts again were on target.

Of course, there are theologies of the Cross other than the one implicit in Gibson's film, but his has enduring emotional power. If Christ atones vicariously for the sins of humanity and if we are healed "by his stripes," then paradoxically the more pain Christ endures, the better. His excruciating torment constitutes a surrogate for the chastisement each and every sinner deserves at the hands of a just, righteous, and gracious God who nevertheless accepts the pain inflicted on Christ as atonement for their sins. Christ is depicted as the only truly acceptable sacrifice by and through whom humanity is to be reconciled to God. This theme is not unrelated to a scene near the end of the film. The Gospel of Matthew reports that immediately after Jesus "yielded up his spirit . . . the curtain of the temple was torn in two, from top to bottom."[5] By contrast, in Gibson's film, the Temple itself is torn asunder, symbolizing divine rejection of the Temple, its priesthood, and the sacrificial system over which the priests presided. The film thereby dramatizes a crucial Christian teaching that only Christ's atoning sacrifice and not the Temple sacrifices could save Israel and humanity.

The Problem of Jewish Unbelief

Clearly, most Jews and most Christians view two very different films when they see *The Passion*.[6] Most Christians view a film whose message is ultimately one of hope, hope for the salvation promised by the suffering and painful death of their Savior. Like the Gospels themselves, *The Passion* conveys "good news," the very best possible good news of salvation. The film was a monumental success and not just because of media hype. Writing from Colorado Springs, Colorado, the Israeli columnist Yossi Klein Halevi reported on the reaction of the overwhelmingly evangelical Christian audience to the film: "People emerged from the screening in what seemed like stunned silence. Clearly, many had just experienced a profound religious encounter."[7] Similar reports of the enthusiastic reception of the film by both Roman Catholic and evangelical Christians came from every part of the United States.

Despite extremely negative portrayals in the film of the Jewish high priest and his priestly entourage, the Pharisees, and the Jewish crowd, Gibson insisted that the film was not "antisemitic" and that some Jews are depicted favorably. He failed to specify that *the "good" Jews all are or become believers in Jesus*. Nor is there any mention in the film of Jesus's popularity among those who came to Jerusalem to celebrate Passover or that he was arrested at night "lest there be a tumult among the people."[8] Apart from Jewish believers in Jesus, Jews in the film are portrayed as cunning, cowardly villains who egg on the Romans to do their dirty work. In the film, as in pre–Vatican II Catholicism, a good Jew is one who has accepted Jesus. This is the essential chasm that historically has divided Jews and Christians.

Jewish "unbelief" has been more of a problem for Christianity from its inception than the "unbelief" of any other community. The first Christians did not claim that theirs was a new religion; rather, they claimed to have the true understanding of God's revelation to Israel in the light of their conviction that the crucified and risen Jesus was truly Israel's Messiah.[9] Even when Christianity became a predominantly Gentile religion, it never claimed that it was a religion foreign to Judaism but instead *the perfection of what God meant Judaism to be.* That people in India and China did not believe in Jesus as Messiah and Son of God was not as grave a problem as Jewish "unbelief." The Jews were Jesus's kinsmen, spoke the same language, and, above all, regarded the same Scriptures as authoritative. Jews were thus in a position, rightly or wrongly, to say to Christians, "He was one of us. We knew him better than you, and we know how to interpret Scripture better than you."

In the language of cognitive dissonance theory, Jews were "disconfirming others."[10] Since early Christians regarded belief in the Lordship of Christ as the indispensable foundation of their religion, culture, and civilization, they found it absolutely necessary to discredit negating witnesses. Thus, the Passion story is both a record of the salvific events and the foundation of the enduring effort to destroy the credibility of Jewish testimony. By their identification with Judas, the disciple who betrays his Lord with a loving kiss, Jews are depicted as untrustworthy even when they appear to be doing good works. Characterizing Jews as "Christ killers" or "God killers" serves to warn the Christian faithful that there is no crime, no matter how heinous, of which the Jews are incapable. The dramatization of these accusations in sacred rituals at certain times and seasons has endowed them with overwhelming emotional power. Jews never could win this contest; they denied the message of the Passion.

Gibson focuses with powerful emotional impact on the traditional fault line separating Judaism and Christianity. To repeat, I believe that Gibson does so not out of malice but out of very strong religious feelings and experience. Nor is it surprising that both Christians committed to ecumenical dialogue and thoughtful Jewish leaders and thinkers have objected to Gibson's focus. Unlike Gibson, who apparently is indifferent to historical biblical scholarship, they know all too well the dangers that lurk at the fault line when its divisiveness is not moderated. What Gibson does know is the emotional power of the Passion narrative as it has been traditionally understood and how to depict the event dramatically with telling effect.

THE EXPOSED FAULT LINE

After the Holocaust, most of the Church's leaders came to understand the full price to be paid for emphasizing the religious otherness of nonbaptized Jews. Their own theology limited what they could do to soften the harshness of that otherness in Christian eyes, for the Church can never abandon its belief that God was somehow incarnate in the person of a Galilean Jew, a belief that Jews faithful to their own tradition can never affirm. Nor could the Church entirely abandon its claim that it is the fulfillment of what God intended Judaism to be. Vatican II represented the Church's well-intentioned effort to maintain its claims while finding a way for Jews to live in freedom and relative security in predominantly Christian lands. The results could not have been entirely satisfactory to either side, but they represented an honest and largely successful attempt to place Jewish–Christian relations on a more harmonious footing than they ever had been before.

The transformation in interreligious relations did not satisfy those Catholics who felt that Vatican II had undermined Christian faith, opened the floodgates of moral relativism, and misrepresented some of the most fundamental Christian beliefs about the Savior and his enemies. Nor would the passing of time result in greater acceptance of Vatican II among conservatives or sectarian traditionalists, such as the late Archbishop Marcel Lefebvre and Hutton Gibson.[11] The latter claims that the post–Vatican II Church is "not a Church but an apostasy" whose "official worship is idolatry."[12] Representatives of the ultra-right-wing Society of Saint Pius X, founded by Lefebvre, have praised Gibson's *Passion* enthusiastically.[13]

Unlike Hutton and Lefebvre, most influential conservative Catholics preferred to work within the Church to modify the reforms of Vatican II. They have an enormous advantage. Their uncompromising version of the Church as an immutable institution and as the sole divinely ordained institution for human redemption offers far greater religious, moral, and emotional security than a version of Christianity that is historically knowledgeable and emphasizes a greater measure of individual responsibility in matters religious and moral. The consecration of an avowed homosexual as a bishop in the Anglican communion and the willingness of the clergy of some Protestant denominations to perform same-sex marriages are not taken by conservatives as examples of the flowering of individual responsibility but rather as object lessons in moral decline and decay. Nor can some conservatives look with favor on the post–Vatican II

Church's attempt to mitigate the deicide accusation, even for contemporary Jews. For them, the fault line between Judaism and Christianity must remain unbridgeable, save for those Jews who cross the line through conversion.

From Father to Brother

The difference between the reactions of most Jews and many Christians to Gibson's *Passion* suggests that Jews and Christians stand on two sides of an important divide, one that separates Christian and Jewish understandings of God, ritual, sacrifice, and, indeed, the nature of the sacred itself. Sigmund Freud[14] suggests that Judaism and Christianity have radically different modes of coping with the domain of the sacred. He identifies Paul of Tarsus, the Pharisee and student of Rabban Gamaliel who became Christianity's first and arguably greatest theologian, as "a man with a gift for religion, in the truest sense.... Dark traces of the past lay in his soul ready to break through into the regions of consciousness."[15] Simply put, Freud implies that *what is repressed or sublimated in Judaism is made manifest in Christianity.*

For example, the denial of all semblance between God and man in Judaism has been called the "ultimate repression."[16] In the earliest childhood of the individual (if not the race), the gods are human figures with whom men and women can identify. Judaism and Islam tend to repress these identifications. By contrast, Christianity makes them available in art, religion, and the general culture. The divine-human figure who became manifest in Christianity was not the Father but Christ, "the firstborn among many brothers."[17] The difference is crucial. Christ as the elder brother may have been a surrogate father, but he elicited a radically different kind of response from his disciples than did the Heavenly Father. Religious Jews never could identify with the Father, in spite of the rabbinic injunction to model oneself after his holiness.[18] The closest relationship one could achieve with the Father in Judaism was obedience and, if one were extremely fortunate, trust but never identification.

By contrast, identification *was* possible with the elder brother. He shared with the younger brothers their defeats, their humiliations, and their complex relations with the mysterious and inaccessible Father. Christ as the elder brother was a preeminently believable model with whom even the lowliest of men could identify. The psychological triumph of the Cross was such that through it no man could be so fallen, degraded, or devoid of worldly accomplishment that he was unable to identify with divinity. Because the elder brother has known the most terrible pain and defeat, any of the other brothers can say, "You are one of us."

It is not surprising that other brothers would want to identify with an older brother who, they believed, experienced the depth of human suffering and then fulfilled the most potent of all human yearnings, the attainment of eternal life. Christ, crucified and resurrected, became the most potent religious model for divine-human identification the Western world has ever known. He experienced the worst that men fear and the most glorious condition for which they hope. If ever there was a film in which men and women of any station and any attainment could identify with "the firstborn among many brothers," it is Gibson's *Passion*—precisely because of the brutal suffering Christ is depicted as enduring. That is the achievement of the film. Unfortunately, that achievement greatly discomforts Jews who dwell on the other side of the fault line.

Nor ought we to wonder that the brothers wanted so badly to identify with the "elder brother" that they were prepared to consume his substance in the Lord's Meal in order to partake of his immortal glory.[19] Fundamental to the Christian message is the hope that the believer derives from identification with both Christ's painful death and his resurrection. This is evident in Paul's characterization of baptism, Christianity's indispensable initiatory rite, as both death and resurrection in Christ:

> Are you ignorant that when we were baptized in Christ Jesus we were baptized in his death? In other words, when we were baptized we went into the tomb with him and joined him in death, so that as Christ was raised from the dead by the Father's glory, we too might live a new life.[20]

Moreover, as bitterly as Paul fought attempts to impose circumcision on Gentile Christians, he never rejected circumcision entirely, for it, too, was identified with Christ's Passion:

> In him you have been circumcised, with a circumcision not performed by human hand, but by *the complete stripping of your body of flesh*. This is circumcision according to Christ. You have been buried with him, when you were baptized; and by baptism, too, you have been raised up with

him through your faith in the power of God who raised him from the dead. You were dead, because you were sinners and had not been circumcised: He (God the Father) has brought you to life with him for he has forgiven us all our sins. (emphasis added)[21]

Here, baptism is identified with circumcision. It is "circumcision according to Christ," a true circumcision "not performed by human hand." It is clearly identified with Christ's Passion, for it is "the complete stripping of your body of flesh." Paul's intent was to contrast Jewish circumcision, in which a small part of the flesh is "stripped off," with Christian baptism-circumcision-burial-with-Christ, which involves the total stripping of the flesh so that the old body may die and be reborn in Christ. For Paul, then, only Christian baptism is true circumcision because it alone is real dying and rebirth.[22]

Paul's defense of baptism as true circumcision implies that sons cannot overcome the judgment of the Father by a painful but localized ordeal. Nothing short of death and rebirth will suffice. Because Jesus, according to Paul, had faced the Father's judgment in its most terrible form without perishing forever, nothing short of death and rebirth would suffice for anyone else. In the New Testament and Gibson's film, Jesus's skin is stripped away as the precondition to a deathless and glorified existence where no further harm ever could come to him. Moreover, Paul does not write that *any* stripping of the body of flesh could rescue men. Their circumcision and death must be that of Christ. Ordinary water will not suffice. The waters must be filled with the Spirit of Christ to effect redemption. Only in that way will men partake of the Resurrection that already has happened to Christ and will ultimately take place for all those who are "in Christ."

Atoning sacrifice, of critical importance in Gibson's *Passion*, is yet another subject in which the fault line between Judaism and Christianity is unbridgeable. There was a time when ritual infanticide was widely practiced on the firstborn in the ancient Middle East; rabbinic Judaism never completely suppressed the repugnant memory of human sacrifice. A very potent reminder appears in the ritual reading from the Torah on the second day of the Jewish new year, Rosh Hashanah. Genesis 22 tells the story of the *Akedah* ("sacrifice"), Abraham's aborted sacrifice of Isaac. On one of their holiest days of the liturgical year, Jews remind themselves that God did not require the death of the tribal patriarch's son because at the last moment God provided a surrogate. Nevertheless, the need to reiterate, under conditions of utmost solemnity, the fact that God was willing to accept a substitute is testimony to the persistence of the very impulse the ritual seeks to ward off. Were the impulse without power, the reading would have ceased to be meaningful.

Christ's sacrifice also is linked typologically to that of Isaac. Although Paul does make an explicit comparison in his extant writings, nonetheless his insistence on Christ as the perfect atonement for the sins of humanity suggests that for Paul as well as for those early fathers of the church who explicitly take up the comparison, *Isaac's Akedah is an aborted Golgotha*. Isaac is depicted as lacking the capacity to redeem humanity because he did not really die on his wooden pyre. In *The Epistle of Barnabas*, God commands that Christ be offered up "as a sacrifice for our sins, in order that the type established in Isaac, who was offered upon the altar, might be fulfilled."[23] Similarly, St. Augustine asks rhetorically who was the ram "caught in a thicket by his horns" that God accepts in place of Isaac.[24] He responds "Jesus, crowned with Jewish thorns before he was offered in sacrifice."[25] The church fathers thus depict Jesus as the perfected Isaac, just as, for them, Christianity is the perfected Judaism. Nevertheless, Christ's suffering and death are the indispensable condition of that perfection. *This fundamental fact about Christianity cannot be altered through interpretation—even if it makes Jews uncomfortable and fearful.*

Coexistence with this impassable theological chasm is part of the price Jews pay for living in predominantly Christian lands. It would be very pleasant indeed if Jews and Christians could live in a conflict-free world, but they do not. The chasm between these intimately related yet widely disparate conceptions of redemption are in important respects unbridgeable. However difficult it may be for Jews like this writer to watch Gibson's unpleasantly graphic depiction of Christ's sufferings, the portrayal appears on course both theologically and emotionally. Without the Christ who suffers and dies the most excruciatingly painful of deaths on the cross, there can be no Christianity. To attack Gibson's film as a contemporary "Nazi-type attack" on the Jews, as did one highly respected Christian leader, is to ignore the fact that there is no way that the Passion narrative can be eliminated from Christianity.[26]

While modern historical scholarship has shown that the Evangelists had pressing political motives to exculpate Pilate for the crucifixion and to affix the blame on the Jews, such scholarship cannot compete in emotional impact with the literal recital of the Passion narratives. Moreover, the imputation of guilt to nonbelieving Jews arguably was an indispensable necessity for the Church because the Church needed to reduce or eliminate the credibility of the one community that plausibly could rejected Jesus's claim to divinity. An entire civilization—radically different from Greco-Roman civilization—was created on the foundation of the belief that the risen Christ is Lord. So much was and perhaps still is at stake that on the Christian side of the fault line there always will remain a potential danger for hostility and the imputation of gross villainy to nonbelieving Jews.

This writer has a profound appreciation of what the Roman Catholic Church, the Evangelical Lutheran Church in America, and other Christian bodies have done to lessen or repudiate the allegation of Jewish guilt for the death of Jesus. Nevertheless, as Gibson amply has demonstrated, the Gospels can lend themselves to the imputation of the worst kind of evil to Jews. In chapter 19 of this volume, the distinguished Jewish thinker Elliot N. Dorff offers us his prescription for "good interfaith relations," which, he argues, are a moral imperative.[27] He reminds us that "creeds created centuries ago have changed continually" and expresses the hope that the "historically evolutionary nature of both faiths" can facilitate interfaith understanding and goodwill. Unfortunately, historical scholarship is a slender reed on which to raise hopes for interfaith understanding. Apart from the powerful rise of a fundamentalism that emphatically rejects such scholarship, even those who took biblical literature courses in college or university hardly are likely to reject Gibson's treatment of the Passion narrative, especially when they perceive their faith to be threatened by nonreligious cultural forces.[28] They are far more likely to regard defense of their traditional faith as a greater moral imperative than "good interfaith relations."

If the Gibson film demonstrates anything, it is that there are limits to two kinds of dialogue: 1) the dialogue of historical scholars with many in their own faith community and 2) the dialogue between Jewish and Christian thinkers. As a Jew, of course, I would have wanted Gibson to present a kinder, gentler Passion. As a scholar of Christian and Jewish theology, however, I cannot wax enthusiastic over the film, but I can understand why Christians do. Nor do I wish to devalue either interfaith dialogue or Vatican II. The latter was an attempt to introduce civility into the religious discourse of Judaism and Christianity.[29] So, too, is much of contemporary interfaith dialogue. Unfortunately, such efforts remain enduringly precarious, especially in times of heightened religious conflict, such as the post-9/11 era.

A final observation: Gibson has added another element to the equation. He is one of those extraordinarily empowered individuals who in the twenty-first century have the resources to challenge and conceivably alter long-established institutions, thereby encouraging sympathetic insiders to join in the enterprise. Through his personal command of powerful communications media, Gibson may be able to restore some of the fault line's harshest features and indeed return to primacy a very conservative reading of the Christian narrative.

Notes

1. Cooperman 2004 reports that according to a telephone survey of 1,703 randomly selected adults conducted by the Pew Research Center from March 17 to 21, 2004 (that is, after the release of Gibson's film), 26 percent said Jews were responsible for Christ's death, up from 19 percent in an ABC News poll that asked the same question in 1997. The greatest increase was among blacks and young people under thirty. Nevertheless, I concur with Jeffrey S. Siker (chapter 10 in this volume) that Gibson's primary focus in producing the film was on "his own identity as a thankful sinner before his crucified and risen Lord."

2. Isaiah 53:5.
3. Fredriksen 27 February 2004.
4. Boyer 2003, 61.
5. Matthew 27:50, 51.
6. See, for example, Prager 2003.
7. Klein Halevi 2004.
8. Matthew 26:5; Mark 14:2.
9. See Siker (chapter 10 in this volume).
10. The social-psychological theory of cognitive dissonance holds inter alia that dissonant items are consistent with each other. This process is known as dissonance reduction. An obvious method of dissonance reduction is to discredit the source of the dissonant item of information. An even more radical method would be to eliminate the source entirely. Both methods have been employed in the history of religion. See Festinger 1956, Festinger 1962, and Aronson 1973.

11. Traditionalist Catholics, including Mel Gibson, reject the modernizing aggiornamento of the 1962–1965 Second Vatican Council and its new openness to ecumenical dialogue with other religious communities, both Christian and non-Christian.

12. Gibson 1997.

13. See Ternisien 2004.

14. Jean-Marie Cardinal Lustiger, archbishop of Paris, denounced the film's violence as the opposite of Jesus's message of love and compassion (Tincq 2004). Lustiger's denunciation preceded by four days the official denunciation of the film by the French Bishops' Conference as potentially antisemitic and a distortion of Christian teaching. See Conférence des évêques de France 2004.

15. Freud 1939, 110.

16. Reik 1952, 264.

17. Romans 8:29.

18. The classical statement is biblical: "Ye shall be holy as I the Lord your God am holy" (Leviticus 19:2).

19. For a full discussion of this issue, see Rubenstein 1972.

20. Romans 6:3, 4. Like Christianity, Judaism also has a ritual of immersion; unlike Christianity, it is a ritual of purification rather than of death and rebirth. In Judaism, immersion is the act of washing performed to correct a condition of ritual impurity and to restore the impure person or object to a state of ritual purity. Total immersion is required of menstrual women at the conclusion of the menstrual cycle. It is also required of the proselyte, but in neither case is there the slightest hint of identification with a divine-human figure. See "Ablution" in *Encyclopaedia Judaica*.

21. Colossians 2:11–13. See Schnackenburg 1964, 67 f.

22. See Sanders 1991, 70–73.

23. Barnabas, "The Epistle of Barnabas," 1919, 7:3.

24. Genesis 22:13.

25. Augustine 1984, 695 (bk. XVI, chap. 32).

26. See Franklin Littell, quoted in Haynes (chapter 14 in this volume).

27. See Dorff (chapter 19 in this volume).

28. See Leslie Smith (chapter 3 in this volume).

29. Few, if any, Catholic thinkers did as much to change the official position of the Roman Catholic Church at Vatican II on such issues as acceptance of religious freedom and pluralism as the late John Courtney Murray, SJ. See Murray 1983; Canavan 1987; Hooper 1993.

CHAPTER SIXTEEN
CRUCIFYING JESUS: ANTISEMITISM AND THE PASSION STORY

Stephen T. Davis

I grew up in the 1940s and 1950s. Because my mother and father were divorced when I was an infant, I was raised in two families. The family with which I spent the most time (my mother, stepfather, five younger siblings, and myself) was nominally Protestant. The other was Catholic. I cannot remember ever being taught, in either family, to hate or disrespect Jews. I do not know when I first heard the canard that all Jews were "Christ killers," but it must have been when I was old enough to recognize the absurdity of the charge because I have never believed it. People are culpable for what they themselves do wrong—not for what other people do.

I would like to make five points in this chapter. The first three concern antisemitism and Christianity, the New Testament and antisemitism, and antisemitism and Christian teachings. Then I will address Christianity and the Passion story. Finally, I ask and try to answer the question, How can we detect antisemitism? My central conclusion is this: Christianity teaches that all human beings—Jews and Gentiles alike—are complicit in the death of Christ. That Jews as a people ought to be singled out for punishment is, in my opinion, contrary to Christian teaching.

Antisemitism and Christianity

The Christian church has been guilty of many egregious faults throughout its history. One of the worst, if not the very worst, is its complicity in antisemitism. I understand the term "antisemitism" to mean prejudice against Jews that expresses itself in hateful attitudes, hateful words, and immoral actions. Looking at our record in the best possible light, the attitudes and actions of Christians toward Jews in the past twenty centuries have been mixed indeed; looked at in the worst light, the record has been despicable. By our own admission and even insistence, Christians are fallible people, capable of evil. Sadly, one area where we have exercised that capacity for evil is in our relations with Jews.

Christian hatred of Jews often has centered on the Passion story in the four canonical Gospels. Accordingly, that story is painful for Jews to hear, and a film about it—especially a movie by a talented and famous filmmaker—inevitably will raise Jewish concerns. My own view is that certain Jews *were* undoubtedly complicit in the death of Jesus. But so were certain Romans; crucifixion was, after all, a Roman punishment determined and carried out by Romans. Were all Jews of Jesus's day responsible for his death? Of course not. Are Jews today responsible for his death? Of course not. Those ideas are so patently absurd, both historically and theologically, that they would not even be worth commenting on except for the sad fact that some misguided people throughout history have believed that the answer to them is yes.

In the New Testament Passion accounts themselves, the responsibility for Jesus's death seems to me to be spread far and wide. One of Jesus's own disciples betrayed him, certain Jewish leaders plotted against him, most of his followers either denied him or abandoned him, the crowd mocked him, Pontius Pilate sentenced him to death, and Roman soldiers brutalized and crucified him. I think the gospel writers (as well as Paul, writing before them) want us to understand that we—all of us, Jew or Gentile, Greek or Barbarian—are responsible for his death. Their view is that he was dying for us.

The New Testament and Antisemitism

I reject the claim that the New Testament is antisemitic. Let me explain why. Most of the New Testament was written when it was becoming clear that there would be an irrevocable split between Christianity and its disapproving parent or elder sibling Judaism. Accordingly, there is a great deal of anti-Judaism in the New Testament. (I define "anti-Judaism" as theological or religious disagreement with Jews or Judaism.) There was less anti-Judaism in the earliest years of the Christian movement, before any decisive break had occurred between early Christians and the Jewish theological establishment. As the Christian movement expanded, it attracted increasing numbers of non-Jews; simultaneously, antagonism between Jewish Christians and mainstream Judaism continued to grow. Eventually, the Christian movement, suffering repudiation and even persecution, became an alternative (and a highly disapproving one) to the rabbinic Judaism that developed after A.D. 70. As such, much of the New Testament is highly critical of those forms of Judaism that reject Jesus.

However, it would be a priori surprising if the New Testament contained much antisemitism (as opposed to anti-Judaism) since most of its authors were themselves Jews. I believe that it is often tacitly assumed that since the New Testament (along with the Hebrew Bible) is the church's scripture, the New Testament is a Christian book. In one sense, that is certainly true: its writers all saw themselves as followers of Jesus of Nazareth. But the New Testament is also largely a Jewish book. Craig Evans rightly points out,

> It is surprising how many fail to perceive the oddness of the assumption that the New Testament and early Christianity were anti-Semitic. Should it not strike us as hard to explain how a first-century Jewish sect, centered around a revered Jewish teacher thought to be Israel's Messiah, God's Son, and fulfillment of Israel's scriptures, within one generation of its founding could mutate into an anti-Jewish, perhaps even anti-Semitic, movement? Surely this is improbable. I suspect that scholars have unconsciously and uncritically read the New Testament through the eyes of the patristic church, which, sad to say, did give vent to anti-Semitic expressions.[1]

Certainly there is material in the New Testament that antisemites can twist in order to buttress their antisemitism. For example, Jesus's attack on "the scribes and Pharisees" in the synoptic Gospels is scathing indeed (see Matthew 23), but it does not necessarily constitute an attack on Pharisaism per se, let alone on Jews or Judaism. Indeed, it has all the earmarks of a conflict within Judaism rather than an exercise in antisemitism. It is similar in tone to criticisms that we find, for example, in the oracles of the prophets Amos or Jeremiah, criticizing the Judaism of their day. Jesus himself was of course a Jew, and he never appears to have doubted the covenant with the patriarchs, the election of Israel as God's chosen people, the divine authority of the Hebrew Bible, or the appropriateness of Temple worship.² He saw himself as fulfilling rather than negating the law and the prophets.³

The apostle Paul himself until his death remained a Jew, proud of his heritage, training, and status as a Jew.⁴ He regarded as irrevocable both Israel's privileges (the covenants, the law, adoption as God's people, the promises, and so on) and Israel's responsibilities, like being a light to the Gentiles.⁵ One passage is often singled out by those who hold that Paul was antisemitic. Speaking of the suffering Judean Christians, Paul says,

> You suffered the same things from your own compatriots as they did from the Jews, who killed both the Lord Jesus and the prophets, and drove us out; they displease God and oppose everyone by hindering us from speaking to the Gentiles so that they may be saved. Thus they have constantly been filling up the measure of their sins; but God's wrath has overtaken them at last.⁶

The language here is polemical and even reveals a degree of anger. But it amounts to a theological argument and an intramural one at that. There is no national, ethnic, or racial hatred here. Paul never turned against the Jewish people or his own Jewish heritage.

The fourth Gospel uses the term "the Jews" in different ways. At times it refers to the entire Jewish nation or to a specific group of Jews, especially where Jewish customs are being explained.⁷ Elsewhere, it refers to Jesus's enemies, those who plotted against him.⁸ So it is possible to develop a mistaken interpretation of the Evangelist to the effect that the entire Jewish nation was somehow responsible for Jesus's death, which was not his intent at all. Notice also Jesus's affirmation in his conversation with the Samaritan woman that "we [Jews] worship what we know" and that "salvation is from the Jews."⁹

The content and limits of Christian Scripture were set long ago. Obviously, there is no way that I have or would ever want to have the authority to change anything in them. But I confess that one text has always troubled me. This is the "blood curse," where the crowd shouts to Pontius Pilate, "His blood be on us and on our children."¹⁰ I believe that Matthew included that statement in his account of the trial because he believed that it had actually occurred.¹¹ I make no judgment at this point on that. But in the light of the horrible implications that this statement has had in Jewish–Christian relations, I often have wondered whether history might have been less harsh for the Jews had Matthew not included that statement in his account.

However, we hardly can blame the New Testament writers for later antisemitism or even genocide since they did not intend to support either, nor had they any idea how their words might later be twisted. In the end, the charge that the New Testament is antisemitic is anachronistic and unhistorical. It is based on the erroneous practice of subjecting first-century writings to categories and ideologies that developed later, some of them much later. It is also based on the practice of holding earlier writers culpable for the ways in which their words (whether innocently or not) were later misinterpreted and misused to help produce unfortunate events.

Antisemitism and Christian Teachings

In one sense, it is surprising that there has existed such a sorry history of Christian antisemitism since that ideology is so obviously contrary to Christian teachings. It is an essential part of the Christian ethic that we are to love all people, even our enemies, and forgive those who sin against us. Thus, Jesus said,

> You have heard that it was said, "You shall love your neighbor and hate your enemy." But I say to you, Love your enemies and pray for those who persecute you, so that you may be children of your Father in heaven.[12]
>
> And Peter came and said to [Jesus]: "Lord, if my brother sins against me, how often should I forgive? As many as seven times?" Jesus said to him, "Not seven times, but, I tell you, seventy-seven times."[13]
>
> But I say to you that listen, Love your enemies, do good to those who hate you, bless those who curse you, pray for those who abuse you. If anyone strikes you on the cheek, offer the other also: and from anyone who takes away your coat do not withhold even your shirt. Give to everyone who begs from you; and if anyone takes away your goods, do not ask for them again. Do to others as you would have them do to you.[14]

Moreover, even the apostle Paul, who, as we have seen, was capable of speaking strongly against his fellow Jews who rejected Christ, firmly believed that God's covenants with Israel still stand, that Christians are like a branch grafted onto the vine of the Jewish people, and that Jews have a continuing role to play in the redemptive purposes of God.[15]

Since antisemitism is not the same thing as disagreeing with Jews (I take it that, at important points, all Christians do that), I will make a bold statement: anyone who practices antisemitism is not practicing Christianity.[16]

Christianity and the Passion Story

There are revisionist Christian theologians today who seem prepared to edit, revise, or even jettison important Christian claims if somebody alleges that they promote evil. The evils usually mentioned are slavery, patriarchy, imperialism, militarism, and antisemitism. Some of the usual suspects for the cause of such evils in the world—especially antisemitism—are Christian practices such as evangelism and Christian beliefs such as "Jesus is the Messiah," "Jesus is the Son of God," or "Jesus's death paid the penalty for our sins." My only point here is that the vast majority of Christians—Catholic, Protestant, and Eastern Orthodox—are not prepared to follow the revisionist path. All Christians recognize that the Passion story raises Jewish suspicions and fears, and for very understandable reasons. But—as I think Jews recognize better than do revisionist Christian theologians—most Christians are quite unwilling to jettison the Passion and death of Jesus as crucial cornerstones of our religion. Moreover, Christians certainly are entitled to give their version—even in a movie—of what happened during Passion Week.

One aspect of the theological revisionism of which I speak is this: certain Christian theologians, clergy, and laypersons no longer seem to accept the theological necessity for any kind of atonement for sin and especially not any kind of atonement that involves sacrifice, substitution, or blood. In their understanding of Christianity, they tend to place much greater emphasis on the teachings of Jesus and on the example of his life than on the death of Jesus. So it is no surprise that many of these more liberal Christians today place little theological emphasis on the Passion story. Accordingly, many of them appear to be shocked and horrified by Mel Gibson's movie. To them, what they see is just meaningless violence. So it is hard for me to imagine that many liberal Protestants, for example, will approve of the film.[17]

Evangelical and other theologically orthodox Christians—the people for whom I am trying to speak in this chapter—are not at all inclined to deemphasize the teachings of Jesus. But most of them are convinced with the church fathers that the Passion, death, and resurrection of Jesus give meaning to what precedes those events in the Gospels rather than vice versa. The very idea of atonement seems gory and premodern to many of our contemporaries. However, most Christians see the atonement accomplished by Christ as much in line with teachings in the Hebrew Bible.[18] Whether it accords with our modern tastes or not, it appears to most Christians that God has chosen to associate atonement with sacrifice and the shedding of blood. Indeed, the writer to the Hebrews can say, "Without the shedding of blood, there is no forgiveness of sins."[19] Thus, the Christian tradition that Jesus was "the lamb of God who takes away the sin of the world."[20] Jesus was not just a guru but also a savior.

There is one additional point that I obviously cannot prove but can only suggest: Christian theological revisionists usually accept some of the more radical findings of Old Testament biblical criticism. (I myself do not at all reject historical-critical biblical scholarship; I just want to see it practiced sensibly.) I often have wondered whether antisemitism becomes more acceptable than it would otherwise have been for a person who rejects the divine authority of the Hebrew Bible, the revealed nature of the Old Testament law, and the uniqueness of Jews as God's chosen people. Once those points are rejected, Jews can easily come to be viewed as a disposable residuum of ancient times, and antisemitism and maybe even genocide can become more thinkable than they might otherwise have been.[21]

How to Detect Antisemitism

In the run-up to *The Passion of the Christ*, I have seen in print many questions about it:

- Is the film antisemitic?
- Is the filmmaker antisemitic?
- Is the film capable of causing Jews pain?
- Is the film capable of reinforcing or legitimating antisemitism?

Having seen the movie and having seen an interview with the filmmaker, I am satisfied that he is not antisemitic and that the movie is not antisemitic. Still, other people—people whom I respect—react otherwise. It is almost as if we saw different movies. Perhaps the essential problem is, as noted, that the symbol of the cross means very different things to Jews and Christians as well as to orthodox and revisionist Christians.

With regard to *The Passion of the Christ*, I am quite sure that the answer to my third and fourth questions is yes. That is, I am sure that the film will cause Jews pain, just as (perhaps for different reasons) it will cause Christians pain. And I am sure that the film will be capable of reinforcing already existing antisemitism in those who already hate Jews. If that happens, it will be unfortunate indeed. As we all know, though, almost anything can reinforce stereotypes and hatreds of that kind. This is not to deny the fact that as human beings we must sometimes be responsible not only for what we say but also for how what we say is likely to be heard. I suspect that rational people will disagree about whether Mel Gibson has satisfied that duty.

Unless signs mislead, antisemitism has been increasing in the world in the past few years. But I do not think the Passion story in the Christian Bible is behind this new antisemitism. Indeed, I suspect that little of it is driven by Christianity. Far more of it, in my opinion, is driven by political and religious extremism in the Islamic world and by the far-reaching implications of the Arab–Israeli conflict. Still, I do not deny for a moment the duty of Jews—and of all morally sensitive people—to be constantly on the watch for antisemitism. As I write this chapter, we are only fifty-nine years past the Holocaust, and it had nothing to do with Arabs or Islam.

When I saw *The Passion of the Christ*, my criterion for testing it was the question, Is the basic message of the film political or spiritual? Judging by his public statements, Gibson himself seems to hope that his movie will cause people to examine themselves and ask to what extent they are guilty, because of their sins, of making the crucifixion of the Son of God necessary. On the other hand, if one thinks that the film explicitly or implicitly urges viewers to take up sides against those evil people the Jews—and I do not think that it does—then one is justified in regarding it as an antisemitic movie.

Like many viewers, I found the unremitting violence of the movie numbing. Gibson, I believe, was trying to depict the sufferings of Jesus as fully and graphically as the medium of cinema allows. One can disagree with various decisions Gibson made about what to include and what to exclude in the film and how to interpret what he included, but my own view is that most of his choices can be defended. I did not especially resonate with the devilish children who taunted Judas, with the hideous baby carried by Satan, or with the raven that pecked out the eye of one of the thieves on the cross.

Still, I found the portrait of Mary and of her sufferings moving. In the Pietà scene at the end, when she stares into the camera, that is, at those of us who are viewing the movie, in my heart I heard her saying, "Look at what you have done." I also appreciated the incisive picture of Simon of Cyrene, who moves from outrage at being forced to carry the cross to determination to bear it and profound sympathy for the one who was to die on it. The flashbacks to the institution of the Eucharist at the Last Supper were also highly meaningful to me since, as an ordained minister, I often have repeated Jesus's words. And there is no denying—well, *I* cannot deny—that the movie constitutes a spiritually gripping portrayal of the agonies that Jesus endured for our sake. In sum, I cannot say that I enjoyed the film, but I learned from it and am glad I saw it.

That all human beings—Jews and Gentiles alike—are complicit in the death of Christ is Christian teaching. That the Jews as a people ought to be hated or singled out for punishment is contrary to Christian teaching.

Notes

As a philosopher of religion, I do not often address in print the topic of relations between Jews and Christians (two brief exceptions are Stephen Davis 1981, 121–29, and Stephen Davis 2000, 71–85), but I have thought a great deal about it and am honored to be part of the distinguished lineup in this book. I would like to thank Professors Jim Butler, Scott Cormode, and Shawn Landres for their helpful comments on an earlier draft of this chapter.

1. Evans and Hagner 1993, 15 n.
2. In my opinion, the Temple incident, recorded in Mark 11:15–19 and elsewhere, was Jesus's attempt to purify rather than repudiate Temple worship. Notice, in Jesus's words on that occasion, the quotations from Isaiah 56:7 and Jeremiah 7:11.
3. Matthew 5:17.
4. See 2 Corinthians 11:22; Philippians 3:4–6; see also Acts 25:8, 26:5, 28:17.

5. See especially Romans 9:4–5, 11:2–29.
6. I Thessalonians 2:14–16.
7. See John 2:6, 13; 3:1, 25; 4:9, 22; 5:1; 6:4; 7:2; 12:9, 11; and so on.
8. See John 5:15–18; 7:1, 13; 9:18, 22; 10:31–33; 18:14, 36, 38; 19:7, 12, 14, 38; 20:19; and so on. There is even one text that asserts that "the Jews were divided" (John 10:19)—some rejected what Jesus had just said, and some believed it.
9. John 4:22.
10. Matthew 27:25.
11. Is it possible that in quoting the crowd as uttering the blood curse, Matthew was implying that the crowd was unknowingly saying more than they intended? Does he want us to understand that the curse was in part a prayer from the members of the crowd that Jesus's blood atone for their sins and the sins of their children?
12. Matthew 5:43–45.
13. Matthew 18:21–22.
14. Luke 6:27–31.
15. See Romans 9–11.
16. There are, of course, Christian thinkers whom I cannot exonerate from the charge of making antisemitic statements, most notably some of the church fathers and Luther. Whatever their authority elsewhere, at this point, in my opinion, they were not practicing Christianity.
17. See Ingersoll (chapter 5 in this volume).
18. See, for example, the institution of the sin offering in Leviticus 5 and of Yom Kippur in Leviticus 16, both of which involved sacrifice.
19. Hebrews 9:22.
20. John 1:29.
21. Consider the admittedly unusual but infinitely depressing case of those few German Old Testament scholars during the 1930s and 1940s who supported National Socialism (Heschel, chapter 13 in this volume). However, I am not suggesting that all who accept the conclusions of radical Old Testament historical criticism are antisemites.

CHAPTER SEVENTEEN
FIVE INTROSPECTIVE CHALLENGES
David M. Elcott

Thousands of Americans have analyzed and criticized Mel Gibson's *The Passion of the Christ*. I leave to my colleagues in this book and elsewhere the task of evaluating the film's historical inaccuracies, its theological fundamentalism, its antisemitic implications, and its political ramifications.[1] My focus is on none of these things. Instead, I investigate what Jews, as individuals and in community, can take from this movie.

Of course, I do agree with those who challenge the anti-Jewish caricatures of *The Passion* and the ways that Mel Gibson used his movie to foster antisemitism. Professor Cornel West was correct to note, in a panel before the Princeton community in which we both participated,[2] that anyone who confuses the imperial, violent, and oppressive power of Rome with the subjugated and oppressed masses of Jews as the key actors in the saga of Jesus's crucifixion must own up to a deeply contorted and arguably antisemitic view. The Jesus of the Scriptures stood with the oppressed, West noted; Mel Gibson stands with the oppressors. This rings true. Nevertheless, as I said, I leave to my colleagues this important analysis. I have chosen to focus on another set of questions.

There are at least five distinct challenges uniquely confronting Jews that grow out of both *The Passion of the Christ* and the debate that has swirled around it, five questions that speak to our engagement with the world and, fundamentally, to our own faith. These are internal questions; I ignore the obvious critiques of the film and the attendant debate with some anxiety. It is easy for Jews to see the ugliness of this movie as an assault and to assume the natural posture of victim. Mel Gibson is a powerful conservative Christian who has used his money and his clout to make and promote a movie with a distinctly anti-Jewish message. Many Jews feel that we are, once again, under attack; our normal reaction is to want to strike back. It is for those Jews to whom I write: Jews like me, whom this alien film first perplexed and then angered and to whom this film seemed to undermine our understandings of Christianity and of antisemitism. We need to ask ourselves five questions:

- Do we as a Jewish community understand modern Christians and their theology?

- Can we, in light of our history, trust our Christian neighbors? What is the cost of not trusting?

- What unique voice do we as Jews have to contribute to the dialogue of faith taking place across North America?

- Do we nourish sacred narratives that could foster hatred or incite violence?

- Are we prepared to stand together with people of good faith to fight against the polarization encouraged by Gibson's movie?

Before I turn to these questions, I want to be clear: looking inward is not a call for retreat. Introspection does not mean that we can cease to be vigilant against those who wish us harm. It means instead, as we publicize and protest against the evils of antisemitism, that we also must probe our community and ourselves. We must take this movie not just as a call to arms against latent antisemitism in our society but also as a call to deep personal and communal introspection.

Do We Understand Modern Christians and Their Theology?

By now it is axiomatic that Jews and Christians who saw *The Passion* saw two very different movies. Many Christians noted the violence on screen but were moved by the gift of Jesus's suffering and love that they experienced Jesus giving the world through his crucifixion. My Jewish colleagues and I saw a very different movie, one that was gratuitously violent, angry, and hate filled.

There is a deeper level of confusion. The Christianity that most Jews recognize does not reflect Vatican II. By the end of the historic Second Vatican Council, called by Pope John XXIII in 1962 and ending in 1965, the Roman Catholic Church had promulgated remarkable changes in its doctrine. Most significant for Jews, in *Nostra Aetate*, the Church definitively rejected contemporary Jewish culpability in the death of Jesus and called antisemitism a sin.[3] Roman Catholics, therefore, do not see *Nostra Aetate* as a concession to Jews but rather understand it as a higher realization of Christian faith. Indeed, many Christians today believe that Christians and Jews share a sacred covenant of God's love.

Many Jews, however, assume that *The Passion* reflects what Christians really believe. They remain unaware or tend to ignore that many Christian scholars and religious leaders have criticized Mel Gibson for his medieval reading of the Passion narrative. In its treatment of Jews, *The Passion of the Christ* does not reflect contemporary Christian doctrine. All mainstream Protestant and Catholic churches have expunged any teaching that "the Jews" as a whole were or that contemporary Jews are responsible for the death of Jesus when it occurred.[4]

We have a strange situation. The Jewish community does not know about these fundamental transformations in Christianity. Very few Jews have read *Nostra Aetate*, nor do we understand the historical context in which it was decided. Indeed, few Jews know about Vatican II at all, let alone understand its implications. So when we see anti-Jewish stereotypes and caricatures, in this movie or elsewhere, many of us presume that Christians are seeing Jews with medieval eyes. We assume that it reminds them, as it reminds us, of medieval Passion plays and the pogroms they inspired. We look for signs of antisemitism of ages past in their responses and even in their choice to see the film, even as we remain unaware that Christian scholars have criticized Gibson precisely for his medieval approach to the blood of Jesus.[5] We are doubly angered if Christians claim to have seen no antisemitism in the movie, fearing that their views somehow hide subconscious (and more dangerous) antisemitism. And we feel only contempt for the cowardice of the church leaders who did not attack the movie publicly. We have created a self-validating system in which, whatever their response, Christians are revealing their true antisemitism.

However, were we to study the seminal Christian theological decisions and documents of the past half century and review the Christian response to *The Passion* with that theology in mind, I think we would understand differently—and better—the Christian response to Gibson's movie. If we are to be good analysts of *The Passion* phenomenon—and good protectors of the Jewish community—we must be educated in modern Christianity so that we might understand the ways Christians teach and learn about Jews and Judaism. There is no doubt that the lens with which we see our Christian neighbors, coworkers, and friends affects the ways we interact and the relationships we seek to establish. It is time for Jews to learn about Christians.

The first step in our own education is to read the documents themselves. The Roman Catholic Church, virtually all the "mainline" Protestant churches, and many evangelical Protestant groups have clear and moving statements about Jews and Judaism, most of which claim that all humanity is responsible for the death of Jesus and define antisemitism as a sin.[6] In today's world, we easily can access these and other statements simply by checking their websites. The next step is to engage Christians, to ask questions and to see how Christians in America live out these responses to Jews and Judaism.

The surprises are everywhere. During a conversation with a young Latino man I have befriended, he told me that the Jews killed Jesus. Carlos then added that, of course, Jesus and all the apostles were Jewish: "There were some bad Jews and some good Jews, just as there are some bad Christians and some good ones. And that was a long time ago." Many of our defense organizations would categorize his statement as antisemitic, even though he clearly is not.[7] I realized once again that I have much to learn by simple engagement with my fellow citizens.

Can We Trust Our Christian Neighbors?

Jews overwhelmingly see *The Passion of the Christ* as stoking the fires of hatred. Recent surveys confirm what one hears in most settings where Jews gather these days that the Jewish world thinks antisemitism is on the rise.[8] However, all signs indicate that the opposite is the case. The most recent Anti-Defamation League audit of antisemitism found no rise in antisemitism; overall, antisemitism is down significantly over the past decade.[9] Moreover, during the first two months following the release of *The Passion*—a period that included Good Friday and Easter Sunday—

there was no discernible increase in attacks on Jews in the United States or even elsewhere in the world. As to specific claims of Jewish culpability for Jesus's death, the fallout from the movie only has reinforced how unacceptable it is in most circles to say that the Jews killed Jesus, at least in the United States.[10] There are indications, at least within certain ethnic communities and among younger Americans, that a rising number of people believe that the Jews killed Jesus.[11] But there is no indication at this point that this historical "fact" translates into antisemitic views or behaviors in general in the United States or even among this population.

Moreover, in our focus on the supposed increase in antisemitism, we forget the suffering of other communities. A recent headline in the Jewish Telegraphic Agency (the Associated Press of the Jewish world) announced that antisemitic incidents against Canadian Jews rose last year. Only in the fourth paragraph of the story does the author mention that of the 583 "incidents" fewer than half resulted in criminal prosecution and that only fifteen involved violence.[12] In the United States in 2002, federally documented hate crimes against Jews—while still too many—comprised only about 10 percent of all those officially recorded.[13] Every incident is serious and warrants our full attention, but the number of hate crimes against Jews pales in comparison to attacks against other minority groups in North America.

Why is it that we believe instinctively that antisemitism is on the rise, given the relative security and comfort in which the North American Jewish community lives? It is painful to realize that, as individuals and as a community, we do not trust Christians. We do not know yet how to deal with the Christian history of violence and persecution against us. We are but one generation from the Holocaust, only a few generations from brutal Passion plays. Too many of us have experienced Christian hatred in our own lifetimes. We have learned well, perhaps too well, the oft-repeated lesson "Never Forget." Because we do remember, it is hard to ask Jews to trust Christian goodwill.

Nonetheless, while it is crucial that we remember the possibility of violence, it is equally important that we remember the sacred Jewish principle of *Teshuvah*, or redemption/forgiveness. Because many Jews still hold contemporary Christians responsible for past violence against us, we have put them in a bind. Nothing they do or say seems able to make up for their history or for the fear that Jews feel when we remember that history.

Many Christian leaders are aware of this. They seem to accept that the body of the Church is, in the metaphor of therapy, a recovering antisemite and, like all who are recovering, must remain ever vigilant about and apologetic for its sometimes quick descent into hatred.

Over the long term, though, a relationship built on these principles is perilous. It is difficult for us to assess the real conditions of our lives, to appreciate what real advances have been made, and to distinguish religious piety from the true antisemitism that remains explosive and alive in many places. If we cannot distinguish the fundamental differences between Mel Gibson and cardinals who did not condemn the movie or between the modern *Passion of the Christ* and its medieval Passion play forebears, then we are doomed to be less effective at defending ourselves against the more serious attacks that come in other ways from other quarters. Moreover, that lack of trust is bound to taint the extraordinary relationships that have brought together Christians and Jews over these past forty years. There must be room for *Teshuvah* for our Christian neighbors.

Yes, I am disappointed that Christian leaders did not adequately criticize the movie for its egregious failure to follow the very guidelines they themselves had promulgated.[14] And I am disheartened that the Vatican did not forcefully defend my friends and colleagues, the many Catholic theologians and scholars who were attacked by the Christian right wing.[15] There still is much work to be done on the interreligious front. But while I continue to mourn the unbearable losses of my own family and the Jewish community at large in Nazi-occupied Europe and in times prior, I know that eternal distrust corrodes the Jewish soul and makes us less effective at discerning and fighting against true antisemitism.

What Unique Voice Do We as Jews Have to Contribute to a Dialogue of Faith?

The Passion has unleashed intense religious conversations—between and among religious groups—across this country. Believing Christians, moved by the movie to a renewed faith in the story of Jesus's generous gift of love and salvation, have turned to us, their Jewish friends and colleagues, and posed a question that many of us are unprepared to answer: "What moves you about your religion? Tell me about your sacred spiritual journey."

FIVE INTROSPECTIVE CHALLENGES

My most recent encounter with this challenge was in a private dialogue between an Episcopalian bishop and his colleagues and a group of Jewish leaders. The Jewish leaders began first by speaking about the pain of Christian antisemitism. The bishop responded by apologizing for the entire history of Christian attacks on Jews. He spoke of his own spiritual path that brought him to the priesthood. My Jewish colleagues, undeterred, again denounced antisemitism. In response to his story of spiritual awakening, they had nothing at all to say except to reiterate the history of antisemitism. What is our Jewish spiritual journey?

We know how to battle those who would destroy us, and we know how to fight hard for the political positions we hold dear. We have honed our skills as defenders of Israel, and I am proud of the influence, political and otherwise, we wield in its support. Yet we have not spent nearly as much energy or time developing our spiritual narratives. In my own work, I employ Krister Stendahl's "holy envy," envy of others that could help lift us up and would inspire us to greater heights.[16] I am awed by the deep faith of many Christians, a faith that for some has been rekindled by Gibson's movie. Moreover, in the spirit of holy envy, I fear that we as Jews do not know what our Judaism teaches us about faith or spirit or where to find sacredness in our lives. I fear that most of us, whatever our level of observance, do not use our Judaism to help us learn what it means to be a religious or spiritual human being.

Before the release of *The Passion*, we feared for our children. We imagined what it would be like for them, in their high schools and colleges, to be asked about this movie. We worried that they would be assaulted with the epithet of "Christ killer." Instead, they are asked to explain their Jewish selves. And they, like we, have precious little religious passion to offer. We have provided them shields for self-protection but no sacred faith with which to engage the world.

We have proven that we can articulate quite effectively what we oppose. But what positive, uniquely Jewish spiritual voice can we offer to ourselves or our children in the religious conversations now taking place across this country? Few of us speak about being partners with God, emulating God's goodness in our acts of justice and righteousness. We seldom speak of the sense of *kedushah*—of holiness—that we can infuse into all aspects of our lives. We do not know to articulate the overarching principle of caring for others and pursuing peace *mipnei darkhei shalom*—for the sake of peace in the world. Yes, we are committed to wonderful values and have learned powerful rituals and observances. We are great political and social justice activists. Yet Christians cannot understand that we ignore the spirit, which for them is the soul of their religious lives. So we must return to our places of learning, to our synagogues, to our communal organizations, and learn about the spiritual home that Judaism provides.

Are There Destructive Sacred Narratives in Our Tradition?

All distinct groups, and especially religious ones, provide sacred narratives both to give meaning to their own communities and to distinguish themselves from others. The Gospels tell the story of the birth, teachings, suffering, death, and resurrection of Jesus. The Koran describes Muhammad's flight from Mecca to Medina, which establishes the Muslim *umma*, the community of the faithful. Buddhists retell the ancient story of Siddhartha, who left power and wealth to find the perfection of inner calm and oneness with the universe. Even nations have sacred narratives. In America, when we recite the words from the Declaration of Independence that "all men are created equal and endowed by their Creator with certain unalienable rights, among them life, liberty and the pursuit of happiness," we retell the sacred narrative of our nation's founding.

Sacred narratives—the holy words, books, and stories we cherish—are powerful vehicles for inspiring faith and commitment. It normally is not our place to undermine the sacred narratives of other faith communities or censor their texts and stories, and, in return, we expect respect for our religious traditions. But if the sacred narrative of one community is used to denigrate or humiliate others, if it is invoked as a source of hatred or violence, then we have a right and, indeed, an obligation to protest.

Christians have used the story of the Passion for centuries to justify the denigration of Jews and Judaism. The triumphant Church demanded the humiliation of my people, inciting violence in the name of Christian faith. It is our duty as human beings to protest this ugliness or any indication of its resurfacing, and nearly all church bodies in this country and around the world have done so. This is not, as some have criticized, religious censorship; it is a challenge to all of us to fight against destructive

FIVE INTROSPECTIVE CHALLENGES

language wherever it rears its head, especially if it does so under the guise of religious conviction.

However—and herein lies the fourth challenge—if we are to demand from Christians that they reinterpret texts and traditions that historically have been used to do damage others, then we must be prepared to evaluate our own traditions with the same care. For approximately eighteen hundred years, our people lived as an oppressed and powerless people. Because we have been a subjugated people for so long, it is hard for us to imagine that our sacred narratives could hurt others. However, we are no longer a landless, victimized people. There is a powerful army in the state of Israel that protects our people daily, in Israel and even abroad. The American Jewish community effectively mobilizes in support of Jews and Jewish interests throughout the world. We are blessed to live in an age when, in spite of continued assaults, we are remarkably strong.

Power demands a different awareness of responsibility. From our position of relative strength at the beginning of the twenty-first century, it is time to reevaluate our sacred texts, especially those that dehumanize non-Jews and call for the destruction of others. For we also have kept alive traditions and texts in our religion that call for the eradication of others in the name of God.

Ten years ago, our family and friends celebrated with a great Purim costume ball as my son, Yaron, became a Bar Mitzvah. We read the complete *Megillah*, the biblical Book of Esther, including the ninth chapter describing how the Jews impaled all of Haman's sons and then killed tens of thousands of their Persian enemies. In the story, killing Haman is the ultimate vindication; in so doing, we wipe out any memory of those who tried to destroy us. This sacred narrative actually begins centuries before when, after a vicious attack by the Amalekites against the Israelites in the desert, God commands us to wipe out each and every Amalekite.[17] Haman, the evil force in the Purim story, is the descendant of the king of the Amalekites. We are commanded to kill Haman and all those who descend from him.

We held this wonderful Purim celebration only to awake Friday morning to the horrifying news that Baruch Goldstein, on completing his own deranged reading of *Megillat Esther*, had murdered twenty-nine Muslims in prayer. He was only one man, and this is only one incident. But his reading of a sacred Jewish text and his choice to act out what he understood as God's command, as contained in that story, demands a *heshbon ha-nefesh*, a spiritual accounting and reevaluation of our sacred narratives, of which this is but one. Baruch Goldstein, in ways we never could have imagined, demonstrated the potential evil of the very sacred Jewish narratives we love.

In 2004, on the tenth anniversary of his death, memorial ceremonies for Goldstein were held in many places.[18] I did not hear voices of protest. Of greater concern, in light of his distorted understanding of the command to kill all Amalekites, is our frequent practice of using Amalek as a metaphor for all those who hate us. This Purim, I read a number of articles that remind us that our enemies—Amalek—lurk in many places, ready to pounce.[19] In some synagogues, we are asked to decide who are the Hamans of our day. Given that the Torah commands us to kill every Amalekite and every Haman and given that Jews are powerful enough today to act on this command, we must be prepared to take responsibility for any Jew who uses our sacred narrative to foment hatred or provoke murder.

This example is only one painful reminder of our duty to engage as a community in a deep and thorough investigation of all our sacred texts. We must make informed and conscious decisions about which texts we continue to teach and how we teach them. This is not a call to rewrite our Scriptures; rather, it is a call to take responsibility for the potential violence and divisiveness in our own sacred narratives, even as we denounce them in those of others.

Are We Prepared to Fight against Polarization?

More than being antisemitic, *The Passion of the Christ* is dangerous because it portrays a harsh and violent account of the last twelve hours of Jesus's life. The movie eradicates the biblical vision that every human is an image of God. In frame after frame, Gibson chooses to focus on a world filled with hateful, cruel human beings. The movie features a dark-cloaked, strange human form—found nowhere in the Gospels' Passion narratives—that Gibson describes as Satan.[20] Through his movie, Gibson has created a world in which we are either one of Jesus's followers or an insidious enemy.

At the end of the screening of *The Passion* to which I was invited, Gibson spoke to the audience of thousands.[21] His words reinforced the movie's fundamental point: not that Jesus was a great teacher or moral leader but that the world is divided between those who believe and those who deny. The opponents of Jesus are dupes of Satan, Gibson said.

The response to the movie has only reinforced this divisive vision. This film has encouraged people to invalidate alternative viewpoints. Radio and television talk shows and myriad websites branded Catholic and Protestant scholars who challenged the movie as "dissident theologians." Christian columnists who challenged the movie were called "Jew lovers" or even "dirty Jews."[22]

Gibson's personal reading of Jesus's death now could become a unifying gospel. Such ugly divisions are far more dangerous than the anti-Jewish stereotypes that pervade the movie. This hate-filled and violent rhetoric is part of a larger assault on the values of pluralism and religious respect in which Americans of goodwill have reached out to each other over the past half century in an unparalleled ecumenical spirit.

The fifth challenge that emerges from *The Passion* requires that we come face to face with this divisive vision and, as a community of Jews and in concert with our neighbors, oppose the polarization while offering an alternative that is respectful and pluralistic. Certainly this movie has moved many people.[23] But religious experiences should not require that the world be divided between them and us, that ugly stereotypes be reintroduced, or that those who challenge the movie be called satanic. We must speak out clearly and constructively against religious polarization that foments cultural warfare. We must be more vigilant than ever to ensure that the words preached in religious settings and the images offered in the name of God not be used, even inadvertently, toward destructive ends.[24] The last thing we can afford at this time is to allow this country and this world to be divided by religion or, in other cases, by ethnicity, race, nationality, or sexual identity.

Rabbi Abraham Isaac Kook, who was chief rabbi of Palestine before the establishment of the state of Israel, offers an important explanation of the rabbinic phrase, "*elu v'elu divrei elohim hayyim hen*"—"many diverse voices make up the words of the living God."[25] The house of humanity is built on this concept, writes Kook, and the supposed contradictions and conflicts resulting from respectful disagreements are all part of the unfolding of the divine plan.[26] An expansive reading of this text focuses us on our roles as citizens who share our love for our republic with fellow

Americans of many faiths, ethnicities, and nationalities. We are called on to nurture respectful dialogue, even as we battle all attempts to invalidate the rich and varied voices of debate that are critical to a thriving democracy. *The Passion of the Christ* is not about Jews; it is about an increasingly polarized America. Religious assaults that divide us into the forces of absolute good and absolute evil are a sure recipe for increased hatred, an environment where antisemitism can flourish.

The Passion of the Christ offers profound challenges to the Jewish community as we struggle to balance our responsibility to protect ourselves vigilantly with our equal obligation to utilize Judaism and Jewish power to improve the world. It requires a more thorough understanding of contemporary Christian theology. It requires a leap of faith and increased trust in our Christian neighbors. It expects from us a willingness to engage more deeply in our own Jewish spiritual quest. It insists that we interrogate our own traditions and ourselves in order to deal honestly with our own sacred narratives that divide or harm. And it obligates us to engage with all our strength to repudiate the polarizing values of the movie. If we do not mobilize on behalf of democratic pluralism and mutual respect, as individuals, in our families, and as a committed Jewish community, we imperil our future and the future of America as well.

Notes

This chapter reflects the views of its author; it is not an official statement of the American Jewish Committee.

1. See chapters 3, 5, 9, 11, 16, and 20 in this volume.
2. Panel Discussion on *The Passion of the Christ*, Office of Religious Life, Princeton University, Princeton, N.J., 2 March 2004.
3. Bishops' Committee for Ecumenical and Interreligious Affairs 2004, 3–4.
4. On 13 April 1986, Pope John Paul II stated explicitly on behalf of the Roman Catholic Church that Jews are Christians' "beloved elder brothers" in faith; in March 1967, the United States Conference of Catholic Bishops Committee for Ecumenical and Religious Affairs published guidelines stating that Jews should not be targeted for conversion, although this report was met with some resistance elsewhere in the Church, as noted in their response "Statement on Catholic-Jewish Relations" (1975). See *The Bible, the Jews and the Death of Jesus*,

inter alia. Some Protestant theologians have begun to reject the doctrine of Christian supersessionism, the principle that Christianity somehow replaced Judaism; see Kathryn Smith (chapter 20 in this volume).

5. See Torjesen (chapter 6 in this volume).

6. See, for example, Broadway 2004; Graham 28 January 2004; Graham 2004; Haggard 2004. See also Haynes (chapter 14 in this volume) and Kathryn Smith (chapter 20 in this volume).

7. See the categories that define antisemitism used by the Anti-Defamation League in its annual surveys.

8. Personal observations gained from sessions in which I spoke across the United States during the first few months of 2004.

9. Anti-Defamation League 2004.

10. Berkofsky 2004.

11. Pew Research Center for the People and the Press 2004.

12. Gladstone 2004.

13. Federal Bureau of Investigation 2003, 17.

14. United States Conference of Catholic Bishops 2004.

15. See William J. Cork (chapter 2 in this volume) and Ingersoll (chapter 5 in this volume).

16. See Marsh 2001. Stendahl has used the term in his public lectures about *The Passion* alongside his "three principles for communal living" (see Wetmore 2004):

1. Let the Other define herself; 75 percent of what our tradition says of another tradition is bearing false witness.

2. Compare equal to equal. We all have our extremists and nuts. Don't compare ideal Christianity with the actual or distorted form of the Other.

3. We will never have good relations without an element of holy envy. Find something in the Other that is beautiful and meaningful and that tells you something about God. You are not called on to absorb it or to pass judgment on it.

17. See Exodus 17:8–16; Deuteronomy 25:17–19; I Samuel 15.

18. *Haaretz* Staff 2004; Shuman 2004.

19. See, for example, Flatow 2004.

20. See Faggen (chapter 8 in this volume) and Morgan (chapter 11 in this volume) for extended discussions of Gibson's "Satan" figure.

21. I was invited to attend a screening on 20 January 2004 at Willow Creek Community Church in South Barrington, Illinois. See Elcott 2004.

22. See Cork (chapter 2 in this volume) and Ingersoll (chapter 5 in this volume).
23. See, for example, Haynes (chapter 14 in this volume).
24. See Dorff (chapter 19 in this volume).
25. Babylonian Talmud *Masekhet Eruvin* 13b.
26. Kook 1962, 330.

CHAPTER EIGHTEEN
NO CRUCIFIXION = NO HOLOCAUST: POST-HOLOCAUST REFLECTIONS ON *THE PASSION OF THE CHRIST*
John K. Roth

As Mel Gibson's excruciatingly bloody scourging of Jesus reaches its climax in *The Passion of the Christ*, one of Pontius Pilate's lieutenants intervenes and chastises the Roman soldiers for excessive brutality. "You weren't supposed to beat him to death!" he exclaims. That moment was only one of many that jarred me when I saw Mel Gibson's film two days after it opened. Given the scourging that Gibson created, the judgment of Pilate's lieutenant seemed ludicrous and incredible. After such a beating, scarcely anyone could have remained alive, as Jesus had to be for his crucifixion to follow. Of course, a caveat in that judgment is needed, and this point is no doubt one that Gibson wanted to make: namely, Jesus was not "anyone"; he was the incarnation of God and thus able to take any punishment, any abuse, that human beings could devise and still triumph over it.

At least four important realizations follow, I believe, from the description I have offered. First, few events, if any, in human history have had more volatile consequences and potent implications than the Roman execution by crucifixion of a then-relatively-obscure Jewish teacher from Galilee whose name was Jesus. To employ one of several shorthand equations that I use in this chapter to put key issues in bold relief, *No crucifixion of Jesus = No Western civilization as we know it.*

Second, the reason why that equation holds is that the crucifixion of Jesus has always played a decisive part in the Christian tradition's understanding of God, the world, and the meaning of our individual lives. These connections are so strong that we may confidently assert another equation: *No crucifixion of Jesus = No Christianity*. Absent Christianity, Western civilization and indeed the world as we know it would be inconceivable.

Taking the New Testament Gospels as the historically accurate source, Mel Gibson's film arrived amidst claims that it truthfully portrayed what really happened during the last twelve hours of Jesus's earthly life. However, as many already have pointed out, Gibson's film is authentic neither as history nor as a representation of the Gospels, at least as far as the details are concerned. To one watching the film, checking the New Testament texts, and tracking Gibson's use of sources, it is apparent that *The Passion of the Christ* is a highly idiosyncratic interpretation of events whose reality remains elusive. Thus, a third key point emerges: beyond the barest of outlines, no one today can be very confident that they know precisely what happened during the last twelve hours of Jesus's life. That Jesus was crucified is not in question, but precisely how and why the crucifixion took place is profoundly contested. Hence, another equation holds: *No crucifixion of Jesus = No Christian–Jewish rivalry*.

Fourth, the Christian–Jewish rivalry had such catastrophic implications that, particularly after the Holocaust, we Christians should be especially careful about how the crucifixion of Jesus is interpreted and portrayed.[1] Nazi Germany's attempt to destroy the Jewish people would have been virtually inconceivable without Christianity's (my tradition's) negative depictions of Jews. That conjunction creates a shameful burden that should shake Christianity to its core. The shame, in turn, should lead not only to repentance about the Christian tradition's long-standing and only very recently reformed stance toward Jews but also to fundamental rethinking about what it should and should not mean to be a Christian after Auschwitz. Among the many shortcomings of Gibson's film, therefore, I believe that none is more egregious than its insensitivity about the Holocaust, its failure to acknowledge the equation *No crucifixion of Jesus = No Holocaust*.

Less than a month after I saw *The Passion of the Christ*, I was teaching my students on an academic travel program in Poland and the Czech Republic. For several days, we worked at the Auschwitz-Birkenau State Museum. Walking through the Auschwitz gate inscribed with the mocking motto *Arbeit Macht Frei*, standing before the crematoria ruins at Birkenau, I thought about the crucifixion of Jesus and about Gibson's interpretation of it. As a Christian, I felt shame and anger—shame for Christianity's complicity in the Holocaust and anger about Mel Gibson's negative portrayals of Jews, which were set forth as if the Holocaust never happened.

No post-Holocaust portrayal of the crucifixion can be trustworthy if it fails to link the crucifixion to that twentieth-century catastrophe. Gibson's film forged no links of that kind. For that reason, every post-Holocaust Christian should be critical of the film, but this is unlikely because the impact of the Holocaust has not been felt sufficiently by most Christians. For that reason, my response to Gibson's movie will concentrate less on the film itself and more on the Holocaust, a reality that Gibson and indeed all of us post-Holocaust Christians would do well to ponder again and again, especially when we confront the New Testament Passion narratives and any artistic or cinematic depiction of the crucifixion of Jesus.

I do not know if Mel Gibson has ever visited Auschwitz or even encountered the echoes of the Holocaust as they are found, for example, in the United States Holocaust Memorial Museum in Washington, D.C. Be that as it may, a visit to such places is a profoundly thought-provoking experience before or after viewing *The Passion of the Christ*, for Christians ought to view Gibson's film—even if he did not—with the following question in mind: how are the Holocaust and Christianity linked together?

In the Holocaust Memorial Museum, biblical words from the prophet Isaiah—"You are my witnesses"—are inscribed on a wall where it is difficult for visitors to miss them.[2] Whenever I visit the museum, I stop for a moment to read that ancient text, which at once expresses an expectation, a commandment, and a fact. Those simple but immensely challenging words make me think about my Christian identity, and after February 2004, they are likely to make me think again about *The Passion of the Christ* in particular. Specifically, Isaiah's words require me to reflect on Christianity's relationship to the Holocaust and to wrestle with the implications of that event for my religious tradition.

Most of my academic life has been devoted to studying the Holocaust. Frequently people wonder how I became involved in that work, which has been my passion for more than thirty years. Sometimes people ask, "Are you Jewish?" perhaps assuming, mistakenly, that dedicated attention to Holocaust history is something that only Jews are likely to pursue. To the question "Are you Jewish?" I would be glad and proud to answer, "Yes," but my identity is different. It is precisely because of my Christian identity that

JOHN K. ROTH

I have immersed myself in the study of the Holocaust, for I believe that my identity (as indeed anyone's contemporary identity as a Christian) is linked to that catastrophe. As I explain what I mean, I also want to suggest how we Christians might reidentify ourselves in a post-Holocaust situation and how we might do so in ways that would give our tradition greater integrity, an integrity that depends in so many ways on solidarity with Jewish tradition and the Jewish people. Meanwhile, the tragedy of Mel Gibson's film is that it subverts and undercuts the very solidarity that Christianity needs to reclaim in order to redeem itself.

To develop these ideas with Gibson's film in mind, follow me from the entry hall in the United States Holocaust Memorial Museum, where Isaiah's words are inscribed, to a smaller but even more solemn place within the museum, a circular space called the Hall of Remembrance. The names of Nazi killing centers, such as Auschwitz and Treblinka, where Jews were gassed, can be found around the perimeter of this hall. The Hall of Remembrance also includes places for memorial candles to be lit in honor and memory of the six million Jewish children, women, and men who were killed, one by one, in those camps of death and destruction. Opposite the entry of this circular hall, an eternal flame burns in a place where soil from camps in Poland, Germany, and other countries has been deposited.

Biblical words appear on the circular walls of the Hall of Remembrance. Shared by Jews and Christians, the three passages from the Hebrew Bible can be read in different sequences, depending on how one's eyes follow the arc that contains them. Consider those three passages (one from Genesis, the other two from Deuteronomy) as guideposts for deepening reflection about identity, integrity, and being a witness, especially as those ideas relate to Christian life after the Holocaust and, as this book's title suggests, after *The Passion* has gone from theaters.

The first biblical quotation says this: "And the Lord said, 'What have you done? Listen; your brother's blood is crying out to me from the ground.'"[3] Those words remind one that witnesses are those who have seen or heard something. They are people who are called to testify. They furnish evidence. Often, they sign their names to documents to certify an event's occurrence or a statement's truth. So, when one reads that verse from the Genesis story of Cain and Abel, God's question calls for testimony and for bearing witness.

NO CRUCIFIXION = NO HOLOCAUST

A Christian who reads those words ("What have you done?") in the United States Holocaust Memorial Museum setting must do some soul-searching about identity and integrity, for the Holocaust's history testifies to a disturbing fact, namely, that while Christianity was not a sufficient condition for the Holocaust, Christianity was a necessary condition for that disaster. That statement does not mean that Christianity caused the Holocaust.[4] Nevertheless, the Holocaust that actually happened is scarcely imaginable apart from Christianity because Nazi Germany's targeting of the Jewish people cannot be explained apart from the anti-Jewish images ("Christ killers," willful blasphemers, unrepentant sons and daughters of the Devil, to name only a few) that have been rooted deeply in Christian practices—and, ominously, reappear in Gibson's film.

After Christianity came to dominate the Roman world in the fourth century C.E., Christian images and institutions that vilified and demonized Jews started laying the groundwork for an increasingly multifaceted antisemitism. Frequently inspired by the New Testament's crucifixion narratives and the interpretations evoked by those texts, these ideas came decisively to define and govern many of Western civilization's most influential worldviews. Well before the Nazi Party struggled its way into existence in the aftermath of World War I, antisemitism was so axiomatic in Christian-dominated cultures that, with few exceptions, Jews could be fully included within Western civilization's fundamentally Christian-defined boundaries of moral obligation only if they first rejected their Jewishness. Understandably, most Jews chose not to do so.

There can be no credible doubt about it: what we can call Christian antisemitism provided essential background, preparation, and motivation for the Holocaust that happened when Germans and their collaborators carried out the "Final Solution" of the so-called Jewish question.[5] "What have you done?"—God's question to Cain—is a question put to Christians, too, and it is put to us Christians in a crucial way after the Holocaust. *The Passion of the Christ* might have underscored this reminder but, unfortunately, did not.

The second biblical quotation in the Hall of Remembrance at the United States Holocaust Memorial Museum says this: "Keep these words that I am commanding you today in your heart. Recite them to your children and talk about them when you are at home and when you are away, when you lie down and when you rise."[6] They are inscribed above the eternal flame that burns in the Hall of Remembrance near the spot where soil from the Nazi death camps has been deposited. In that place, standing before those words should make deep impressions on Christians, and, at least for me, they do. Those impressions involve, once again, identity, integrity, and being a witness.

The words inscribed from Deuteronomy are calls to living witness, which entails not only personal and communal experience but also memory of it, so that one's witnessing has specific content that can be passed from one generation to another. Such calls are crucial because when we remember and bear witness, we can contribute to humankind's redemption.[7] That outlook, of course, is not referring to just any kind of bearing witness. In the Deuteronomist's view, bearing witness should keep ourselves and our children close to God and on the right path.

To be a witness, a living witness, one has to have something about which to bear witness. Such work is hard but immensely important. Specifically, bearing witness, from generation to generation, calls us post-Holocaust Christians back to our roots in ways that remind us about who we are and who we ought to be when we are at our best. Indeed, given the historical proximity of the Holocaust to our own lives, current post-Holocaust Christians have a unique opportunity and responsibility to be living witnesses of a distinctive kind. Here I can clarify my meaning by emphasizing that what drew me to study the Holocaust was a growing conflict between two features of my experience. On the one hand, although not without qualification, I have experienced Christianity as something good. On the other hand, I know that Christianity, my tradition, has not been good for everyone; the Holocaust bears witness to that. Thus, I found myself wanting to know where things had gone so badly wrong and how they might best be corrected, especially insofar as Christians and Jews have been concerned. In the ongoing process of self-definition, I came to believe that we Christians have lost sight of our close and essential ties to Jewish tradition.

Very few people anywhere—American or not—would be among the world's two billion Christians if it were not for a centuries-old Christian mission whose history includes Holocaust-related hostility to Jews and Judaism, even if many Christians are not as aware of this fact as we ought to be. Lest I be misunderstood, I am not suggesting that anti-Judaism was or is the underlying force behind the evangelism that made Christianity a global religion. Rather, Christians still need to come to terms fully with the fact that antipathy toward Jews and Judaism has been embedded persistently throughout global Christianity. Here honesty requires post-Holocaust Christians to underscore that it is neither sufficient nor indeed historically accurate to say that Christians who have harbored anti-Jewish sentiments or even antisemitism have not been real Christians. Significant signs of change for the better can be found today, but, in fact, the mainstream of Christianity long has been anti-Jewish, if not antisemitic, including the greatest leaders of the Christian churches, such as Augustine of Hippo and Martin Luther, to cite but two. Post-Holocaust reform of the Christian tradition is far from finished and continues to be necessary. It is good that Christians have post-Holocaust theologies that denounce anti-Judaism and that identify antisemitism as a sin, but we Christians must also recognize that such outlooks are, on the whole, new to our tradition. Our commitment is required to ensure that they endure.

Many contemporary Christians—like those of us who live in the United States and flocked to see Mel Gibson's film—may wonder why we need to remember Christianity's role in the Holocaust. After all, we might argue, that involvement took place long ago and far away. It was part of Europe's "Old World" corruption. In our country, we twenty-first-century Americans may be tempted to say, things have been different; we made a new beginning, and we broke away from fallen European ways. The Holocaust was not—could not have been—any responsibility of ours, especially if, like me, we live in Mel Gibson's California, which is about as far away from Auschwitz as one can get.

The problem is that Gibson's film has much more in common with pre-Holocaust Christian animosity toward Jews than it does with post-Holocaust reconciliation between Christianity and Judaism. Judging by polls that differentiate between Americans who have seen the film and those who have not,[8] *The Passion* leaves no doubt that Jews were the instigators and unrelenting advocates of that gruesome death. To be sure, Gibson and his supporters have claimed that all of humanity, not any group in particular, is responsible for the crucifixion of Jesus and the suffering of God. However, such universalizing is too easy, too convenient, as a way out of the dilemmas that attend narratives that are unavoidably particular and specific. Christianity, like Judaism, does not regard God primarily as a universalizing, cosmic metaphysician but as One who acts in very specific and concrete ways within history. If the responsibility is universal and therefore everyone's but no one's in particular, then Gibson's authority for saying that his account is faithful to the New Testament is in double jeopardy: once for going far beyond the texts and twice for not taking them seriously enough. And if Gibson wanted to advance an account of universal human responsibility for the crucifixion, his film does a very poor job of making that case.

Let us return to the words from Deuteronomy that are inscribed above the eternal flame in the Hall of Remembrance at the Holocaust Museum. The commandment to bear witness contained in the words from Deuteronomy immediately follows other words that say, "Hear, O Israel: The Lord is our God, the Lord is One. You shall love the Lord your God with all your heart, with all your soul, and with all your might."[9] When the Christian New Testament reports that Jesus was asked which commandment was the first of all, he paraphrased those words in reply, adding in true Jewish fashion that the second is to love your neighbor as yourself.[10] Then, when Jesus was asked to define who is one's neighbor, he told the parable of the Good Samaritan,[11] a figure who epitomizes what it ought to mean to be a Christian. The key point here, however, is that we Christians have our identity because the workings of history put before us a relationship with God that can be understood neither apart from Jewish history nor (and this is very important) apart from the ongoing vitality of Jewish life.

We Christians came to know God through the Jewish tradition as Jesus and his followers made that tradition accessible to us and grafted us into it.[12] As time passed, changes distorted those connections, and, tragically, the full price of those distorted connections would not be exacted or known until the Holocaust scarred the earth. Nevertheless, the basic point was there to be recognized all along: if Christians are the followers of Jesus, a faithful Jew, then our responsibility is to love God and to love our neighbors—most emphatically including Jesus's own Jewish people—as ourselves. As we Christians interpret the identity of Jesus, the bottom line comes back to those words from Deuteronomy that are inscribed above the eternal flame in the Hall of Remembrance, including the way in which they point to God. Christian reidentification after the Holocaust, I believe, can lead to a deepened integrity for Christian life just to the extent that there is a Christian *Teshuvah*, a repentant returning to a love of our rootedness in Jewish tradition.[13]

This returning needs to emphasize something very different from the negative pictures of Jews highlighted by Mel Gibson's *Passion*. That is,

NO CRUCIFIXION = NO HOLOCAUST

Jews are not indebted to Christians; rather, we Christians are indebted to them. As Clark Williamson, a thoughtful Christian thinker, has put it, we Christians should think of ourselves as guests in the house of Israel and behave accordingly.[14] Gibson's filmmaking in *The Passion of the Christ* does not fit that description.

Finally, as my eyes follow the Hall of Remembrance's arc from left to right, from words that question "What have you done?" to words, illuminated by an eternal flame, that encourage one to live and bear witness, a third inscription requires attention as well. Its words, attributed to Moses, say this: "I have set before you life and death. . . . Choose life so that you and your descendants may live."[15] As I think about those words, I am reminded of Pope John Paul II's special concert at the Vatican in April 1994 to commemorate the Holocaust.[16] It was a night of "firsts," although not entirely a cause for celebration because the "firsts" were so late in coming.

On that occasion, for example, the chief rabbi of Rome was invited for the first time to co-officiate at a public function in the Vatican. For the first time, a Jewish cantor sang in the Vatican. For the first time, a 500-year-old Vatican choir sang a Hebrew text in performance—Leonard Bernstein's *Chichester Psalms*. Late though these "firsts" turned out to be, the music at the Vatican's interfaith concert was moving, and the pope's concluding words went to the heart of the matter when he asked the concert's listeners to observe silence and to "hear once more the plea, 'Do not forget us,'" a plea rising from the Holocaust's victims, the dead and the living. Calling it "powerful, agonizing, heartrending," Pope John Paul II also suggested that no memory can be worthy of that plea unless remembering leads people to resist what he called "the specter of racism, exclusion, alienation, slavery, and xenophobia" and to act so that "evil does not prevail over good," as it did for millions of Jews during the Holocaust.

The music, the pope's words, and particularly the *Chichester Psalms* accented a very important point: the value of beliefs (Christian or Jewish) must be measured by the justice or injustice, the good or evil, they inspire. Therefore, we must measure our Christian beliefs—including beliefs surrounding the Passion of Jesus—against both their contributions to the Holocaust and their responsiveness to it. Such a test leaves Christianity wanting in ways that should make my religious tradition much less triumphalist and much more modest than it has been in the past and still often is. More than ever, Christianity requires honesty, candor, and atonement—indeed, living witness that protests against injustice and that tries its best to protect those who fall prey to evil.

The post-Holocaust condition that is most necessary for us Christians is a spiritual and ethical turning, a soul-searching (personal and communal) that leads us to ask, What should it mean for me, for us, to be a Christian after Auschwitz? Sound Christian responses to that question are still taking time to form. Christianity will have the identity and integrity that it needs only to the extent that these responses are formed well. Those responses should focus on three points:

1. Our answer to the question, What have you done?

2. Our acknowledgment that Christians are followers of the Jew named Jesus

3. Our responsibility to choose life

Thinking and acting well with regard to these points will qualify Christians to respond authentically to the Deuteronomic charge that we bear witness in everything that we do. Only to the extent that we post-Holocaust Christians make that response an honest one will our identity and integrity become what they ought to be.

My identity—perhaps the identity of each of us—is in its own way inseparable from Christianity, but that proposition does not mean that either our personal identities or the nature of Christianity is set in concrete. I could abandon Christianity, but I choose not to do so because Christianity includes affirmations that I value, and it does so in the ways that are most familiar to me. The Passion and resurrection of Jesus are key parts of that tradition. Nevertheless, we must rethink, reform, and at times reject the ways that the narratives about those events have been understood in the past and are presented here and now. It is in that spirit that I suggest that we reject Mel Gibson's *Passion* precisely because it fails the tests I described previously.

As the twenty-first century begins, we Christians most definitely do not need a version of Jesus's crucifixion that imputes guilt and responsibility unfairly and that implies Christian triumphalism after the Holocaust. Instead, we need a narrative that shows how Christians can affirm Jews as Jews and that opens a way for Jews to find that the cross and the crucified

Jesus are neither alien nor threatening. This can occur only when those who claim to follow Jesus as Lord practice with persistence and humility what he preached: that we should love God and love our neighbors as ourselves. Were such a story real and then told again in film, it still might not get the hype and the huge box office receipts heaped on the Gibson movie. But such a film, especially if it were informed by deep awareness of the Holocaust, would help show that *The Passion* has gone because it would have been eclipsed by something far more deserving of attention.

Notes

1. The Vatican Commission for Religious Relations with Jews (1985) and the National Conference of Catholic Bishops (1988) have published guidelines for just this purpose.

2. Isaiah 43:10. The following paragraphs in this chapter are derived from Roth 2000 and 2001 and Rubenstein and Roth 2003.

3. Genesis 4:10.

4. A related theme is stressed in the important 2000 document "*Dabru Emet*: A Jewish Statement on Christians and Christianity" endorsed by rabbis and other Jewish scholars across the United States: "Without the long history of Christian anti-Judaism and Christian violence against Jews, Nazi ideology could not have taken hold nor could it have been carried out. . . . But Nazism itself was not an inevitable outcome of Christianity" (Frymer-Kensky et al. 2000).

5. See Heschel (chapter 13 in this volume) for an extended discussion of the ways that German theologians buttressed the Nazi's anti-Jewish agenda.

6. Deuteronomy 6:6–7.

7. Here my claim echoes the saying attributed to the Baal Shem Tov, the founder of Hasidism: "In remembrance resides the secret of redemption."

8. See, for example, Pew Research Center for the People and the Press 2004.

9. Deuteronomy 6:4–5.

10. See Matthew 22:34–40.

11. Luke 10:25–37.

12. The apostle Paul reflects a version of this idea in Romans 11.

13. Compare Elcott (chapter 17 in this volume).

14. See Williamson 1993.

15. Deuteronomy 30:19.

16. The references and quotations that follow are from Levine 1994.

CHAPTER NINETEEN
THE PASSIONATE ENCOUNTER: THE ETHICS OF AFFIRMING YOUR FAITH IN A MULTIRELIGIOUS WORLD
Elliot N. Dorff

If we take Mel Gibson at his word, he intended his movie *The Passion of the Christ* to stir Christians to a deeper understanding and commitment to their faith. Christians, though, do not live alone in this world any more than do adherents of any other faith or of no faith; and so Gibson's movie raises important questions about how we may and should affirm our own faith without harming others. That is not a new question; people have been grappling with how to understand themselves in relation to others from the very beginnings of human recorded history. The movie, though, is an especially intense formulation of Christian faith presented in a medium that is by its very nature graphic, and so it makes the moral issues of interfaith relations especially vivid and critical.

Self and Others

Every group has pride in its own identity. Sometimes that pride is justified by the group's accomplishments, but just as often groups take pride in themselves simply as an expression of their self-esteem. "My country right or wrong" has similar echoes in religious doctrines that portray one's own religion as the correct one and better than any other, however one measures or justifies such judgments.

Self-esteem is important for any individual or group. Indeed, lack of self-esteem is often at the root of criminals' behavior, for it is hard to respect others if one does not respect oneself. In its extreme, lack of self-esteem tempts people to commit suicide. On the other hand, valuing only oneself can just as surely lead to criminal behavior, with the Nazis illustrating the shocking extent of this danger. In essence, then, as the first-century Jewish sage Hillel said, "If I am not for myself, who will be for me? But if I am only for myself, what kind of person am I?"[1]

The same dynamic applies to religious groups. Religions, in fact, sometimes serve to motivate and justify harmful behavior, for they speak in the name of a group's perception of ultimate truth and value, and they deal with some of our worst fears and most cherished hopes.[2] How can anyone who disagrees with us about such fundamental matters be right or good? Why should we even tolerate them, let alone seek to build strong relations with them? Worse, if another group played a negative role in your group's story, why should I even let them live? Since the Gospels blame Jesus's death at least in part on the Jews, Passion plays in the past have been the occasion for Christian rampages of killing and mayhem against the local Jews. That history is the source of many Jews' consternation about the effects of this film, which is much more graphic than those plays ever were and which will be seen by far more people.

The truth, though, is that Jews, no less than Christians, experience the tension between pride in their own religion and culture on the one hand and openness to people of other faiths and cultures on the other.[3] For that matter, the violence perpetrated over the past several years against the West by some Muslims and denounced by others is a vivid, contemporary example of this tension, and the same issues affect Asian religious groups as well. Since *The Passion* is about Jews and Christians, however, I shall focus on this issue as it affects them.

Historical, Philosophical, and Theological Grounding for Good Interfaith Relations

Clearly, the question of how Jews should interact with non-Jews does not arise in matters of justice, commerce, or charity, for there what governs Jewish behavior are Jewish conceptions of God as the Creator of us all and Jewish laws insisting that all people be treated fairly.[4] Later Jewish law went further: in order to establish good relations between Jews and non-Jews, Jews must help the poor and the sick of all religions and aid in burying their dead and in comforting their mourners.[5] That kind of care for others is unusual even for peoples in the modern world. Moreover, the ways in which Christians and others persecuted Jews throughout history make this high standard of civility in traditional Judaism remarkable: Jewish theology, unlike some versions of Christian and Muslim theology, did not blind its believers to the human necessity of being honest, fair, and caring toward others who believed differently.

The deeper questions, then, the ones on which the ethics of interfaith relations rests, are these: How can and should Jews understand the truth status of other religions? How shall we understand their moral claims and practices? Are other peoples simply deluded, or may their religions contain truths and values from which Jews themselves can learn? On the other hand, if other religions do contain truths and commendable values, why should Jews remain Jewish? Answering such questions about one's own religion clearly and convincingly is critical for people of all faiths. It is especially important if religious people (and nonreligious people) ever hope to go beyond persecuting others, offending them, avoiding them, or, at best, merely tolerating them and to advance to the point of actually understanding and appreciating them while at the same time retaining their own convictions and sense of identity. I suggest three foundations for accomplishing this: history, philosophy, and theology.

History

Historically, Christianity has been subject to change and redefinition at least as much as Judaism has, if not more. Within both faiths, even within the same denomination, creeds created centuries ago have changed continually, sometimes through outright amendment; sometimes through new interpretations, emphases, or applications; and sometimes through simply ignoring them. This constantly evolving nature of both Judaism and Christianity makes some of the faithful uneasy; they long for certainty and stability. Each religion, though, has retained its relevance and its dynamism only by opening itself to change.

The same is true about each faith's understanding of others. The Second Vatican Council's repudiation of blaming Jews living then or now for the death of Jesus and the recent rejection by the Evangelical Lutheran Church in America of Martin Luther's many antisemitic writings are relevant cases in point. Conversely, few modern Jews dismiss other faiths out of hand as being theologically false and morally bad, as Jews did in the past; on the contrary, my own work has been but one of many attempts to create a new Jewish conception of other religions.[6]

At the same time, history does not undermine a religious community's ability to draw boundaries and to take a strong stand on what it believes. Even though the contemporary Jewish community is much exercised over the question of who is a Jew, for example, it has determined uniformly and authoritatively that members of groups such as Jews for Jesus decidedly are *not* Jews.

The historically evolutionary nature of both faiths and the rampant borrowing from one to the other should, however, help contemporary Jews and Christians get beyond the feeling that the present articulation of their faith is the only one possible for a decent person to have. On the contrary, history should teach us that people of intelligence, morality, and sensitivity most likely exist in other faiths too.[7] Thus, even if relations between people of specific faiths have not been good in the past, we *can* reshape those relations in the present and future, for all religions change over time.

It is this historical awareness that, unfortunately, is missing from Gibson's film. I recognize the difficulty of portraying the gospel story, which is inherently anti-Judaic and to some degree antisemitic, in a way that is both authentic to the story and yet manages to avoid the negative implications that that story has had for Jews. However, historical awareness that the Gospels themselves were written many decades after the events they portray and that the Gospels are indeed interpretations of those events—what Jews would call *midrash*—should have made it possible for Gibson to capture the religious meaning of the story for Christians without repeating the Gospels' slurs against the Jews.

Philosophy

In my book on Jewish social ethics, *To Do the Right and the Good*, I explain and justify the position of epistemological relativity in contrast to absolutism on the one side and relativism and subjectivism on the other. Relativity, when applied to interfaith relations, asserts that all human beings, whatever their background or creed, suffer from the same limitations on human knowledge. Many of us have sacred texts and traditions that, for us, reveal God's nature and will—or, for nontheological traditions, ultimate reality and morality—as clearly and fully as we think possible. We all must recognize, though, that other peoples make the same claim for their sacred texts and traditions. Moreover, we have no grounds outside the various traditions to provide shared criteria to judge them; medieval Western philosophers tried to use reason to justify and compare all three Western faiths, but we now know that the rules of reason themselves vary with cultures and over generations. Therefore, either we must resort to vacuous and disingenuous debates, such as the disputations of the Middle Ages about whose tradition is right, or we must finally confront the fact that none of us can know God's nature or will with absolute certainty.

At the same time, just as historical considerations such as the interactions of nations and cultures do not make all faiths the same or spoil the significance of living by one specific faith, so, too, philosophical factors such as the relativity of human knowledge do not undermine faith altogether. We may think that our particular understanding of God and all other religious topics is the correct one for all people, *as far as we can tell*. We may also advance arguments toward convincing others of its truth and worth and even of its preeminence over other faith claims. We must do so, however, knowing ahead of time that no human argument on these matters can be conclusive, for no person is omniscient and no human vantage point can claim inherent superiority over all others.

Moreover, we must recognize that part of the reason that the arguments for my faith seem most persuasive to me is because it is, after all, *my* faith and that of my family and my people.[8] One need not deny cognitive meaning to religion to take such a position, as A. J. Ayer, R. B. Braithwaite, and others did in the middle of the twentieth century,[9] for people of all faiths are trying to respond to objective reality as they see it. One need be humble only enough to recognize that none of us sees the world through transparent lenses, that we all view it through the filter of our particular religion or philosophy of life, and that our autobiographical backgrounds inevitably do and perhaps should play a role in determining what we see and how we respond to it.[10]

Gibson's movie, of course, intends to dramatize a particular religious story, not to make a philosophical statement. Still, someone with this awareness of the limits of human knowledge might have ensured that however powerful a particular tenet such as the Passion of Christ is in his life, one must take care to ensure that in telling the story one does not harm others. After all, even though it may seem crystal clear to Gibson that the Passion took place as he portrays it and has the implications that he draws from it as a Christian, awareness of the limits of human knowledge requires enough humility to make sure that one's claims minimally do not harm others.

Precisely that kind of epistemological humility and care for others forms the basis for pluralism and democracy. Those who instead insist that only they can be right have adopted a position that not only is philosophically unfounded and intellectually fascist—often leading, when such people have power, to political fascism—but also, in essence, an idolatrous worship of their own intelligence and views. Perhaps the greatest gift that the United States has given to the world is a healthy pluralism, in which people of all faiths and none can live together in harmony. A film that ignores the need to tell one's story without harming others is both epistemologically and morally wrong, and it threatens that specifically American brand of pluralism.

Theology

In addition to these historical and philosophical considerations, Judaism contains some important theological tenets that we can use to lay the groundwork for a genuine appreciation of others. I discuss these at length in *To Do the Right and the Good*, but a few examples will make the point. So, for example, the rabbis assert that in creating us, God made both the bodies and thoughts of each individual unique and, as such, each individual must be respected and valued, just as the original painting costs more than any copy. Similarly, biblical and rabbinic sources indicate that Jews learned about theological and moral matters from their discussions with non-Jews. Thus, despite the fact that Job and his friends were not Jewish,[11] the Sages intentionally included the Book of Job in the biblical canon, undoubtedly because they knew that Job's discussion did indeed increase our knowledge of God and His ways. Indeed, much of the Bible, and especially the Wisdom literature (Proverbs, Job, Ecclesiastes, and so on), reflects the significant influence of the ancient cultures near which the Jews were living.[12] Furthermore, the Talmud records a number of conversations between the rabbis and non-Jews on theological and moral topics, including, for example, the theological questions posed by Tineius Rufus, the Roman governor of Palestine, to Rabbi Akiba.[13] In all these biblical and talmudic conversations with heathens, the Jews involved are stimulated by the non-Jews' questions and thoughts to real learning.

Nonetheless, traditional Jewish sources assign non-Jewish views to a clearly secondary status; for them, only the Jews know what is objectively correct and good. This is not only how *Jews* understand God's will but also the reason why Jews commit all their energies and, indeed, their very lives to Jewish belief and practice. Despite this nationalistic side of the Jewish tradition, however, what ultimately rings through it are Jewish sources that acknowledge and respect the Other. The Sages assert that non-Jews fully meet God's expectations by obeying the Seven Noahide Laws—that is, prohibitions against murder, idolatry, incest, eating a limb torn from a living animal, blasphemy, and theft, together with the positive duty to establish laws and courts[14]—and they declare that "the pious and virtuous of all nations participate in eternal bliss."[15] Moreover, affirmation of pluralist approaches to God within the Jewish community also can be applied, without too much tampering, to intercommunal relations as well. Therefore, theological as well as historical and philosophical considerations can and should make Jews open to serious interfaith discussions and motivate them to participate in many interfaith activities on behalf of the general good.

Moral Duties to Those of Other Faiths

If these historical, philosophical, and theological factors call on us not only to tolerate people of other faiths but also to care about them and to learn from them while still affirming our own identity, how should we do that?

1. *Avoid triumphalism.* It is, admittedly, a hard thing to balance pride in oneself and one's own tradition with respect for others. After all, if you did not believe that your faith is right at least for you and perhaps for others as well, why would you affirm it in the first place? Still, the three factors described in the previous section require that we gain the maturity to take pride in our own tradition and yet appreciation for others. This does not preclude a passionate portrayal of one's own faith, such as Gibson intended to create.

2. *Avoid harm to others.* What the three factors do preclude, however, is harming others in the act of expressing our own faith. If we recognize that history, philosophy, and theology all require

us to be less than cocksure about our own faith commitments, we must at least make sure that our present version of our faith does not provoke hatred and harm for others. It is here that Passion plays throughout history failed badly, and Gibson's movie unfortunately did not do much better.

3. *Choose interpretations with respect for others in mind.* How do traditions change? In response to interactions with other faiths or new conditions, sometimes traditions borrow from other faiths, with or without modification, and sometimes they instead fight against such influences. Either way, exponents of the faith learn to interpret their sacred texts and traditions in new ways in order to formulate an apt response. Sometimes that means actively rejecting a previous text, as the Evangelical Lutheran Church did in 1996 in repudiating Luther's antisemitic comments. More often, leaders use one part of their tradition to modify another, as the Second Vatican Council and the authors of later papal statements have done in affirming that Judaism is the root of Christianity and is to be respected as such. Sometimes teachers help adherents drop a bad interpretation of the faith, as the Second Vatican Council did in asserting that not all Jews at the time of Jesus and none since were responsible for Jesus's death. Sometimes, masters of the tradition simply ignore parts of the tradition ("benign neglect") and focus on (or "lift up") others in order to change the tradition's conceptions and practices in ways the leaders deem desirable. Awareness of the three factors discussed in the previous section should enable the faithful to recognize that they have a *choice* in how they shape their tradition and put it into practice, that they do *not* have to blindly repeat the prejudices and harmful practices of the past, and that their *ability* to change imposes a *moral duty* to interpret their tradition in ways that respect others and do not harm them.

From all that he has said, Mel Gibson did not intend to be antisemitic, and yet he produced a movie that repeats some of the same negative stereotyping of Jews that has been part of Christianity since the Gospels. May our multiple, modern interactions with people of other faiths and our awareness of the moral duty to respect them in the telling of our own stories and the exercise of our own faith foster more morally sensitive and responsible articulations of our faith commitments in the future?

Notes

1. M. *Avot (Ethics of the Fathers)* 1:14 (hereafter, M. = Mishnah [edited c. 200 C.E.]; B. = Babylonian Talmud, edited c. 500 C.E.; M.T. = Maimonides' *Mishneh Torah*, completed in 1177 C.E.; and S.A. = Joseph Karo's *Shulhan Arukh*, completed in 1565 C.E.).

2. I discuss the ways in which religion contributes to both immorality and morality in Dorff 2003, chapter 1.

3. For a description of the tension between nationalism and universalism in Jewish sources, see Dorff 2002, chapter 3.

4. According to the Talmud (B. *Bava Metzia* 59b), the commandment to love the stranger and not to wrong him occurs thirty-six times in the Torah, perhaps most explicitly, "When a stranger resides among you in your land, you shall not wrong him. The stranger who resides with you shall be to you as one of your citizens; you shall love him as yourself, for you were strangers in the land of Egypt; I am the Lord your God" (Leviticus 19:33–34). Furthermore, "There shall be one law for the citizen and for the stranger who dwells among you" appears often in the Torah (for example, Exodus 12:49; Leviticus 24:22; Numbers 15:15–16). These principles, together with the need to avoid the enmity of non-Jews, made Jews treat non-Jews with the same principles of justice that they used for themselves and even to bury the non-Jewish dead and to provide for the basic needs of the non-Jewish poor. See the next note.

5. B. *Gittin* 61a; M.T. *Laws of Gifts to the Poor* 7:7; *Laws of Idolatry* 10:5; *Laws of Mourning* 14:12; *Laws of Kings* 10:12; S.A. *Yoreh De'ah* 335:9, 367:1.

6. For some other modern Jewish formulations of the Jewish–Christian relationship, see Rothschild 1990, which includes excerpts on the subject by Leo Baeck, Martin Buber, Franz Rosenzweig, Will Herberg, and Abraham Heschel; Neusner 1993.

7. Some modern Christian attempts to reformulate the Jewish–Christian relationship include Hick 1989 and Van Buren 1980, 1987, 1995.

8. Judah Halevi made this point. He has the Kuzari say that he does not believe the arguments presented for Christianity and Islam and that the only way he could is if he had grown up with them: "Here is no logical conclusion; nay, logical thought rejects most of what you [the Christian] say. It is only when both

appearance and experience are so palpable that they grip the whole heart, which sees no way of contesting, that it will agree to the difficult, and the remote will become near.... As for me, I cannot accept these things, because they have come upon me suddenly, seeing that I have not grown up with them. My duty is, therefore, to investigate further" (Judah Halevi, *The Kuzari*, Book I, para. 5). Compare also paragraph 6, where the Kuzari tells the Moslem scholar, among other things, that "if your book [the Koran] is a miracle, a non-Arab, like me, cannot perceive its miraculous character because it is written in Arabic!"

9. The two nonperspectivists mentioned, A. J. Ayer (1946, 114–20) and R. B. Braithwaite (1955), share the view that religion does not make true or false assertions but rather motivates one emotionally, but the former thinker sees this as a major limitation on religion, while the latter thinks that this description is both accurate and fine.

10. James William McClendon (1974) and Michael Goldberg (1982, esp. 66–70, 91–95; 1985), among others, have emphasized the role of biography—one's own and that of others—in theology along with other stories that inform a tradition.

11. According to Job 2:11, Eliphaz is a Temanite, Bildad is a Shuhite, and Zophar is a Naamathite. Only the fourth interlocutor, Elihu, bears a name that appears Jewish; see Job 32:2. On the religious status of Job and his friends, see Gordis 1965, 65–67, and chapter 6 generally. On the international influences on the Book of Job, see Gordis 1965, 53–64; Pope 1962, 911–25, esp. 914–17; Matthews and Benjamin 1991, 201–26, esp. 219–26.

12. As the biblical scholar M. H. Pope writes, "The recovery of the literatures of the ancient Near East, of Egypt, Mesopotamia, Syria, and Anatolia has shed much light on the OT [Old Testament]. It is no longer possible to study the OT in isolation from the larger world in which it originated. Wisdom literature of the OT in particular has so much in common with similar literatures of Egypt and Mesopotamia that international influence appears likely" (1962, 914).

13. See, for example, B. *Bava Batra* 10a, on whether God would support human efforts to help the poor; B. *Sanhedrin* 65b (= *Genesis Rabbah* 11:5 and *Tanhuma*, Ki Tissa 33), on whether the Sabbath is incumbent on non-Jews in the hereafter; and *Tanhuma*, Tazria 5 and 7, on whether God's creations or man's are more beautiful, given that a male human is born uncircumcised.

14. T. *Avodah Zarah* 8:4; B. *Sanhedrin* 56a, 60a.

15. T. *Sanhedrin* 13:2, and, concerning the children of Gentiles, T. *Sanhedrin* 13:1. Later Jewish tradition follows Rabbi Joshua in both passages. See also M. *Avot* 4:29 and *Lamentations Rabbah* on Lamentations 3:23, both of which seem to assure life after death to people generally, and B. *Eruvin* 19a and *Ecclesiastes Rabbah* to Ecclesiastes 3:9, both of which promise the Garden of Eden to the

righteous and Gehinom to the wicked, without mention of any restriction to Jews. One source, in fact, specifically limits the punishment of Gehinom to the children of *wicked* Gentiles: "With respect to the children of wicked gentiles, all agree that they will not enter the World to Come" (B. *Sanhedrin* 110b). Some rabbinic sources express the opposite extreme: "The Resurrection is reserved for [the People] Israel" (*Genesis Rabbah* 13:6; compare M. *Sanhedrin* 10:1). These undoubtedly reflect times in which Gentiles were oppressing Jews and the consequent need during such times to reinforce Jewish commitment with the promise of future reward; they may also reflect the concern of Jewish leaders that some of their number would be attracted to Hellenistic or Christian beliefs and practices. Restricting the reward of the World to Come to Jews alone would encourage Jews to persevere in their faith, despite oppression or the lures of foreign ideas. That does not erase, though, the remarkably universalistic passages that appear in rabbinic literature, some of which are noted at the beginning of this note, and the clear aversion to missionizing embedded in Jewish law and practice for at least the last two thousand years.

CHAPTER TWENTY
REFRAMING DIFFERENCE: EVANGELICALS, SCRIPTURE, AND THE JEWS
Kathryn J. S. Smith

Within evangelical Christianity, there exist several streams of thought regarding Jewish people and the Gospels and with regard to reading the texts of Scripture. Both sets of differences—approaches to Jewish people and approaches to Scripture—are important if we are to understand the ways that evangelicals read the Passion stories in the Gospels and how those readings affect Jewish–Christian relations.

Many are not aware of the great diversity that exists within evangelicalism. There are fundamentalists and Anabaptists, Charismatics and Reformed, dispensationalists and Wesleyans, social Conservatives and pacifist Liberals. Nowhere are these varieties of viewpoints more noticeable than when we look at evangelical views about Israel and the Jewish people.

There is one very large group of evangelicals, known as dispensationalists, whose proponents are probably the most vocal about Israel and are the most familiar to contemporary American Jews. Dispensationalists contend that the consummation of the ages is imminent and that it will result in a catastrophic, apocalyptic end centering on the nation of Israel. Because of this apocalyptic focus, dispensationalists identify themselves as "premillennialists," asserting that Jesus will return in glory to set up a thousand-year reign—a millennial reign.[1] It is this group that has been the most vocal supporter of Israel for reasons that will be discussed in this chapter.

Evangelicalism in the nineteenth century was largely postmillennial. Nineteenth-century evangelicals also looked forward to a thousand-year reign of God's people on earth, but postmillennialists expect Jesus to return at the end of that reign rather than at the beginning. Thus, in the very forward-looking nineteenth century, postmillennialist evangelicals held themselves responsible for inaugurating the millennium. They were at the forefront in developing volunteer organizations and in spearheading efforts to eradicate poverty. The twentieth century, marked by two world wars, genocide, and unremitting poverty, led to a pessimism that proved to be fertile ground for premillennial dispensational ideology.

Dispensationalists argue for consecutive ages, or "dispensations," in which God replaces one dispensation with another, the new one annulling and superseding the previous dispensation. This movement, which became widely popular in the twentieth century, generally is associated with fundamentalism and is noted for its categorical insistence on the strict distinction between Israel and the Christian church. While this distinction may seem welcome to contemporary Jews, it is based on a dualistic understanding of the cosmos in which the promises to the Jews are earthly and material, while the promises to the church are spiritual and divine. Thus, dispensationalists set up a structured anthropology that accepts and expands on the ancient Christian assertion that the church is spiritual and divine while Israel is earthly and carnal.[2]

Premillennial ideas are among those that cause the greatest concern to contemporary Jews—and for some very good reasons. On the one hand, premillennial dispensationalists are very strong in affirming that Israel's covenant relationship with God is eternal, albeit for the last two thousand years marked by an age or dispensation in which Israel has been largely irrelevant in history. In fact, premillennialists themselves have been largely ahistorical in their theology. The world is evil and irredeemable, and Christ soon will come to do away with it.

Despite this ahistorical perspective, premillennialists were nevertheless a major force in the early twentieth century for supporting the establishment of the state of Israel. They viewed the establishment of the state as a sign that God was reentering history and that the age of the church was ending. Throughout that century and into the present, premillennial Christians were and are extremely vocal against antisemitism. This support carries over beyond the realm of mere words. Modern dispensationalists contribute virtually millions of dollars to social and medical programs in Israel.

On the other hand, there are troubling elements within their philosemitism. Many evangelicals—and this extends beyond premillennialists—

tend to romanticize and idealize Jews in ways that make contemporary Jews very uncomfortable—and rightly so. If Israel has reentered divine history through the establishment of the modern state of Israel, as dispensationalists contend, then the Israeli government's actions are representative of God's own work on earth. This results in an extreme idealization at one end of the spectrum and, potentially, an extreme disenchantment at the other end of the spectrum should the Israeli government not perform in a manner consistent with these elevated expectations.

Further, dispensationalists have a clearly developed, internal definition of Jewish identity and Jewish calling. Dispensationalists are not likely to acknowledge that Jews themselves must be about their own self-determination. Consequently, dispensational evangelicals are not prone to deeply engage Jewish scholars and theologians about what it is to be Jewish and what Israel means as a theological category for contemporary Jews. They already possess a well-developed dogma about Israel's significance and fate. The outcome of this is that many premillennial dispensationalists tend to box the contemporary state of Israel into their expectation of an end-time cataclysm that involves catastrophic, apocalyptic devastation—for Israel. With friends like these, some have wondered, who needs enemies?

Finally, premillennial Christians share with many other evangelicals the desire to see all the Jews "saved" *as they define it*. Inherent in evangelicalism is this very strong theological focus on evangelism. And for this, evangelicals have no need to be apologetic. The problem is that it has come at the expense of recognizing that, according to the Scriptures that premillennialists claim to interpret literally, the Jewish people have their own corporate covenant commitments. Here, evangelicals face a dilemma, as do many other Christians in this post-Shoah world. Evangelicals, like other Christians, have largely recognized that there are deep problems with the notion that the church has superseded Israel as the people of God. However, they also have been slow to develop an alternative theology to account for social-historical Israel (I define social-historical Israel as a socially historically definable people with a shared collective memory—a people that possesses its own theology of landedness and sacred space that is deeply tied to its own self-understanding). What results is that evangelicals make claims about Jews being chosen—but the way they define Jewish chosenness is to be marked for conversion out of their status as Jews—out of their status as social-historical Israel. Moreover, if these Christians were successful in their evangelistic endeavors, it would result in the disappearance of Jews as a collective group. This is the great irony, for this is precisely the phenomenon that those same evangelicals would claim to not want to see. The focus on individual "salvation" by evangelical churches ignores the notion that corporate identity for Jewish people is theologically central. In the end, I do applaud the strong support of Israel on the part of premillennial dispensationalists, but I am troubled by these implications of dispensational theology and soteriology.

This is not to say that evangelism should not be a part of the commitment of evangelicals. Every group has the right to perpetuate itself and to contend for its ideas in the larger world of theological opinion. However, if dispensationalists claim that social-historical Israel is to be taken seriously as a theological category that matters today, then they need to go back to the theological drawing board with respect to their anthropology and their soteriology.

To be sure, there are other types of evangelicals for whom the Jewish people are simply irrelevant. That is not good news for contemporary Jews because these evangelicals have little historical perspective about the church's past treatment of Jews. Their very ignorance is a kind of supersessionism because it assumes that they themselves are the "true Israel" and that social-historical Israel is an inert and obsolete theological category. This type of evangelical acknowledges God as creator but ignores the indications that Scripture presents a God who claims to want to be known to the world through a people—a particular people in history.[3] We still live in the shadow of the Shoah. As such, this perspective, too, is troubling to me.

In the end, what comes forth from evangelicalism regarding Jews and Israel contains all sorts of internal paradox and contradiction, and this is why it makes many Jewish people today very uncomfortable. Nevertheless, there are those evangelicals who do take Israel seriously theologically without abandoning their own claims about Jesus. They also take the New Testament seriously as inspired Scripture. These evangelicals, who come from a variety of denominations, are thinking critically in this post-Shoah world about the church's history of triumphalism toward Israel and about the church's massive and catastrophic failures in this regard. Among these are evangelicals who acknowledge that when Christians took over Israel's story as their own, they deeply and shamefully distorted their own understanding of God, of history, and of the nature of the people of God.

Several scholars within traditions that share much with evangelicalism are engaged in serious dialogue with Jewish scholars and theologians. Among them are R. Kendall Soulen, Douglas Harink, and Terence Donaldson. The late John Howard Yoder, an Anabaptist, was another important voice in this Jewish–Christian dialogue. These theologians argue that social-historical Israel is a central theological category for their own self-definition as Christians. They are actively engaged in listening to Jews and talking to Jews, and they are formulating their theology out of those discussions. For many of these scholars, the God of Abraham, Sarah, and the ancestors can be known through the children (at least the symbolic children) of Abraham, Sarah, and the ancestors—the contemporary people of Israel and the Jewish diaspora. For them and for the growing number of evangelicals to whom they speak, in order to know the God of Israel, you have to have a relationship with the people of Israel—real, flesh-and-blood people. There is a very real, incarnational aspect to this understanding—God, incarnated in and to the world through and for a people.

Naturally, this incarnational theology of Israel deeply affects the way these groups interpret the Gospels. If we are to assume that Israel also was a significant theological category for those ancient gospel communities, then those Gospels are not in the first instance a Gentile story. They are Israel's story, written by Jews and for Jews as well as for those Gentiles who were willing to associate with Jews and with the God of the Jews. Such an understanding radically changes the meaning for contemporary reading and hearing communities. The story of the Scriptures is the story of Israel: if Israel is read out of the story, then there is no story. As R. Kendall Soulen has stated, "The problem of supersessionism coincides with the way in which Christians have traditionally understood the theological and narrative unity of the Christian canon as a whole."[4] Likewise, if Israel is read out of history, as the church has done for the past two thousand years, then history itself becomes an inert theological category. History loses its place as a site, a locus, for the incarnational self-revelation of God to humanity.[5]

Let me give you an example of how this incarnational reading affects our understanding of the Gospels. Jesus, throughout the Gospels, preaches the "kingdom" (in Hebrew, the *malkhut*), or the realm of God on earth. However, if you disembody Jesus from his Israel-centered focus and identity, then the result will be what we often see today—a construal of Jesus's preaching that results in a focus only or primarily on personal piety and an internalized inner life. This is a very different understanding than that derived from seeing the Gospels as Israel's story. If they are read as Israel's story, then the reader sees in Jesus's preaching a very strong political and economic dimension—his concern was with collective Israel, and he preached with concern for Israel's welfare front and center. The Gospel of Matthew quotes Jesus as saying, "I was sent only to the lost sheep of the house of Israel";[6] in the Gospel of John, Jesus says, "Salvation is of the Jews."[7] These statements, argue a growing number of scholars, make perfect sense when understood with the assumption that the earliest Jesus communities valued social-historical Israel as a central theological category.

This raises a challenge for contemporary evangelicals. As Gentile Christians, they are beginning to construct a theological identity for themselves in relation to Israel. Israel indeed becomes their collective Other, but it does so in the sense of helping Christians define themselves. This results in an empathetic reading rather than an alienating reading. The way God reveals God's love of creation is through Israel. This gives rise to a conviction among some that solidarity with Israel is theologically essential for Christians.

This brief summary demonstrates why there is such great diversity among evangelicals not only regarding Israel but also regarding the Christian tradition itself. Because the evangelical movement is highly traditional with respect to biblical interpretation, many evangelicals do not critically reflect on the implications of their teaching. They uncritically accept the traditional reading of texts without an awareness of the historical problems that have long been associated with those traditional readings. For instance, despite great improvements over the past decade, egregious cases of anti-Jewish stereotyping are still common in evangelical Sunday school materials. Pharisees, almost universally depicted as opponents and enemies, often are dressed in strikingly Jewish garb, with characteristically striped prayer shawls covering their heads. Illustrations frequently depict Jesus and his disciples bareheaded and wearing no distinctively Jewish clothing. The message is clear. The Jews are the enemy, and they are not "Us."

At the same time, because of this increased focus on Israel and the Jewish people among evangelicals that I discussed previously, more and more Sunday school material is emerging that presents the opposite picture. The new material focuses clearly and perceptibly on the Jewish character of Jesus and his disciples and presents them as distinctively Jewish members of their social and religious worlds. This diversity shows up in approaches to reading the Bible as well. A popular approach is the literalist-fundamentalist, or inerrantist, approach, which argues for a radical kind of positivism in its interpretation. Its adherents claim that, because the Bible is God's divine Word, it cannot contain human depictions that are inaccurate as defined by the fundamentalists' positivist, historicist perspective. The argument goes something like this. The Scriptures teach us that they are inerrant in their original autographs, meaning that an implied individual author penned the first manuscripts. The notion of an original autograph in itself is deeply problematic. If a particular "author"—and such a term has been widely problematized with respect to ancient, traditional texts as well as to contemporary texts—pens one letter and then makes a slight change in another version of the same letter, which version is the "original autograph?" This is only one problem among many in the inerrantist claims.

Of course, inerrantists do acknowledge the large number of historical and literary inconsistencies and errors in the manuscripts that we possess, but they contend that these discrepancies were not present in the original autographs. Indeed, these errors and inconsistencies are not significant theologically—unless you are an inerrantist. Then they become vastly significant. In the inerrantist understanding of the development of Scripture, the presence of even a minute error would be a theological impossibility. As such, when inerrantists are presented with examples of text critical discrepancies, they answer that those discrepancies could not have been present in the original autographs. However, none of the original autographs has been preserved for our observation. There is therefore no physical evidence to support the inerrantists' claim. There is only their theologically dogmatic supposition, which, they assert, is based in Scripture. Here is where the argument begs the question: inerrantists claim that their assertions arise from the original autographs of Scripture, to which they acknowledge they have no access.

Happily, there are other approaches to Scripture within evangelicalism. Many of these other evangelical approaches affirm that God acts in concert with humanity to convey Scripture to human beings. As such, the historical eras during which these human agents live, their cultures, and their theological and ideological hopes and dreams shape their perceptions. These perceptions and values predictably become enshrined within the text of Holy Scripture. And Scripture itself, in another sense, becomes incarnational: God joins with humanity to bring the story of redemption to God's creatures.

In light of this approach, many evangelical scholars claim that the Gospels and specifically the Passion narratives are not about telling positivist history according to contemporary rules of historiography; they are about telling a story—a theological story about Jesus, about Israel, and about suffering. Thus, there is no problem in recognizing that, of the four authors of the canonical Gospels, each provides a unique and distinctive story. To be sure, each author contributes a different perspective, indeed a different story, to a grander theological narrative that these various perspectives enrich and nourish. The gospel writers were not about writing history according to the conventions of contemporary historiography. Why impute to them motives and expectations that they did not presume on themselves?

Nowhere is the importance of this issue more palpable than in the question of how Christians read the crucifixion story and how that reading relates to contemporary Jewish communities. What do we know? Elsewhere in this volume, my colleagues have explained the social/historical setting that makes some sense of why some first-century Jewish people (the gospel writers) could be so hostile to their own.[8] We also know that the Gospels were written decades after the events they record and that styles of rhetoric in the first-century Greco-Roman world generally were harsh and offensive in all kinds of discourse—not just the Gospels. In fact, two of the Gospels—Matthew and John—share a common literary formula called "Promise-Fulfillment." Matthew and John often employ a formulaic phrase such as, "And this was to fulfill the Scripture." These formulaic phrases then are followed by a reference to a passage from the Scriptures, usually the Prophets.[9] Both Matthew and John, when searching to understand the significance and meaning of the events they related, looked to the one body of material that was ultimately true to them—the Scriptures of Israel. They adopted their idiom, worldview, and harsh rhetoric from the Prophets. It is these two Gospels—Matthew and John—that most often are called antisemitic. Ironically, these two Gospels draw most closely from ancient Jewish expressions, language, and values. This shows how important the study of ancient rhetoric is in understanding the Gospels.

What else do we know about first-century Judaea and its environs? We know that by the time of the writing of the Gospels, the Romans had destroyed the Temple in Jerusalem and that the Jesus people were frustrated by their fear that their hopes would not be fulfilled. Their Jewish renewal movement was a movement totally explainable within the world of the contemporary Judaisms of that time and that place. The members of these Jesus communities had anticipated that their own Jewish renewal movement would sweep over the people of Israel and would become widely popular—theologically, socially, economically, and politically—but their hope had turned to frustration and disappointment.

This explains much of the harsh rhetoric as well as the Gospels' depictions of the bloody despot Pontius Pilate as such a sweet guy. After all, by the end of the first century, Jesus's followers were taking this message to Roman citizens. How do you convince Roman citizens to follow the man whom you claim to be the promised redeemer of the world but who, inconveniently, has been executed in the most ignoble fashion known at the time—by Rome? How do you convince those Roman citizens that they will not be forced to share that same fate? You tell them that they have nothing to fear—that this new movement is completely consistent with Roman law (and you downplay the fact that its leader and some of its main proponents have been executed according to Roman law). This is precisely what occurs in our Gospels.

We also can understand why the Gospels depicted the chief priests and Sadducees as largely implicated in the death of Jesus. Interestingly, neither the Gospel of Mark nor that of Luke implicates the Pharisees in Jesus's death. This may indicate that those Pharisees who may have been members of the Sanhedrin at the time refused to participate in the proceedings. Moreover, in the Gospel of Luke, it is not the crowds that mock Jesus but the leaders. Luke makes a very real effort to distinguish the crowds from the leaders, implying that, for him, the real guilt lay at the feet of a very specific group among the leaders. So, in his gospel, the crowds, after witnessing the crucifixion, "turned back, beating their breasts."[10]

Moreover, we have reports from Josephus and even from the Talmud and Tosefta that paint the members of the high priestly party of that time as horribly corrupt and oppressive of their own people—many of the Jewish people, suffering under their oppression, hated them. A Jewish diatribe preserved in the Babylonian Talmud and the Tosefta accuses the high priests in the first century of enslaving their people, casting spells and incantations, creating libels and slanders against their enemies, embezzling and stealing from the Temple treasury, and having their servants beat the people with staves.[11] This particular group of chief priestly families was in collusion with the Romans, and they participated in excessive taxation, fraud, graft, corruption, and the exploitation of their own people. In other words, they were an easy target at the end of the first century—a target that few in Israel were willing to defend—especially after their power base had been destroyed in 70 C.E. with the destruction of the Temple.

Even if we can understand and locate the reasons for the hostile rhetoric, the problem remains. We know that the contemporary communities that read and interpret the texts are the ones who determine meaning. Once a text is circulated within the public realm, its writers or the community that produced it can no longer control its meaning. This is true regardless of all these social or historical elements in the story that we have discussed in this volume. People are going to interpret the Gospels in light of what they know—and most Christians simply do not know all these contextual elements. They do not even realize that ignoring Israel, which many Christians see as benign, is a kind of supersessionism in itself.

Unfortunately, there is no real protection from this characteristic of textuality. In fact, the only protection is to insist that communities read texts in light of their own history (the good and the bad) and, in this post-Shoah world, in light of their own past history of biblical interpretation. This is where there can be some hope, for even fundamentalists have learned a thing or two. And although today's evangelicals have a long way to go as far as assessing the significance of social-historical Israel for their own theology, many know, at the very least, that they come from a tradition that has sinned deeply against Israel. They often do not really understand how; they tend to excuse it in themselves, but they know it happened. Moreover, they have become convinced that it is their own sin that has crucified Jesus—not that of the Jews, not that of the Romans but their own.[12]

For these reasons, I am ambivalent about Mel Gibson's movie *The Passion of the Christ*. Certainly, evangelicals have reason to question the lack of historical context in the film as well as the unrelenting and exaggerated violence in the film. Classical Christian theology asserts Jesus as fully God and fully human. Hence, his ability to endure suffering did not exceed that of other human beings. The movie, however, embellishes and exaggerates his suffering to the point of caricature. What emerges is a Christ whose humanity is discounted while his divine ability to endure inhuman pain, suffering, and loss of blood is emphasized. This is the traditional *Christus Victor*, not the Christ of history.

What is more, I know firsthand that most evangelical Christians, including many students who enter my classroom for the first time, do not have a clue about the church's treatment of the Jews over the centuries and thus are bound to repeat the errors and sins of the past. At the same time, I know that despite their cluelessness, they will not see how Gibson's *The Passion* displays antisemitism or, more specifically, anti-Judaism. They will not see the historical embellishments and artistic license taken by the producers. In this world of personal and individualistic piety, they will see Christ dying and enduring immeasurable suffering because of *their* sin and their sin alone.

There is much work to be done in raising awareness, but there also are many evangelicals who are committed to that task and who are working tirelessly to that end. For those reasons, I think there is some hope, and, maybe, by bringing this issue to the fore, this movie will advance our discussion, however inadvertently on the part of the movie's producers.

Notes

1. It is possible, however, to be premillennial but not dispensationalist.
2. On the ways in which late antiquity Judaism simultaneously responded to and assimilated the notion of "carnal Israel," see Boyarin 1993.
3. See Soulen 1996, 55.
4. Soulen 1996, 33. The result of such a reading is what Soulen calls a "structurally supersessionist [system] *because it unifies the Christian canon in a manner that renders the Hebrew Scriptures largely indecisive for shaping conclusions about how God's purposes engage creation in universal and enduring ways*" (31).
5. For the development of this incarnational theology, see Wyschogrod 1996.
6. Matthew 15:24; compare also 10:6.
7. John 4:22.
8. See, especially, Stephen Davis (chapter 16 in this volume).

9. See, for instance, Matthew 1:22; 2:15; 3:15; 8:17; 12:17; 13:35; 21:4; 26:54, 56; 27:9; John 12:38; 13:18; 18:9, 32; 19:24, 28; among others.

10. Luke 23:48. Beating the breast is a traditional sign of repentance, contrition, or mourning. See Luke 8:52, 18:13, 23:27.

11. B. *Pesachim* 57:1; Tosefta *Menachot* 13:21.

12. Interestingly, the New Testament texts themselves focus on another explanation for the death of Jesus—that he willingly gave up his own life. See John 6:51; Galatians 2:20; Ephesians 5:2, 25; Hebrews 7:27, 9:14, 10:10.

AFTERWORD: THE PASSION OF WAR
Mark Juergensmeyer

Everything has a context. As several writers in this volume correctly have pointed out, if we wish to understand the historical context of the death of Jesus, we must fully take into account the records of the Roman occupation and historical accounts written decades later in various parts of the Roman Empire in addition to the reports of the gospel writers themselves. As other writers in this volume also have indicated, the subsequent retellings of the gospel narratives—whether they are in iconography, in print, or in a film such as Mel Gibson's *The Passion of the Christ*—also have social contexts. One of these contexts is the recent era of globalization. In a multicultural milieu, as a number of authors in this volume have demonstrated amply, the biases of the storytellers and film-makers reflect modern ethnic and religious tensions, even when those writers and producers attempt to be "true to history."

Another facet of the contemporary global context is the political one—the war on terror. The cinematic retelling of an ancient morality play may seem far removed from current political tensions and the violent resistance to a form of globalization that is perceived as Americanization. Yet I think that that the current preoccupation with religious terrorism is at least one factor in explaining the phenomenal interest in Mel Gibson and his *Passion*, especially in the United States. My suggestion is that the deep emotions evoked by the film among some Americans are due, in part, to the religiosity of the present-day mood of militarism, which in turn is linked with religion's long tradition of complicity in war and political violence.

One clue to the film's popularity is the very intensity of its bloodshed and gore. There have been other cinematic portrayals of the last days of Jesus—including the deeply moving adaptation by Martin Scorsese of the novel by Nikos Kazantzakis, *The Last Temptation of Christ*, and Pier Paolo Pasolini's socially engaging *The Gospel according to St. Matthew*, which faithfully reproduces the biblical text.[1] Although Mel Gibson filmed part of his own version of the Passion of Jesus in the same Italian towns that Pasolini chose for his settings, the cinematic versions could not be more different. What Gibson portrays is not the life or teachings of the Christ but the intense physical suffering of the human Jesus. He shows not just the psychological trauma of the man but every whiplash, nail-pounding, and thorn-penetrating moment. It almost would be the stuff of a horror movie if it were not couched in such a religious setting.

In many ways, though, it *is* a horror movie, an orgy of bloodshed that goes far beyond the Christian tradition's norm for portraying the agony and sacrifice of Jesus. Since sacrifice is about redemption and purification, neither of which this film portrays, one might conclude that the Gibson movie is not really about sacrifice at all but about victimization.[2]

In fact, from a cinematic point of view, the Gibson film has less in common with other religious films than it has with Gibson's other movies, like the *Lethal Weapon* series, many of which traffic in gratuitous violence. Some indeed are well crafted—one thinks of Gibson's Academy Award–winning *Braveheart*, for example, which chronicled Scottish freedom fighters in their bloody encounters. The film was Gibson's previous attempt at portraying over-the-top graphic violence and scenes of dismemberment in a curiously artful fashion. The film was said in a BBC radio report to have captivated the minds of Chechnyan rebels in 1999 who viewed it as emblematic of their own struggle.[3]

What the Chechnyan rebels saw in *Braveheart* was a film not just about gore but also about struggle. That film fits into a pattern of recent war movies that attempt to portray not only the valor of fighting but also its agony and horror. One thinks of the opening scene in Steven Spielberg's *Saving Private Ryan*, for example, the image of a Marine's corpse being dragged through the streets of Mogadishu in *Black Hawk Down*, and some of the more gripping moments in Vietnam War films such as *The Deer Hunter*, *Hamburger Hill*, and *Platoon*.

AFTERWORD

These are films about war but especially about the tragedy of war—particularly about the suffering of the innocents. They are about men dying young, their vitality squandered in the insanity of violent conflict. Even when the films point to an ultimate triumph of heroic proportions—as in *Braveheart*—what the films focus on for what seems to be an interminable period of time is the suffering and victimization of war.

The young Jesus in *The Passion of the Christ* could be one of these innocent victims of war. More than innocent, Jesus is the very exemplar of purity *sans pareil*. He is the sacrificial offering, and yet, as I mentioned before, there is something about the excessive gore and the oppressive sense of victimization that makes this film more about Jesus's victimization than his sacrifice. It would seem, then, to be a kind of war movie—but what kind of war? Who are the enemies?

The shadowy, bearded figures of the Sanhedrin portrayed in Gibson's film provide a clue to these answers. They are the enemy. They have manipulated Jesus into a position of torture. He is the innocent victim of a plot meant to ravage innocence and intimidate the population. They are, in a sense, biblical terrorists.

In this sense, then, *The Passion of the Christ* is indeed a war movie but a movie that works especially well for those who think in terms of a war on terrorism. The innocent figure of Jesus so maligned and shredded could have been one of the office workers in the top floors of the World Trade Center, a secretary in the Pentagon, or a child in the day care nursery in Oklahoma City's Murrah Federal Building. For many who have viewed the movie, Jesus could stand in for all Americans and indeed all citizens of the globe who have felt violated, even distantly, by savage acts of terrorism.

It is paradoxical in this regard that the perpetrators of terrorism in the Gibson film are Jewish rather than Muslim—the shadowy, bearded and robed figures lurking in the background in the movie are, of course, members of the Jewish Sanhedrin and not the Muslim al-Qaeda. But is it such a stretch to imagine that in Middle America, any bearded, robed enemy of Christendom might be viewed as a part of a generic "Other" capable of the most hideous anti-American terrorist acts? Perhaps, in the minds of many who viewed the film, the Sanhedrin figures also could be Muslim: they could be any of the shadowy, bearded and robed figures in America's image of terrorist activists—the Ayatollah Khomeini of the Iranian revolution, Sheik Omar Abdul-Rahman of the 1993 bombing of the World

Trade Center, Sheik Abdul Yassin of Hamas, or Osama bin Laden of al-Qaeda.[4] Jewish or Muslim, they are enemies of Christianity, and ultimately they are enemies of Christendom's social order.

Allied with these shadowy robed terrorists are the uniformed members of the sinister states that protect them. In the film, it is the Roman officials who bend to the will of the Sanhedrin. In the broader American imagination about terrorist networks, these devious officials could be any of those states that "harbor terrorism," as Afghani officials—and then Iraqi—were alleged to have done. The Roman officials in Gibson's film could have been members of Afghanistan's once-official Taliban or Iraq's Ba'ath Party, whom most Americans still mistakenly regard as having been in league with Osama bin Laden prior to the U.S. invasion of Baghdad in 2003. The weak capricious Pontius Pilate in Mel Gibson's film could be confused with Saddam Hussein.

The experience of innocent victimization associated with terrorism of the al-Qaeda sort undoubtedly augmented the popularity of Gibson's *Passion*. But this does not mean that Gibson consciously intended his film to be a parody of the war on terrorism. Clearly, he had many other purposes in mind, including the vindication of his own traditionalist Catholic vision of the suffering Christ. In that sense, *The Passion* has much in common with the iconography of traditional Central American Catholic churches, where at the side of the main sanctuary one often can find a glass-lidded coffin through which worshippers can peer at a wooden full-size figure of the dead Jesus, colorfully painted with bloody thorn marks and embedded nails from his torture on the cross.

Gibson's Jesus actually moves, however, and in doing so re-creates his experience of torture. Hence, it is appropriate to compare his iconography not just with folk images but also with other films, including his own, that often portray such scenes of violence in times of war. Again, though, there is no indication that Gibson consciously was trying to create a war movie for the current war on terror, even though it serves that purpose brilliantly. In the same way, the creators of the science fiction movies in the 1950s may not have been aware that the popularity of their cinematic tales was due to the anticommunist paranoia of the Cold War. The enormous fear evoked among 1950s Americans who watched as cinematic creatures from outer space inhabited human bodies and made them into zombies in part was due to conservative Americans' obsession over finding commies among ordinary citizens during the early years of the Cold War. Like the zombies, communists were thought to be automatons controlled by an alien power—they might look like everyday citizens, but inside they were the communist "pinkos" who were hell-bent on destroying the American way.

Today's pinkos are terrorists. They are more recognizable than the zombielike communists who infiltrated American society several decades ago, but in the imaginations of those who fear them as inexplicable agents of evil, they are just as lethal, just as hell-bent on destroying the American way. You can recognize them by their bearded, robed mien. One can ignore the niceties of the ideological and political distinctions among them—these shaggy, shadowy Islamic enemies are Osama bin Laden, Saddam Hussein, the Ayatollah Khomeini, and Sheik Yassin of Hamas. No matter that they quarrel and disagree with one another, they are America's new global foes. And they look a lot like Gibson's Sanhedrin.

Gibson's *The Passion of the Christ* is also a war movie in that it portrays the struggle between good and evil, which are made absolute polar opposites through the simple moral dichotomy that is always war's way of thinking about conflict. Jesus, of course, is the perfect symbol of good. The agents of his torture, so dramatically portrayed in the film, therefore must be construed as absolutely evil as Jesus is antiseptically good. The movie's protagonists present such a stark image of evil—it is one as clear and unchallenged as President George W. Bush's characterization of terrorists following September 11. This view, shared by others in the neoconservative war cabinet of the American president, is aptly summarized in the title of a recent book by the leading theorist of this group, Richard Perle, whose book subtitled "how to win the war on terror" is titled *An End to Evil*.[5]

War simplifies the struggle of opponents into a contest of good and evil for which there can be no easy compromise. Like Perle's view of terrorists, Gibson's portrayal is that the enemies of Jesus are, simply, purely evil. There is no need to explore their worldview, their understanding of the situation, or their reasons for wanting to see their enemies accused and punished. By the very definition of their evilness, they have no moral basis for their views, whatever they might be, so there is no need to waste time in trying to understand them. This is a war view, and war makes moral positions easy to understand.

Such is the attraction of war, especially a view of war that is all-encompassing, one that embraces the fundamental struggle between good and evil that is part of every religious tradition. I call such notions "cosmic war."[6] They are cosmic in that they loom larger than life. They evoke great battles of the legendary past, and they relate to metaphysical conflicts between good and evil. Notions of cosmic war are intimately personal but can also be implanted on a social plane. Ultimately, though, they transcend human experience.

Long before Gibson's *Passion*, the idea of warfare has had an eerie and intimate relationship with religion. History has been studded with overtly religious conflicts such as the Crusades, the Muslim conquests, and the wars of religion that dominated the politics of France in the sixteenth century. Although these usually have been characterized as wars in the name of religion rather than wars conducted in a religious way, historian Natalie Zemon Davis uncovered what she calls "rites of violence" in her study of religious riots in sixteenth-century France. These constituted "a repertory of actions, derived from the Bible, from the liturgy, the action of political authority, or from the traditions of popular folk practices, intended to purify the religious community and humiliate the enemy and thus make him less harmful."[7]

The interesting thing about this understanding of what might be called the religionization of violence is the exaggeration of the act of physical mutilation as a way of heightening its symbolism. Just as in Gibson's film, Davis observed that violence in the religious riots of sixteenth-century France was "aimed at defined targets and selected from a repertory of traditional punishments and forms of destruction." According to Davis, "even the extreme ways of defiling corpses—dragging bodies through the streets and throwing them to the dogs, dismembering genitalia and selling them in mock commerce—and desecrating religious objects" had what she called "perverse connections" with religious concepts of pollution and purification, heresy and blasphemy.[8]

The anthropologist Stanley Tambiah showed how the same "rites of violence" were present in the religious riots of southern Asia. In some instances, a crowd would snatch up innocent bystanders and burn them alive. According to Tambiah, these horrifying murders of defenseless and terrified victims were carried out ritualistically, in "mock imitation of both the self-immolation of conscientious objectors and the terminal rite of cremation."[9]

In a macabre way, the riotous battles described by Davis and Tambiah were, like Gibson's portrayal of the death of Jesus, religious events. But given the prominence of the rhetoric of warfare in religious vocabulary, both traditional and modern, one could also turn this point around and say that religious events often involve the invocation of violence. One could argue that the task of creating a vicarious experience of warfare—albeit one usually imagined as residing on a spiritual plane—is one of the main businesses of religion.

Virtually all cultural traditions have contained martial metaphors. The ideas of a Salvation Army in Christianity or a *Dal Khalsa* ("army of the faithful") in Sikhism characterize disciplined religious organizations. Images of spiritual warfare were even more common. The Muslim notion of jihad was the most notable example, but even in Buddhist legends great wars abounded. In Sri Lankan culture, for instance, virtually canonical status was accorded the legendary history recorded in the Pali Chronicles, the Dipavamsa, and the Mahavamsa that related the triumphs of battles waged by Buddhist kings. In India, warfare contributed to the grandeur of the great epics, Ramayana and the Mahabharata, which were tales of seemingly unending conflict and military intrigue. More than the Vedic rituals, these martial epics defined subsequent Hindu culture. Whole books of the Hebrew Bible were devoted to the military exploits of great kings, their contests related in gory detail.[10] Although the New Testament did not take up the battle cry, as Gibson's movie shows, the suffering of Jesus often is portrayed in Christian iconography as the wounds of a soldier in battle. Moreover, the later history of the church supplied Christianity with an abundance of martial images and the bloody record of crusades and religious wars.

Religion does not relegate the idea of warfare to legendary historical narratives, however; many contemporary religious symbols continue to evoke images of blood and battle. Though Gibson evokes the Roman Catholic portrayals of the bloody sacrifice of Jesus, Protestant Christianity also has been vigorous in its images of bloodshed. Though the reformed tradition was strongly pacifist with regard to military conscription and actual fighting, it is interesting to note that martial images abounded in the rhetoric and symbolism of the faith, especially as churches developed in the nineteenth-century American frontier. There Protestant preachers encouraged their flocks to wage war against the forces of evil, and their homilies were followed with hymns about "Christian soldiers," fighting "the good fight," struggling "manfully onward."[11] One scholar of popular Protestantism, Harriet Crabtree, surveyed the images that were prominent in what she called the "popular theologies" projected in the hymns, tracts, and sermons of modern Protestant Christianity and found the "model of warfare" one of the most enduring.[12]

What was significant about the popular Protestant talk about war, Crabtree states, is that the image was meant to be taken more than metaphorically. When the writers of hymns urged "soldiers of the Cross" to "stand up, stand up for Jesus," this was interpreted as a requirement for real, albeit spiritual, combat. Protestant writers such as Arthur Wallis claim that "Christian living is war." Wallis explains that the warfare was not "a metaphor or a figure of speech" but a "literal fact"; the character of the war, however—"the sphere, the weapons, and the foe"—were "spiritual rather than material."[13] Crabtree asserts that the image of warfare is attractive because it "situates the listener or reader in the religious cosmos."[14]

The busloads of pious middle-aged American church folk who are carted to Mel Gibson's gory spectacle of Jesus's victimization in his final earthly hours are treated, in a sense, to a vision of religious war. They enter into the age-old drama of good and evil personified, in combat, with all its savage intensity. Though they all know—or believe, through faith—that good finally will reign victorious, in the meantime they want to experience vicariously the pain that evil can inflict. After all, they have seen it already in the crumbling of the World Trade Center towers, the devastation of American embassies in Africa, and the mutilation of American soldiers in Iraq. They have seen the terror wars of the twenty-first century, but now they know that it is part of an age-old template of Christian experience. They know that in the end, good will prevail because, as Gibson's movie so amply demonstrates, God already has entered the struggle. Though humiliated and assaulted, just as we have been, ultimately he will win.

Notes

1. See Baugh (chapter 12 in this volume).
2. See Elcott (chapter 17 in this volume).
3. "The World" (British Broadcasting Corporation, 28 October 1999). See also Karny 1999.
4. Even the photographs of Saddam Hussein after his arrest featured him with a beard.

5. Frum and Perle 2004.
6. See the chapter on cosmic war in Juergensmeyer 2003. The following paragraphs in this chapter are based on sections of this book.
7. Natalie Davis 1973, 52–53.
8. Natalie Davis 1973, 81–82.
9. Tambiah 1996, 310–11.
10. It therefore is unsurprising that Gibson would consider the apocryphal Book of Maccabees—which contains some of Judaism's most enduring martial images—as a possible follow-up film project.
11. For an analysis of "Onward Christian Soldiers" and other hymns of America's frontier revival movements, see Sizer 1978.
12. Crabtree 1991. She summarizes her findings with regard to warfare in Crabtree 1989–1990, 6–27.
13. Wallis 1973, 10.
14. Crabtree 1989–1990, 7.

BIBLIOGRAPHY

"Against the Heresies: Judaism"
  Catholic Apologetics Information. 24 January 2004, http://www.catholic apologetics.info/Heresies.htm#Judaism.

Agence France-Presse
  "Catholic Cardinal Warns against New European Anti-Semitism." 21 December 2003.

Alessio, Mark
  "Christ Crucified: An Update on the Controversy Surrounding Mel Gibson's Film—Passion." *The Remnant: A Catholic Fortnightly*, 23 September 2003. 24 March 2004, http://ourworld.compuserve.com/homepages/remnant/passion1.htm.
  "The "Passion" Debacle: Mammon Meets the Gospel-Haters." *The Remnant: A Catholic Fortnightly*, 14 October 2003. 24 March 2004, http://ourworld.compuserve.com/homepages/remnant/adl.htm.
  "The Rise & Fall of Mel Gibson's Critics: But They're Not Done Yet." *The Remnant: A Catholic Fortnightly*, 4 January 2004. 24 March 2004, http://our world.compuserve.com/homepages/remnant/critics.htm.

Allen, John L., Jr.
  "Update on 'The Passion.'" The Word from Rome. *National Catholic Reporter* 3:22 (23 January 2004). 26 April 2004, http://www.nationalcatholicreporter.org/word/pfw012304.htm.

Altmann, Alexander
  Moses Mendelssohn: A Biographical Study. University: University of Alabama Press, 1973.

BIBLIOGRAPHY

Ambrose
: Letter LX [to Theodosius]. "Nicene and Post-Nicene Fathers." Series II, Vol. X. 16 April 2004, http://www.ccel.org/fathers2/NPNF2-10/Npnf2-10-52.htm#P7967_2116073.

Ammerman, Nancy
: *Bible Believers: Fundamentalists in the Modern World.* New Brunswick, N.J.: Rutgers University Press, 1987.

Anisfeld, Sharon Cohen, and Cynthia Terry
: "Is Suffering Redemptive? Jewish and Christian Responses." In *Irreconcilable Differences? A Learning Resource for Jews and Christians*, ed. David F. Sandmel, Rosann M. Catalano, and Christopher M. Leighton. Boulder, Colo.: Westview Press, 113–33.

Anselm of Canterbury
: *Cur Deus Homo.* Edited by Jasper Hopkins and Herbert Richardson. Toronto: Edwin Mellen Press, 1976.

Anselm, and S. N. Deane
: *Basic Writings: Proslogium; Monologium; Gaunilon's on Behalf of the Fool; Cur Deus Homo.* La Salle, Ill.: Open Court Publishing, 1962.

Anti-Defamation League
: "ADL Audit Finds Anti-Semitic Incidents Remain Constant; More Than 1,500 Incidents Reported across U.S. in 2003" [press release]. 24 March 2004. 28 March 2004, http://www.adl.org/PresRele/ASUS_12/4464_12.htm.

: "ADL Screens Mel Gibson's 'The Passion of the Christ'; Says Film's Portrayal of Jews 'Painful to Watch'" [press release]. 22 January 2004. 22 January 2004, http://www.adl.org/PresRele/ASUS_12/4444_12.htm.

: "ADL Statement on Mel Gibson's 'The Passion'" [press release]. 24 June 2003. 25 June 2003, http://www.adl.org/PresRele/Mise_00/4275_00.asp.

Archdiocese of Denver
: Home page. 28 January 2004, http://www.archden.org/.

Armstrong, Chris
: "The Fountain Fill'd with Blood." *Christianity Today*, March 2004, 42.

Aronson, Elliot
: "The Rationalizing Animal." *Psychology Today*, May 1973, 46–52.

Arroyo, Raymond
: "The Greatest Story, Newly Told." *Wall Street Journal*, 7 March 2003, W13.

Associated Press
"Mel Gibson Brings Movie to Colorado for a Screening with Religious Leaders." State and Local Wire. 27 June 2003.

Augustine
Concerning the City of God against the Pagans. Translated by Henry Bettenson. Harmondsworth: Penguin Books, 1984.

Ayer, A. J.
Language, Truth, and Logic. London: V. Gollancz, 1946.

Ballard, M. Russell
"The Gospel of Inclusion." *The Ensign*, May 2001, 65.

Bamberger, Felix, et al., eds.
Gesammelte Schriften. Jubiläumsausgabe. Stuttgart-Bad Cannstatt: F. Frommann, 1971–.

Bammel, Ernst
"Christian Origins in Jewish Tradition." *New Testament Studies* 13 (1966/67): 317–35.

Barnabas
"The Epistle of Barnabas." In *The Apostolic Fathers*, ed. and trans. Kirsopp Lake. London: W. Heinemann, 1919. 30 March 2004, http://www.early christianwritings.com/text/barnabas-lake.html.

Barrett, Cameron
"Anatomy of a Weblog." 26 January 1999. 22 March 2004, http://www.camworld.com/archives/001177.html.

Bartlett, Anthony W.
Cross Purposes: The Violent Grammar of Christian Atonement. Harrisburg, Pa.: Trinity Press International, 2001.

Barton, Bruce
The Man Nobody Knows: A Discovery of the Real Jesus. Indianapolis: Bobbs-Merrill, 1925.

A Young Man's Jesus. Boston: Pilgrim's Press, 1914.

Baugh, Lloyd
Imaging the Divine: Jesus and Christ-Figures in Film. Kansas City, Mo.: Sheed & Ward, 1997.

"Palestinian Braveheart: The Atonement Theology of Mel Gibson's *Passion*." *America*, 23 February 2004, 17–21.

BIBLIOGRAPHY

Bellinger, W. H., and William Reuben Farmer
Jesus and the Suffering Servant: Isaiah 53 and Christian Origins. Harrisburg, Pa.: Trinity Press International, 1998.

Benson, Ezra Taft
"To the Youth of the Noble Birthright." *The Ensign*, May 1986, 43.

Berenbaum, Michael
"In 2003, We Are Strong: In 1933 We Were Weak." *Jewish Journal of Greater Los Angeles*, 5 December 2003. 26 April 2004, http://www.jewishjournal.com/home/preview.php?id=11470.

"The Top Ten Reasons Why Today Is Different." *Jewish Journal of Greater Los Angeles*, 5 December 2003. 28 April 2004, http://www.jewishjournal.com/home/preview.php?id=11471.

Berger, David
"Religion, Nationalism, and Historiography: Yehezkel Kaufmann's Account of Jesus and Early Christianity." In *Scholars and Scholarship: The Interaction between Judaism and Other Cultures*, ed. Leo Landman. New York: Yeshiva University Press, 1990, 149–68.

Berkofsky, Joe
"One Poll Finds 'Passion' Makes Viewers Less Likely to Blame Jews for Crucifixion." Jewish Telegraphic Agency. 17 March 2004. 29 March 2004, http://www.jta.org/page_view_story.asp?intarticleid=13889.

Berners-Lee, Tim
"The World Wide Web: A Very Short Personal History." 15 March 2004, http://www.w3.org/People/Berners-Lee/ShortHistory.

Berry, Jason, and Gerald Renner
Vows of Silence: The Abuse of Power in the Papacy of John Paul II. New York: Free Press, 2004.

Bieler, Ludwig, ed.
The Irish Penitentials. Dublin: Dublin Institute for Advanced Studies, 1975.

Bishops' Committee for Ecumenical and Interreligious Affairs (BCEIA)
The Bible, the Jews and the Death of Jesus: A Collection of Catholic Documents. Washington, D.C.: United States Conference of Catholic Bishops, 2003.

Blankenship, Cassie
Comment 22301. Posted at See the Passion.com: An Independent Website in Support of "The Passion of the Christ." 21 April 2004, http://www.seethepassion.com/public_view.php?page=1488.

Blood, Rebecca
    The Weblog Handbook: Practical Advice on Creating and Maintaining Your Blog. Cambridge, Mass.: Perseus Publishing, 2002.

    "Weblogs: A History and Perspective." 7 September 2000. 22 March 2004, http://www.rebeccablood.net/essays/weblog_history.html.

Board of Rabbis of Southern California
    "Rabbis' Reflections on 'The Passion.'" February–March 2004. 9 May 2004, http://www.jewsforjudaism.org/web/passion/commentaries.pdf.

Bonaventure, Isa Ragusa, and Rosalie B. Green
    Meditations on the Life of Christ: An Illustrated Manuscript of the Fourteenth Century. Princeton, N.J.: Princeton University Press, 1961.

Bondanella, Peter E.
    Italian Cinema: From Neorealism to the Present. New York: Continuum, 1990.

Boteach, Shmuley
    "The Gospel Untruth." *Jerusalem Post*, 13 November 2003, 15.

Bowles, Scott
    "Fans Have the Muscle to Shape the Movie." *USA Today*, 19 June 2003. 1 July 2003, http://www.usatoday.com/life/movies/2003-06-19-movies-cover_x.htm.

Boyarin, Daniel
    Carnal Israel: Reading Sex in Talmudic Culture. Berkeley: University of California Press, 1993.

Boyer, Peter J.
    "The Jesus War: Mel Gibson's Obsession." *The New Yorker*, 15 September 2003, 58–67. 9 April 2004, http://www.wcnet.org/~bgcc/gibson.htm.

Boys, Mary C., et al.
    "Dramatizing the Death of Jesus: Issues That Have Surfaced in Media Reports about the Upcoming Film, *The Passion*." 17 June 2003. Boston College Center for Christian Jewish Learning. 29 June 2003, http://www.bc.edu/research/cjl/meta-elements/texts/news/dramatizing_the_death_of_jesus.htm.

    "Report of the Ad Hoc Scholars Group Reviewing the Script of *The Passion*." 2 May 2003. Boston College Center for Christian Jewish Learning. 2 March 2004, http://www.bc.edu/research/cjl/meta-elements/texts/education/Passion_adhoc_report_2May.pdf.

Braithwaite, Richard Bevan
    An Empiricist's View of the Nature of Religious Belief. Cambridge: Cambridge University Press, 1955.

BIBLIOGRAPHY

Brennan, Phil
"Crucifying Mel Gibson." NewsMax.com. 26 March 2003. 16 April 2004, http://www.newsmax.com/archives/articles/2003/3/25/200221.shtml.

Broadway, Bill
"The Evangelical-Israel Connection: Scripture Inspires Many Christians to Support Zionism Politically, Financially." *Washington Post*, 27 March 2004, B9.

Brown, Dan
The Da Vinci Code: A Novel. New York: Doubleday, 2003.

Brown, Raymond Edward
The Death of the Messiah: From Gethsemane to the Grave: A Commentary on the Passion Narratives in the Four Gospels. New York: Doubleday, 1994.

Buber, Martin
Hasidism and Modern Man. New York: Horizon Press, 1958.

Buchanan, Patrick J.
"The Passion and Its Enemies: The Campaign against the Movie Bespeaks Deeper Animus." *The American Conservative*, 26 April 2004. 21 April 2004, http://www.amconmag.com/2004_04_26/feature.html.

Bugg, Richard
"Passion of Christ Shows Humble Love for Humanity." *The University Journal Online*, 4 March 2004. 21 April 2004, http://www.suujournal.com/vnews/display.v/ART/2004/03/04/4047a0c288182?in_archive=1.

Burkett, Delbert Royce
The Son of Man Debate: A History and Evaluation. Cambridge: Cambridge University Press, 1999.

Butler, Jon
Awash in a Sea of Faith: Christianizing the American People. Cambridge, Mass.: Harvard University Press, 1990.

Bynum, Caroline Walker
Jesus as Mother: Studies in the Spirituality of the High Middle Ages. Berkeley: University of California Press, 1982.

"Violent Imagery in Late Medieval Piety." *Bulletin of the German Historical Institute* 30 (spring 2002): 3–36.

Cain, Michael
"'It' Depends on What 'Is' Was!" *The Daily Catholic*, 21 January 2004. 12 February 2004, http://www.dailycatholic.org/issue/04Jan/ed012104.htm.

"A Man of His Word True to the Word." *The Daily Catholic*, 10 February 2004. 12 February 2004, http://www.dailycatholic.org/issue/04Feb/feb10 ed.htm.

Calasso, Roberto
The Marriage of Cadmus and Harmony. New York: Knopf, 1993.

Canavan, Francis, SJ
"Religious Freedom: John Courtney Murray, S.J. and Vatican II." *Faith & Reason*, summer 1987. 2 April 2004, http://www.ewtn.com/library/HUMANITY/FR87203.TXT.

Card, Orson Scott
"The Passion of the Christ—Three Reviews and a Letter." Civilization Watch. *The Ornery American*. 29 February 2004. 21 April 2004, http://www.ornery.org/essays/warwatch/2004-02-29-1.html.

Carroll, Michael P.
The Cult of the Virgin Mary: Psychological Origins. Princeton, N.J.: Princeton University Press, 1986.

Catchpole, David R.
The Trial of Jesus: A Study in the Gospels and Jewish Historiography from 1770 to the Present Day. Leiden: E. J. Brill, 1971.

Catholic League for Religious and Civil Rights
"ADL Attack on *The Passion* Is Unfair" [press release]. 12 August 2003. 30 March 2004, http://www.catholicleague.org/03press_releases/quarter3/030812_passion.htm.

"ADL Attacks Mel Gibson" [press release]. 25 June 2003. 30 March 2004, http://www.catholicleague.org/03press_releases/quarter2/030625_adl.htm.

"Catholic Bishops Did Not Attack Gibson Movie" [press release]. 1 July 2003. 30 March 2004, http://www.catholicleague.org/03press_releases/quarter3/030701_gibson.htm.

"*The New Republic* Libels Mel Gibson" [press release]. 21 July 2003. 30 March 2004, http://www.catholicleague.org/03press_releases/quarter3/030721_gibson.htm.

"Reaction to Mel Gibson's Film Reaches Hysterical Level" [press release]. 27 August 2003. 30 March 2004, http://www.catholicleague.org/03press_releases/quarter3/030827_hikind.htm.

BIBLIOGRAPHY

Cattan, Nacha
"Christians Launch Effort to Counter Film's Impact." *The Forward*, 30 January 2004. 27 April 2004, http://www.forward.com/main/article.php?ref=cattan 200402181242.

"'Passion' Critics Endanger Jews, Angry Rabbis Claim, Attacking Groups, Foxman; Hier Responds: Charges 'Despicable.'" *The Forward*, 5 March 2004. 27 April 2004, http://www.forward.com/main/article.php?ref=cattan 200403031140.

Chamberlain, Houston Stewart
The Foundations of the Nineteenth Century. Translated by John Lees. London: John Lane Company, 1911.

Chaput, Charles
"Mel Gibson, 'The Passion,' and Critics Who Can't Wait." *Denver Catholic Register*, 28 May 2003. 16 April 2004, http://www.archden.org/dcr/news.php?e=26&s=2&a=594.

"'The Passion of the Christ': See This Film." *Denver Catholic Register*, 28 January 2004. 9 April 2004, http://www.archden.org/dcr/news.php?e=64&s=2&a=1526.

Charen, Mona
"Seeded Images." *Washington Times*, 2 March 2004. 16 April 2004, http://www.washtimes.com/commentary/20040301-085725-2974r.htm.

Christensen, Carl C.
Art and the Reformation in Germany. Athens: Ohio University Press; Detroit: Wayne State University Press, 1979.

Ciaccio, Edward
"The Ascent of Zion: Part One." *The Daily Catholic* 14:31 (June 2003). 30 July 2003, http://www.dailycatholic.org/issue/junfms1.htm.

Ciaccio, Giacinto
"Fedele Al Racconto, Non All'ispirazione Del Vangelo Il Film Di Pasolini." *L'Osservatore Romano*, 6 September 1964, 6.

Clifton, James
The Body of Christ in the Art of Europe and New Spain, 1150–1800. Munich: Prestel, 1997.

Conférence des évêques de France [Conference of Bishops of France]
"Position du Comité permanent pour l'information et la communication sur le film "La Passion du Christ" de Mel Gibson." 30 March 2004. 30 March 2004,

http://www.cef.fr/catho/actus/communiques/2004/commu20040330_passionduchrist.php.

Connor, Kevin
"Dr. Bob Gray, Pastor, Is Your Church a Cult?" *The Baptist Magazine*, March–April 1998. 21 April 2004, http://www.lbtministries.com/The%20Baptist%20Magazine/March%20April%201998/cult.htm.

Connor, Tracy
"Mel Says No Hate in Jesus Film." *Daily News*, 14 June 2003, 3.

Cooperman, Alan
"Ideas about Christ's Death Surveyed Growing Minority: Jews Responsible." *Washington Post*, 3 April 2004, A3. 3 April 2004, http://www.washingtonpost.com/wp-dyn/articles/A45637-2004Apr2.html.

Corbett, Julia Mitchell
Religion in America. 4th ed. Upper Saddle River, N.J.: Prentice Hall, 2000.

Cork, William J.
"The Passion of The Christ: Crisis and Opportunity in Jewish-Catholic Relations." 13 February 2004, http://wquercus.com/passion.htm.

Corliss, Richard, and Jeff Israely
"The Passion of Mel Gibson: His Jesus Film Is Bloody, Bold—and in Aramaic: Here's an Exclusive Look." *Time*, 27 January 2003, 54.

Coulter, Ann
"The Passion of the Liberal." Anncoulter.com. 3 March 2004. 9 May 2004, http://www.anncoulter.org/columns/2004/030304e.htm.

Crabtree, Harriet
The Christian Life: Traditional Metaphors and Contemporary Theologies. Harvard Dissertations in Religion. Minneapolis: Fortress Press, 1991.

"Onward Christian Soldiers? The Fortunes of a Traditional Christian Symbol in the Modern Age." *Bulletin of the Center for the Study of World Religions* 16:2 (1989–1990): 6–27.

Cunningham, Philip A.
"Gibson's *The Passion of the Christ*: A Challenge to Catholic Teaching." Boston College Center for Christian-Jewish Learning. 25 February 2004. 16 March 2004, http://www.bc.edu/research/cjl/meta-elements/texts/reviews/gibson_cunningham.htm.

BIBLIOGRAPHY

D'Ambrosio, Dan
"Denver Pastor Creates Furor with Sign Blaming Jews for Crucifixion." The Associated Press State and Local Wire. 26 February 2004.

Davis, Natalie Zemon
"The Rites of Violence: Religious Riots in Sixteenth-Century France." *Past and Present* 59 (May 1973): 52–53.

Davis, Stephen T.
"Evangelical Christians and Holocaust Theology." *American Journal of Philosophy and Theology* 2:3 (September 1981): 121–29.

"The Question of Miracles, Ascension, and Anti-Semitism." In *Jesus' Resurrection: Fact or Fiction?*, ed. Paul Copan and Ronald K. Tacelli, 71–85. Downers Grove, Ill.: InterVarsity Press, 2000.

Deberg, Betty
UnGodly Women: Gender and the First Wave of American Fundamentalism. Minneapolis: Fortress Press, 1990.

Delitzsch, Franz
Jesus und Hillel: Mit Rücksicht auf Renan und Geiger. Erlangen: Verlag von Andreas Deichert, 1866.

Dobson, James
"The Greatest Story Ever Told." *Dr. Dobson's Newsletter*, February 2004. Family.org: A Website of Focus on the Family. 10 April 2004, http://www.family.org/docstudy/newsletters/a0030580.cfm.

Dodd, Patton
"Whose Passion? Mel Gibson's Christ Movie Began with Small, Secretive Screenings Deep in the Heart of Evangelical America." *Killing the Buddha*, 25 February 2004. 27 April 2004, http://www.killingthebuddha.com/critical_devotion/passion.htm.

Donaldson, Terence L.
Paul and the Gentiles: Remapping the Apostle's Convictional World. Minneapolis: Fortress Press, 1997.

Donohue, William A.
"The Passion: Nothing but Love" [letter to the editor]. *New York Times*, 17 August 2003, B2.

Dorff, Elliot N.
To Do the Right and the Good: A Jewish Approach to Modern Social Ethics. Philadelphia: Jewish Publication Society, 2002.

Love Your Neighbor and Yourself: A Jewish Approach to Modern Personal Ethics. Philadelphia: Jewish Publication Society, 2003.

Douin, Jean-Luc
"Jésus Superstar: Certains Préfèrent L'invisible." *Le Film Religieux—Cinémaction No. 49.* Paris: Corlet, 1988.

Drake, Tim
"Catholics Are 'Blogging' on the Internet . . . to Evangelize." *National Catholic Register*, 9–15 June 2002. 12 March 2004, http://www.ncregister.com/Register_News/061102blo.htm.

Dreher, Rod
"Did the Vatican Endorse Gibson's Film—or Didn't It?" *Dallas Morning News*, 22 January 2004, A19.

Drew, Spencer
"Kinder, Gentler Passion." *Sightings*, 6 November 2003. Martin Marty Center, University of Chicago Divinity School. 21 April 2004, http://marty-center.uchicago.edu/sightings/archive_2003/1106.shtml.

Easterbrook, Gregg
"An Apology." Easterblogg. *The New Republic Online*, 16 October 2003. 20 October 2003, http://tnr.com/easterbrook.mhtml?pid=868.

"Take Out of the Gore and *Kill Bill* Is an Episode of 'Mighty Morphin' Power Rangers.'" Easterblogg. *The New Republic Online*, 13 October 2003. 20 October 2003, http://tnr.com/easterbrook.mhtml?pid=844.

Eckstein, Yechiel
"A Jewish Response to Mel Gibson's 'Passion of the Christ.'" International Fellowship of Christians and Jews. 16 February 2004. 21 April 2004, http://www.ifcj.org/site/News2?page=NewsArticle&id=5249.

"A Jew's Insights from 'The Passion of the Christ.'" International Fellowship of Christians and Jews. 9 April 2004. 21 April 2004, http://www.ifcj.org/site/News2?page=NewsArticle&id=5703.

Ehrenstein, David
The Scorsese Picture: The Art and Life of Martin Scorsese. New York: Carol Publishing Group, 1992.

Elcott, David
"Gibson's Polarizing *Passion*." *Boston Globe*, 12 February 2004. 28 March 2004, http://www.boston.com/news/globe/editorial_opinion/oped/articles/2004/02/12/gibsons_polarizing_passion/.

BIBLIOGRAPHY

Emmerich, Anna Katharina
The Dolorous Passion of Our Lord Jesus Christ. London: Burns & Oates, 1911.

Emmerich, Anne Catherine
The Dolorous Passion of Our Lord Jesus Christ. London: Burns, Oates & Washbourne, 1928.

The Dolorous Passion of Our Lord Jesus Christ. Rockford, Ill.: Tan Books and Publishers, 1983.

The Dolorous Passion of Our Lord Jesus Christ [n.d.]. 17 April 2004, http://www.emmerich1.com/DOLOROUS_PASSION_OF_OUR_LORD_JESUS_CHRIST.htm.

Encyclopaedia Judaica
CD-ROM edition. Jerusalem: Judaica Multimedia, n.d.

Evans, Craig A., and Donald A. Hagner
Anti-Semitism and Early Christianity: Issues of Faith and Polemic. Minneapolis: Fortress Press, 1993.

Ewald, Heinrich
Geschichte des Volkes Israel. Göttingen: Dieterischen Buchhandlung, 1864.

"Übersicht der 1857–1858 erschienenen Schriften zur Biblischen Wissenschaft." *Jahrbücher der biblischen Wissenschaft* 9 (1858): 94–275.

Falk, H., trans. Seder Olam Rabba ve-Zuta, Appendix
Journal of Ecumenical Studies 19:1 (winter 1982): 108–9.

Farrell, Steve
"The 'Dark' Passion." Meridian: The Place Where Latter-day Saints Gather. *Meridian Magazine*, 26 February 2004. 21 April 2004, http://www.meridianmagazine.com/arts/040226dark.html.

Federal Bureau of Investigation
Hate Crime Statistics 2002. Washington, D.C.: U.S. Department of Justice, 2003. 28 March 2004, http://www.fbi.gov/ucr/hatecrime2002.pdf.

Festinger, Leon
"Cognitive Dissonance." *Scientific American* 207 (October 1962): 93–102.

When Prophecy Fails. Minneapolis: University of Minnesota Press, 1956.

Field, Geoffrey G.
Evangelist of Race: The Germanic Vision of Houston Stewart Chamberlain. New York: Columbia University Press, 1981.

Finaldi, Gabriele, et al.
The Image of Christ. London: National Gallery. Distributed by Yale University Press, 2000.

Finke, Roger, and Rodney Stark
The Churching of America: Winners and Losers in America's Religious Economy. New Brunswick, N.J.: Rutgers University Press, 1992.

Flatow, Stephen M.
"'The Passion' and Purim." *The Jewish Week*, 5 March 2004. 28 March 2004, http://www.thejewishweek.com/top/editletcontent.php3?artid=3313.

Flesher, Paul V. M., and Robert Torry
"Filming Jesus: Between Authority and Heresy." *SBL Forum*, Society for Biblical Literature. 7 March 2004, http://www.sbl-site.org/Article.aspx?ArticleId=226.

Focus on the Family Website
"Mel Gibson's 'The Passion of the Christ.'" 9 April 2004, http://www.family.org/topics/A0029433.cfm.

Fortner, Don
"The Passion of Christ: The Movie." Institute for Theonomic Reformation. Commentary on Passion of the Christ Movie. 24 March 2004, http://www.hisglory.us/commentary/the_passion_of_christ.htm#fortner.

Forward, The
"Clues and Illusions" [unsigned editorial]. *The Forward*, 12 March 2004. 27 April 2004, http://www.forward.com/main/article.php?ref=20040310902.

Fox, Richard Wightman
Jesus in America: Personal Savior, Cultural Hero, National Obsession. New York: HarperCollins, 2004.

Frankl, Razelle
"Televangelism." In *The Encyclopedia of Religion and Society*, ed. William Swatos, 512–18. Walnut Creek, Calif.: AltaMira Press, 1998.

Franklin, Robert M.
"Black Theology and the Passion." *Sightings*, 19 February 2004. Martin Marty Center, University of Chicago Divinity School. 21 April 2004, http://marty-center.uchicago.edu/sightings/archive_2004/0219.shtml.

Fredriksen, Paula
"Mad Mel: The Gospel according to Gibson." *The New Republic*, 28 July 2003, 25–29. 26 March 2004, http://www.tnr.com/doc.mhtml?pt=Fsjrgo3Y%2BNbA6C9EgznUeQ%3D%3D.

"Pain Principle," *The New Republic Online*, 27 February 2004. 30 March 2004, http://www.tnr.com/docprint.mhtml?i=express&s=fredriksen022704.

Freud, Sigmund
Moses and Monotheism. Translated by Katherine Jones. New York: Knopf, 1939.

Frum, David, and Richard Perle
An End to Evil: How to Win the War on Terror. New York: Random House, 2004.

Frymer-Kensky, Tikvah, et al.
"*Dabru Emet*: A Jewish Statement on Christians and Christianity." September 2000. 17 April 2004, http://www.icjs.org/what/njsp/dabruemet.html. Republished in *Christianity in Jewish Terms*, ed. Tikvah Frymer-Kensky et al. (Boulder, Colo.: Westview Press, 2000), xv–xviii. Also republished in *Irreconcilable Differences: A Learning Resource for Jews and Christians*, ed. David F. Sandmel, Rosann M. Catalano, and Christopher M. Leighton (Boulder, Colo.: Westview Press, 2001), 11–14.

Funkenstein, Amos
Perceptions of Jewish History. Berkeley: University of California Press, 1993.

Geiger, Abraham
"Antwort an Delitzsch." *Jüdische Zeitschrift für Wissenschaft und Leben* 10 (1872): 309–11.

"Das Judentum und seine Geschichte." In *Zwölf Vorlesungen. Nebst einem Anhange: Ein Blick auf die neuesten Bearbeitungen des Lebens Jesu*. Breslau: Schlettersche Buchhandlung, 1864.

"Das Judentum und seine Geschichte." *Jüdische Zeitschrift für Wissenschaft und Leben* 2 (1864): 161–229; 3 (1865): 1–78.

"Das Judentum und seine Geschichte." In *Vierunddreißig Vorlesungen*. Breslau: Wilhelm Jacobsohn, 1910.

Das Judentum und seine Geschichte bis zur Zerstörung des zweiten Tempels. Nebst einem Anhange: Renan und Strauß. Breslau: Schlettersche Buchhandlung, 1865.

"Das Judentum und seine Geschichte von der Zerstörung des zweiten Tempels bis zum Ende des zwölften Jahrhunderts." In *Zwölf Vorlesungen. Nebst einem Anhange: Offenes Sendschreiben an Herrn Professor Dr. Holtzmann*. Breslau: Schlettersche Buchhandlung, 1865.

Judaism and Islam: A Prize Essay. Translated by F. M. Young. Madras: M.D.C.S.P.C.K. Press, 1898; 2nd ed., New York: Ktav, 1970.

Judaism and Its History, in Two Parts. Translated by Charles Newburgh. New York: Bloch Publishing, 1911.

Urschrift und Übersetzungen der Bibel in ihrer Abhängigkeit von der innern Entwickelung des Judenthums. Breslau: Julius Heinauer, 1857; 2nd ed., Frankfurt am Main: Verlag Madda, 1928.

Was hat Mohammed aus dem Judenthume aufgenommen? Eine von der Königl. Preussischen Rheinuniversität gekrönte Preisschrift. Bonn, 1833; 2nd ed., Leipzig: M. W. Kaufmann, 1902.

Geiger, Ludwig
"Zunz im Verkehr mit Behörden und Hochgestellten." *Monatsschrift für Geschichte und Wissenschaft des Judentums* 60 (1916).

Gellman, Marc, and Thomas Hartman
"'Passion' Seen through Others' Eyes." *Newsday*, 18 February 2004, A27.

Gibson, Hutton
Letter, 27 July 1997. "Repair My Church: Responses and Evaluation." 30 March 2004, http://www.geocities.com/prakashjm45/rmc/rmchugi1.html.

Gibson, Mel, dir.
The Passion of the Christ. Los Angeles: Icon, 2004.

Ginzberg, Louis, ed.
Ginze Schechter: Genizah Studies in Memory of Doctor Solomon Schechter. 3 vols., vol. 1. New York: Jewish Theological Seminary, 1928.

Girard, René
The Scapegoat. Baltimore: Johns Hopkins University Press, 1986.
Violence and the Sacred. Baltimore: Johns Hopkins University Press, 1977.

Giussani, Luigi
Why the Church. Montreal: McGill-Queen's University Press, 2001.

Gladstone, Bill
"Anti-Semitism Report in Canada Finds Highest Levels in Two Decades." Jewish Telegraphic Agency. 16 March 2004. 28 March 2004, http://jta.org/page_view_story.asp?intarticleid=13883.

Gleason, Ron
"The 2nd Commandment and 'The Passion of the Christ.'" *PCANews.com: The Web Magazine of the Presbyterian Church in America.* 24 March 2004, http://www.christianity.com/partner/Article_Display_Page/0,,PTID23682|CHID125043|CIID1716514,00.html.

BIBLIOGRAPHY

Glenn, David
"Scholars Who Blog: The Soapbox of the Digital Age Draws a Crowd of Academics." *Chronicle of Higher Education*, 6 June 2003. 12 March 2004, http://chronicle.com/free/v49/i39/39a01401.htm.

Goldberg, Michael
Jews and Christians, Getting Our Stories Straight: The Exodus and the Passion-Resurrection. Nashville: Abingdon, 1985.

Theology and Narrative: A Critical Introduction. Nashville: Abingdon, 1982.

Gordis, Robert
The Book of God and Man: A Study of Job. Chicago: University of Chicago Press, 1965.

Graham, Franklin
"The Point of 'The Passion.'" *Decision Magazine*, March 2004. Billy Graham Evangelistic Association. 28 March 2004, http://www.billygraham.org/article.asp?i=417&s=55.

Unpublished letter to Abraham Foxman. 28 January 2004.

Greenberg, Blu
"Rabbi Jacob Emden: The Views of an Enlightened Traditionalist on Christianity." *Judaism* 27 (1978): 351–63.

Greenberg, Eric J.
"Burning 'Passion': Some Say Film Could Stick Jews in Middle of Internal Christian Battle." *The Jewish Week*, 8 August 2004. 26 April 2004, http://www.thejewishweek.com/news/newscontent.php3?artid=8302.

Grundmann, Walter
"Das Messiasproblem." In *Germanentum, Christentum und Judentum: Studien zur Erforschung ihres gegenseitigen Verhältnisses*, ed. Walter Grundmann. Vol. 2: *Sitzungesberichte der zweiten Arbeitstagung des Instituts zur Erforschung des jüdischen Einflusses auf das deutsche kirchliche Leben vom 3. bis 5. März 1941.*

Haaretz Staff
"Kach Members Mark 10th Anniversary of Hebron Massacre." *Haaretz*, 7 March 2004. 27 March 2004, http://www.haaretz.co.il/hasen/spages/401734.html.

Haggard, Ted
"NAE Resists Anti-Semitism" [press release and statement]. 24 February 2004. 28 March 2004, http://www.nae.net/index.cfm?FUSEACTION=editor.page&pageID=31.

Hallow, Ralph Z.
"Jewish Americans Wary of Bush Evangelical Base." *Washington Times*, 17 March 2004. 26 April 2004, http://www.washtimes.com/national/20040316-102301-7749r.htm.

Harding, Susan Friend
The Book of Jerry Falwell: Fundamentalist Language and Politics. Princeton, N.J.: Princeton University Press, 2000.

Hare, Douglas R. A.
The Son of Man Tradition. Minneapolis: Fortress Press, 1990.

Harink, Douglas
Paul among the Postliberals: Pauline Theology beyond Christendom and Modernity. Grand Rapids, Mich.: Brazos Press, 2003.

Hatch, Nathan O.
The Democratization of American Christianity. New Haven, Conn.: Yale University Press, 1989.

Haynes, Stephen R.
The Bonhoeffer Phenomenon: Portraits of a Protestant Saint. Minneapolis: Augsburg Fortress, 2004.

Reluctant Witnesses: Jews and the Christian Imagination. Louisville, Ky.: Westminster/John Knox, 1995.

Hein, Anton, and Janet Hein, eds.
"Mormonism." Apologetics Index. 24 November 2001. 21 April 2004, http://www.apologeticsindex.org/m04.html.

Hempel, Johannes
"Chronik vom Herausgeber." *Zeitschrift für alttestamentliche Wissenschaft* Neue Folge 18 (1942–1943): 209–15.

Henning, Jeffrey
"The Blogging Iceberg." *Perseus Blog Survey*, 26 November 2003. 20 March 2004, http://www.perseusdevelopment.com/blogsurvey/thebloggingiceberg.html.

Henry, Michael
"Entretien Avec Martin Scorsese Sur *La Dernière Tentation du Christ*." *Positif* 332 (October 1988): 6–10.

Herbert, James
"Public Eye." *San Diego Union-Tribune*, 24 September 2002, E3.

BIBLIOGRAPHY

Heschel, Susannah
Abraham Geiger and the Jewish Jesus. Chicago Studies in the History of Judaism. Chicago: University of Chicago Press, 1998.

"Revolt of the Colonized: Abraham Geiger's *Wissenschaft des Judentums* as a Challenge to Christian Hegemony in the Academy." *New German Critique* 77 (spring/summer 1999): 61–86.

"Theology as a Vision for Colonialism: From Supersessionism to Dejudaization in German Protestantism." In *Race and Imperial Fantasy in Modern Germany: An Anthology in Memory of Susanne Zantop*, ed. Marcia Klotz, Lora Wildenthal, and Eric Ames. Lincoln: University of Nebraska Press, 2004.

Hess, Jonathan M.
Germans, Jews and the Claims of Modernity. New Haven, Conn.: Yale University Press, 2002.

"Sugar Island Jews? Jewish Colonialism and the Rhetoric of 'Civic Improvement' in Eighteenth-Century Germany." *Eighteenth-Century Studies* 32:1 (1998): 92–100.

Hick, John
"Trinity and Incarnation in the Light of Religious Pluralism." In *Three Faiths—One God: A Jewish, Christian, Muslim Encounter*, ed. John Hick and Edmund S. Meltzer. Albany: State University of New York Press, 1989, 197–210.

Himmelfarb, Gertrude
"A 'Passion' Out of Proportion." *Washington Post*, 7 March 2004, B7.

"Hippolytus's Account of the Baptismal Service."
Creeds of Christendom. 6 April 2004, http://www.creeds.net/ancient/Hippolytus.htm.

Hirsch, Marianne
The Mother/Daughter Plot: Narrative, Psychoanalysis, Feminism. Bloomington: Indiana University Press, 1989.

Hirsen, James
"Attack on Mel Gibson Continues." Newsmax.com. 11 March 2003. 16 April 2003, http://www.newsmax.com/archives/articles/2003/3/11/135646.shtml.

Holtzmann, H. J.
"Jüdische Apologetik und Polemik." Review of *Das Judentum*, vol. 1, *Protestantische Kirchenzeitung* 10 (11 March 1865): 225–37.

BIBLIOGRAPHY

Hooper, J. Leon, SJ
"John Courtney Murray, S.J., and Religious Pluralism." *Woodstock Report* 33 March 1993. 29 July 2004, http://www.georgetown.edu/centers/woodstock/report/r-fea33.htm.

Hunter, James Davison
Culture Wars: The Struggle to Define America. New York: Basic Books, 1991.

Ingersoll, Julie
Evangelical Christian Women: War Stories in the Gender Battles. New York: New York University Press, 2003.

International Fellowship of Christians and Jews
"Noted Rabbi Cautions Jewish Community against Overreation to Gibson's 'Passion'" [press release]. 12 February 2004. 26 April 2004, http://www.ifcj.org/site/News2?page=NewsArticle&id=5697.

Jackson, Peter, dir.
The Lord of the Rings. Los Angeles: New Line Cinema, 2001–2003.

Jacoby, Jeff
"Is 'The Passion' Anti-Semitic?" *Boston Globe*, 24 February 2004, A19.

Jensen, Peter
"The Good News of God's Wrath." *Christianity Today*, 24 March 2004, 45–47.

"Jews against Jesus?"
Christianity Today [unsigned editorial]. 30 October 2003. 31 October 2003, http://www.christianitytoday.com/ct/2003/011/21.43.html.

Joffé, Roland, dir.
The Mission. Great Britain: Columbia-Canon-Warner, 1986.

Judah, and N. Daniel Korobkin
The Kuzari: In Defense of the Despised Faith. Northvale, N.J.: Jason Aronson, 1998.

Juel, Donald
Messianic Exegesis: Christological Interpretation of the Old Testament in Early Christianity. Philadelphia: Fortress Press, 1988.

Juergensmeyer, Mark
Terror in the Mind of God: The Global Rise of Religious Violence. 3rd ed. Berkeley: University of California Press, 2003.

BIBLIOGRAPHY

Karny, Yo'av
"Undying Enmity: The Chechen Leaders Thrive on Perpetual, Idealized War." *Washington Post*, 10 October 1999, B1.

Kazantzakis, Nikos
Ho Teleutaios Peirasmos [The Last Temptation of Christ]. Athens: Diphros, 1955.
The Last Temptation of Christ. New York: Simon and Schuster, 1960.

Kellstedt, Lyman, et al.
"Evangelicalism." In *The Encyclopedia of Religion and Society*, ed. William Swatos, 175–78. Walnut Creek, Calif.: AltaMira Press, 1998.

Kelly, Mary Pat
Martin Scorsese: A Journey. New York: Thunder's Mouth Press, 1991.

Kennedy, Randy
"'Passion' Film Is Incendiary, 2 Jewish Leaders Report." *New York Times*, 23 January 2004, A12.

Keyser, Lester J.
Martin Scorsese. Twayne's Filmmakers Series. Toronto: Twayne, 1992.

Kintz, Linda
Between Jesus and the Market: The Emotions That Matter in Right-Wing America. Durham, N.C.: Duke University Press, 1997.

Klein Halevi, Yossi
"Jews and Christians after 'The Passion,'" *Jerusalem Post*, 4 March 2004. 5 March 2004, http://www.jpost.com/servlet/Satellite?pagename=JPost/JPArticle/ShowFull&cid=1078373359933.

Kohler, Judith
"Pastor Whose Sign Ignited Furor Apologizes to 'Jewish People.'" Associated Press State and Local Wire. 2 March 2004.

Kook, Abraham Isaac
Seder Tefilah Im Perush Olat Re'iyah. Vol. 1. Edited by Zevi Judah Kook. Jerusalem: Mosad ha-Rav Kook, 1962.

Krauss, Samuel
Das Leben Jesu nach jüdischen Quellen. Berlin: S. Calvary, 1902.

Krauthammer, Charles
"Gibson's Blood Libel." *Washington Post*, 5 March 2004, A23.

Kravitz, Bentzion
"A Passionate Distortion of Truth." Jewishpassion.com [n.d.]. 9 May 2004, http://www.jewishpassion.com/documents/n_distortion.htm.

LaHaye, Tim F., and Jerry B. Jenkins
Left Behind: A Novel of the Earth's Last Days. 12 vols. Wheaton, Ill.: Tyndale House, 1995–2004.

Landres, J. Shawn
"Just Say Wait: A First Look at the *True Love Waits* Campaign." In *The Power of Gender in Religion*, ed. Georgie Ann Weatherby and Susan A. Farrell. New York: McGraw-Hill, 1996, 109–18.

"Passion Response Do's and Don'ts." *Jewish Journal of Greater Los Angeles*, 13 February 2004. 26 April 2004, http://www.jewishjournal.com/home/preview.php?id=11801.

"When the Medium *Isn't* the Message: The *True Love Waits* Campaign." *Religion & Education* 23:1 (spring 1996): 25–33.

Landsbaum, Mark
"Gibson's *The Passion of Christ* Faithfully Represents the Gospels." Concerned Women for America. 13 January 2004. 11 April 2004, http://www.cwfa.org/articledisplay.asp?id=5084&department=CWA&categoryid =misc.

Lane, Jennifer
"Compassio: Participation in the Passion and Late Medieval Pilgrimage." Doctoral diss., Claremont Graduate University, 2003.

Lapin, Daniel
"Just Wait till the Muslims See It." *Toward Tradition: The American Alliance of Jews and Christians*. 21 April 2004. 9 May 2004, http://www.towardtradition.org/article_Wait_Till_Muslims.htm.

"Protesting Gibson's Passion Lacks Moral Legitimacy." 22 September 2003. 9 May 2004, http://www.towardtradition.org/article_Mel_Gibson.htm. Excerpted as "Selective Outrage Mustn't Fritter Away Friendship." *The American Enterprise Online: Politics, Business and Culture*, January/February 2004. 30 April 2004, http://www.taemag.com/issues/articleid.17815/article_detail.asp.

Lawler, Michael G.
"Sectarian Catholicism and Mel Gibson." *Journal of Religion and Film* 8:1 (February 2004). 30 March 2004, http://www.unomaha.edu/~wwwjrf/2004Symposium/Lawler.htm.

BIBLIOGRAPHY

Leffler, Siegfried
Christus im Dritten Reich der Deutschen: Wesen, Weg und Ziel der Kirchenbewegung "Deutsche Christen." Weimar: Verlag DC, 1935.

Lehmann, Chris
"Picturing *The Passion:* Is it Porn, Horror, or Infotainment?" *The Revealer: A Daily Review of Religion and the Press*, 9 March 2004. 27 April 2004, http://www.therevealer.org/archives/feature_000240.php.

Lerner, Michael
"Gibson's The Passion: A Plea to Christians to Respond with a Gospel of Love and Hope in Place of This New Fundamentalism." *Tikkun: The Current Thinking* 10 (March 2004). 28 April 2004, http://www.tikkun.org/index.cfm/action/current/article/220.html.

Let God Be True
"The Animated Crucifix: A Bible Critique and Alternative View of Mel Gibson's 'The Passion of the Christ.'" Let God Be True, But Every Man a Liar. 5 March 2004. 24 March 2004, http://www.letgodbetrue.com/Todays World/passion.htm.

Levine, Bettijane
"Scholars Concerned about Film's Fallout: Some Express Fear That Gibson's 'The Passion,' about Christ's Last 12 Hours, Could Ignite Animosity between Christians and Jews." *Los Angeles Times*, 22 April 2003, E3.

Levine, Gilbert, dir.
The Papal Concert to Commemorate the Holocaust. Royal Philharmonic Orchestra. Houston: Justice Records, 1994.

Liebeschütz, Hans
Das Judentum im deutschen Geschichtsbild von Hegel bis Max Weber. Tübingen: Mohr Siebeck, 1967.

Limbaugh, David
"Mel Gibson's Passion for 'The Passion.'" 9 July 2003. 21 April 2004, http://www.townhall.com/columnists/davidlimbaugh/dl20030709.shtml.

Linafelt, Tod, ed.
A Shadow of Glory: Reading the New Testament after the Holocaust. London: Routledge, 2002.

Lindsay, Richard P.
"Church Issues Statement on Controversial New Movie." Public Communications Department, Church of Jesus Christ of Latter-day Saints. *Church News*, 20 August 1988, Z4.

Linner, Rachel
  "St. Blog's Church: America's Most Vibrant Parish?" *Commonweal* 131:4 (27 February 2004). 10 March 2004, http://www.commonwealmagazine.org/2004/february272004/022704st.htm.

Lipman, Steve
  "Film's Greatest Danger Seen in Asia, Africa: Threat Seen in Countries 'Least Familiar' with Shoah; Anti-Jewish Incidents in U.S." *The Jewish Week*, 5 March 2004. 17 April 2004, http://www.thejewishweek.com/news/newscontent.php3?artid=9158.

Little, Steve
  "'The Passion of the Christ' Is Historically Accurate, Not Anti-Semitic." Interview with Ted Haggard. Christian World News. CBN.com. 8 August 2003. 26 April 2004, http://cbn.org/CBNNews/CWN/080803tedhaggard.asp.

"Live Chat with LA Cardinal Roger Mahony: Transcript of Beliefnet's February 20 Online Chat with the Leader of America's Largest Catholic Diocese." Beliefnet.com. 20 February 2004. 24 February 2004, http://www.beliefnet.com/story/140/story_14062_1.html.

Ludolph the Saxon
  The Hours of the Passion: Taken from the Life of Christ. Translated by Henry James Coleridge. London: Burns & Oates, 1887.

Lundwall, N. B.
  The Fate of the Persecutors of the Prophet Joseph Smith. Being a Compiliation of Historical Data on the Personal Testimony of Joseph Smith, His Greatness, His Persecutions and Prosecutions, Conspiracies against His Life, His Imprisonments, His Martyrdom, His Funeral and Burial, the Trial of His Murderers, the Sorrow and Mourning of His Followers, the Fate of Those Who Persecuted and Killed Him, and the Attitude of His Followers Who Also Endured and Passed through Many of These Experiences. Salt Lake City: Bookcraft, 1952.

Maimonides, Moses
  Eight Chapters.
  Epistle to Yemen.
  Guide of the Perplexed.
  Mishneh Torah.

Malone, Guy
  "The Passion Movie Presents a False Jesus Christ." 24 March, 2004, http://www.guymalone.com/thepassion.htm.

BIBLIOGRAPHY

Manin, Giuseppina
"Sul Cinema Chiesa in Malafede." *Corriere della Sera*, 25 February 1996, 014.

Marsden, George
Fundamentalism and American Culture. Oxford: University Press, 1980.

Understanding Fundamentalism and Evangelicalism. Grand Rapids, Mich.: Eerdmans, 1991.

Marsh, Molly
"Developing Holy Envy." *Sojourners: Faith, Politics, Culture*, September–October 2001. 30 March 2004, http://www.sojo.net/index.cfm?action=magazine.article&issue=soj0109&article=010932f.

Marsh, W. Jeffrey
"Another Perspective on *The Passion of Christ*." Meridian: The Place Where Latter-day Saints Gather. *Meridian Magazine*, 27 February 2004. 21 April 2004, http://www.meridianmagazine.com/arts/040227Perspective.html.

Marty, Martin E.
"Not My Passion." *Sightings*, 9 February 2004. Martin Marty Center, University of Chicago Divinity School. 21 April 2004, http://marty-center.uchicago.edu/sightings/archive_2004/0209.shtml.

Matthews, Victor Harold, and Don C. Benjamin
Old Testament Parallels: Laws and Stories from the Ancient Near East. New York: Paulist Press, 1991.

Mauss, Armand L.
The Angel and the Beehive: The Mormon Struggle with Assimilation. Urbana: University of Illinois Press, 1994.

May, John R.
"Visual Story and the Religious Interpretation of Film." In *Religion in Film*, ed. John R. May and Michael S. Bird, 23–43. Knoxville: University of Tennessee Press, 1982.

McClendon, James William
Biography as Theology: How Life Stories Can Remake Today's Theology. Nashville: Abingdon, 1974.

McConkie, Bruce R.
The Mortal Messiah, Book 4: From Bethlehem to Calvary. Salt Lake City: Deseret Book Company, 1981.

McDannell, Colleen
The Christian Home in Victorian America, 1840–1900. Bloomington: Indiana University Press, 1986.

McLaren, Brian
"Passionate, but Not for Mel's Movie." *Christianity Today*, 9 March 2004. 3 April 2004, http://www.christianitytoday.com/leaders/newsletter/2004/cln 40309.html.

McNeil, John T., and Helena M. Gamer
Medieval Handbooks of Penance. New York: Columbia University Press, 1938.

Meacham, Jon
"Who Killed Jesus?" *Newsweek*, 16 February 2004. 27 March 2004, http://www.msnbc.msn.com/id/4212741/.

Medved, Michael
"Controversial Film: *The Passion.*" Washingtonpost.com, 6 August 2003. 6 August 2003, http://www.washingtonpost.com/ac2/wp-dyn?pagename=article&node=&contentId=A21289-2003Aug5.html.

"Crucifying Mel Gibson." 24 December 2003. *The American Enterprise Online: Politics, Business and Culture*, January/February 2004. 30 April 2004, http://www.taemag.com/issues/articleid.17815/article_detail.asp.

"'Passion' Elicits Unfair Conflict." USAToday.com, 21 July 2003. 26 April 2004, http://www.usatoday.com/news/opinion/editorials/2003-07-21-medved _x.htm.

"'Passion' Will Inspire Other Religious Films." USAToday.com, 14 March 2004. 26 April 2004, http://www.usatoday.com/news/opinion/editorials/ 2004-03-14-medved_x.htm.

Meier, John P.
A Marginal Jew: Rethinking the Historical Jesus. 3 vols. New York: Doubleday, 1991.

Mendelssohn, G. B., ed.
Moses Mendelssohns Gesammelte Schriften. 7 vols. Leipzig: F. A. Brockhaus, 1843–1845.

Mendelssohn, Moses
"Unpublished notes on Lavater, March 1770." In *Gesammelte Schriften, Jubiläumsausgabe*, ed. Felix Bamberger, Alexander Altmann et al. Stuttgart-Bad Cannstatt: F. Frommann, 1971–.

BIBLIOGRAPHY

Merrill, Keith
"Passionate Choice." Meridian: The Place Where Latter-day Saints Gather. *Meridian Magazine*, 16 February 2004. 21 April 2004, http://www.meridianmagazine.com/arts/040216Passionate.html.

Miesel, Rick, ed.
"Mormonism: Christian or Cult?" Bible Discernment Ministries [n.d.]. 20 April 2004, http://www.rapidnet.com/~jbeard/bdm/Cults/mormon.htm.

Miles Jack
Christ: A Crisis in the Life of God. New York: Knopf, 2001.

Milton, John
"Areopagitica." In *The Complete Prose Works of John Milton, Volume Two*, ed. Ernest Sirluck, 486–570. New Haven, Conn.: Yale University Press, 1959.

Mitchell, Margaret M.
"Special Gibson." *Sightings*, 11 March 2004. Martin Marty Center, University of Chicago Divinity School. 21 April 2004, http://marty-center.uchicago.edu/sightings/archive_2004/0311.shtml.

Mohler, Albert
"Furor over 'The Passion': Mel Gibson and His Critics." Weblog. Crosswalk.com, 1 October 2003. 9 May 2004, http://www.crosswalk.com/news/weblogs/mohler/?adate=10/1/2003.

Morgan, David
Protestants and Pictures: Religion, Visual Culture, and the Age of American Mass Production. New York: Oxford University Press, 1999.

The Sacred Gaze: Religious Visual Culture in Theory and Practice. Berkeley: University of California Press, 2005.

Visual Piety: A History and Theory of Popular Religious Images. Berkeley: University of California Press, 1998.

Mork, Gordon R.
"Christ's Passion on Stage—The Traditional Melodrama of Deicide." *Journal of Religion and Film* 8 (2004). 4 March 2004, http://www.unomaha.edu/~wwwjrf/2004Symposium/Mork.htm.

MovieWeb: The Internet Movie Network
Daily Grosses for "The Passion of the Christ." April 2004. 26 April 2004, http://movieweb.com/movies/box_office/daily/film_daily.php?id=577.

Murray, John Courtney, SJ
Religious Liberty: Catholic Struggles with Pluralism. Edited by J. Leon Hooper. Louisville, Ky.: Westminster/John Knox, 1983.

Nason, Pat
"Hollywood Digest." United Press International. 23 September 2002.

National Association of Evangelicals
"NAE Defends Gibson's New Film, *The Passion*" [press release]. 22 July 2003. 26 April 2004, http://www.nae.net/index.cfm?FUSEACTION=editor.page&pageID=11.

National Conference of Catholic Bishops
Criteria for the Evaluation of Dramatizations of the Passion. Washington, D.C.: Office of Publishing and Promotion Services, United States Catholic Conference, 1988.

Bishops' Committee for Ecumenical and Interreligious Affairs. *Criteria for the Evaluation of Dramatizations of the Passion.* Washington, D.C.: Bishops' Committee for Ecumenical and Interreligious Affairs, National Conference of Catholic Bishops, 1988. 3 March 2004, http://www.usccb.org/seia/criteria.pdf.

Statement on Catholic-Jewish Relations. Washington, D.C.: Office of Publishing and Promotion Services, United States Catholic Conference, 1975. 29 July 2004, http://www.bc.edu/research/cjl/meta-elements/texts/documents/catholic/NCCB_Statement.htm.

Neff, David
"The Passion of Mel Gibson." *Christianity Today*, March 2004. 16 March 2004, http://www.christianitytoday.com/movies/commentaries/passion-passionofmel.html.

Nelson-Stowell, Amelia
"Critics Agree: 'Passion' Is Violent." *The Daily Universe*, 19 March 2004. 21 April 2004, http://nn.byu.edu/story.cfm/49336.

Neusner, Jacob
A Rabbi Talks with Jesus: An Intermillennial, Interfaith Exchange. New York: Doubleday, 1993.

Neven, Tom
"The Passion of the Christ." *Focus on the Family Magazine*, 2003. 12 April 2004, http://www.family.org/fofmag/cl/a0029428.cfm.

BIBLIOGRAPHY

Newhouse, Alana
"The Bare Light of Personal Belief: Mel Gibson Offers Up a Provocative and Problematic Version of History." *The Forward*, 20 February 2004. 28 April 2004, http://www.forward.com/main/article.php?ref=20040218644.

Norris, Christopher
Deconstruction: Theory and Practice. London: Routledge, 1982.

Norris, Pippa
"The Bridging and Bonding Role of Online Communities." 16 February 2004. *The Harvard International Journal of Press/Politics* 7(3): 3–8. 22 March 2004, http://ksghome.harvard.edu/~.pnorris.shorenstein.ksg/Acrobat/bridgingandbonding.pdf.

Norris, Richard A.
The Christological Controversy. Philadelphia: Fortress Press, 1980.

North American Mission Board, Southern Baptist Convention
"The Passion of the Christ: Churches Going beyond The Passion of the Christ to Tell the Rest of the Story." 2004. 26 April 2004, http://www.passionchrist.org.

Novak, David
Jewish-Christian Dialogue: A Jewish Justification. New York: Oxford University Press, 1989.

Noxon, Christopher
"Is the Pope Catholic . . . Enough?" *New York Times Magazine*, 9 March 2003, 50.

Personal correspondence. 24 January 2003.

Oaks, Dallin H., and Marvin S. Hill
Carthage Conspiracy: The Trial of the Accused Assassins of Joseph Smith. Urbana: University of Illinois Press, 1975.

Oppenheimer, Mark
Knocking on Heaven's Door: American Religion in the Age of Counterculture. New Haven, Conn.: Yale University Press, 2003.

O'Reilly, Bill
Interview with Marvin Hier. *The O'Reilly Factor.* FOX News Channel, 13 March 2003.

Interview with Mel Gibson. *The O'Reilly Factor.* FOX News Channel, 13 January 2004. "Transcript: Mel Gibson Talks to O'Reilly while Filming 'The

Passion.'" 24 February 2004. 30 March 2004, http://www.foxnews.com/story/0,2933,112307,00.html.

Origen
Against Celsus. Edited and translated by Henry Chadwick. Cambridge: Cambridge University Press, 1953.

Parker, J. Michael
"The Story of Jesus and Its Many Versions: Passionate Debate: Mel Gibson's Movie 'The Passion of Christ' Stirs Concerns about Anti-Semitism before It's Even Released." *San Antonio Express-News*, 1 November 2003, 7B.

Parkin, Scott
Review of *The Passion of the Christ* [online posting]. 29 March 2004. AML-List, The Association for Mormon Letters. 21 April 2004, http://mailman.xmission.com/pipermail/aml-list/2004-March/000076.html.

Pasolini, Pier Paolo, dir.
Il Vangelo secondo Matteo [The Gospel according to Saint Matthew]. Rome: Arco Film, 1964.

Pasolini, Pier Paolo, and Jon Halliday
Pasolini Su Pasolini: Conversazioni Con Jon Halliday. Parma: Guanda, 1992.

"Passion Jewelry"
Share The Passion.com: The Website of Official Licensed Products for Mel Gibson's Movie *The Passion of the Christ* [Internet store]. 21 April 2004, http://www.sharethepassionofthechrist.com/jewelry.asp.

"Passion Movie Inspired Gear"
ThinkWow. Cafepress.com: Design, Print, and Sell Custom Products [Internet store]. 12 April 2004, http://www. cafeshops.com/thinkwow/242584.

Pope Paul VI
"Declaration on the Relation of the Church to Non-Christian Religions *Nostra Aetate*." Vatican City. 28 October 1965. 2 April 2004, http://www.vatican.va/archive/hist_councils/ii_vatican_council/documents/vat-ii_decl_19651028_nostra-aetate_en.html.

Pax, Salam
Salam Pax: The Clandestine Diary of an Ordinary Iraqi. New York: Grove Press, 2003.

Penslar, Derek J.
Shylock's Children: Economics and Jewish Identity in Modern Europe. Berkeley: University of California Press, 2001.

BIBLIOGRAPHY

Peretti, Frank E.
Piercing the Darkness. Westchester, Ill.: Crossway, 1989.
This Present Darkness. Westchester, Ill.: Crossway, 1986.

Perry, L. Tom
"That Spirit Which Leadeth to Do Good." *The Ensign,* May 1997, 68.

Pettit, Peter A.
"Challenge of 'Passion' Is to See Jesus as the Last Victim." *The Morning Call* (Allentown, Pa.), 25 February 2004, A13.

Pew Research Center for the People and the Press
"Belief That Jews Were Responsible for Christ's Death Increases: Prevalent among Young People, Minorities and 'Passion of Christ' Viewers." 2 April 2004. 9 April 2004, http://people-press.org/reports/display.php3?ReportID=209.

Phillips, Stone
"Dateline Special Report: The Last Days of Jesus." *Dateline NBC,* 20 February 2004. 27 March 2004, http://reprints.msnbc.com/id/4315203/.

Philo of Alexandria
Embassy to Gaius. Loeb Classical Library. Cambridge, Mass.: Harvard University Press, 1971, 294–309.

Piper, John
The Passion of Jesus Christ: Fifty Reasons Why He Came to Die. Wheaton, Ill.: Crossway, 2004.

Pope, M. H.
"Job, Book Of." In *The Interpreter's Dictionary of the Bible; an Illustrated Encyclopedia Identifying and Explaining All Proper Names and Significant Terms and Subjects in the Holy Scriptures, Including the Apocrypha, with Attention to Archaeological Discoveries and Researches into the Life and Faith of Ancient Times.* Vol. 2. Edited by George Arthur Buttrick. New York: Abingdon, 1962, 911–25.

Prager, Dennis
"The Passion: Jews and Christians Are Watching Different Films." Townhall.com, 28 October 2003. 21 April 2004, http://www.townhall.com/columnists/dennisprager/dp20031028.shtml. Republished as "Mel Gibson's Two Movies" (Beliefnet.com, 28 October 2003, 30 March 2004, http://www.beliefnet.com/story/135/story_13565.html); "The Passion:

Jews and Christians Are Watching Different Films." (Hollywood Prayer Network, 6 November 2003, 21 April 2004, http://www.hollywoodprayernetwork.org/news/news_detail.cfm?NEWS_ID=21); and "How Jews, Christians See Gibson's Film" (*Jewish Journal of Greater Los Angeles*, 7 November 2003, 17 April 2004, http://www.jewishjournal.com/home/print.php?id=11324).

Ray, Darby Kathleen
Deceiving the Devil: Atonement, Abuse, and Ransom. Cleveland: Pilgrim Press, 1998.

Rees, Robert A.
"Unremitting Passion." *Sunstone Magazine*, 131 (March 2004): 66–71.

Reid, Julie
"One Man's Passion: An Interview with Mel Gibson." *Worship Leader: Movie Guide to The Passion of The Christ*, January/February 2004.

Reik, Theodore
Myth and Guilt. New York: George Braziller, 1952.

Reinhartz, Adele
"Passionate Moments in the Jesus Film Genre," *Journal of Religion and Society* 6 (2004): 1–10. 16 April 2004, http://moses.creighton.edu/JRS/2004/2004-3.html.

Ribuffo, Leo
The Old Christian Right: The Protestant Far Right from the Great Depression to the Cold War. Philadelphia: Temple University Press, 1983.

Rich, Frank
"The Greatest Story Ever Sold." *New York Times*, 21 September 2003, B1.

"Mel Gibson Forgives Us for His Sins." *New York Times*, 7 March 2004, B1.

"Mel Gibson's Martyrdom Complex." *New York Times*, 3 August 2003, B1.

"The Pope's Thumbs Up for Gibson's 'Passion.'" *New York Times*, 18 January 2003, B1.

Rittner, Carol, and John K. Roth, eds.
"Good News" after Auschwitz? Christian Faith within a Post-Holocaust World. Macon, Ga.: Mercer University Press, 2001.

Robinson, Stephen, and Craig I. Blomberg
How Wide the Divide? A Mormon and an Evangelical in Conversation. Downer's Grove, Ill.: InterVarsity Press, 1997.

BIBLIOGRAPHY

Rose, Jacqueline
Sexuality in the Field of Vision. London: Verso, 1986.

Rosenblatt, Gary
"The Passion of Abe Foxman: Was the ADL Leader's Aggressive Criticism of Mel Gibson's Film a Major Misstep?" *The Jewish Week*, 5 March 2004. 28 April 2004, http://www.thejewishweek.com/news/newscontent.php3?artid=9152.

Roth, John K.
Holocaust Politics. Louisville, Ky.: Westminster/John Knox, 2001.

"What Does the Holocaust Have to Do with Christianity?" In *The Holocaust and the Christian World: Reflections on the Past, Challenges for the Future*, ed. Carol Rittner, Stephen D. Smith, and Irena Steinfeldt. London: Kuperard, 2000, 5–10.

Rothschild, Fritz A.
Jewish Perspectives on Christianity: Leo Baeck, Martin Buber, Franz Rosenzweig, Will Herberg, and Abraham J. Heschel. New York: Crossroad, 1990.

Rubenstein, Richard L.
After Auschwitz: History, Theology, and Contemporary Judaism. 2nd ed. Baltimore: Johns Hopkins University Press, 1992.

After Auschwitz: Radical Theology and Contemporary Judaism. Indianapolis: Bobbs-Merrill, 1966.

My Brother Paul. New York: Harper and Row, 1972.

Rubenstein, Richard L., and John K. Roth
Approaches to Auschwitz: The Holocaust and Its Legacy. Rev. ed. Louisville, Ky.: Westminster/John Knox, 2003.

Ruddy, Christopher
The Strange Death of Vincent Foster: An Investigation. New York: Free Press, 1997.

Rudin, A. James
"Jump-Starting the Conversation between Jews and Catholics." *National Catholic Reporter*, 4 October 2002. 30 March 2004, http://natcath.org/NCR_Online/archives2/2002d/100402/100402t.htm.

Ruether, Rosemary Radford
Christianity and the Making of the Modern Family. Boston: Beacon Press, 2000.

Faith and Fratricide: The Theological Roots of Anti-Semitism. New York: Seabury Press, 1974.

Rush, George, et al.
"Mel's Next Mission: Cinema Savior." *Daily News*, 6 August 2002, 18.

Russell, James C.
The Germanization of Early Medieval Christianity. Oxford: Oxford University Press, 1994.

Rutten, Tim
"'Passion': Christians Join the Call." *Los Angeles Times*, 11 February 2004, E1.

Saddleback Church
"What an Easter! More Than 39,000 People Attend Easter Services at Saddleback." Saddleback Family.com. 21 April 2004, http://www.saddleback family.com/home/todaystory.asp?id=6538.

Saddleback Church Bulletin
Saddleback Church, Lake Forest, California. 28–29 February 2004.

Safire, William J.
"Not Peace, but a Sword." *New York Times*, 1 March 2004, A21.

Said, Edward W.
Orientalism. New York: Pantheon Books, 1978.

Samuelsen, Eric
"Unremitting Passion." *Sunstone Magazine* 131 (March 2004): 68–71.

Sanders, E. P.
Paul and Palestinian Judaism: A Comparison of Patterns of Religion. London: S.C.M., 1977.

Paul: A Very Short Introduction. New York: Oxford University Press, 1991.

Sawyer, Diane
"From Pain to Passion: A *PrimeTime* Event." Interview with Mel Gibson. *PrimeTime Live*. New York: ABC News, 16 February 2004.

Interview with Maia Morgenstern. *Good Morning America*. New York: ABC News, 25 February 2004.

Schlichting, Günter
Ein jüdisches Leben Jesu: Die verschollene Toledot-Jeschu-Fassung Tam u-mu'ad. Tübingen: J. C. B. Mohr, 1982.

BIBLIOGRAPHY

Schnackenburg, Rudolf
Baptism in the Thought of Saint Paul. Translated by G. R. Beasley Murray. Oxford: Basil Blackwell, 1964.

Schroeder, Rev. H. J.
Canons and Decrees of the Council of Trent. Translated by H. J. Schroeder, OP. St. Louis: B. Herder Book Co., 1941.

Schultz, Walter (Bishop)
Letter to President Rönck of Thuringian Church, August 2, 1944 re. Pich's Denkschrift, *Der Jude Schaul.* Landeskirchen Archiv Thüringen, Personalia: Leffler, Grundmann: Institut, 1938–1944.

Schweitzer, Albert
The Quest of the Historical Jesus: A Critical Study of Its Progress from Reimarus to Wrede. Translated by W. Montgomery. London: A. & C. Black, 1910.

Von Reimarus zu Wrede, Eine Geschichte der Leben-Jesu-Forschung. Tübingen: J. C. B. Mohr, 1906.

Scorsese, Martin
The Last Temptation of Christ. Los Angeles: Universal Pictures, 1988.

Scorsese, Martin, David Thompson, and Ian Christie
Scorsese on Scorsese. London: Faber and Faber, 1990.

"See The Passion"
Home page. 17 April 2004, http://www.seethepassion.com.

Segal, Alan F.
Rebecca's Children: Judaism and Christianity in the Roman World. Cambridge, Mass.: Harvard University Press, 1986.

Senior, Donald
The Passion of Jesus in the Gospel of Mark. Wilmington, Del.: Michael Glazier, 1984.

Serafin, Gerard
"Some Catholic Blogs (Sometimes Referred to as 'St Blog's Parish')." 28 March 2004, http://praiseofglory.com/blogs.htm.

Serre, Olivier
"Le Point De Vue De Chrétiens-Médias." *Le Film Religieux—Cinémaction No. 49.* Paris: Corlet, 1988.

Shapiro, James
Oberammergau. New York: Vintage, 2000.

Shipps, Jan
: *Mormonism: The Story of a New Religious Tradition.* Urbana: University of Illinois Press, 1985.

Shuman, Ellis
: "Kach Activists 'Celebrate' 10th Anniversary of Baruch Goldstein Massacre." *israelinsider: Israel's daily newsmagazine*, 7 March 2004. 30 March 2004, http://web.israelinsider.com/bin/en.jsp?enDisplay=view&enDispWho=Article%5El3393&enDispWhat=object&enZone=Politics&enPage=ArticlePage&.

Siciliano, Enzo
: *Pasolini: A Biography.* New York: Random House, 1982.

Silk, Mark
: "Gibson's Passion: A Case Study in Media Manipulation?" *Journal of Religion and Film* 8:1 (February 2004). 15 April 2004, http://www.unomaha.edu/~wwwjrf/2004Symposium/Silk.htm. Also published in *Journal of Religion and Society* 6 (2004). http://moses.creighton.edu/JRS/2004/2004-4.html.

Sim, Stuart
: *The Icon Critical Dictionary of Postmodern Thought.* London: Routledge, 2001.

Simon Wiesenthal Center
: "Background to a Dilemma." 16 February 2004. 28 April 2004, http://www.wiesenthal.com/social/press/pr_item.cfm?ItemID=8933.

: "Wiesenthal Center on Gibson Film: Going Back to Pre-Vatican II May Give Rise to Anti-Semitism" [press release]. 7 March 2003. 12 April 2004, http://www.wiesenthal.com/social/press/pr_item.cfm?ItemId=7306.

Singer, Tovia
: "Will 'The Passion' Crucify the Jews?" *The Tovia Singer Show: Talk Radio on the Edge*, 25 September 2003. 9 May 2004, http://www.toviasingershow.com/RantArchives8.aspx.

Sizer, Sandra
: *Hymns and Social Religion: The Rhetoric of Nineteenth-Century Revivalism.* Philadelphia: Temple University Press, 1978.

Sloyan, Gerard S.
: *The Crucifixion of Jesus: History, Myth, Faith.* Minneapolis: Fortress Press, 1995.

Soulen, R. Kendall
: *The God of Israel and Christian Theology.* Minneapolis: Fortress Press, 1996.

BIBLIOGRAPHY

Spiegel, Paul, Karl Lehmann, and Wolfgang Huber
"Gemeinsame Stellungnahme zum Film 'Die Passion Christi'" [joint statement on the film *The Passion of the Christ*]. Central Council of Jews in Germany, German Bishops' Conference, and the Evangelical [Lutheran] Church in Germany. 18 March 2004. 9 May 2004, http://dbk.de/presse/pm2004/pm2004031801.html.

Stack, Peggy Fletcher
"Clergy Screen 'Passion.'" *Salt Lake Tribune*, 25 February 2004, A1.

St. Joseph's Men Society: Defending the One True Faith
"Bishops Sell Out to the Jewish Christophobes Again." 29 February 2004, http://www.stjosephsmen.com/articles/AmBishops.

Stammer, Larry B.
"'Christ' and the Gospel Truth; With 'The Passion of the Christ,' Mel Gibson Displays Reverence for the Gospels—Perhaps to a Fault." *Los Angeles Times*, 25 February 2004, E1.

Steinfels, Peter
"Beliefs: In the End, Does 'The Passion of the Christ' Point to Christian Truths, or Obscure Them?" *New York Times*, 28 February 2004, A13.

Strobel, Lee
The Case for a Creator: A Journalist Investigates Scientific Evidence That Points toward God. Grand Rapids, Mich.: Zondervan, 2004.

The Case for Christ: A Journalist's Personal Investigation of the Evidence for Jesus. Grand Rapids, Mich.: Zondervan, 1998.

The Case for Easter: A Journalist Investigates the Evidence for the Resurrection. Grand Rapids, Mich.: Zondervan, 2004.

The Case for Faith: A Journalist Investigates the Toughest Objections of Christianity. Grand Rapids, Mich.: Zondervan, 2000.

Strobel, Lee, and Garry Poole
Experiencing the Passion of Jesus. Grand Rapids, Mich.: Zondervan, 2004.

Support Mel Gibson!
Home page. 26 April 2004, http://www.supportmelgibson.com/.

Swanson, R. N.
Religion and Devotion in Europe c.1215–1515. Cambridge: Cambridge University Press, 1995.

Tackett, Del
    Letter to Paul Lauer, Icon Productions 11 July 2003. Family.org: A Website of Focus on the Family. 21 April 2004, http://family.custhelp.com/cgi-bin/family.cfg/php/enduser/fattach_get.php?p_tbl=9&p_id=3611&p_created=1061309929.

Talmage, James E.
    Jesus the Christ. Salt Lake City: Deseret Book Company, 1915.

Tambiah, Stanley
    Leveling Crowds: Ethnonationalist Conflicts and Collective Violence in South Asia. Berkeley: University of California Press, 1996.

Tapia, Andres
    "Reflections on 'The Passion'—What I Would Tell My Jewish Friends." *Pacific News Service*, 1 March 2004. 11 August 2004, http://www.pacificnews.org/news/view_article.html?article_id=e8bbf5d3713b0e4e959da2d71ad05620. Reprinted in *The National Catholic Reporter* 40:20 (19 March 2004): 22.

Ternisien, Xavier
    "Pour les disciples de Mgr Lefebvre, la violence du film est 'porteuse de sens.'" LeMonde.fr., 30 March 2004. 31 March 2004, http://www.lemonde.fr/web/recherche_articleweb/1,13-0,36-359243,0.html.

The Daily Universe
    Brigham Young University, editions of 7 March 2004 and 18 March 2004.

"The Jews and the Passion"
    Society of St. Pius X. 28 February 2004, http://www.sspx.org/controversies.htm.

"The Mormon Cult"
    Fellowship of the Mystery: An Internet Outreach Ministry Revealing the Truth about the End Times Apostasy to the World Wide Web [n.d.]. 21 April 2004, http://www.fellowshipofthemystery.com/deception.html.

"The Passion of the Christ, the Greatest Story Ever Told"
    LifeWay Christian Resources. 25 March 2004, http://www.lifeway.com/passion.

"The Secret of the Masons"
    January 1954. The Crusade of Saint Benedict Center for Slaves of the Immaculate Heart of Mary. 12 February 2004, http://www.catholicism.org/pages/masonjews.htm.

BIBLIOGRAPHY

Thiessen, Mark
"Jewish Group Says Mormon Practice of Baptizing Holocaust Victims Continues." Associated Press. 9 April 2004.

Thomas, Wendi C.
"Jews Didn't Kill Jesus; He Gave His Life for Us." *Memphis Commercial Appeal*, 2 March 2004, C1.

Thurston, Herbert
The Stations of the Cross: An Account of their History and Devotional Purpose. London: Burns & Oates, 1906.

Tincq, Henri
"Mgr Lustiger contre le 'sadisme' du film de Gibson." LeMonde.fr, 27 March 2004. 31 March 2004, http://www.lemonde.fr/web/imprimer_article/0,1-0@2-3208,36-358438,0.html.

Trewhella, Matthew
Missionaries to the Preborn. Home page. 24 February 2004, http://www.missionariestopreborn.com/.

"*The Passion of the Christ* or The Emperor's New Clothes." Institute for Theonomic Reformation. Commentary on Passion of the Christ Movie. 24 February 2004, http://www.hisglory.us/commentary/the_passion_of_christ.htm#treweller.

United States Conference of Catholic Bishops
"Ecumenical and Interreligious Committee Responds to News Report" [press release]. 11 June 2003. 25 June 2003, http://www.usccb.org/comm/archives/2003/03-119.htm.

"*The Passion of the Christ*." 28 March 2004, http://www.usccb.org/movies/p/thepassionofthechrist.htm.

Urekew, Robert
"Is It as It Was?" *Midstream*, April 2004, 22–23.

Van Buren, Paul Matthews
A Theology of the Jewish Christian Reality: Discerning the Way. 3 vols., vol. 1. New York: Seabury Press, 1980.

A Theology of the Jewish Christian Reality: A Christian Theology of the People Israel. 3 vols., vol. 2. San Francisco: Harper and Row, 1987.

A Theology of the Jewish-Christian Reality: Christ in Context. 3 vols., vol. 3. Lanham, Md.: University Press of America, 1995.

Vargas Llosa, Mario
Aunt Julia and the Scriptwriter. New York: Farrar, Straus & Giroux, 1982.

Vatican Commission for Religious Relations with Jews
"Notes on the Correct Way to Present the Jews and Judaism in Preaching and Catechesis in the Roman Catholic Church." 1985. 17 February 2004, http://www.bc.edu/research/cjl/meta-elements/texts/documents/catholic/Vatican_Notes.htm.

Verhoeven, Michael, dir.
Das schrekliche Mädchen [The Nasty Girl]. Germany: Filmverlag der Autoren, 1989.

Vermes, Geza
Jesus in His Jewish Context. Minneapolis: Fortress Press, 2003.

Viano, Maurizio Sanzio
A Certain Realism: Making Use of Pasolini's Film Theory and Practice. Berkeley: University of California Press, 1993.

Vieth, Gene Edward
"Passion Play: How Did a Realistic Movie about the Death of Jesus Get to Be So Controversial?" Citizen Magazine: A Website of Focus on the Family. 10 April 2004, http://www.family.org/cforum/citizenmag/webonly/A0029427.cfm.

Wall, James M.
"Biblical Spectaculars and Secular Man." In *Celluloid and Symbols*, ed. John Charles Cooper and Carl Skrade, 51–60. Philadelphia: Fortress Press, 1970.

Wallis, Arthur
Into Battle: A Manual of Christian Life. New York: Harper and Row, 1973.

Walther, Andrew
"Bishops Apologize to Mel Gibson over *The Passion*." *National Catholic Register*, 22–28 June 2003. 22 June 2003, http://www.ncregister.com/Register_News/061503_1.htm.

Warren, Rick
"Catching the Passion Wave." *Christianity Today*, 16 March 2004. 3 April 2004, http://www.christianitytoday.com/leaders/newsletter/2004/cln40316.html.

The Purpose-Driven Church: Growth without Compromising Your Message and Mission. Grand Rapids, Mich.: Zondervan, 1995.

The Purpose-Driven Life: What on Earth Am I Here For? Grand Rapids, Mich.: Zondervan, 2002.

"Understanding the Passion—Part 1: What the Passion of Jesus Tells Us about God." Sermon Notes, 21–22 February 2004.

Watanabe, Teresa
"'Passion' Stand Mishandled, Some Jewish Leaders Say: Gibson's Movie Is Called Unlikely to Fan Hatred and a Beneficiary of Its Foes' Critical Comments." *Los Angeles Times*, 23 February 2004, A1.

Weaver, J. Denny
The Nonviolent Atonement. Grand Rapids, Mich.: Eerdmans, 2001.

Weaver, Mary Jo, and R. Scott Appleby, eds.
Being Right: Conservative Catholics in America. Bloomington: Indiana University Press, 1995.

Weber, Cornelia
Altes Testament und völkische Frage. Forschungen zum Alten Testament 28. Tübingen: Mohr Siebeck, 2000.

Weber, Timothy P.
Living in the Shadow of the Second Coming. Chicago: University of Chicago Press, 1987.

Wetmore, Andrew
"Rhode Islanders Consider 'The Passion.'" Episcopal News Service 03104-1, 1 March 2004. 30 March 2004, http://www.episcopalchurch.org/3577_29963_ENG_Print.html.

White, David Allen
"Reflections on *The Passion of the Christ*." *The Remnant: A Catholic Fortnightly*, 15 March 2004. 16 March 2004, http://ourworld.compuserve.com/homepages/remnant/doc.htm/.

"Who Really Killed Jesus?"
Religion and Ethics Newsweekly. Episode 725. Washington, D.C.: Public Broadcasting Corporation, 20 February 2004.

Wiese, Christian
Wissenschaft des Judentums und protestantische Theologie im wilhelminischen Deutschland. Tübingen: Mohr Siebeck, 1999.

Wiesel, Elie
  Night. New York: Avon Books, 1960.

Williams, James G.
  The Bible, Violence, and the Sacred: Liberation from the Myth of Sanctioned Violence. Pbk. ed. Valley Forge, Pa.: Trinity Press International, 1995.

Williams, Natalie
  "Gibson's 'Passion' Puts Christ on the Big Screen." *The Daily Universe*. Brigham Young University. 26 February 2004. 21 April 2004, http://nn.byu.edu/story.cfm/48693.

Williamson, Clark
  A Guest in the House of Israel: Post-Holocaust Church Theology. Louisville, Ky.: Westminster/John Knox, 1993.

Willow Creek Community Church
  Home page. 19 April 2004, http://www.willowcreek.org.
  "I'm New—Willow Creek Community Church." 19 April 2004, http://www.willowcreek.org/im_new.asp.

Winfield, Nicole
  "ADL Asks Vatican to Condemn 'The Passion.'" Associated Press. 18 February 2004.

Winter, Michael M.
  The Atonement. Collegeville, Minn.: Liturgical Press, 1995.

Wolpe, David
  "The Real Tragedy of *The Passion*: Gibson's Portrayal of Jews Is Worrisome." In *The Passion Papers: Making Sense of the Movie and the Crucifixion*, 100–104. New York: Beliefnet.com/Waterfront Media, 2004.

WorldNetDaily
  "Billy Graham Screens 'The Passion of the Christ.'" WorldNetDaily, 26 November 2003. 26 March 2004, http://www.worldnetdaily.com/news/article.asp?ARTICLE_ID=35826.

Wuthnow, Robert
  The Restructuring of American Religion. Princeton, N.J.: Princeton University Press, 1988.

Wyschogrod, Michael
  The Body of Faith: God and the People of Israel. Northvale, N.J.: Jason Aronson, 1996.

BIBLIOGRAPHY

Yoder, John Howard
The Jewish-Christian Schism Revisited. Edited by Michael G. Cartwright and Peter Ochs. Grand Rapids, Mich.: Eerdmans, 2003.

Yusko, Alan
"Mel Gibson's Catholic Movie: The Passion." Bible Prophecy and the Rapture Report. 8 March 2004, http://www.geocities.com/Athens/Rhodes/7895/cathpassion04.html.

Zahn, Paula
Interview with William Donohue and Marvin Hier. *Paula Zahn Now.* Atlanta: CNN, 4 February 2004.

Zenit News Agency
"Christ's Agony as You've Never Seen It." 6 March 2003. 23 January 2004, http://www.Zenit.org/english/visualizza.phtml?sid=32330.

"Controversy Swirls around Mel Gibson's 'Passion.'" 30 May 2003. 23 January 2004, http://www.Zenit.org/english/visualizza.phtml?sid=36393.

"Production of 'Passion' Under Way." 19 November 2002. 23 January 2004, http://www.Zenit.org/english/visualizza.phtml?sid=27885.

INDEX

abortion, 21, 49, 77, 81, 83, 87n20
absolutism: moral, 20, 48, 258; rhetoric of, 55, 58n39
Ad Hoc Scholars Group, 27–29, 33, 36, 37, 45n19
Albacete, Lorenzo, 12, 89–90
Alessio, Mark, 86n15, 87n23
Allen, John, Jr., 30
Amalek, Amalekites, 175, 237–38
Anabaptists, 267, 271
Anselm of Canterbury, 98–99, 100, 143, 147n15
anti-Catholicism, 37, 40, 77
Anti-Defamation League (ADL), 2, 3, 9, 19, 27, 29–30, 36, 37, 40, 232, 241n7
anti-Judaism, 91, 195–96, 220–21, 231, 247, 253n5; in the New Testament and Christianity, 129, 140–42, 187, 198–99, 200, 203, 248–49, 253n4, 258, 272; in *The Passion of the Christ*, 12, 90, 129–31, 133, 201, 229–30, 239, 277; in Sunday school materials, 272–73

antisemitism, 1–3, 4, 14, 25, 38, 125–36, 169n3, 170n21, 176, 179, 185, 187, 197–98, 203, 230, 233–34, 240, 241n7; in the New Testament and Christianity, 9, 13, 31, 70–71, 77, 80, 91, 106–8, 112, 113n4, 171n26, 184, 191n18, 205n13, 219–28, 231–32, 235, 247, 249, 257–58, 262, 268, 274; in *The Passion of the Christ*, 3, 5, 10, 12, 16, 21, 32, 37, 40, 44n14, 54–55, 64, 69, 75, 89, 90, 105, 115, 122, 164, 174–75, 195–96, 200–201, 204, 207, 209, 218n14, 229, 238, 277
apocalyptic, 71, 140, 146n8, 267, 269
art, devotional/religious, 90, 96, 99, 100, 101, 115, 119, 122, 149–50
Aryan Jesus, 173, 178, 181–85, 191n18, 192n22
atonement: substitutionary, 78, 79, 98, 101, 215; theology of, 21, 66–68, 71, 85, 89, 92, 97, 100, 101, 104n23, 111, 126, 134n3, 140, 143–45, 147n15, 152, 157, 165,

331

INDEX

168, 208–9, 214–15, 224–25, 228n11, 251
Auschwitz, 199–200, 244, 245, 246, 249, 252
Auschwitz-Birkenau State Museum, 244
Ayer, A. J., 259, 264n9

Baptists, Southern, 8–9, 39, 40
Barabbas, 130
Barton, Bruce, 150
Baugh, Lloyd, 12, 91–92
Beer, Georg, 184
Benson, Ezra Taft, 61, 63, 72
Bernstein, Leonard, 251
Bible: as literature, 264n12; as reflection of cultural contexts, 106, 260; extra- and non-biblical materials in *The Passion of the Christ*, 20, 22, 40, 48, 57n5, 65, 82, 83, 91, 127, 129, 131, 152, 165, 171n26, 189, 195, 196; Hebrew (*see* Hebrew Bible); inerrancy of, 7, 8, 48, 49, 51, 64, 65, 69, 70, 191n13, 273; interpretation of, 11, 15, 64, 83, 86n16, 110, 111, 116, 135n19, 137, 183, 184, 210, 228, 272, 276; Mormon use of, 62, 66, 70; quoted at United States Holocaust Memorial Museum, 246–48; use of in *The Passion of the Christ*, 26, 56, 128, 134n17
bin Laden, Osama, 282, 283
Bishops' Committee for Ecumenical and Interreligious Affairs (BCEIA), 27, 37, 44n8, 113n5, 240n4
Black Hawk Down, 280
blog, 20, 35–45
Bonhoeffer, Dietrich, 204

Boyer, Peter, 8, 30, 208
Boys, Mary, 27
Braithwaite, R. B., 259, 264n9
Braveheart, 32, 102, 280, 281
Buchanan, Patrick, 8, 9, 14, 32, 169n3
Bugg, Richard, 68, 73n21
bulimia, theological. *See* theological bulimia
Butler, Jim, 227

Caiaphas, 119, 121, 123n21, 131, 135n27, 165, 171n26
Cain and Abel, story of, 246, 247
Calvary, 32, 82, 105, 153, 155, 165, 200
canonicity, 182, 260, 277, 285; Mormon, 61, 62, 66, 74n26
capitalism, 54
Card, Orson Scott, 63–65, 67, 71, 73n21
Catholic Church. *See* Catholicism; Roman Catholic Church
Catholic League for Religious and Civil Rights, 9, 29, 33n16, 37
Catholicism: mainstream, 29, 75–77, 108; Roman (*see* Roman Catholic Church); traditionalist, 2, 3, 7, 19, 20, 25, 36, 38, 48, 67, 75, 77, 78, 86n15, 90, 92, 108, 109, 116, 150, 156–57, 208, 209, 211, 282
Chamberlain, Houston Stewart, 183–84, 191nn18–19, 192n28
Chaput, Charles, 28, 33n22
Charen, Mona, 31
Charismatics, 267
Chichester Psalms, 251
chief priests. *See* Sadducees
Christian Coalition, 49
Christian Right, 57n9, 60, 63, 65, 68, 69, 77, 78, 234

INDEX

Christian Zionism, 9, 267, 268–69, 272
Christianity, muscular. *See* muscular Christianity
Church Age, 86n6
Church of Jesus Christ of Latter-day Saints (LDS Church), 12, 21, 60, 62, 65–66, 71, 72, 74n30
Civil War, American, 149
cognitive dissonance, 210, 217n10
Connor, Tracy, 33n16
conservatism: Christian, 4, 31, 46n31, 47, 48–49, 56, 85, 104n25; social, 267
consumerism, 20, 48, 52–54, 56, 58n29
consummation of the ages, 267
conversion, 16n28, 20, 47–49, 51, 52, 55, 74n30, 103n10, 141, 190n2, 212, 222, 240n4, 269
co-redemptrix. *See* Mary, mother of Jesus
Cork, James, 36
Cork, William, 12, 20, 29, 33n18, 44n7, 191n19
Cormode, Scott, 227
counterhistory, 173, 178–80, 186–87
covenant, 90, 120, 121, 126, 131, 141, 142, 222, 223, 231, 268, 269
Crossan, John Dominic, 39
Crowley, Aleister, 50
culture war, 6, 8, 12, 14, 19, 23, 31, 32, 54, 64, 79, 84, 86n15, 191n19, 283
Cunningham, Philip, 80

Dabru Emet, 1, 253n41
Danziger, Harry, 202–3
The Da Vinci Code, 112
Davis, Natalie Zemon, 284
Davis, Stephen, 13, 174, 227

Day, Dorothy, 7
The Deer Hunter, 280
dejudaization, 173, 183–85, 188, 192n28
demons, 79, 86n14, 93, 152, 154
DeNiro, Robert, 203
Derenbourg, Joseph, 181
Derrida, Jacques, 132
Deuteronomy, 118, 246, 248, 250
dialogue, interreligious, 6, 9, 11, 27, 36, 40, 41, 42, 44n7, 45n29, 71, 142, 174, 179, 180, 185, 186, 195, 198, 210, 216, 217, 218n11, 230, 234–36, 240, 251, 255–65, 271
diaspora (Jewish), 271
dispensationalism, 77, 86n6, 267–70, 277n1
dissonance, cognitive. *See* cognitive dissonance
Dobson, James, 39, 55, 56, 78
Donaldson, Terence, 271
Donohue, William, 9, 29, 33n16, 37, 38, 44n14
Dorff, Elliot, 13, 176, 216
Dowd, Maureen, 39
dualism (dualistic), 268
Dziwicz, Stanislaw, 30, 170n20

Easterbrook, Gregg, 130
Eckstein, Yechiel, 32
Elcott, David, 13, 175, 241n21
Emden, Jacob, 179
Emmerich, Anne Catherine (Anna Katharina), 41, 102n1, 129, 130, 131, 135n31, 153, 166, 171n26
emotion, emotionalism, 20, 38, 41, 48, 51–52, 56, 68, 90, 94, 97, 106–7, 108, 109–10, 112, 151, 152, 153, 157, 169, 174, 196, 208, 210, 211, 215, 216, 264n9, 279

INDEX

erasure, 90, 132, 133, 134n14
evangelicalism, 20–21, 47–58, 63, 76, 77, 78–79, 84–85, 86n6, 89, 100, 101, 104n23, 136n40, 143, 176, 200, 209, 225, 267–78; diversity within, 176, 267, 272, 273; and Mormonism, 59–60, 63–64, 65–66, 71, 72
Evangelical Lutheran Church in America, 216, 257, 262
evangelism, 48, 53, 55, 75, 133, 174, 204, 224, 248, 269, 270
Evans, Craig, 221
experience, religious, 52, 56, 69, 78, 99, 101, 109–12, 122, 164–66, 209, 213, 230, 239, 264n8, 285–86

Faggen, Robert, 12, 90, 134n4
Falwell, Jerry, 7, 78, 169n31
Farrell, Steve, 69, 74n23
Finke, Roger, 75, 76, 81
Fisher, Eugene, 27–28, 44n8
Flossenbürg, 204
Focus on the Family, 39, 51, 55, 56
formulas (formulaic), 95, 274
Fredriksen, Paula, 29, 208
Freud, Sigmund, 212
fundamentalism, 6, 7, 12, 13, 14, 21, 49, 75–76, 78, 104n23, 128, 143, 160, 169n3, 197, 216, 229, 268, 273, 276
fundamentalist critique of *The Passion of the Christ*, 81–84, 85

Geiger, Abraham, 181–83, 186, 187, 190n12, 191n15
gender, 21, 77, 84, 85, 104n23, 155–56, 187, 188
Gethsemane, Garden of, 66, 67, 69, 100, 154

Gibson, Hutton, 2, 24, 25, 202, 211
Gilbert, Gary, 12, 90–91
globalization, 4, 279
Gnosticism, 90, 112
Goldstein, Baruch, 237, 238
Good Samaritan, Parable of, 250
The Gospel According to Saint Matthew, 92, 159, 161, 280
Graetz, Heinrich, 181, 184
Graham, Billy, 78–79
Gray, Patrick, 202
Great Commission (Matthew 27:51), 49
Grundmann, Walter, 184, 185, 189

Haggard, Ted, 9, 16n35, 45n22
Halevi, Judah, 179, 263–64
Hamburger Hill, 280
Harink, Douglas, 271
Haynes, Jean, 205
Haynes, Stephen, 12, 174
Hebrew Bible, 117, 119, 120, 178, 185, 221, 222, 225
Heidegger, Martin, 132
Heschel, Susannah, 12, 16, 113, 142, 173
Hier, Marvin, 2, 3, 4, 9, 16n32, 19, 26, 27
Himmelfarb, Gertrude, 32
history, practice of, 116–17, 178–81 *passim*, 256–58, 268–78 *passim*
Hitler, Adolf, 178, 185
Hollywood, 4, 14, 19, 21, 25, 31, 48, 56, 64, 71, 75, 85, 102, 174, 177, 195
Holocaust, 1, 2, 3, 6, 8, 9, 40, 74n30, 91, 141, 175–76, 185, 187, 196, 197, 200, 204, 205n1, 211, 226, 233, 243–53, 269, 270, 276
Holtzmann, Heinrich Julius, 183

holy envy, 235, 241n16
homosexuality, 10, 21, 49, 77, 162, 163, 170n13, 211
humility, epistemological, 176
Hunter, James Davison, 79, 84
Hybels, Bill, 78

iconography, 127, 149, 156, 157n1, 164, 279, 282, 285
idolatry, 22, 83, 180, 211, 260, 261
incarnational theology. *See* theology, incarnational
Ingersoll, Julie, 12, 21–22, 57n7, 104n23
Institute for the Study and Eradication of Jewish Influence on German Church Life, 184, 185, 189
interfaith dialogue. *See* dialogue, interreligious
Internet, 9, 12, 20, 25, 35–46 *passim*, 195
interreligious dialogue. *See* dialogue, interreligious
Iraq War, 6, 35, 44n4, 189, 282, 286
Irons, Jeremy, 203
Isaiah, interpretation of, 73n18, 120, 123n17, 140, 146n7, 208, 245–46
Israel, 2, 4, 5, 9, 16n35, 31, 41, 45n22, 46n31, 108, 197–98, 235, 237, 239; "carnal Israel," 268, 277n2; in Christian theology, 71, 74n29, 111, 118, 131, 138, 176, 187–88, 189, 191n22, 209, 210, 221, 222, 223, 251, 267–78

Jacoby, Jeff, 31
Jesus: Aryan (*see* Aryan Jesus); historical, 12, 110, 173, 177, 180, 182, 190n10; life and teachings of in *The Passion of the Christ*, 2, 5, 91, 144, 165–66, 177, 227; masculinity of, 91, 150, 155, 156; resurrection of in *The Passion of the Christ* and other films, 5, 79, 80, 91, 92, 106, 153, 166–69
Jesus of Montreal, 129
Jewish people: as category in Christian theology, 9, 16n35, 74n29, 135n20, 200, 222, 224, 246, 250, 267, 269, 270, 273, 274, 276
Job, Book of, 260, 264n11
John Paul II, Pope, 30–31, 51, 164, 170n20, 240n4, 251
John (Gospel of), 95, 117, 121, 129, 135n27, 152, 154, 272, 274
Josephus, 202, 275
Jost, Isaac, 181
Juergensmeyer, Mark, 13

Kazantzakis, Nikos, 159, 160, 280
kingdom of God, 86n6, 163
Kintz, Linda, 55
Kittel, Gerhard, 184
Klein Halevi, Yossi, 209
Kook, Abraham Isaac (Rav), 239
Korn, Eugene, 27, 29, 44n8
Krauthammer, Charles, 184
Kuhn, Karl Georg, 184

Landres, J. Shawn, 58n31, 58n41, 87n27, 227
Lapin, Daniel, 8, 16n28, 29, 31
The Last Temptation of Christ, 60, 63, 64, 92, 129, 159, 161, 280
Lawler, Phil, 37, 38
Lefebvre, Marcel, 211
Left Behind series, 63, 71, 86n14
Legion of Christ, 26, 33n8
legitimacy, evangelical, 55–56

INDEX

Lerner, Michael, 4
Lethal Weapon, 94, 280
Limbaugh, David, 64, 65
Limbaugh, Rush, 33n11
Luke (Gospel of), 95, 138–39, 152, 186, 275
Luther, Martin, 249, 257, 262

Mahony, Roger (Cardinal), 34n32, 169n3
Maimonides (Moses ben Maimon), 179, 190n8
Mark (Gospel of), 95, 126, 131, 135n30, 146n8, 170n25, 227n2
Marsh, W. Jeffrey, 69
Marty, Martin E., 5, 81
Mary Magdalene, 150, 152, 156, 160, 168
Mary, mother of Jesus (Virgin Mary), 57n5, 73n22, 77, 78, 82, 83, 84, 85, 91, 99, 109, 150–54, 156, 157n7, 166, 168, 227; as co-redemptrix, 83, 84, 87n27, 152
Mass (Eucharist), 22, 77, 82, 87n22, 101, 146, 151, 156, 227
materialism, 20, 54, 58n29
Matthew (Gospel of), 64, 70, 90, 95, 125, 126, 131, 135n30, 145, 152, 161–63, 169, 170n8, 170n25, 196, 205n3, 208–9, 221, 222, 223, 228n11, 272, 274
Mauss, Armand, 59, 63, 68
McConkie, Bruce R., 66, 67
media coverage of *The Passion of the Christ*, 2, 5, 12, 19, 20, 23, 26, 30, 31, 33n13, 34n32, 36, 77, 116, 125, 165, 193, 194, 209
Medved, Michael, 8, 16n32, 29, 31
megachurch, 50, 52

Megillah, Megillat Esther, 237
memorabilia, 53
Mendelssohn, Moses, 179, 190n6, 190n9
Meridian Magazine, 73n11
Merrill, Keith, 63, 64, 65, 68, 73n11, 73n21
Miles, Jack, 5, 15, 120
millennialism. *See* premillennialism; postmillennialism
millennium, 267
Miller, Brett, 58n31
Millet, Robert, 63, 72n5, 73n21
Milton, John, 122
The Mission, 203
Mohler, Albert, 8, 40
Moral Majority, 49
Morgan, David, 12, 17, 91
Morgenstern, Maia, 117
mother, motherhood: and compassion, 151, 153, 157; and domestic formation, 156; mother-son relationship in *The Passion of the Christ*, 150–54; Victorian ideal of, 150
Motion Picture Association of America (MPAA) rating system, 61–62, 69
muscular Christianity, 149

Naomichana, 40
National Socialism (Nazi Party), 178, 180, 183, 184–85, 186, 228, 234, 244, 246, 247, 248, 253n4, 253n5
nativism, 77. *See also* anti-Catholicism
Navarro-Valls, Joaquín, 170n20
New Testament, 10, 40, 83, 112, 117, 119, 120, 129, 134n5, 135n19, 143, 145, 150, 170n16, 174, 179, 181,

182, 184, 185, 186, 189, 202, 214, 219, 220, 221, 223, 244, 245, 247, 250, 270, 278n12, 285

The New York Times, The New York Times Magazine, 6, 19, 24, 26, 29, 33n16, 32n5, 36

The New Yorker, 8, 30, 125, 208

Newsmax.com, 26, 33n11

Nicolosi, Barbara, 37–38, 39 *passim*

Norris, Pippa, 41, 42

Nostra Aetate, 3, 108, 231

Noxon, Christopher, 19, 24–25, 26, 27, 36

Oberammergau, 115, 126

O'Connor, John (Cardinal), 169n3

Oedipus complex, 155, 188

Old Testament: as Christian categorization of Hebrew Scriptures, 112, 141, 185

O'Reilly, Bill

The O'Reilly Factor, 24

pacifist Liberals, 267, 285

Palestine (Roman province), 93, 142, 162, 170n24, 260

Parkin, Scott, 68, 73n21

Pasolini, Pier Paolo, 12, 92, 161–64, 165, 168, 169, 170n13, 170n19, 280

Passion: narrative of, 2, 6, 90, 99, 106, 107, 110, 126, 145, 174, 178, 210, 215, 216, 231, 238, 245, 274; Passion plays, 41, 36n31, 89, 93, 94, 106, 108, 111, 115, 126, 127, 128, 134n9, 202, 231, 233, 234, 256, 262

The Passion of the Christ, early screenings of, 29, 31, 33n22, 37–38, 47, 75, 144–46, 238–39, 241n21

Paul, 95, 118–19, 126, 147n17, 182, 185, 186, 189, 212–15 *passim*, 220, 223–24, 253n12

Perry, L. Tom, 61

Pharisees, 108, 118, 128, 181–82, 186, 191n13, 191n15, 209, 212, 221, 272, 275

philosemitism, 136n40, 268

philosophy, 109, 113n9, 119, 132, 176, 227, 256, 257, 258–60, 261

Pietà, *Pietà*, 39, 82, 109, 152, 168, 227

Pilate, Pontius, 95, 113n4, 116, 119, 121, 126, 128, 129, 130, 134n5, 135n27, 143, 152, 153, 165, 170n24, 171n26, 189, 216, 220, 222, 243, 275, 282

Platoon, 280

pluralism, 49, 56, 175, 218n29, 239, 240, 260, 261

polarization, 8, 14, 38, 64, 175, 230, 238, 239, 240

postmillennialism, 7, 86n6, 267, 268

postmodernism, 13, 48, 50, 52–54 *passim*, 55, 90, 132, 133

Poupko, Yehiel, 27

Prager, Dennis, 14, 19, 31

premillennialism, 7, 77, 86n6, 267, 268, 269, 270, 277n1

"Promise-Fulfillment," 268, 274

Protestantism, 75–77, 156, 286; evangelical (*see* evangelicalism); mainline, 1, 7, 11, 65, 142, 179, 182, 183, 186, 224, 232

protestantization: of Mormonism, 12, 21, 59, 60, 63, 65, 68, 72; of the Roman Catholic Church, 156

INDEX

psychoanalysis, 12, 153, 154, 155, 157n7

racism, 183, 191n19, 191–92n22, 197, 251, 222
rationality, 13, 48, 49, 154
redemption, 104n23, 143, 144, 156, 211, 214, 248, 253n7, 274, 280; difference between Jewish and Christian views of, 2, 6, 215, 233; of sinners, 80, 91, 146
Rees, Robert, 68
Reformation, Protestant, 100, 156
Reform Judaism, 173, 182, 187
reformed tradition, 82, 267, 285
Reinhartz, Adele, 129
The Remnant, 78, 87
rhetoric: Greco-Roman, 274–75, 276, 285; Mormon, 63–65
Rhodes College, 202
Rich, Frank, 24, 29, 32n41
rites of violence. *See* violence, rites of
Robertson, Pat, 78, 169n3
Roman Catholic Church, 1, 2, 8, 14, 26, 34n32, 77, 100, 108, 134n16, 135n20, 142–43, 146, 159, 216, 218n29, 231, 232, 240n4; protestantization of. *See* protestantization
Romans, 6, 9, 16n35, 21, 37, 67, 80, 91, 93, 95, 96, 97, 98, 103n7, 112n4, 119, 120, 121, 129, 132, 135n29, 142, 144, 145, 151, 153, 168, 170n24, 187, 189, 197, 209, 220, 243, 247, 260, 275, 276, 279, 282
Romans (Epistle to), 123n14, 147n17, 218n20, 253n12
Rosenberg, Alfred, 183, 185
Roth, John, 13, 175–76

Rubenstein, Richard, 12, 174, 178, 191n19
Ruether, Rosemary, 57n9, 129, 141

Saddleback Church, 52–53, 78
Sadducees, 70, 138, 275, 276
Safire, William, 31
St. Blog's Parish, 44n7
Sallman, Warner, 100
salvation, 47, 65, 67, 80, 100, 140, 143, 146, 156, 184, 189, 200, 207, 209, 222, 234, 270, 272
Samuels, Shimon, 197
Samuelsen, Eric, 12, 21
Sanhedrin, 128, 135n27, 275, 281–82, 283
Satan, Satanic, 49, 54, 79, 82, 91, 97, 119, 151, 152, 160, 185, 189, 201, 207, 227, 238, 239, 241n20; as counter-mother in *The Passion of the Christ*, 154–55; traditional definition of, 123n15
Saving Private Ryan, 280
Sawyer, Diane, 117
Scholars' Committee, Scholars' Report. *See* Ad Hoc Scholars Group
Scofield Reference Bible, 86n6
Scorsese, Martin, 12, 60, 63, 92, 159–61, 163, 165, 167–69 *passim*, 170n7, 280
Second Temple. *See* Temple, Second
Second Vatican Council. *See* Vatican II
sectarianism, 21, 75, 76–77, 81, 211, 221
seekers, 52, 53, 189, 193
September 11 (9/11), 13, 177, 189, 197, 217, 283
Shea, Mark, 37, 38, 45n19
Shipps, Jan, 59

INDEX

Shoah. *See* Holocaust
Siker, Jeffrey, 12, 91, 217n1
Silk, Mark, 12, 14, 19, 20, 191n19
Simon Wiesenthal Center, 2, 3, 9, 26, 71, 197
Smith, Joseph, 62, 73n7, 73n20
Smith, Kathryn, 13, 176
Smith, Leslie, 12, 20
Society of Saint Pius X, 211
sola scriptura, 90, 111
soteriology, 51, 171n27, 270
Soulen, R. Kendall, 271, 277n4
Southern Baptists. *See* Baptists, Southern
Stark, Rodney, 75, 76, 81
Stations of the Cross, 22, 67, 82, 100, 156
Stendhal, Krister, 235, 241n16
Streete, Gail, 202
Strobel, Lee, 50–52
suffering, 233, 281; of Jesus in *The Passion of the Christ*, 5, 55, 69, 91, 94–95, 101–2, 127, 144–46, 151, 152, 153–57 *passim*, 174, 189, 195, 202, 207, 208, 209, 213, 215, 226, 230, 277, 280, 282; Jewish, 2, 6, 200, 276; theology of, 5–6, 66–68, 81, 83, 89, 91, 95–100, 101, 102, 103n9, 104n23, 106, 109, 120–21, 122, 135n32, 139, 140, 143, 146n8, 166, 167, 199–200, 202, 203, 204, 208, 213, 215, 236, 249, 274, 277, 285
"suffering servant," "suffering Son of Man," 120, 123n17, 139, 145, 146n8
Sunstone, 63, 68, 69
supercessionism. *See* supersessionism
supernaturalism, 20, 48, 179, 180, 182
supersessionism, 90, 129, 144, 200, 241n4, 268–71, 276, 277n4

Tackett, Del, 51, 52
Talmage, James, 66, 67
Talmud, 191n13, 260, 263n1, 263n4, 275, 276
Tambiah, Stanley, 284
Temple, Second, 80, 93, 108, 112n4, 120, 121, 144, 147n9, 171n26, 181, 184, 187, 190n7, 222, 227n2; destruction of, 91, 126, 131, 135n28, 142, 145, 165, 170n25, 209, 275, 276
terrorism, 189, 279, 281–83, 286
Teshuvah, 175, 233–34, 250
theological bulimia, 189
theology: incarnational, 271, 277n5; penitential, 5, 6, 12, 89, 92, 97–100, 102, 103n10
Torjesen, Karen, 5, 12, 89
Tosefta, 275, 276
tradition: as a religious category, 106–7, 110–12, 236–40, 246, 248, 249, 250, 258–59, 261, 262, 264n10
traditionalist Catholicism. *See* Catholicism, traditionalist
Treblinka, 246
Trent, Council of, 156
Trewhella, Matt, 83–84
triumphalism, 176, 251, 252, 261, 270

United States Conference of Catholic Bishops (USCCB), 3, 19, 27, 28, 29, 33n19, 36, 37, 44n8, 80, 134n17, 160, 240n4
United States Holocaust Memorial Museum, 245–48

Vargas Llosa, Mario, 105
Vatican II, 2, 26, 32n6, 76, 77, 78, 80, 100, 101, 107, 108, 111, 144, 146,

INDEX

156, 170n12, 207, 209, 211, 217, 218n29, 231
Veronica, 82, 93, 156, 157
victimhood, 4, 14
victimization, 21, 55, 95, 97, 152, 187, 237, 280–82, 286
violence: in *The Passion of the Christ*, 21, 44n14, 48, 54, 65, 67, 69, 78, 80, 82, 89, 101, 102, 153, 154, 157, 165, 171n26, 174, 195, 201, 202, 203, 208, 218n14, 224, 226, 230, 238, 239, 277, 280, 282; potential for, 9, 40, 238; rites of, 284
Virgin Mary. See Mary, mother of Jesus
von Harnack, Adolf, 183, 191n18, 191n19

Wallis, Arthur, 286
Wallis, Jim, 7
Warner, Kurt, 50
Warren, Rick, 53, 78
Wasserman, Lew, 169n3
weblog. *See* blog

Weiss, Judith, 41, 45n29, 45n31
Weiss, Steven I., 46n30
Welborn, Amy, 36
Wellhausen, Julius, 183
Wesleyans, 267
White, James, 40
Wiesel, Elie, 2, 196, 198, 200
Wildmon, Don, 169n3
Williamson, Clark, 251
Willow Creek Community Church, 50, 52, 57, 78, 241n21
Wissenschaft des Judentums, 181
women, 55, 77, 84, 85, 87n27, 104n23, 190n2, 218n20
Wuthnow, Robert, 79, 81, 84

Yoder, John Howard, 271
Yusko, Alan, 82

Zeffirelli, Franco, 160, 169n4, 170n13
Zenit News Agency, 26, 28, 33n16
Zionism, Christian. *See* Christian Zionism
Zunz, Leopold, 181

ABOUT THE CONTRIBUTORS

Msgr. Lorenzo Albacete is currently the U.S. National Ecclesiastical Director of the International Catholic Movement "Communion and Liberation." He has been professor of theology at St. Joseph Seminary in Yonkers, New York, and president of the Pontifical Catholic University of Puerto Rico. He was also one of the founders of the Washington, D.C., campus of the John Paul II Institute for Studies in Marriage and Family, where he was professor of theology and executive assistant to the dean. A lecturer and writer, Msgr. Albacete's articles have appeared in the *New York Times Magazine*, *The New Yorker*, and *The New Republic*. He is a columnist of the Italian news and opinion magazine *Tempi*. His latest book is *God at the Ritz* (2002).

Lloyd Baugh, SJ, a Canadian Jesuit priest, is ordinary professor of theology and film at the Pontifical Gregorian University in Rome. He has published widely in the areas of film and theological reflection, film and moral issues, film and spirituality, and film and intercultural–interreligious dialogue, and he serves on the editorial boards of two theological journals: *Gregorianum* and *Consacrazione e Servizio*. He teaches regularly in theology faculties in his native Canada, the United States, and the Philippines. In Rome, he serves as adviser to the Pontifical Council for Culture and the Pontifical Council for Social Communications. Author of *Imaging the Divine: Jesus and Christ-Figures in Film* (1997), he is at present completing a book on the ten *Decalogue* films of Krzysztof Kieslowski, examining them from the point of view of their treatment of the fundamental moral law of love.

ABOUT THE CONTRIBUTORS

Michael Berenbaum is director of the Sigi Ziering Institute: Exploring the Ethical and Religious Implications of the Holocaust and an adjunct professor of theology at the University of Judaism. He is the former president and chief executive officer of the Survivors of the Shoah Visual History Foundation. He was the director of the United States Holocaust Research Institute at the U.S. Holocaust Memorial Museum and the Hymen Goldman Adjunct Professor of Theology at Georgetown University in Washington, D.C. From 1988 to 1993, he served as project director of the U.S. Holocaust Memorial Museum, overseeing its creation. He has written and edited fifteen books on the Holocaust, most recently *A Promise to Remember: The Holocaust in the Words and Voices of Its Survivors* (2003).

William J. Cork, DMin, is the creator of *Ut Unum Sint . . . Iustus ex Fide Vivit: An Ecumenical Blog*. He is director of young adult and campus ministry, Catholic Diocese of Galveston-Houston. He attended Atlantic Union College (BA, 1984), the Lutheran Theological Seminary at Gettysburg (MAR in church history 1986; MDiv, 1989), and the Graduate Theological Foundation (DMin in ecumenism, 1998). He has been pastor of Lutheran parishes in Pennsylvania and Vermont and a chaplain in the Army Reserve, a parish director of religious education, and a Catholic campus minister at the University of California, Santa Barbara (UCSB). He has been a member of interfaith associations in Montpelier, Vermont, and Riverside, California, and was chair of the UCSB Interfaith Council and a member of the program committee for the 16th National Workshop on Christian–Jewish Relations (Houston, 1999). He has been creating personal and office Web pages for seven years and has been blogging for two years.

Stephen T. Davis is the Russell K. Pitzer Professor of Philosophy at Claremont-McKenna College. He is the author of some thirteen books and over sixty articles. He writes mainly in the philosophy of religion and in Christian theology. An ordained minister in the Presbyterian Church (USA), he is the author of *Risen Indeed: Making Sense of the Resurrection* (1993) and *God, Reason, and Theistic Proofs* (1997) and coeditor of *The Incarnation* (2002) and *The Redemption* (2004).

Elliot N. Dorff is rector of the University of Judaism and Distinguished Professor of Philosophy. A Conservative rabbi, he serves on the Law

ABOUT THE CONTRIBUTORS

Committee of the Rabbinical Assembly and is one of the world's leading authorities on medical ethics. He is the author of several books, including *Matters of Life and Death: A Jewish Approach to Modern Medical Ethics* (1998) and *To Do the Right and the Good* (2002), the latter of which won the National Jewish Book Award in Jewish Thought for 2003.

David M. Elcott is the U.S. director of interreligious affairs for the American Jewish Committee. He holds a PhD from Columbia University in political psychology and Middle East studies with a specialty in Islam and Arab culture and has additional academic expertise in Islamic and Jewish studies. Author of *A Sacred Journey: The Jewish Quest for a Perfect World* (1995) and of numerous articles and monographs, he was both trained at and has taught at the Reform movement's Hebrew Union College–Jewish Institute of Religion and the Conservative movement's University of Judaism. He previously served as vice president of the National Jewish Center for Learning and Leadership.

Robert A. Faggen is professor of literature at Claremont-McKenna College, where he has taught since 1988. Among his courses is the Bible as literature. He is the author of *Robert Frost and the Challenge of Darwin* (1997) and has edited the *Cambridge Companion to Robert Frost* (2001) and *Striving for Being: The Letter of Thomas Merton and Czeslaw Milosz* (1997). He serves as the general editor of the Harvard edition of the *Collected Writings of Robert Frost* and is writing a book titled *The Sparks Fly Out* on the work of American novelist and cultural icon Ken Keasey. He has an AB from Princeton and an MA and a PhD from Harvard.

Gary Gilbert is assistant professor of religious studies at Claremont-McKenna College and coordinator of the Jewish Studies program at the Claremont Colleges. He received his bachelor's degree in classics from Haverford College and his doctorate in biblical studies from Columbia University with additional studies in ancient Jewish history and literature at the Jewish Theological Seminary and New Testament and early Christianity at Union Theological Seminary. He has published numerous articles on the New Testament and ancient Judaism and is currently completing a book on the influence of Roman political propaganda on early Christian thought.

ABOUT THE CONTRIBUTORS

Stephen R. Haynes, associate professor of religious studies at Rhodes College, holds a PhD in religion and literature from Emory University, an MDiv from Columbia Theological Seminary, an MA from Florida State University, and a BA from Vanderbilt University. His publications include *Reluctant Witnesses: Jews and the Christian Imagination* (1995), *Noah's Curse: The Biblical Justification for Slavery in America* (2001), and *The Bonhoeffer Phenomenon: Portraits of a Protestant Saint* (2004). He offers courses on the Holocaust, religion and racism, and religion and literature. In addition to these subjects, he has research interests in Jewish–Christian relations, Dietrich Bonhoeffer, and religion and higher education.

Susannah Heschel is the Eli Black Associate Professor of Jewish Studies and chair of the Jewish Studies program at Dartmouth College. She is the author of numerous studies of modern Jewish thought, including *Abraham Geiger and the Jewish Jesus* (1998), which won the National Jewish Book Award and an award from the University of Potsdam and has been translated into German. She is also coeditor of *Insider/Outsider: American Jews and Multiculturalism* (1998) and *Betrayal: German Churches and the Holocaust* (1999). She is the editor of a classic collection of essays, *On Being a Jewish Feminist* (1995), and in 1996 she published an anthology of her father's writings titled *Moral Grandeur and Spiritual Audacity: Essays of Abraham Joshua Heschel* (1996). She has recently completed a book titled *When Jesus Was an Aryan: Theologians in Nazi Germany* (in press). Heschel has published essays in *Tikkun, Dissent, The Nation*, and the *New York Times Book Review*. Since 1999, she has served on the Academic Advisory Committee of the Research Center of the U.S. Holocaust Memorial Museum and as cochair, with Michael Lerner and Cornel West, of the Tikkun Community.

Julie Ingersoll is associate professor of religious studies at the University of North Florida in Jacksonville, where she teaches courses on the relationship between religion and culture in America. She holds a PhD in religious studies from the University of California, Santa Barbara. Her publications include *Evangelical Christian Women: War Stories in the Gender Battles* (2003) and *Baptist and Methodist Faiths in America* (2003) as well as several articles.

ABOUT THE CONTRIBUTORS

Mark Juergensmeyer is director of global and international studies and professor of sociology and religious studies at the University of California, Santa Barbara. He is an expert on religious violence, conflict resolution, and South Asian religion and politics and has published more than two hundred articles and a dozen books. He is the author of *Terror in the Mind of God: The Global Rise of Religious Violence* (rev. ed., 2003), *The New Cold War? Religious Nationalism Confronts the Secular State* (1993), and *Gandhi's Way* (2002). He is the editor of *Global Religions* (2003) and *A Handbook of Global Religion* (2004). Juergensmeyer has received research fellowships from the Woodrow Wilson Center, the Harry Frank Guggenheim Foundation, the United States Institute of Peace, and the American Council of Learned Societies. He is the 2003 recipient of the Grawemeyer Award for contributions to the study of religion, and in 2004 he received the Silver Award of the Queen Sofia Center for the Study of Violence in Spain.

J. Shawn Landres is a research fellow at the Sigi Ziering Institute: Exploring the Ethical and Religious Implications of the Holocaust at the University of Judaism in Los Angeles, California. He has taught at the University of Judaism; Matej Bel University in Banská Bystrica, Slovak Republic; and the University of California, Santa Barbara (UCSB). He coedited and contributed to *Personal Knowledge and Beyond: Reshaping the Ethnography of Religion* (2002). He was cochair of the American Academy of Religion's (AAR's) consultation on religion in central and eastern Europe and is incoming cochair of the AAR's Anthropology of Religion Group. From 2002 to 2004, he comanaged the UCSB-Fulbright American Studies Institute on "Religion in the United States: Pluralism and Public Presence." He was a Capps Junior Fellow at UCSB's Walter H. Capps Center for the Study of Religion and Public Life and a Keith Murray Senior Scholar in Lincoln College, Oxford. He has published numerous scholarly articles and book chapters as well as essays for the popular press; his most recent article is "Jewish Communities in the Americas," in *A Handbook of Global Religions* (2004).

David Morgan is Phyllis and Richard Duesenberg Professor in Christianity and the Arts and professor of humanities and art history in Christ College, the undergraduate humanities honors college of Valparaiso University. He edited *Icons of American Protestantism: The Art of Warner Sallman* (1996)

ABOUT THE CONTRIBUTORS

and coedited (with Professor Sally M. Promey) *The Visual Culture of American Religions* (2001). He is the author of *Visual Piety: A History and Theory of Popular Religious Images* (1998) and *Protestants and Pictures: Religion, Visual Culture, and the Age of American Mass Production* (1999). His *The Sacred Gaze: Religious Visual Culture in Theory and Practice* will be published in 2005. Morgan is an editor and cofounder of *Material Religion: The Journal of Objects, Art, and Belief.*

John K. Roth is the Edward J. Sexton Professor of Philosophy and director of the Center for the Study of the Holocaust, Genocide, and Human Rights at Claremont-McKenna College. He is recognized as one of the preeminent Christian scholars on the Holocaust and a pioneer in the field of Holocaust ethics. He is the author or editor of more than thirty-five books on the Holocaust and on American religion and philosophy. Among them are *Holocaust Politics* (2001), *Approaches to Auschwitz: The Holocaust and Its Legacy* (with Richard L. Rubenstein [1987, 2003]), *Different Voices: Women and the Holocaust* (edited with Carol Rittner [1993]), *Holocaust: Religious and Philosophical Implications* (edited with Michael Berenbaum [1989]), and *Ethics after the Holocaust: Perspectives, Critiques, and Responses* (1999). In 1988, Roth was named U.S. Professor of the Year by the Council for Advancement and Support of Education and the Carnegie Foundation for the Advancement of Teaching.

Richard L. Rubenstein is president emeritus, Distinguished Professor of Religion, and life member of the Board of Trustees at the University of Bridgeport. He is also Lawton Distinguished Professor Emeritus of Religion at Florida State University. He received the master of Hebrew literature and rabbinic ordination from the Jewish Theological Seminary (Conservative), the master of theology (STM) from Harvard Divinity School, and the PhD from Harvard. In 1977, Florida State University named Rubenstein Distinguished Professor of the Year, the university's highest academic honor. In February 2001, the university created the Richard L. Rubenstein Professorship of Religion. In 1987, the Jewish Theological Seminary conferred the degree of doctor of Hebrew letters, *honoris causa*, on him at its Centennial Convocation. In 1999, Grand Valley State University conferred on him the degree of doctor of humane letters, *honoris causa*.

ABOUT THE CONTRIBUTORS

Eric R. Samuelsen, associate professor and head of creative writing in theater and media arts at Brigham Young University (BYU), is a playwright and novelist with sixteen professional productions of his work, including productions in New York, Los Angeles, and Indiana. Samuelson is recognized as a scholar of Ibsen, and his dissertation dealt with Ibsen's brand in Norwegian culture. He serves as dramatic arts editor of *BYU Studies* and has published in such journals as *Scandinavian Studies*, *Western European Stages*, and *Nineteenth Century Theatre at BYU*. He received his PhD from Indiana University and taught at Wright State University before moving to BYU in 1992.

Jeffrey S. Siker is professor of New Testament and chairs the Department of Theological Studies at Loyola Marymount University (LMU), Los Angeles, where he has taught since 1987. He received his BA and MA from Indiana University, an MDiv from Yale Divinity School, and his PhD in New Testament from Princeton Theological Seminary. His expertise includes the areas of early Jewish–Christian relations, the history of biblical interpretation, and uses of the Bible in ethical debates. He was the organizing chair of the Society of Biblical Literature's section on early Jewish–Christian relations. At LMU, among other courses, he regularly teaches a course on Jesus in film. He is the author of many articles and several books, including *Disinheriting the Jews: Abraham in Early Christian Controversy* (1991), *Homosexuality in the Church: Both Sides of the Debate* (1994), and *Scripture and Ethics: 20th-Century Portraits* (1997).

Mark Silk is associate professor of religion and public life and director of the Leonard E. Greenberg Center for the Study of Religion in Public Life at Trinity College, Hartford, Connecticut. He is the author of *Spiritual Politics: Religion and America since World War II* (1989) and *Unsecular Media: Making News of Religion in America* (1998). He is also editor of the journal *Religion in the News* and of Religion by Region, a nine-volume series of books on religion and public life in contemporary America.

Kathryn J. S. Smith currently serves as chair of the Department of Biblical Studies at Azusa Pacific University. She received her PhD in early Judaism and New Testament at the Claremont Graduate University and did much of her graduate work in Midrash at Hebrew Union College, Los

ABOUT THE CONTRIBUTORS

Angeles. She holds a bachelor's degree in Jewish studies from the University of Washington. She speaks and publishes on issues of gender, social boundaries, and early Judaism and Christianity.

Leslie E. Smith is a doctoral student in religious studies with an emphasis in women's studies at the University of California, Santa Barbara, studying gender and modern conservative Christian thought. She has taught courses coinciding with these research interests at Southwest Missouri State University, Drury University, and Pepperdine University. From 2002 to 2004, she was a researcher for the Ford Foundation's Religious Pluralism in Southern California Project, focusing specifically on the use of religious tolerance rhetoric in public school classrooms. She is the author of "Complicating Things: Material Culture and the Classroom," featured in the American Academy of Religion's "Spotlight on Teaching" section of *Religious Studies News* (May 2003), and "Divine Order, Divine Myth: Uncovering the Mythical Construction of Gender Ideals in Protestant Fundamentalist Circles" (*ARC: The Journal of the Faculty of Religious Studies*, 2002).

Karen Jo Torjesen is the Margo L. Goldsmith Professor of Women's Studies in Religion, director of the Women's Studies in Religion program, chair of the Department of Religion, and codirector of the Institute for Antiquity and Christianity. Her research interests include constructions of gender and sexuality in early Christianity, authority and institutionalization in the early churches, hermeneutics and rhetoric in late antiquity, and comparative study of Greek and Latin patristic traditions. During her tenure as assistant professor of patristic theology at the University of Göttingen (Germany), her book *Hermeneutical Procedure and Theological Structure in Origen's Exegesis* (1986) was published. Her most recent book is *When Women Were Priests: Women's Leadership in the Early Church and the Scandal of Their Subordination in the Rise of Christianity* (1993).